Labour Euroscepticism: Italian and Irish Unions' Changing Preferences Towards the EU

Labour Euroscepticism: Italian and Irish Unions' Changing Preferences Towards the EU

by Darragh Golden

ecpr PRESS

Published by ECPR Press
European Consortium for Political Research
Harbour House
6–8 Hythe Quay
Colchester CO2 8JF
United Kingdom

British Library Cataloguing in Publication Data
A catalogue record for this book is available from the British Library.

Paperback ISBN: 978-1-910259-89-4

Hardback ISBN: 978-1-78661-052-2

Per Francesca

Table of Contents

Preface & Acknowledgements

In writing a book, George Orwell, a person who knows a thing or two about this process, said it is 'a horrible, exhausting struggle'. The accuracy of this sentiment has of late begun to ring through. The genesis of this book can be traced back to my days in Italy whilst toiling in an (Italo-)Irish pub and engaging in political discussions on all things 'European' from the dark days of Nazi-Fascism to the ideal of a federalised Europe. Subsequently, I returned to university, reading European Studies at University College Cork where, under the guidance of Dermot Keogh (RIP) and Diarmuid Whelan (RIP), to name but two, I developed a deep fascination for what is to my mind is one of the most ambitious political projects to date. European integration is a wieldy subject to study and to fully appreciate it I believe it necessary to return to those days where the shadow of Nazi-Fascism loomed large. With the passing of the decades, historical memories inevitably become fainter and fainter and as the shadow of jingoistic nationalism fades there is the distinct danger of forgetting and unlearning the lessons of the past. What the eminent historian, Eric Hobsbawm, dubbed the Short Twentieth Century concluded in 1991, precisely when European integration was re-launched as a political economic endeavour, most notably with the creation of common currency, which came into circulation as I was working in Italy and where trepidation and excitement existed in equal amounts. Hence, you could say that since the 2000s, when the common currency entered circulation, replacing the *Lira* and the *Punt* I have been a 'participant observer' of European integration.

Organised labour has been integral to the reconstruction of Western Europe and has contributed to the public debate on European integration, particularly around important milestones including the question of membership and EU treaties, which underpin the EU's constitutional evolution. The largest Irish and Italian unions initially viewed the project with a good deal of scepticism, albeit from different vantage points. By the time of the Maastricht Treaty (1992) there was a pro-European consensus amongst Irish and Italian trade unions. This consensus remained intact until the mid-2000s, when during debates surrounding the Lisbon Treaty, labour Euroscepticism emerged in Ireland, but not in Italy. This development, which grew against the backdrop of the 'Great Recession', piqued my interest and understanding the changing preferences of Irish and Italian unions towards European integration across time became the subject of my doctoral research.

It was against the backdrop of the 'Great Recession' that I embarked on my doctoral journey, under the mentorship of Roland Erne who encouraged me to satisfy my intellectual curiosities rather than developing an expertise in a singular academic discipline. Whilst this can inevitably generate more questions than answers, it became apparent that labour politics, which *per se* is multi-dimensional, has become unmoored from broader sociological and economic debates. One objective of this book is to bring labour politics and the social question back together by viewing them through the prism of European integration, which is in and of itself a transformative socio-economic phenomenon. In particular, I'm interested in labour mobility, not least because of my own personal experience, and how it is refracted through national institutions, which are integral to unions' *raison d'être* and the idea of social protection. These institutions, or Polanyian fixes as I term them, have been under attack by neoliberal ideologues since the 1980s as being too rigid and outdated. Their contribution to off-setting social dumping and ensuring 'a fair day's pay ...' is overlooked and there is a danger, I argue, that where transnational labour 'markets' go unpoliced and social dumping practices unchecked, the likelihood of anti-EU sentiment increases. This lesson is all the more important in light of Brexit and the rise of ethno-culturalist political parties.

As much as the writing of this book was a solitary endeavour, it would not have been possible without the collaboration of many others. First and foremost, a great deal of gratitude is owed to those who generously afforded me their time to conduct an interview, although the encounter was always less of an interview and more of a conversation. I spent six months at IRES, Bologna and must thank Volker Telljohan, Francesco Garibaldo, Cesare Mighini, and Floinda Rinaldini. Following my participation in two projects at the Centre for Advanced Studies, Oslo, and University College Dublin (UCD), I would like to thank Knut Kjeldstadli, for his generosity of spirit, Sabina Stan, Andreas Bieler, Idar Helle, Tiago Mathos, Imre Szabó, Vincenzo Maccarrone, Mary Naughton and Costanza Galanti for critical comments on key chapters and their camaraderie. Colleagues at UCD, John Geary, Bill Roche and Colm McLaughlin, provided important guidance for which I'm grateful. At ECPR Press I would like to pay gratitude to Deborah Savage and Kate Hawkins for their professionalism in shaping this manuscript. Finally, both the Irish and Norwegian Research Councils are to be thanked for their fundamental financial support, without which this research would not have been possible.

Darragh Golden,
Oslo, Summer, 2024

List of Tables and Figures

TABLES

FIGURES

List of Abbreviations

AFL	American Federation of Labor
ANCE	Associazione Nazionale Costruttori Edili
ATGWU	Amalgamated Transport and General Workers Union
CGIL	Confederazione Generale Italiana del Lavoro
CISL	Confederazione Italiana Sindacati dei Lavoratori
CIU	Congress of Irish Unions
CSO	Central Statistical Office
DC	Democrazia Cristiana
DG ECFIN	Directorate General for Economic and Financial Affairs
DURC	Documento Unico di Regolarità Contributiva
EC	European Commission
ECB	European Central Bank
ECSC	European Coal and Steel Community
ECT	European Constitutional Treaty
EEC	European Economic Community
EFBWW	European Federation of Building and Wood Workers
EMS	European Monetary System
EMU	Economic and Monetary Union
ERM	European Exchange Rate Mechanism
ERT	European Round Table of Industrialists
ETUC	European Trade Union Confederation
EU	European Union
FENEAL	Federazione Nazionale Lavoratori Edili Affini e Del Legno
FILCA	Federazione Italiana Lavoratori Costruzioni e Affini

FILLEA	Federazione Italiana Lavoratori Costruzioni e Legno
FIOM	Federazione Impiegati Operai Metallurgici
(F)WUI	(Federated) Workers Union of Ireland
ICTU	Irish Congress of Trade Unions
IMF	International Monetary Fund
ISTAT	Istituto Nazionale di Statistica
MRC(I)	Migrant Rights Centre (Ireland)
PCI	Partito Comunista Italiano
PD	Partito Democrático
PPSN	Personal Public Service Numbers
QCA	Qualitative Comparative Analysis
QMV	Qualified Majority Voting
REA	Registered Employment Agreement
SEA	Single European Act
SIPTU	Services Industrial Professional and Technical Union
TEC	Treaty establishing the European Community
TEEU	Technical Engineering and Electrical Union (now Connect)
TGWU	Transport and General Workers Union
TUC	Trade Union Congress
UIL	Unione Italiana del Lavoro

Chapter One

Quo Vadis, Europa? The Politics of European Integration

Our Union is undivided and indivisible

(Rome Declaration, 25 March 2017).

INTRODUCTION

It takes a deathly tragedy of unimaginable proportions, and of human doing too, to foment sufficient political resolve that aspires to ensure that a vile, atavistic ideology, such as Nazi-Fascism, never again finds fertile soil. The Schuman Plan, with the creation of the European Coal and Steel Community, did enough to pave the way to a deeper, more meaningful relationship between the six founding member-states. Going beyond the supranational governance of coal and steel was by no means a straightforward process. Complex and intense negotiations required adept brinksmanship from pre-eminent federalist visionary, Jean Monnet, culminating in 1957's Treaty of Rome, which established what today we call the European Union (EU). Such is the Frenchman's indelible mark on the European integration process that the mere mention of his name is like evoking a being of quasi-mythical status. Whilst the 'scope and limits of Monnet's influence are a complex issue' (Duchêne 1994: 199), there are at least two aspects or characteristics that have secured Monnet's status in Europe's political pantheon. First, there is the cameo role that the perspicacious Frenchman attributed to crises in driving integration further: 'Europe will be forged in crisis and will be the sum of the solutions adopted for those crises' were prophetic words of Monnet (1978: 488) that continue to ring true (White 2020a: 189). Second, there is the technocratic-elitism that Monnet vigorously pursued.

A 'rather anonymous, technocratic figure' (Duchêne 1991: 184), Monnet 'worked among élites only' (Anderson 2009:16), which included the leaders of national organised labour. Akin to his compatriot and like-minded

1

federalist Robert Schuman, 'a militant supporter' of the 'trade union movement and of trade union rights' (Milward 2000 [1992]: 290), Monnet was
also a 'forceful advocate of strong organized labour representation' (*ibidem*:
296). Well aware that 'any new impetus toward integration had to come from
those who held national power' (Yondorf 1965: 889), Monnet established
the Action Committee for the United States of Europe. This elite group was
composed of 'a highly select group' of political leaders and trade union leaders from the Christian-democrat, liberal and (moderate) socialist traditions
(*ibid.*). The objective was simple, namely, to fashion supporters of sup¬na-
tionalism out of the leaders of national labour movements. Hence, from the
outset, organised labour has been integral to the idea of European integration,
its legitimation and promulgation, as well as its contestation.

For Monnet, a single market alone would never suffice. 'Via money, Europe
could become political', Monnet is reported as having told a friend, but the
political will was never really there in his lifetime for such a significant step
to transpire. Circumstances were very different when Jacques Delors became
President of the European Commission in the mid-1980s. After Monnet,
Delors is the personage associated most with furthering the supranational
project. A 'consummate technocrat with a strong ideological commitment
to the European project' (Hodson 2016: 213), Delors is considered by many
as having taken up Monnet's mantle in the pursuit of European unification.
Certainly, his overtures towards organised labour were equal to those of Monnet; however, as a former trade unionist, Delors had greater insight into the
exigencies of organised labour, which resided at both the supranational and
national levels. His famous quip that 'one cannot fall in love with a market'
was music to the ears of trade unionists; it meant that Delors inherently
understood the social deficit that laid at the heart of the EU and he sought to
remedy this by promoting the notion of a 'European social model'.[1]

Against the backdrop of ascending Reaganomics and Thatcherism, the idea
of a *European* social model was of great interest to labour movements across
Europe; and it is why, for many trade unionists, Delors remains 'the most able
president the European Commission has had' (Milward 2004: 146). Nevertheless, Delors himself remained critical of the EU's most ambitious objective to
date, namely, monetary union in the absence of political union (Jabko 2006).
Notwithstanding, on 1 January 1999, Ireland and Italy, along with nine other
member states, abandoned their national currencies and adopted the euro.

As the EU was preparing to celebrate the ten-year anniversary of the single
currency, the design flaws of monetary union were brutally exposed. An ensuing economic and social turmoil ravaged the European continent, threatening
to tear the EU apart. There emerged the group of so-called PIIGS countries,
which, other than Ireland and Italy, included Portugal, Greece and Spain.
The PIIGS were financially unstable, and the weakness of their economies

put the entire common currency community at risk. Such was the profundity of financial crisis that comparisons with the 1930s were regularly made by commentators. To boot, neo-fascist parties have made inroads in a number of European states, including Finland, France, Italy, Germany, Greece, the Netherlands and, most reprehensibly, the UK with the advent of Brexit. From the EU's perspective, two important events occurred against the backdrop of a rising Euroscepticism, namely, the awarding of the Nobel Peace Prize in 2012 and the celebration of the sixtieth anniversary of the Treaty of Rome in 2017. Both occasions served as an opportunity to refocus the minds of political leaders away from the day-to-day dilemmas of European and national crisis governance and back towards the broader and loftier ambitions of Jean Monnet, Robert Schuman and Jacques Delors, to name but a few of Europe's visionaries.

In December 2012, national leaders, including German Chancellor, Angela Merkel, French President, Francois Hollande, Ireland's Taoiseach, Enda Kenny and Italy's technocratic Prime Minister, Mario Monti, convened in Oslo for the Nobel award ceremony. So too did leaders of the various European institutions, such as Martin Schulz, President of the European Parliament, and Commission President, José Manuel Barroso. Speeches were peppered with pro-integration platitudes that recalled the post-war reconciliatory spirit embodied by Monnet and Schuman. Barroso (2012) described the euro as 'one of the most visible symbols of our unity'. This unity, he continued, must be grounded in 'a deeper sense of a community of destiny'. Angela Merkel (2012), in a statement, affirmed

> ... that this is now the perfect time to think about what our predecessors put in place: from Konrad Adenauer to Helmut Kohl, from Robert Schuman to Jean Monnet and many, many others ... Everybody automatically thinks of the United States of America when they hear that. But I do think we need more that is shared, that is common, and that we must cooperate even more closely (www. bundeskanzlerin.de).

Despite intimating the need for deeper co-operation, neither personality offered any greater insight as to what 'a deeper sense of a community of destiny' might look like.

Attempts to forge such post-national vistas suggests that there may well be a desire for deeper integration: but this desire stops a good way shy of support for a federal superstate. In the run-up to the Brexit referendum in 2016, the foreign ministers of the six founding member states met for an informal conflab in Rome. A joint communiqué underlined how they were 'concerned about the state of the European project' but reiterated their resolve 'to continue the process of creating an ever closer union' and that 'the European

Union remains the best answer we have for today's challenges' (Foreign Affairs Ministers of Belgium, Germany, France, Italy, Luxembourg and the Netherlands 2016). Whilst the founding members underlined the need for strengthening cohesion in the EU, they noted that the EU 'allows for different paths of integration' (*ibid.*). Is the possibility of 'different paths of integration' compatible with Merkel's vision for the EU? More recently again, and by way of response to the result of the Brexit referendum, the then-leader of the German Social Democrats (and former President of the European Parliament), Martin Schultz, sought to extol the virtues of the EU by negotiating 'a new constitutional treaty to establish the United States of Europe' (*Financial Times*, 7 December 2017). Leaving little scope for 'different paths of integration', Schultz warned that member states which fail to approve it 'will automatically have to leave the EU' (*ibid.*)!

Clearly, Schultz's proposal differs from the position of the six foreign ministers outlined above, which differs again from the vision promoted by Merkel. It would appear that the EU is searching for a new soul, but diverging views are undermining such attempts or at the very least complicating them. The sixtieth anniversary of the EU provided an opportunity to rekindle the debate on the *finalité*, or destination, of European integration. Despite being riven by divisions resulting from the euro-crisis, which were exacerbated by the so-called refugee crisis, the member states' leaders convened in the same opulent marbled chamber where the Treaty of Rome was signed sixty years previously. The EU's founding principles were reasserted as national leaders renewed their vows and committed to pushing integration forward. The carefully stage-managed signing of the Rome Declaration masked the backstage haggling that went on in the weeks preceding the ceremony. Similarly, the post-ceremony press conference was well choreographed, with no opportunity allowed for probing questions from pesky and inquisitive journalists (*Politico* 25 March 2017). Perhaps the EU is too sacred, or too fragile, to place under scrutiny?

To mark the occasion of the EU's sixtieth anniversary, the European Commission then presided over by Jean-Claude Juncker issued a White Paper (EC 2017) on the future of the EU. Whilst the imminent challenges of the euro-crisis might have been overcome, its authors acknowledged that, in principle, 'Europe's challenges show no sign of abating' (EC 2017: 6). To this end, the EU is promoted as the best way to confronting collective challenges; however, five different scenarios for the EU are outlined. These are i) carrying on; ii) nothing but the single market; iii) those who want more do more; iv) doing less more efficiently; and v) doing much more together (EC 2017). Surely, there are advantages and disadvantages to each scenario? Which scenario, by way of thought experiment, might the different personalities mentioned above choose? Would their choice be hindered by the political party to which they are committed? For instance, would a Christian-democrat, such as Merkel, opt for a different scenario to that of a social-democrat, such as Schultz? Or would their preferences converge on account of their Germanness rather than their political persuasion? And, importantly for this book, what position might Irish and Italian organised labour opt for? And how might this preference be articulated?

Morgan (2005) argues that the EU suffers from a justificatory deficit (*see also* Glencross 2009a; Dimitrakopoulos 2011), which is problematic if we consider the EU and European integration to be a fundamentally normative project that periodically requires legitimation to ensure its continuance (Eriksen and Fossum 2000; Pagden 2000; Bellamy and Castiglione 2003; Hayward 2002, 2003; Morgan 2005; Føllesdal 2006; Glencross 2009a and 2000b; Sternberg 2013; Bellamy and Weale 2015). There is considerably less knowledge about the question that really matters 'what is the justification for a European polity?' (Morgan 2005: 22) This requires a discussion on the *finalité* of European integration. The recurring question of 'what should the European Union become?' should prompt intense debate; all too often, however, it is fudged. Mair (2007) is critical of the mainstream political parties for perpetuating such a non-debate. The 'EU construct', for Mair, is 'the house that party politicians built' so as to 'avoid the emergence of institutional competitors' (2005: 17–24). As a result of this tacit agreement between mainstream parties, 'the giant is not only sleeping, but has been deliberately sedated' (2007: 13). Similarly, Hyman (2010) posed an awkward question of the trade union leadership by querying whether their preferences towards European integration were 'out of step' with the inclinations of the membership?

Whilst a quiet technocratic elitism might well be a necessary condition when it comes to reconfiguring territorial spaces and communities (Bartolini 2005: ch. 2), it cannot be indefinitely banked-upon or taken for granted (Mair 2007; Majone 2009; Hyman 2010). Regrettably, economic and monetary integration was never going to be a panacea for social conflicts and, with the passing of time, mass–elite linkages on EU-related questions have started to break down, thereby imperilling the future of the EU. The post-functionalist turn in EU Studies (Hooghe and Marks 2009) is problematic not least because 'integration' as a transnational socio-economic dynamic has been marginalised (Manners and Rosamond 2018: 29). Following Vauchez (2015: 5), this book 'explores the *institution* of Europe's polity as the contingent and conflictual *historical* process of symbolic, cognitive and practical unification of a variegated set of European constructions'. This is done by exploring the preferences of Irish and Italian organised labour on the changing nature of European integration across time. This inevitably implies a historical process-tracing of transformations both on a material and on an ideational plain. In so doing, this book is in keeping with the broader tradition of comparative historical sociology that conceptualises the EU as a 'reciprocal relationship between market construction and polity construction' (McNamara 2010: 130; *see also* Marks 1997, 2004; Bartolini 2005; Schmitter 1996, 2009; Bourdieu 2014; Trenz 2016).

As the attendant challenges associated with EU membership and the complex phenomenon of European integration become more diffuse, there is a need to shift between levels of analysis (Bieler 2006; Erne 2008; Bechter, Brandl and Meardi 2012; Taggart 2006; Zurn 2019) so as to determine whether or not there is a feedback loop between how European integration is being experienced on the ground and how it is being articulated in public discourse. Trans-frontier mobility, integral to European integration, has transformed and continues to transform the historic subject-matter of societies and 'undermin[e] endogenous social structures', which have generally been seen to temper socio-political conflict and reproduce capitalism (Urry 2000: 1). If the concept of the 'social' as society, whatever its value in the past, is no longer 'especially relevant as the organising concept of [political] sociological analysis' (*ibid.*), then how should this transformative phenomenon be studied (*see also* Fligstein 2008; Trenz 2016). This is, of course, a methodological question, which I will briefly deal with in the following section and more substantially in Chapter Three. Suffice to say here that for those interested in the contemporary politicisation and democratisation of the EU, the meso- or sectoral level is advantageous to the production of knowledge and our understanding of *labour* Euroscepticism (Bartolini 2000; Bechter, Brandl and Meardi 2012).

Whereas the Great Financial Crisis of 2008–9 understandably grabbed the attention of policymakers and scholars, there are lessons that remain unlearned from the rejection of the Lisbon Treaty and its predecessor, the European Constitutional Treaty (ECT). The former was 'even more surprising than the negative votes of three years before' (Majone 2009: 4) and in the immediate aftermath it was 'indeed difficult to see how the Irish voters could be induced to change their minds' (*ibid.*: 6). Were it not for the onset of the Great Financial Crisis, which placed Ireland in the eye of a brutal economic maelstrom, who is to know which way the second vote would have gone? Had another rebuff emerged there is no doubt that the EU would have been plunged into a deep constitutional crisis (and there would have been no Article 50 for the British Conservative government to trigger!). Counterfactuals aside, I argue that there are lessons that remain unlearned from the Irish rejection of the Lisbon Treaty. Should these go unheeded, or at least unacknowledged, there is a distinct danger that the consequences could one day come home to roost. Perhaps they already have, if the Brexit vote is anything to go by (Schmidt 2016). Hitherto, the exit option never really featured in national discourses, but the decision of the British has rendered the debate about EU *finalité* all the more important and raises the conundrum anew: *quo vadis, Europa?*

PUZZLING TIMES: POLITICISATION
AND PREFERENCES ACROSS TIME

This book is about the genesis of European integration, on the one hand, and Italian and Irish organised labour, on the other. More precisely, it is about Italian and Irish organised labour's views *on* European integration and *within* contemporary European integration. Broadly speaking, it is about the emergence, disappearance and re-emergence of labour Euroscepticism, which speaks to two inter-related concepts or processes, namely, preference-formation and politicisation. The term labour Euroscepticism is used quite simply to differentiate it from the well-studied phenomenon of party Euroscepticism, which is a veritable cottage industry. When it comes to labour Euroscepticism, however, there is a dearth of knowledge. That said, there are overlaps. For instance, within labour Euroscepticism there can exist both 'hard' and 'soft' variants (Taggart 1998; Taggart and Szczerbiak 2008a, 2008b). The question of membership was to be, and remains, 'the ultimate litmus test' of 'hard' Euroscepticism (*ibid.*: 240); 'soft' Euroscepticism, on the other hand, is defined simply as opposition to the further deepening of European integration in favour of the *status quo*. Both variants of labour Euroscepticism are of relevance for this book; however, the former variant is relatively short-lived and often overstated (*see* Chapter Four). Its disappearance was followed by a pro-European consensus, which, paradoxically, emerged at a time when European integration was being politicised and party Euroscepticism was emerging. The re-emergence of labour Euroscepticism in Irish organised labour, but not Italian, still requires an adequate explanation, as does Euroscepticism in organised labour more generally (Fitzgibbon, Leruth and Startin 2017; Mathers, Milner and Taylor 2017).

I have chosen to focus on the critical junctures that punctuated the European integration process, namely, the seven EU treaties, which are useful yardsticks for gauging actors' preferences on European integration at different points across time. This is important because the 'EU's evolution as both a 'polity' and 'regime' has been an ongoing process of multiple negotiations over the normative issues raised by integration' (Bellamy and Castiglione 2003: 8). Consequently, EU treaties generate broad political debate and actors' justifications are best studied 'in the form of public debates involving a mass audience and the media' (Trenz 2016: 83). This is more the case with EU treaties than it is with European policymaking, which rarely enters the public sphere. However, it is important to note that the numerous EU Treaties are debated in different ratification contexts (Hodson and Maher 2018) or embedded in different phases of European integration (Hutter and Grande 2014). Regarding the latter, I argue that it is possible to identify three distinct phases of European integration.

Figure 1.1 is a visual representation, in the broadest terms, of the research puzzle at the heart of this book. Here, we can see that the EU has been reinvented on at least two occasions and, in each instance, such changes are legitimised by 'skilled social actors … who mobilize cooperation among others' (Stone Sweet *et al.* 2001: 8). I distinguish between three qualitatively different phases. Coincidentally, each phase commences with a two-term Commission President whose vision leaves a lasting impression. These are Walter Hallstein (1958–67), who worked closely with Jean Monnet; Jacques Delors (1985–95), who, as mentioned above, introduced, *inter alia*, monetary union; and José Manuel Barroso (2004–14), who oversaw the EU's 'big bang' enlargement and was at the helm for the EU's deepest crisis to date. Each of these phases had a flagship project requiring the energies of the EU institutions and commanding the attention of organised labour. Each of these developmental phases can be broadly mapped on to the different kinds of 'consensuses' that underpinned European integration across time and feature extensively in the EU academic literature. Phase one is characterised by the free movement of goods, which was underpinned by a 'permissive consensus'. Establishing monetary union, and the free movement of (financial) capital, is the defining feature of phase two, which was buttressed by an active 'pro-European consensus' insofar as organised labour is concerned. Promoting labour mobility, a core component of EU citizenship, is the defining characteristic of phase three. It is in this phase that we see the 'pro-European consensus' being replaced by a 'constraining dissensus', at least in the Irish case.

For simplicity's sake, I 'aggregate' the preferences of Italian and Irish unions at three different 'critical junctures' across the different phases, namely: on the question of accession to the EEC; the Maastricht Treaty in 1992; and the Fiscal Treaty in 2012. The crude weighting of preferences – pro-EU, EU-critical and anti-EU – is based on the position adopted by the major unions, using total membership as a guideline, minus the contrasting position adopted by other, numerically less powerful unions. For example, on the burning question of EU membership, both the Italian unions *Confederazione Italiana Sindacati Lavoratori* (CISL) and *Unione Italiana del Lavoro* (UIL) were in favour of Italy's participation in European integration. However, the *Confederazione Generale Italiana del Lavoro* (CGIL) was strongly opposed. As the latter was the dominant union in Italy at the time, in terms of membership, we can argue that *overall* the Italian trade union movement was critical of membership. Similarly in Ireland, the largest union, the Irish Transport and General Workers Union (ITGWU and SIPTU today) (along with other unions), was opposed to accession. Hence, a similar stance, broadly speaking again, was adopted by organised labour in Ireland on the question of membership.

Observing the trajectories of Irish and Italian unions, we can see that between the question of membership and the Maastricht Treaty, both Italian and Irish labour movements converged on a pro-EU position. This raises a number of questions. For instance, what explains the anti-EU stance in the first place? Secondly, what factors explain the shift to a pro-EU stance in Phase II by both Irish and Italian labour movements? Both labour movements have been exposed to similar EU-associated challenges, such as the budgetary constraints associated with economic and monetary union (Baccaro and Howell 2017; Hancké 2013; Hardiman 2002; Regan 2012a) or the challenges associated with labour mobility following the EU's enlargement in the 2000s (OECD 2012), yet by the time of the EU's response to the euro crisis by way of the Fiscal Compact (*see* Chapter Eight), a number of large Irish unions – Unite and Connect, but also SIPTU – campaigned against it. Hence, the aggregate position of the Irish unions reverted back to an EU-critical position whilst the Italian unions continued to maintain a pro-EU stance. What explains this divergence?

Figure 1.1 Irish and Italian Unions' EU changing preferences across time

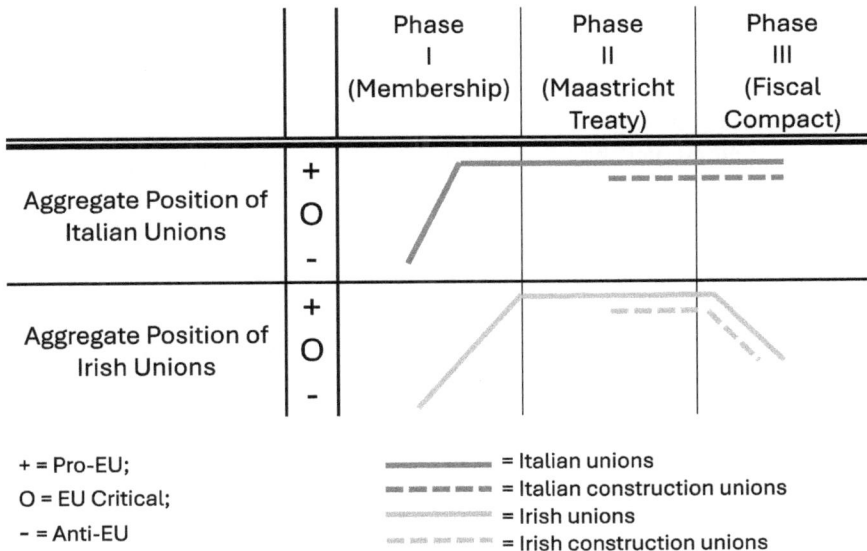

+ = Pro-EU;

O = EU Critical;

- = Anti-EU

━━━━━━ = Italian unions

━ ━ ━ ━ = Italian construction unions

═══════ = Irish unions

▬ ▬ ▬ ▬ = Irish construction unions

Source: Own

Continuing to focus on the right-hand frame of Figure 1.1, which is embedded in the broader context of the Great Financial Crisis, there are a number of EU-related developments that are of immediate concern to organised labour and which render this puzzle all the more perplexing. This requires a little contextualisation. Following the announcement that the EU was to be awarded the Nobel prize for peace, the *New York Times* (12 December 2012) wrote, '[F]or all the talk of unity ... a variety of signals suggested the opposite.' Two such 'signals' directly concern organised labour. The first 'signal' brings us to the streets of Dublin, where, in November 2010, 100,000 people took part in one of the largest demonstrations ever organised by the Irish Congress of Trade Unions (ICTU) to protest against the terms and conditions of the EU's €85 billion bailout. ICTU's General Secretary, David Begg, in the closing speech, used incendiary language to paint a hitherto unorthodox portrait of the EU: 'Our gallant allies in Europe have arrived 95 years too late and uninvited, and instead of guns to help the revolution they have brought economic weapons of mass destruction.' The 'gallant allies in Europe' reference is a controversial excerpt from the 1916 Proclamation, a founding document of the Irish state, and refers to the German Empire, which had supplied the Irish rebels with arms to fight British imperialism. Resorting to such provocative language, tinged with nationalist overtones, and only a stone's throw from where the Proclamation was first publicly read, marked a new departure from the accustomed portrayal of the EU by the leadership of Irish organised labour.

The second 'signal' has to do with a departure from the EU's traditional approach to collective problem-solving and the introduction of a new economic governance regime (Erne 2015). In March 2011, the Treaty on Stability, Coordination and Governance in the Economic and Monetary Union was signed by all the member states, with the exception of the Czech Republic and the United Kingdom. Unlike previous 'grand bargains', the Fiscal Compact, as it became publicly known, is an intergovernmental treaty and technically not an EU treaty. Additional legislation, known as the Six- and Two-pack, provided the foundation for a new economic governance regime which allows the European Commission to intervene in policy areas that hitherto were closely guarded national prerogatives, namely, labour market policy and collective wage bargaining mechanisms (Erne 2015). In other words, two policy areas where the EU does not have competence and that are of immediate concern to organised labour, everywhere. The new agenda is clearly laid out in in a DG ECFIN (2012: 104) policy paper: 'The new and political instruments of control must be used with the aim of reducing the wage setting power of trade unions.'

Albeit an important actor from a legitimacy standpoint, the ETUC is generally considered as being weak and over-reliant on the goodwill of the

Commission (Turner 1996: 344; Bartolini 2005: 292; Gajewska 2009 117). Notwithstanding this, and other drawbacks, such as being beleaguered by internal differences (Dølvik 1997), which were exacerbated following the EU's eastern enlargement (Seeliger and Wagner 2018), the ETUC opposed the Fiscal Compact in 2012. Critical of the 'semi-secret negotiations ... [which] ignored the democratic scrutiny that should normally characterise any reform of the Union', the ETUC 'deplore[d]' the 'undemocratic process', which 'will undermine the support of the population for European integration' (ETUC 2012). In opposing the Fiscal Compact, a historical precedent was set by the ETUC; but did such an approach herald a new departure in the relationship between the EU and organised labour? And, if so, how did it manifest in different national contexts, generally, and within national labour movements, particularly?

Despite the aforementioned weaknesses, the ETUC was successful in orchestrating a Europe-wide Day of Action on 14 November 2012. Co-ordinating simultaneous strike action in six EU countries, along with mass demonstrations and symbolic acts of solidarity in most other member states, is seen as an important step in the politicisation of a European working class (Helle 2015). 'Although this kind of transnational strike had already occurred at sectoral level, it was *unprecedented* at a cross-sectoral level' (Dufresne 2015: 152, emphasis added). Rather surprisingly, ICTU did not participate in the transnational day of action in any way. This lack of action is entirely at odds with the tone of the message delivered by its General Secretary two years before on the streets of Dublin. There was also a unusual lack of trade union unity in Italy. Whereas the largest union, CGIL, called a four-hour strike, the other two confederations, CISL and UIL, did not participate. What politics lay behind these aberrations in Ireland and Italy? Furthermore, in Italy, but not in Ireland, we have the enshrining of a debt brake into the Italian Constitution, which is tantamount to an institutionalisation of the austerity-inspired rules of the Stability and Growth Pact (Moschella 2017). Even here, the Italian unions, particularly the CGIL, remained uncharacteristically quiet on the issue and there was little debate (Gago 2018). What explains this reticence by Italian organised labour to politicise these issues? This in and of itself presents an interesting research puzzle. However, for two reasons, I would caution against using the most recent period as a point of departure.

The first reason is that it would be ahistorical. 'History', as Lacan writes, 'is not the past. History is the past in so far as it is historicised in the present – historicised in the present because it was lived in the past' (cited in Miller 1988: 12). Unfortunately, historical accounts are largely absent from the general literature on European integration. As historians Gilbert (2008: 641) and Ludlow (2009: 25) respectively note, 'the story of the EU is being told in over-simplified and unhistorical ways' and 'attention has for the most part focused on the making of institutions and policies and not upon their wider impact.' Consequently, 'the views of those who may have been affected by the integration process ... have seldom been taken into account' (Ludlow 2009: 25). I would argue that, in many regards, organised labour finds itself at the sharp end of the uneven European integration process; but their responses remain overlooked by the academic literature on the EU.

The same ahistorical bent can be attributed to the study of political preferences, of which Euroscepticism is a sub-set. As a Euroscepticism scholar writes, '[D]uring the first four decades of European integration, opposition or hostility to the European project was not on the agenda of scholars in the field of EU studies' (Leconte 2015: 251; *see also* Crespy and Verschueren 2009). Studying basic or fundamental preferences is important as they

> ... act as cognitive maps that allow political actors to make sense of the context in which they operate ... they provide normative templates that enable actors to choose between appropriate and inappropriate options. They legitimise some forms of political action but not others (Dimitrakopoulos 2011:15).

That said, 'the origin of preferences of political actors with regard to European integration has remained under-researched' (*ibid.*: 3; *see also* Hall 2005; Kassim, Saurugger and Puetter 2019). Here, obvious exceptions include national governments (*see*, for example, Moravcsik 1998; Fioretos 2011) and political parties (*see*, for example, Featherstone 1988; Dunphy 2004) albeit with some limitations (*see* Mair 2000, 2005, 2007). The question of Irish and Italian organised labour on European integration remains under-explored, as does the phenomenon of labour Euroscepticism, which occupies 'a structural role in the integration process' (Usherwood and Startin 2013: 2). Following Vasilopoulou and Dimitrakopoulous, 'we need to focus on how [labour] Euroscepticism has changed over time' (Vasilopoulou 2013: 154) and '[E]xploring the historical origins of the preferences of key actors is a *conditio sine qua non,* both for understanding their current views and for assessing how far they are prepared to go in terms of the reform of the EU.' (Dimitrakopoulous 2011: 3).

The second reason I would caution against using the most recent period as a point of departure has to do the logic of comparative analysis typical of synchronic, comparative research designs (*see* Przeworski and Teune 1970). The latter predominantly deploy systemic-level explanatory factors or indicators to explain variation. Here, the risk is that certain national-level factors are overemphasised while other sub-national or meso-level factors are overlooked. Domestic political-economic institutional factors, for example, can be employed to explain different political preferences (*see*, for example, Binegar *et al* 2004), but a word of caution is necessary here. To demonstrate this, let us take the work of Baccaro and Howell (2017) in *Trajectories of Neoliberal Transformation*. Both European integration and EMU are identified as the driving forces behind 'a convergent, liberalizing trajectory to European political economies' (Baccaro and Howell 2017: 186–7, 148; *see also* Scharpf 1999). Hence, political-economy institutions are not as static as once believed. Considering that the EU is *the* most globalised region, this might not be so surprising, but it does raise dilemmas with regards to how we study political economies, in general, and processes of politicisation and preference-formation, in particular.

Baccaro and Howell (2017: ch. 7) single out Italy as having gone further than any other member state in restructuring its political economy, particularly in the name of monetary union. Such is the extent of 'restrictive measures' (*ibid.*: 140–1; *see also* Rutherford and Frangi 2018), many of which are inimical to workers' rights (such as abolition of wage-indexation), that it 'is like looking at pictures from two different geological eras' (*ibid.*: 121). Given this scenario, is it not paradoxical that Italian unions remain staunch supporters of the European project? Ireland, on the other, is considered to have benefited greatly from the membership of the EU (Hardiman 2002; Laffan and O'Mahony 2008; Regan 2012a; O'Riain 2004, 2014), not only in economic terms, 'becoming one of the most open economies in the world' (2014: 39), but also in terms of labour–state relations, which were consolidated in the 1990s against the backdrop of EMU. Yet, it is in Ireland that we see labour Euroscepticism emerge in the 2000s.

This paradox is all the more striking if we consider *the* most contentious rulings by the Court of Justice of the EU (CJEU) for organised labour to date. The Viking (C 438/05) and Laval (C-341/05) rulings sent shockwaves through European trade union circles, primarily because the CJEU found that transnational economic freedoms trump nationally embedded social rights and, in particular, the right to strike. The rulings seemed to affirm Fritz Sharpf's earlier prognostication that 'the only solution that could be uniformly imposed would be the Anglo-American form of deregulated and disembedded capitalism' (1999: 193). Writing on these landmark cases, Schapf (2010: 235) notes that the rulings 'will have *the least effect* on the institutions and practices of L[iberal] M[arket] E[conomie]s' (emphasis added). If this is the case, as Scharpf, as well as Baccaro and Howell (2017: 188), all argue, we would expect to see increased hostility towards the EU and European integration originating in the member states for whom economic internationalisation and monetary union has come at a greater socio-political cost. Yet this is not the case. But explanations of this remain elusive.

Following the rejection of the ECT, a 'new politicisation' strand of literature emerged (*see* Zurn 2016 for an overview). In particular, there was the 'post-functionalist turn' associated with the work of Hooghe and Marks (2009), two well-established EU scholars, who coined the term 'constraining dissensus'. The 'post-functionalist theory of integration' places an emphasis on the cultural dimension of the politicisation process of the EU (*see also*, McLaren 2006; Inglehart and Welzel 2005). In other words, a primordial attachment to the nation-state. This line of argument chimes with the *Euroclash* thesis of economic sociologist Neil Fligstein (2008), who provides a convincing argument for focusing on 'social fields', whereby attention is focused on 'what were previously separate national fields [but now] have become European fields' (2008: 2). Rather than focusing on political-economic institutional factors, Fligstein instead uses micro-level data to explore how different social groups view European integration. Drawing on Eurobarometer data, Fligstein finds that there are 'high levels of support for the EU amongst the middle- and upper-middle-class citizens of Europe ... Less-well-off citizens oppose the EU as they have not shared the fruits of economic integration' (*ibid.*: 245). In other words, 'Europe' 'is clearly a social class project' (*ibid.*: 251). The *Euroclash*, therefore, is between the winners of the EU's project, on the one hand, and the losers, who remain 'wedded to the national worldview', on the other (*ibid.*: 207; *see also* Kriesi *et al.* 2012). In other words, it is a dispute between enlightened cosmopolitans on one side and xenophobic nationalists on the other. This dichotomy is problematic for reasons I will return to below.

For the time being, let us evaluate the predictive validity of Eurobarometer data, which I believe to be too weak or insufficiently strong to construct a robust argument. Take, for example, the 2008 Eurobarometer data for Ireland. The most positive opinions on the image of the EU and on their country's membership of the EU are registered in Ireland (65 per cent and 73 per cent respectively). Ireland has constantly scored high on being supportive of the EU. Yet, when the Irish public was asked to vote on the Lisbon Treaty in June of the same year, the Eurobarometer data was found wanting. This is because Eurobarometer data is limited and does not consider broader political developments in the EU, such as the landmark ECJ rulings mentioned above.

Thus far, it should be clear that there are limitations when it comes to analysing or comparing political preferences at the macro-, that is, institutional, or the micro-, that is, individual levels. This is especially the case as European integration becomes more diffuse across time. Here, we would expect the likelihood of political conflict to grow and, as a consequence, the number of voices contributing to EU domestic debates to increase (Fitzgibbon 2013). In other words, the more European integration becomes part and parcel of domestic economic life, the more prone it is to being politicised. This is by no means a straightforward process and assessing such a proposition might not be captured by remaining at the same level of analysis. Instead, by shifting the level of analysis from the national to the sectoral level, we are better able to determine the nature of European integration as a 'moving target' (Marks

1997, 2004) as well as the scope for any political conflict that might arise as a result. That said, political conflict needs to be mobilised. Here 'actors can shift the central logic of a political conflict' by framing a specific issue more strategically (Grande *et al.* 2016: 181; *see also* Erne 2008; Statham and Trenz 2013).

In order to mitigate the shortcomings of a synchronic-comparative research design, I have not only adopted an historical approach but I also incorporate a meso-level analysis into the research design. This is because the meso- or sectoral level is more sensitive to the diffusive effects of contemporary European integration (Bieler 2006; Erne 2008; Bechter, Brandle and Meardi 2012; Meardi 2012a, 2012b) as well as the differential effects of political conflict and politicisation (Bartolini 2000; de Wilde, Michailidou and Trenze 2016). Paul Taggart, an early scholar of Euroscepticism, laments that within Euroscepticism scholarship there 'remains something of an academic Berlin Wall between those who study European domestic processes and the process of European integration' (2006: 20). In other words, research is being conducted at different levels with little or no dialogue. If this is to be remedied, then 'we need more systematically to integrate the study of European domestic politics with the study of the politics of the European integration process' (*ibid.*: 8). A prominent politicisation scholar, Zurn (2019: 987), re-echoing Taggart (2006), notes that there is an argument for observing politicisation at two levels: 'A focus on only one political level in the study of politicization runs the danger of overlooking counter-trends on the other political levels.'

Empirical observations on EU debates can be made at the individual (micro-), organisational (meso-) and national (macro-)levels. Hitherto, the majority of politicisation studies have focused either on the individual level, by analysing survey data (for example, Fligstein 2008) or the systemic (macro-)level by analysing media debates (for example, Kriesi *et al.* 2008, 2012; Grande and Hutter 2016; *see* Zurn 2016 for an overview). Despite politicisation studies having proliferated in the past decade or so, 'our empirical knowledge on the *level* of politicization, its *timing* and its *driving forces* is still insufficient' (Hutter and Grande 2014: 1002, emphasis in original). Given the historical role of organised labour in the creation of collective social rights (Marshall 1964); and political cleavages (Ebbinghaus 1993; Bartolini 2000) – as well as the politicisation of market relations not least within the national context (Korpi 1983; Crouch 1993; Hyman 2001a) but also within the broader European context (Marginson and Sisson 2004; Erne 2008) – it is remarkable that organised labour has not really featured in the politicisation debate. Take, for example, the edited volume *Politicising Europe* (Hutter *et al.* 2016; *see also* Hoeglinger 2016), which contains barely any reference to organised labour. This is partly because the focus is on 'protest politics' or the 'electoral arena' and partly a reflection of the times we live in rather than a deliberate omission. As Colin Crouch (2015: 3) notes '[F]or several decades now the study of labour issues has been a specialized field, rather cut off from the rest of sociology and economics.' The objective of this book is to bring labour politics and the social question back together and view them through the prism of a transformative socio-economic phenomenon, namely, European integration.

Studying organised labour is the bread and butter of industrial relations scholarship, where much of the analysis takes places at the sectoral level. The advantage of a sectoral or a comparative industrial relations approach is that transnational socio-economic processes are best observed at the meso-level (Bechter, Brandl and Meardi 2012). This level 'has been traditionally fundamental for the governance of labour markets' (*ibid.*: 186). As noted above, the third phase of European integration was characterised by a level of labour mobility the EU had never before experienced. That said, the phenomenon of labour mobility was 'strangely neglected by industrial relations scholars' (McGovern 2007: 218) and theories of European integration (*see* Chapter Three). Consequently, our understanding of the main factors responsible for politicising labour mobility 'is still unsatisfactory' (Grande *et al.* 2019: 1445). By addressing this lacuna, we are better able to understand not only how organised labour offsets challenges associated with labour mobility but also to what extent the experience informs broader preferences towards the EU generally and labour Euroscepticism in particular. In other words, comparative industrial relations and the sectoral level offer 'the best balance between parsimony and complexity' (Marginson and Sisson 2004: 317).

By focusing on a substantive transnational aspect of European integration, namely, labour mobility, within a specific temporal frame and within an economic sector, such as construction, it is possible to determine whether organised labour's regulatory and non-regulatory coping mechanisms (*see* Chapter Seven) are sufficient to offset the challenges associated with labour mobility, such as social dumping practices (Menz 2005). Social dumping is defined as 'the practice, undertaken by self-interested market participants, of undermining or evading existing social regulations with the aim of gaining a competitive advantage' (Bernaciak 2015: 2).

Arguably, experiences on the ground will at the very least inform debates on the future direction of European integration (*see* Chapter Three). In effect, I am making the argument that the more European integration becomes a *dis-embedding* force *à la* Polanyi (*see* Chapter Two), the more the likelihood of contestation increases. However, what shape this contestation takes depends largely on the extent of engagement with European representative structures as well as domestic political factors. Ironically, it is the more liberally-oriented economic and political orders that are at greater risk from social dumping, which can be conceptualised as a consequence of disembedding. Should this contestation be misdiagnosed, or go unchecked, there is the distinct possibility that 'morbid symptoms' (Gramsci 1971) will become the driving force of the next social transformation (Polanyi 2001[1944]). Scholars, too. have a responsibility in this regard, which is the theme of the next section.

POLITICISATION: A FORM OF HERESY?

Surveying the politicisation literature, Zurn notes that 'much of research on EU considers politicization a problem' rather than an 'enabling condition that can lead to democratization' (2019: 984, 986). Certainly, this is the case when it comes to Andrew Moravcsik, who argues that the recent politicisation of the EU is 'a self-inflicted wound' resulting not from 'the EU's policies, or its constitutional structure', but from 'its constitutional discourse' (*ibid.*: 237). For Moravcsik, 'the existing European constitutional settlement is not just pragmatically more successful, but also normatively more desirable, than politicization through "democratic" reform' (*ibid.*: 222). Clearly an apostle of technocracy and the *status quo*, Moravscik argues that 'the EU's greatest tactical advantage is that it is, in a word, so *boring*' (2006: 238, emphasis in original) and it therefore should remain arcane to citizens and ultimately 'depoliticized' (*ibid.*: 237–9). Speaking of 'modern constitutional systems', Moravcsik does so as though they have been fashioned out of thin air. Clearly, no role is envisaged for agency, or democratising agency at that, which is problematic if we consider that the EU is an increasingly contested project (Fligstein 2008; Hooghe and Marks 2009; Kriesi *et al.* 2012; Grande *et al.* 2016; Hoeglinger 2016; Grande *et al.* 2019). Even less aware is he of the structuring condition of transnational socio-economic dynamics, or that organised labour, to quote Marx (1852), 'make their own history, but they do not make it as they please; they do not make it under self-selected circumstances, but under circumstances existing already, given and transmitted from the past'. Perhaps Moravcsik's hesitancy towards greater democratic legitimacy is because '[P]rocesses of democratization always require a redistribution of power. Rulers have therefore rarely initiated them' (Erne 2008: 19).

Following the rejection of the ECT, Moravcsik (2006: 227) wrote that '[F]orcing participation is likely to be counterproductive, because the popular response is condemned to be ignorant, irrelevant and ideological'! This is to be contrasted with the 'educated' 'enlightened' and 'cosmopolitan' elite that support deeper integration. As Fligstein (2008: 178) writes:

> At its core, one of the reasons that educated people support the European project is because the European values they espouse are identical with the Enlightenment values that have been a hallmark of educated people for over two hundred

years. Indeed, if Europe stands for anything, it is the completion of the Enlightenment project of democracy, rule of law, respect for the differences of others, and the principles of rational discourse and science.

Consequently, the educated masses are the 'the real moral engine of the EU' (*ibid.*). However, and somewhat contradictorily, they also 'believe in democracy and peacefully adjudicating political issues' and 'also care about rational debate, having tolerance for other people's points of view, and using discourse to settle grievances' (*ibid.*,178–9).

Clearly, academics occupy the upper echelons of European society (Béthoux, Erne and Golden 2018: 19); however, they are urged not to awaken the sleeping giant. For instance, Moravscik (2006: 221) argues that there is a need to 'counsel skepticism toward those who recommend politicization, deliberation and mass plebiscitary democracy to promote political legitimation and effectiveness' (*ibid.*). A similar note of caution is issued by the political theorist Andreas Føllesdal:

> Normative political theory may ... contribute significantly to promoting long term stability [in the EU]. However, normative political theory is double edged. If theorists were to find that there is no common good for Europe, or that the present regime or particular institutions fail to secure these objectives and values to a reasonable extent, what diffuse support there was may corrode further. The regime may then not warrant obedience. Normative political theory may bring that out in the open, adding pressure to the need for regime reform rather than popular acquiescence to a political order that fails to respect all as equals (2006: 463).

First and foremost, there is an onus on scholars and researchers to pursue an objective truth. This is by no means a straightforward task, given the complexity of social reality. There is, however, a danger in taking political shibboleths at face value. This is especially the case with Euroscepticism, a term invented by UK journalism in the mid-1980s (Harmsen and Spiering 2004: 14), which subsequently became a buzzword or label used to discredit political opponents, typically through the media, as nationalistic and xenophobic. Take, for instance, the idea of the 'Polish plumber', which became a trope for a social dumping threat and a defining characteristic of the French debate on the ECT and was supposedly instrumentalised by 'Eurosceptics' to scare voters into rejecting the treaty (Favell 2008; Etzioni 2007; Nicolaïdis and Schmidt 2007).

A lesser-known fact is that the spectre of the 'Polish plumber' entered the referendum debate at a late stage, following a controversial press conference with EU Commissioner, Fritz Bolkestein (Sciolino 2005). The strategic imputation was clearly an attempt to label leftist opposition to the ECT as nationalistic and narrow-minded rather than a necessary ingredient of democratic politics (Béthoux, Erne and Golden 2018) and a similar tactic was used by Bolkestein against those critical of his Services Directive, not least organised labour (Fischbach-Pyttel 2017). A similar line was adopted by the *Financial Times*, which accused the opposing labour leaders of 'simple xenophobia' (Arnold 2005). This negative cultural framing of Euroscepticism has proven influential; and while the *Financial Times* might have a hidden pro-liberal agenda, one might expect greater empirical substantiation from academic scholars. This, unfortunately, has not been the case, as the 'Polish plumber' trope has also featured in the academic literature to explain the 'great electoral reward to be had by populist politicians using the "threat" of open doors eastwards' (Favell 2008: 703).

The quest for EU democratisation is central to the work of Roland Erne in his book *European Unions*. The overarching theme can be read in the book's subtitle: *Labor's Quest for a Transnational Democracy*. Drawing on the work of labour historians E. P. Thomson and Eric Hobsbawm, Erne (2008) argues rather convincingly that just as in the national experience, organised labour's plea for democratic legitimacy within the EU might not be the ultimate objective but rather the means to an end. Erne is critical of the existing EU integration scholarship for having overlooked democratisation, which, for all intents and purposes, is a form of politicisation. Extant scholarship 'see[s] further integration as a product of the incremental political action by elites carried out behind the backs of European citizens' (*ibid.*: 20). Erne terms this Euro-technocratisation, which is disconnected from partisan politics and is by no means an accident. Erne (*ibid.*: 18) is critical of the ideology of technocracy, whether it be at the European level or at the national level, and, in particular, the efficiency-oriented view of legitimacy. Erne argues, *contra* Scharpf (1999), that to apply the term 'democracy' to output-oriented legitimacy is tantamount to concept-stretching, only the consequences are greater than invoking the charge of having committed academic misconduct.

Erne's line of argumentation is not dissimilar to that of Mair's outlined above. The latter lamented that 'virtually no attention is paid to the question of how Europe may have provoked fissures within parties' (Mair 2000: 27). The same can be said for national labour movements on the question of European integration, with some rare exceptions (for example, Bieler 2006; Erne 2008). An objective of this book is to address this gap in the literature. Hence, this book seeks not only to understand the origins and subsequent mutations of broad preferences towards the EU but also to conduct an empirical investigation into the substantive nature of European integration, so as to grasp why it is that labour Euroscepticism is emerging amongst some trade unions but not others. As Trenz (2016: 91) states:

There is no sense in researching Euroscepticism as an attribute of particular actors or parties. Instead of a descriptive account of Euroscepticism and its various manifestations, we need to engage in a critical inquiry of the structural and material conditions that empower or disempower particular population strata and generate collective responses.

However, collective responses to socio-economic phenomena need to be articulated or incorporated into a broader strategy, which could lead to the politicisation of European integration.

To this end, I argue in favour of a) conceptualising Euroscepticism and politicisation as polity-contestation; and b) focusing on the micro-foundations of contemporary European integration in different, but comparable, contexts. In doing so, this book contributes to a societal understanding of European politics (Polanyi 2001[1944]); Gramsci 1971; de Wilde 2011; de Wilde and Trenz 2012; Trenz 2016), whilst bearing in mind that society is no longer limited to one country (Urry 2000; Beck and Grande 2007; Fligstein 2008). Albeit latecomers to EU studies (*see* Ross 2011), sociological approaches are a welcome development in the burgeoning academic scholarship of EU studies. Yet the dearth of attention to labour politics continues (Crouch 2015). Notwithstanding, the natural home of labour-oriented scholarship, that is, comparative industrial relations, has much to offer (*see* Hyman 2001b; Almond and Connolly 2019). By analysing transnational transformative processes, within a specific socio-economic field (Bechter, Brandl and Meardi 2012), and through the prism of organised labour's regulatory and non-regulatory coping mechanisms, it is possible to determine the extent to which there is a feedback loop between experiences of European integration, as a transnational socio-economic process, and attendant changing preferences on the EU. In other words, there is a 'dual ontology' (Bellamy and Castiglione 2003; Dobson 2006) which can produce an admixture of socio-economic and national issues.

STRUCTURE OF THE BOOK

This book is divided into three parts, following this introductory chapter. Part I contains two chapters. Chapter Two deals with the theory of European integration and its limitations when it comes to preference-formation and politicisation. Here, I draw on the work of economic sociologist Karl Polanyi (2001[1944]), whose concepts of (dis)embedding and countermovement are particularly useful for understanding European integration as a transnational socio-economic process that facilitates market expansion and attendant responses by social actors. Chapter Three discusses the benefits of a diachronic research design over a synchronic one; and, through qualitative comparative analysis, it explains how it is possible to systematically exclude a number of potential explanatory factors when accounting for changes in preferences across time. The case is also made for incorporating a sectoral analysis into the research design. Part II consists of three empirical chapters. Chapter Four considers Irish and Italian labour's attitudes to and during the first and longest phase of European integration. Chapters Five and Six relate to the second phase of European integration. Here, we see Irish and Italian organised labour following a similar trajectory between phase one and phase two, when labour Euroscepticism gives way to a more positive stance *vis-à-vis* European integration. Part III is focused primarily on the most recent phase of European integration, noteworthy for the free movement of labour and services, in the context of EU enlargement. As transnational socio-economic processes are constituted locally (Amoore 2002), a more fine-grained approach is required. Chapter Seven presents a study of the Irish and Italian construction sector, in which the unions' respective 'coping mechanisms' are assessed. Chapter Eight looks at the debates surrounding the European Constitution, its successor the Lisbon Treaty and the Fiscal Treaty. It is during this phase that labour Euroscepticism re-emerges in Irish unions, but not in their Italian counterparts. The Conclusion identifies the factors that shape the preferences of Irish and Italian organised labour on European integration.

PART I

STUDYING PREFERENCES ON EUROPEAN INTEGRATION: THEORY AND PRAXIS

Chapter Two

Theories of Political Preferences on European Integration: A Neo-Polanyian Approach

The Community shall have as its task ... to promote throughout the Community a harmonious, balanced and sustainable development of economic activities, a high level of employment and of social protection, equality between men and women, sustainable and non-inflationary growth, a high degree of competitiveness and convergence of economic performance, a high level of protection and improvement of the quality of the environment, the raising of the standard of living and quality of life, and economic and social cohesion and solidarity among Member States (Article 2, Treaty of Rome, emphasis added).

INTRODUCTION

The concept of 'constructive ambiguity' is engineered into the DNA of the EU. Article 2 of the Rome Treaty, above, demonstrates this point well. This 'constructive ambiguity', a term coined by Henry Kissinger, has acted as a mask for politics and ideologies even to this day (Crespy and Vanheuverzwijn 2019) and has served the bridging of different -isms, in the name of jettisoning one of the most abhorrent -isms of them all, namely, fascist nationalism. Yet there is an inherent tension or contradiction. The ideologies shaping the EU were defined exactly by their hostility to ideological conflict. Informed by an idea of the supranational as a technocratic realm beyond ideological division, efforts to transcend ideological conflict and its cross-border variant were bound up in an apparent contradiction. As White (2020a: 2) states, 'the EU has been built on ideology, and also against it.' Scholarship, too, has been instrumental in obfuscating ideological rivalries. This was especially the case with Ernest Haas (1958) and neo-functionalism, which introduced an integrative ideology termed 'Europeanism'. The other dominant theory of European integration is that of liberal intergovernmentalism, which is closely associated with the work of Andrew Moravcsik (1998). According to liberal intergovernmentalism, greater attention should be paid to geopolitical ideology. In shaping a member state's geopolitical ideology, economic interests are 'primary' and pressure from economic interest groups, including trade unions, are of greater importance than 'security concerns and the ideological visions of politicians and public opinion' (Moravcsik 1998: 6–7). Other theoretical contributions have come from critical political economists who draw on the work of Italian Marxist, Antonio Gramsci, to shed light on the EU's constructive ambiguity or, in their words, 'the contradictions that have characterized the European economic and financial integration since at least the 1992 Maastricht Treaty' (van Apeldoorn and Horn 2019: 196). The post-Maastricht period is associated with the 'awakening of the Giant' and the rise of Euroscepticism. Accounting for this has produced the most recent theoretical contribution to EU studies, which is termed post-functionalism (Hooghe and Marks 2009). The subject of preference-formation on the question of European integration has been theorised by these different schools of thought, albeit indirectly and usually unsatisfactorily. Instead, I argue that the 'institutionalist' approach of Karl Polanyi (2001 [1944]) is well placed to help us grasp the emerging phenomenon of contemporary labour Euroscepticism.

In the following sections, I will briefly assess the strengths and weaknesses of the different theories on the question of political preferences *vis-à-vis* the EU. In the first section, the contributions of neo-functionalism and liberal intergovernmentalism will be presented. Following on, the more recent contributions to the theoretical debate on preference-formation will be laid bare. Whilst an advancement in the theorisation is discernible, there remains scope for enrichment. To this end, I draw on the *magnum opus* of economic sociologist Karl Polanyi, his *The Great Transformation*, which was published just as the second world war was entering its final stage. However, Polanyi's work has never been of greater relevance than in the most recent phase of European integration.

NEO-FUNCTIONALISM AND LIBERAL INTERGOVERNMENTALISM: A QUESTION OF PREFERENCE?

Theories of European integration are characterised by two dominant schools of thought: neo-functionalism and liberal intergovernmentalism. Neo-functionalism is heavily influenced by an admixture of pluralism and functionalism. Rather than making assumptions about state interests, as intergovernmentalists do, the neo-functionalist tradition conceptualises the state as an arena in which socio-economic and political actors seek to realise their interests. Should these actors deem their interests to be best served by a supranational institution, then the focus will shift to the European level and regional integration is thereby propelled forward (Haas 1958). A mutually reinforcing process, known as spillover, will drive the process further and result in political reordering as regional integration opens up new possibilities for socio-political actors within both national and supranational arenas. Haas (1958: 16) believed that economic integration would be followed by a political integration process 'whereby political actors in several distinct national settings are persuaded to shift their loyalties, expectations and political activities towards a new centre'. Obliquely, this implies a pro-EU preference *tout court*, which is shaped, first and foremost by functionalist forces, and generates a shift in preferences for the supranational level over the national one. Haas (1958: 356) specifically implicated trade unions in this process, as 'they tend to compromise competing national viewpoints in the interest of international labour unity'. Whilst this capacity might be there, it is not automatic (Bieler *et al.* 2015: ch. 1).

For neo-functionalists, '[T]he end result of a process of political integration is a new political community, superimposing over the pre-existing ones' (Haas 1958: 16). Arguably, the 'superimposing' aspect is important from a preference perspective. For starters, it does not imply a replacement of preferences for national political or industrial relations systems, which might be considered too dramatic in terms of transformation. The use of the term is also in keeping with the 'end of ideology' thesis (White 2020a), which is intrinsic to neo-functionalism and its integrative ideology, which 'blunts domestic ideological conflict and permits a measure of harmony to develop in spite of a tenacious group struggle' (Haas 1958: 20). As Haas (1968) noted a decade later in the second edition of *The Uniting of Europe*, 'the supranational scheme does not call for a conflict of loyalties between the nation and the European Community' (*ibidem* xvii) and, as a consequence, 'the conditioning impact of nationalism was defined out of existence' (*ibid.* xiv). In other words, 'high politics' were replaced by a technocratic logic that would move the EU towards economic integration and social harmonisation: in sum, political integration or a form thereof. Simple interdependence blunted the sword of unilateralism, with the odd exception from de Gaulle – 'a true nineteenth-century nationalist' *(ibid.* xviii) – but 'Europeanism', as Haas (1958: 19–28) termed it, had sufficient devotees to ensure that 'the economic technician could play his [sic] role within the shelter of the politicians' support' (Haas 1968: xxi). There was, to evoke Dahl's term (1965: 19), a 'surplus of consensus', which supported technocratic fixes and assuaged concerns about a premature politicisation of European integration.

Neo-functionalism was more concerned with institutional form rather than socio-economic content, with the latter being portrayed broadly as a benevolent force. The 'spillover' effect was seen as being the driving force behind increasing the authority of supranational institutions, which would offset potential political conflicts through technocratic means. The technocratic aspect is important in maintaining or modifying the preferences of (national) socio-economic actors as well as their identities. Neo-functionalism envisaged that such actors would, upon their return to their national capitals, promote their recalibrated functional interests and the supranational-technocratic *modus operandi*. By doing so, a pro-European stance would be consolidated. As Haas (1958: xiii) put it: 'group pressure will spill over into the federal sphere and thereby add to the integrative impulse'. The technocratic process is important not only in circumventing political conflict but also by not arousing public concerns and achieving a 'permissive consensus' (Lindberg and Scheingold 1970).

Whilst neo-functionalists such as Haas, and his students Lindberg and later Schmitter, believed that politics are rooted primarily in society, national governments and societal actors are seen as implicitly buying into the supranational political process. However, these actors often have conflicting interests and ideologies, which could potentially result in diverging preferences about European integration. Also, societal interests are perceived more as functional experts willing to engage in technocratic processes rather than organised interests whose preferences are the result of class struggles. In other words, 'the theory emphasized the power of the expert ... But ... had no explanation for which groups should succeed, form coalitions, mobilize interests, have access to policy-makers, and affect policy' (Caporaso 1998: 9). Finally, neo-functionalism placed too strong an emphasis on the prospect of labour internationalism. Post-war labour internationalism was far from unified and instead was plagued by ideological divisions (Pasture 2001). This aspect will be examined further in Chapter Four; however, once ideological divisions were eventually overcome the scope for 'market-correcting' responses resulting from spillover would be limited (Scharpf 1999).

Against the backdrop of ebbing European integration, known as Eurosclerosis, Haas (1975) somewhat paradoxically wrote of the 'obsolescence of regional integration theory', precisely at a time when labour movements were overcoming their ideological differences and establishing the European Trade Union Confederation (ETUC). Following its creation in 1973, the ETUC had the potential to engage with the technocratic process and the different European institutions. Kirchner's study of the ETUC (Kirchner 1977) represents one of the first systematic studies of interest group systems in the emerging decision-making centre. Kirchner's argumentation rested on two fundamental points. First, that the ETUC emerged so as to counter the mobilisation of business interests at the European level. And second, that interest-group mobilisation begets more interest-group mobilisation. This sounds more like a corroboration of neo-functionalism than its obsolescence. Notwithstanding Kirshner's work, scholars' interest in organised labour at the EU level waned in favour of developments, particularly neo-corporatism, at the national level (Streeck and Schmitter 1991). Haas's 1975 essay was critical of the fact that neo-functionalism was ill-equipped to explain shifts in political preferences towards European integration.

> In large measure, the disappointment resulted from not allowing for the possibility that actors' motives change, that interests and values considered salient and positively linked to integration may give way to different interests and to values with a more equivocal impact on integration (Haas 1975: 8).

What Haas does not ask is what stimuluses might underpin a change of heart? And are they rooted in cultural or socio-economic explanations?

Turning to liberal perspectives: these also have a pluralist facet but tend towards an individualist conception of supranational relations. Here, European integration is seen from the standpoint of nation-states in search of mutually advantageous pacts or understandings. The importance of domestically defined state interests distinguishes liberal intergovernmentalism from the realist school of international relations, which typically theorises state preferences as unitary and fixed (Moravcsik 1998: 20). Hence, state–society relations are considered but their treatment remained, as discussed here, rather limited. Intergovernmentalist scholars, most notably Hoffmann (1966), rarely identified a clear set of preferences for member governments, other than a principled apprehension about the ceding of national sovereignty. Following the so-called relaunch of European integration in the mid-1980s, debates on the nature of European integration were revived. Andrew Moravcsik's (1991, 1993, 1997, 1998) work built on intergovernmentalism by introducing a liberal model of preference-formation when discussing the development of the EU. Contrary to his previous work on the Single European Act, which was criticised for its state-centric ontology and for excluding social forces altogether from the analysis, Moravscik (1997) made the case for 'taking preferences seriously' and, to this end, introduced a liberal component into intergovernmentalism. Bound up in international relations, the focus is on the most powerful member states within the EU, their national agendas and their bargaining strategies. However, Moravcsik went beyond the realist interpretation of the international system. States 'do not automatically maximize fixed, homogeneous conceptions of security, sovereignty, or wealth *per se* (as realists assume) … Instead … they pursue particular interpretations and combinations of security, welfare and sovereignty preferred by powerful groups' (Moravscik 1997: 519).

For Moravcsik, powerful groups' interests are bound up with economic interests. Writing in the *Choice for Europe*, Moravcsik (1998: 3) claims that European integration 'evolved slowly in response to structural incentives in the global economy'. For Moravcsik, the integration process proceeds in three stages. In the first stage, organised interests are seen to shape government outcomes: 'groups articulate preferences; governments aggregate them' (Moravcsik 1993: 8). Hence, unlike intergovernmentalists before, state–society relations are now considered. In the second stage, the member states bring their formed national preferences to the European bargaining table. And in the third stage we have the outcome of these negotiations, which decides the extent of sovereignty-pooling and the institutional design required to implement supranational policies necessary for market regulation (Moravcsik 1998: 5–10). There is a fourth stage, namely, the ratification process, in which Ireland is a unique case as a plebiscite is necessary and this affords actors the opportunity to politicise the EU and European integration.

Notwithstanding the consideration of state–society relations with regard to the first stage, liberal intergovernmentalism remains problematic on a number of fronts. Firstly, the second and third stages remain bound up in neo-realist state-centrism. Secondly, (federalist) ideas are not considered as being important, or of marginal importance at best (Moravcsik 1998: 4), despite the fact that the project of European integration is underpinned by a grand idea (Morgan 2005) Consequently, liberal intergovernmentalism 'overly rationalises the negotiation process through a reductionist emphasis on the role of national governments' (Armstrong and Bulmer 1998: 33). In doing so, there is little or no scope for politicisation of the process, during either the formulation stages or the ratification stage. Thirdly, supranational and transnational actors, such as the Commission and the ETUC, are ignored, as are the day-to-day politics of the EU and routine policymaking. Despite 'social purpose' appearing in the subtitle of *The Choice for Europe*, and attempts being made to bring domestic politics into the analysis, serious issues remain with a liberal theory of state–society relations. I will return to this in the following section, where I discuss the merits of neo-Gramscian theory in the formation of preferences. Lastly, the emphasis of liberal intergovernmentalism is on 'producer groups', which national governments tend to favour over 'consumers, tax-payers, third-country producers, and also potential future producers' (Moravcsik 1998: 36). To this list we can add organised labour, which is overlooked in favour of business groups and rendered a passive passenger in the development of the EU (*see also* Fioretos 2011). In other words, there is 'no interest in the *balance* of social forces (emphasis in original) and how this might be *changing over time*' (van Apeldoorn 2002: 40, emphasis added). The 'changing over time' aspect is emphasised as it is of import for this book: any change in the direction of greater political integration is seen as being dependent on a shift in preferences of business groups in Europe's leading states.

(NEO-)GRAMSCI AND THE THEORISATIONS OF EUROPEAN INTEGRATION, SOCIETY AND ITS STRUGGLES

First-order theories of European integration – neo-functionalism and intergovernmentalism – have serious shortcomings when it comes to the theorisation of preference-formation and the potential for change. This is because these 'scholars are not always explicit about [their] metatheoretical commitments, which makes it hard to identify what is on offer, what is being rejected, and what is at stake' (Jupille 2006: 220). Neo-Gramscian scholars, in particular, are critical of the lack of 'society' in European integration theories and research and, drawing on the work of Robert Cox (1987), they argue that 'state and society must be conceived as a relational whole' (van Apeldoorn 2002: 310). Otherwise, there is a likelihood that the underlying political structure of societies is oversimplified or even overlooked. The 'neo-' prefix of Gramsci-inspired scholarship can be traced back to the work of Cox (1981, 1983) and van der Pijl (1984) for their work on intra-class factions and the emergence of a transnational capitalist class that, for all intents and purposes, is 'superimposed upon national class structures' (Cox 1981: 147, cited in Bieler 2005: 516). From the use of term 'superimposed', one can perhaps detect a sympathy with neo-functionalism (*see above*); and, whilst its proponents certainly consider that interest groups are important actors in developing a transnational society, the concept, as far as neo-Gramscians are concerned, remains under-theorised. 'Transnational society is introduced as a concept but there is no *theory* of transnational society' (van Apeldoorn 2002: 38 emphasis in original). Hence, neither neo-functionalism nor liberal intergovernmentalism can sufficiently address the question of social purpose.

A neo-Gramscian perspective argues that '[P]olitical orders are always open to contestation and need to be constantly re-created' (Bieler 2006: 14).

Hence, European integration is driven by an open-ended political struggle in which different interest groups construct and advance different interests and related projects in a bid to create their vision of a European order. Here, there are multiple ways in which actors' preferences can be strategically pursued. By focusing on the *problématique* of social purpose, neo-Gramscian scholars pose a question that is not adequately addressed by established approaches to European integration. As the following quotation illustrates, a different direction is envisaged, one that addresses some of the shortcomings in the more established approaches to European integration.

> As a critical theory of European transformation it [a neo-Gramscian perspective] asks the question of how the current European order – which is both a political-institutional as well as a socio-economic order – came about; how this order differs from previous 'European orders' and what the conditions for its future transformation are (van Apeldoorn 2002: 34).

Since the mid-1990s, neo-Gramscian theories have featured in debates on European integration, critiquing neo-functionalism and liberal intergovernmentalism for their 'conceptual determinism' in the notions of spillover and state centrism, respectively (Bieler 2005). These theories were also criticised for prioritising the institutional structure of the emerging Euro-polity, rather than its social purpose (van Apeldoorn 2002: 34–44; Bieler 2000: 3–8). Instead, a neo-Gramscian approach argues that we can only come to a full understanding of the EU's political limits and their implications for future European governance if we 'analyse not just the changing institutional form but above all the socio-economic content or underlying social purpose of the integration' (Drahokoupil, van Apeldoorn and Horn 2009: 2). In other words, we need to ask to what extent does economic integration further the interests of a particular social force?

A basic distinction can be drawn between national social forces of capital and labour, born originally of national production sectors. Traditionally, these social relations of production take place within both the state and the market (Bieler and Morton 2003: 476; Bieler 2005: 516); however, the post-Cold-War context has led to the emergence of new social forces engendered by the transnationalisation of production and finance. Hence, a further distinction neo-Gramscians make is between *nationally* oriented capital and labour, which reside in domestic (production) sectors, and *internationally* oriented capital and labour, which produce for the international market.

Whether social forces, be they labour or capital, national or transnational, are located in the wider, transnational structure of the social relations of production, this 'do[es] not determine but [instead] shape[s] their interests and identity' (Bieler and Morton 2001: 17). Importantly, however, the 'uncovering and explanation of actual strategies of social forces remains the task of an empirical investigation' (Bieler 2005: 517). In sum, an understanding of the transformation of the European political economy 'can only be developed based on detailed empirical studies of transformation in different locations' (Pistor 2005: 120).

Naturally, neo-Gramscian scholarship owes a great deal to the philosophical writing of the Italian Marxist, Antonio Gramsci, and his conceptualisation of hegemony. Hegemony is a form of dominance that relies less on coercion and more on constructing a consensus. It is shaped by phases of stability and conflict (Bieler 2006: 31) and can be constituted on different levels, including regional orders. Bieler (*ibidem*) identifies three important factors in the struggle for hegemony. These are, first, ideas and ideology; second, material capabilities and power resources; and third, institutions, which are a combination and a product of the previous two and important for establishing a degree of order. Of particular importance to neo-Gramscians is the changing nature of class struggle and the material structure of ideas.

Another Gramscian concept of import is that of 'organic intellectuals', who emerge from and represent particular factions of social forces. The 'organic' implies 'an awareness of its own function not only in the economic but also in the social and political fields' (Gramsci 1971: 5). These organic intellectuals play an important role in the struggle for hegemony, within which ideas can play an important role. Ideas become part of the social structure in the form of intersubjective meanings and are important for linking the world of production with the political realm. Hence, ideas are 'produced by human agency in the context of social power relations' (van Apeldoorn 2002: 19). As hegemony is continually contested and requires continuous reaffirmation, '[O]rganic intellectuals do not simply produce ideas, but they concretise and articulate strategies in complex and often contradictory ways' (Bieler 2006: 36). This implies that understanding the role of ideas and their articulation, through organic intellectuals, requires empirical investigation.

NEO-GRAMSCIAN APPROACHES AND PREFERENCE-FORMATION

Studying the EU as a political-institutional construction and European integration as a transnational socio-economic process is an important analytical distinction. To this end, neo-Gramscian scholarship has made some advances. Preferences towards the EU, as a political system, are inevitably bound up with questions relating to social forces and the question of power resources, which are, in turn, bound up with transnational socio-economic processes. This relationship is by no means straightforward, nor linear. The work of van

Apeldoorn (2002) is of significance with regard to the role of *transnational* social forces and their preferences in developing a supranational political system from the mid-1980s onwards; Bieler's (2006) work is important as it examines the impact of transnational socio-economic processes on the preferences of organised labour on the question of EMU. Whilst the subject of van Apeldoorn and Bieler's work is quite different, however, both offer insights that further the theoretical development of preference-formation on the EU. Not coincidentally, the term 'struggle' is present in the title of both of their books; but it is their contribution to the theorisation of political preferences that makes discussion of their works so worthwhile here.

Van Apeldoorn (2002) is more concerned with how the post-Maastricht EU order came about, that is, the political-institutional aspect and the shift, on the ideological plane, from Keynesianism to 'embedded neoliberalism' within the transnational capitalist class. In doing so, he goes beyond the debate on whether the shape of European integration is determined by intergovernmental co-operation, or whether its development is shaped by transnational actors and supranational institutions that are underpinned by a functionalist logic. Instead, the argument is made that the EU is to be studied as an 'international state' (*ibid*: 46) with a 'unique system of governance' (*ibid*: 42); however, this should be complemented by a 'more *political* conceptualisation of transnational society' (*ibid*: 38 emphasis in original). Hence, by adopting a historical-materialist approach, society is brought back into the analysis. According to such a perspective, capitalist societies are structured 'to a significant degree' (*ibid*: 45) by the transnational relations of production, but not entirely. By extending the transnational 'dynamics of capitalist society to the realm of ideas and ideology, it focuses on the strategic action and struggles of social forces as a key constitutive factor' (*ibid.*). Typically, the struggle is between rival (trans)national social forces, notably labour and capital. However, on important questions these groups can also be the site of struggle and are not necessarily homogenous or unified subjects. Hence, preference-formation is 'about a *process*, which cannot be really understood if an ahistorical and static picture is taken' (*ibid*: 44, emphasis in original).

On the specific question of preference-formation, other insights can be drawn from van Apeldoorn's (2002) study of the European Roundtable of Industrialists (ERT). Despite the focus being on the transnational capitalist class, there are noteworthy lessons. Van Apeldoorn advances the claim that 'power ... takes the form of political and ideological agency' (2002: 46), which is used in the pursuit of its own preferences. How it is used, though, is a question for empirical investigation. Second, different ideological and strategic orientations are shaped by i) the geographical scale of the industry, ii) the sectoral characteristic in which the industry is embedded and iii) the national institutional context. These last two factors capture the historicity of social struggles that took place within national contexts and which shaped, *inter alia*, the emergence of industrial relations systems. Third, that the changing of preferences 'is indeed *a gradual process*' (*ibid*: 48, emphasis added). However, the underlying objective remains the same, to influence the shape of 'the emergent transnational and multi-level state–society complex of the EU' (*ibid*: 48).

Within the space of ten years, the ERT changed its position *vis-à-vis* European integration from a defensive attitude to global competition to a new, embedded neo-liberal orientation. Whilst the contours of embedded neo-liberalism are interesting and of consequence for the evolution of the EU (*see* van Apeldoorn 2002: 181–2), the process by which the preference is formulated concerns us here, at least from a theoretical standpoint. Identifying broad preferences is important because '[A]t the level of discourse, these models [or preferences] can be argued to function as reference points in ideological struggle' (*ibid*: 78). Following the 'constructivist turn' in EU studies (*see* Christiansen *et al.* 2001) van Apeldoorn rejects the 'structuralist perspective that merely focuses on the structural domination of capital over labour' (*ibid*: 21) and instead advances a critical theory that, similar to (social) constructivism, 'historicises the present social structures' (*ibid*: 16). This 'critical constructivism' not only brings (transnational) society back into the analysis, but it also places emphasis on 'the intersubjective making of social reality' as it is here that 'we find the role of ideas' (*ibid*: 14). As Risse and Wiener (1999: 780) write, drawing on the seminal work of Offe and Wiesenthal (1979):

> ... the *shared experience* and social structure of a society contribute to whether, and if so how, actors know their interests. As Offe and Wiesentahl point out, the rationale of collective actors differs crucially. The difference is, however, not simply based on given interests. Instead, it changes according to experience, i.e., *position in relation to other actors and in relation to larger structures* (cited in van Apeldoorn 2002: 43, emphasis added).

I will return to the relational aspect below. Here, I want to dwell momentarily on the questions regarding the articulation of 'shared experiences'. This articulation is down to what Gramsci termed 'organic intellectuals' (*see above*), who play an important role in making sense of complex reality by connecting social forces with ideas. These ideas are not fixed but can be amended in the interest of constructing an 'historic bloc' or, in the case of the ERT, transnational class solidarity.

Bieler (2006), on the other hand, focuses on organised labour in five countries and the development of their preferences with regards to EMU. Whereas van Apeldoorn (2002) engages and critiques orthodox theories of European integration, Bieler (2006) reserves criticism for the 'varieties of capitalism' (Hall and Soskice 2001) school of thought which has risen to prominence in academic scholarship over the past two decades. The 'varieties of capitalism' approach is critiqued for adopting a state-centric approach and understating the extent of globalisation, which is treated as an exogenous challenge. Also, the 'varieties of capitalism' conceptualisation of organised labour is seen as operating at the national level *vis-à-vis* other national actors, including the government, instead of being 'understood as being part of a wider restructuring changing the international state system' (Bieler 2006: 27). Bieler is keen to emphasise the restructuring nature of globalisation processes and its role in shaping the preferences of organised labour.

Much, Bieler argues, depends on how globalisation is defined (*ibid.*: 24). He defines globalisation as 'the transnationalisation of production and finance at the material level and the shift from Keynesianism to neo-liberal ideas at the ideological level' (*ibid.*: 199). This phenomenon is then studied through the prism of EMU, which is seen to reinforce certain tendencies introduced by economic internationalisation. Hence, 'EMU is regarded as a vehicle to assess trade unions' options and possibilities to respond to global structural change and participate in the formation of the future economic-political system of the EU' (*ibid.*: 1). Adopting a strategic-relational approach, Bieler concretely investigates how unions struggle for an alternative Europe, by comparing the positions of Austrian, British, French, German and Swedish unions on the question of EMU. Bieler is interested in assessing i) confederal pluralism and the interplay between ideology and the position on EMU; ii) how the internal politics of national confederations are characterised by unions in transnationalised sectors and unions in more sheltered sectors; and iii) whether unions engage in European co-ordination strategies and, if so, whether the strategies are pursued through the ETUC, or if alternative avenues are sought out.

Bieler finds that 'the vast majority of transnational sector unions ... supported EMU', however, 'unions' positions cannot be read off from their location in the production process' and that production is 'determining only in the first instance' (Bieler 2006: 151, 35). This may appear confusing or even contradictory; however, this is where the strategic-relational aspect comes in. Class, in and of itself, is a relational concept that originates in the structure of the social *relations* of production and generates the basic division between labour and capital. These divisions may be structural but they are not fixed, as confirmed by van Apeldoorn and Bieler: they can coexist *within* a class, be it capital or labour, and produce diverging preferences on European questions. The internationalisation of the economy has complicated this aspect, giving rise to a functional difference between financial capital, on the one hand, and productive capital, on the other (van der Pijl 1998: ch. 2). The extent of transnationalisation is another aspect that can have a bearing on how a class faction reacts, or formulates a preference, on an impending question, which could carry implications for inter- and intra-class relations. Here, 'the agency of these elites becomes a critical factor in understanding transnational political phenomena inasmuch as they seek to set the agenda and shape policies' (van Appeldoorn 2002: 3). These 'organic' elites have a degree of strategic autonomy or selectivity available, which can vary across space and time. It is for this reason that the sphere of production, be it national or transnational, is only the starting point for investigation, not necessarily the end point. Hence, 'there are always several potential strategies actors can choose from and that, by extension, future development is open-ended' (Bieler 2009: 236). For starters, there is the state, which 'is the framework within which various different strategies are possible' (*ibid*: 237; *see also* Jessop 1990). Additionally, there are other institutions that might shape strategic behaviour, such as the industrial relations system. Alternatively, there remains the transnational or European level (Erne 2008). Together, these can be termed the political opportunity structure of the EU (Marks and McAdam 1996). Ascertaining which avenue actors choose to realise a preference requires empirical investigation.

By and large, neo-Gramscians are concerned with the hegemonic spell of neo-liberal restructuring and its 'articulatory practice' (Laclau and Mouffe 1985). The contributions of van Apeldoorn (2002) and Bieler (2006) highlight how preferences towards economic and monetary integration are formed, in the first instance, and how preferences can change across time. A recent appraisal of the neo-Gramscian scholarship observes that 'most neo-Gramscian research was – and perhaps still is – on the emergence and reproduction of neoliberal hegemony ... most scholars have taken into consideration the processes of globalisation, financialization and digitalization and the changing patterns of production, but also highlighted the more explicitly political manufacturing of a transnational consensus' (Bieler and Bieling 2019: 51–2). Whilst being quite comprehensive in its scholarship, there is scope for complementary research. The first, and most obvious, is by extending the cases under study. I do this by studying the Irish and Italian labour movements across time. How globalisation is defined, as Bieler (2006) rightly points out, is very important; however, globalisation is not just about the transnationalisation of supply chains and finance. There is another dimension, which has more recently came to the fore in the EU, namely, transnational migration or, as I term it, labour mobility. As prominent scholars of globalisation, such as David Held and others, note '[O]ne form of globalization is more ubiquitous than any other – human migration' (Held *et al.* 1999: 283, ch. 6). To boot, the idea of counter-hegemony remains undertheorised. As Bieler (2005: 522) notes, 'too little attention has been paid to the potential of resistance to neo-liberalism.' In the following two sections, I look to develop a theoretical framework that will help to explain why labour Euroscepticism (re-)emerges in some countries but not in others. This is achieved by drawing on the work of Karl Polanyi, who conceptualises why it is that resistance to neo-liberalism might materialise.

LIMITATIONS OF NEO-GRAMSCIAN APPROACHES IN AN ENLARGED EU

In the 2000s, the EU underwent an enlargement, just as it had with every passing decade since the 1970s. This enlargement, however, under the presidency of José Manuel Barroso, was of considerable significance and qualitatively different by comparison to previous ones. The Eastern enlargement of the EU differed for a variety of reasons. The most obvious reason is the sheer number of accession states and the dramatic increase in the EU's (working) population. Since the 1970s, the EU had undergone an enlargement every decade and the 'magic' number of new entrants each time had been three. The first decade of the new millennium, by contrast, saw the EU's membership almost double: from 15 to 27 member states. Secondly, previous enlargements differed because of the geographical proximity of the new entrants to the existing bloc of member states. Geographical proximity is an important factor with labour mobility as this usually overlaps with cultural and historical links. When labour mobility was introduced in the late 1960s, Italy, as a labour-sending country, shared only a small border with France. Of the subsequent enlargements in the 1970s, 1980s and 1990s, only one out of three of the joining countries shared a frontier with an existing member state[1]. The new member states in 2004 shared borders with Finland, Germany, Austria, Greece, and Italy. In addition, both the push and the pull factors were particularly strong (Fassmann, Haller and Lane 2009). Put simply, there was a considerable wage gap between the 'old' and the 'new' member states. The availability of low-cost travel and improved infrastructural linkages greatly facilitated labour mobility as 'old' destinations were replaced by 'new' destinations. Social networks, established during the 1990s, also facilitated the process of labour mobility from East to West (Ban 2009; Perotta 2011).

Although neo-Gramscian scholars have not fully engaged, to my knowledge, with labour mobility as a restructuring phenomenon of neo-liberalism, there has been some engagement with the concept of EU citizenship in the context of the Lisbon agenda, which is loosely related and rightly acknowledges that labour mobility inevitably produces 'changes in the spatial structuration of capitalist production and reproduction affecting territorially defined social relations' and leads to 'the commodification of the social existence of people through a relentless expansion of market practices' (Pellerin and Overbeek 2001: 137). Labour mobility has produced the transformation of the labour process, making it possible to use mobile labour in the most integrated and fixed sectors of the European political economy. It is in these sectors, such as construction, that a recourse to practices such as subcontracting, outsourcing and 'posting' have become all the more prevalent (*see* Part III). Posting involves a worker who is sent by their employer to provide a service in another EU member state on a temporary basis and is commonplace in construction, as Menz's study of the sector notes: 'German employers engaged in a two-tier strategy: employ foreign subcontractors, pay them Portuguese wages, and try to block any minimum wage the union might propose' (2005: 191).

As a structural phenomenon, labour migrants not only participate in and rely on, but also contest and negotiate, the social relations of capitalist (re) production and are therefore intrinsically linked to the neo-liberal restructuring of the European political economy. Understanding this phenomenon requires an empirical investigation into the concrete, contingent and situated practices of transnational labour migration. Only by doing so will we be in a position to better comprehend the contradictions, conflicts and tensions that are brought about by transnational labour markets. This social transformation, I contend, is feeding into labour Euroscepticism, which can also be interpreted as a misplaced expression of hostility to the social effects of neo-liberalism and the deregulation of labour markets (Schmidt 2016).

For scholars who draw on the work of Gramsci, the point of departure is the social question: society and social transformation. 'In the Gramscian ontology, social relations and social structures are the primary elements to be considered, for they alone constitute the limits of the potential space for change to take place' (Amoore 2002: 52). For Gramsci, the principal terrain of social transformation is the national level. Neo-Gramscians, as noted above, identify the supranational terrain as an additional level upon which social transformations can be enacted. On both the national and supranational levels, the intersubjective realms of ideas, knowledge, theory and social institutions are central to processes of social transformation (*see* van Apeldoorn 2001). Whilst there is no doubt whatsoever that the question of labour migration is shaped by socio-political forces at the supranational and national levels, the effects of it can be felt, first and foremost, locally, on the ground. Hence, it is at the meso- or sub-national level that social transformation is most visible (Bechter *et al.* 2012). This experience inevitably shapes, for better or worse, the intersubjective realms of ideas, knowledge, theory and social institutions and could well provoke (or constrain) social contestation, conflict and discord. As noted above, this social reality is articulated by 'organic intellectuals'; such a person is, in Gramsci's words

... a creator, an initiator; but he [sic] neither creates from nothing nor does he move in the turbid void of his own desires and dreams ... What 'ought to be' is therefore concrete; indeed it is the only realistic and historicist interpretation of reality, it alone is history in the making and philosophy in the making, it alone is politics (Gramsci 1971: 172).

Hence, the essence of politics, and the processes of politicisation, are to be found in the contests and struggles that shape the world of work. Understanding this requires bringing EU studies closer to the social practices resulting from European integration. Amoore problematises this by focusing on the sociological aspect of economic internationalisation as praxis.

It is in the realms of everyday thought and practice that competing interests confront one another, and where the contradictions and tensions of social transformation are expressed. Indeed, we might say that the 'everyday' realm is one where the boundaries of national/transnational, local/global, economics/politics and states/markets are both constituted and confounded (Amoore 2002: 55).

Labour migration is 'experienced, given meaning, reinforced/challenged in the everyday social practices of individuals and groups at multiple levels' (Amoore 2002: 7). Adopting a practice-centred view of economic restructuring permits the perception of transnational migrant labourers (and their native counterparts) not as passive but rather as agential subjects. In the following chapter, I make a case for studying the meso-level when studying the question of labour mobility; suffice to say here that it is at this level that collective tensions emerge and the material structure of ideas is constituted. However, the articulation of this 'reality', or its politicisation, depends on political factors (*see* Chapter Three). The next section outlines the theoretical rationale underpinning such a selection by drawing on the work of Karl Polanyi.

ACCOUNTING FOR LABOUR EUROSCEPTICISM: A NEO-POLANYIAN APPROACH

Attuned to the subtleties surrounding the power of ideas, and their sociological re-formulation (*see below*), neo-Gramscian scholars focus on globalisation as a driving force for economic restructuring. However, there is a need to problematise European integration as an intense regional form of globalisation from the vantage point of labour mobility; the latter thus far remains undertheorised by European integration scholars, in general, and neo-Gramscian scholars, in particular. To this end, the work of Karl Polanyi can be useful and complementary to the work of Antonio Gramsci, as van Apeldoorn (2002: 160) notes: 'Polanyi's ideas can very well be integrated with a Gramscian historical materialist framework.' Although both men suffered at the hands of fascism, they are rarely considered together. Yet, 'their engagement with historical forces is inseparable from their theoretical development' (Burawoy 2003: 201). Gramsci and Polanyi both 'converged on the same idea from very different experiences' (*ibid.*: 200). Both 'endow their notions of society with historical specificity', which 'occupies a specific institutional space within capitalism between economy and the state' (*ibid.*: 198). This institutional space is populated by political parties, voluntary associations, religious organisations and *trade unions*. Whereas Gramsci conceptualises society in terms of its complex relationship to the state, Polanyi sees society primarily in relation to the market; but Polanyi also acknowledges the state as a terrain for struggle. Gramsci's concept of hegemony as the organisation of class struggle is convincing and is the basis of the neo-Gramscian work cited above; however, the idea of counter-hegemony or resistance in the EU is undertheorised (Bieler 2005: 522; Crespy and Verschueren 2009: 279).

In *The Great Transformation* (2001 [1944]), Polanyi posits that markets are embedded in political and social institutions, which, in turn, are the construct of open-ended political struggles. Although Polanyi himself hardly used the concept of embeddedness (Krippner 2001: 779), many scholars have since borrowed and developed the concept (for example, Ruggie 1982; Granovetter 1985; Esping-Andersen 1990; Blyth 2002; van Appeldoorn 2002). Another useful Polanyian concept is that of the 'double movement', which follows attempts to disembed the market from society or to subject 'fictitious commodities', such as labour, to market dynamics (*see also* Thomson 1963). Whereas neo-Gramscian scholars have focused their analysis on the construction of hegemony at the transnational level (for example, van Apeldoorn 2002), a neo-Polanyian approach facilitates an analysis of transnational markets at the local and national level. Should a disembedding dynamic develop, we might expect to see resistance, which can take the form of a counter-hegemonic movement. The articulation of such grievances against the corrosive effects of markets falls to 'organic intellectuals', who, through their close ties with the working class, posit an alternative hegemony. How this materialises requires empirical investigation, ideally at the meso-level.

According to Polanyi, an efficient, unregulated and free-market system is a utopian concept. Moreover, '[S]uch an institution could not exist … without annihilating the human and natural substance of society' (Polanyi 2001 [1944]: 1). Attempts to create a 'self-regulating market' are not only utopian; such attempts will inevitably lead to a counter-movement by social forces. Polanyi (2001 [1944]: 130) wrote, 'for a century the dynamics of modern society were governed by a double movement: the market expanded continuously, but this movement was met with a counter-movement, checking the expansion in definite directions.' Thus, the 'double movement' was structured by two organising principles, namely, liberalism and social democracy or, in Polanyi's terminology, social protection.

The principle of economic liberalism, that is, the establishment of a self-regulating market, relies on the support of the trading classes and uses *laissez-faire* and free trade as its methods. The principle of social protection is the conservation of society, in terms of equality and fair treatment, and is reliant on those willing to articulate the grievances of those most affected by the deleterious action of the market (*ibid*: 138–9). This falls to 'organic intellectuals' or, to use Polanyi's term, 'enlightened reactionaries' (*ibid*: 160–74). Whilst the two poles of Polanyi's dialectical argument – a free, self-regulating market and a wholly socialised market – are ideal-types and therefore fanciful, there is a constant political battle between social forces in the space between these two poles.

The 'enlightened reactionaries' pursuing a 'protective response' are primarily, but not exclusively, the labour class. The 'double movement' dialectic goes a considerable way to explain the emergence of social institutions at the national level, which not only shaped interest representation but also determined the shape that contemporary welfare states and industrial relations systems have taken (Esping-Andersen 1990; Crouch 1993). Typically, 'welfare-state regimes and employment regimes tend to coincide' (Esping-Andersen 1990: 159) and can be seen as two sides of the European social model coin. These welfare and employment regimes, or industrial relations systems, can be conceptualised as Polanyian fixes, which have an embedding function and not only underpinned a cross-class consensus at the national level (Ruggie 1982) but also served to bolster the cross-country consensus at the supranational level (Milward 2000 [1992]). This order proved resilient in the face of distributive struggles at the national level: until the mid-1980s, that is, when the forces of economic liberalism coalesced at the European level (van Apeldoorn 2002) and advocated transnational market expansion, both in terms of network industries, most of which were in public hands, and in terms of geographical expansion. The creation of a common currency is also central to this agenda. These developments inevitably impacted on national labour markets and their governance (*see below*).

As noted in the work of van Apeldoorn (2002) 'embedded *neo*liberalism' (emphasis in original) characterised European integration from the 1990s onwards. The 'embedded' aspect involved the creation of complementary Polanyian fixes at the supranational level. These fixes emerged during what I term the second phase of European integration, which is closely associated with Commission President, Jacques Delors, and ensured that a pure or orthodox neo-liberalism never materialised. In other words, these Polanyian fixes undergirded the compromise that is 'embedded neo-liberalism'. A former trade unionist, Delors implicitly understood the teachings of Polanyi, having famously quipped that 'one cannot fall in love with the single market'. Appeasing proponents of a neo-liberal and social Europe required a great deal of political brinksmanship and political creativity by the European Commission (*see* Jabko (2006) for a detailed account). This involved creating Polanyian fixes at the supranational level, which, concretely, meant establishing sectoral social dialogue, creating structural and cohesion funds for underdeveloped regions and formulating a raft of socially oriented Directives that improved the working lives of EU workers. These Polanyian fixes went a considerable way to establishing a pro-European consensus amongst proponents of a social Europe.

Few would deny that labour markets have, over the past decades, undergone significant changes. Whilst macro-societal changes in the composition of the workforce and technological advancements have played their part, economic internationalisation, directly, and monetary union, indirectly, have also had considerable impact on (national) labour markets. Economic internationalisation intensified 'regime competition' (Scharpf 1999; Bieler 2006), thereby putting Polanyian fixes at the national level under pressure as the balance of power shifted in favour of capital. Also, the introduction of EMU brought pressure to bear on the welfare state–industrial relations nexus. This pressure became more explicit against the backdrop of the post-2008 'Great Recession' when national governments pursued 'internal devaluations' so as to regain competitiveness (*see* Erne *et al.*, 2024). Whilst these developments carry consequences for the social institutions that embed the market, the empirical focus of this book is on the effects of enlargement. This development not only intensified 'regime competition' (Bohle 2006), further strengthening capital's hand, but also heralded the mass movement of workers from East to West. A similar competitiveness discourse, put forth by a neo-liberal elite, underpinned the rationale for labour migration. As Menz (2016: 639) notes, 'the new discursive association with economic growth and competitiveness helped ensure public support or at least acquiescence' for labour migration.

With impending enlargement, Polanyian fixes were envisaged. These fixes were important in terms of securing a consensus; however, they were a national prerogative and could only be temporary in nature (*see* Chapter Seven). As labour-market stakeholders, organised labour seeks to influence the dynamics of supply and demand so that workers are not left at the mercy of market forces (Kjeldstadli 2015). Unions see labour markets less as marketplaces and more as embedded networks of individuals engaged in employment relations, which are, or at least ought to be, governed by a mutual contractual agreement between the employer and the employee (Hyman 2012: 66–7). In other words, trade unions implicitly view labour as a 'fictitious commodity', which necessitates social protection (Polanyi 2001 [1944]; Esping-Andersen

1990). Labour mobility, in an enlarged EU, introduced challenges which are of a different order than, say, the challenges associated with the free movement of goods or capital or the Maastricht criteria and EMU. Appreciating the nature of these challenges requires assessing labour mobility as a potential disembedding force, through the prism of unions' coping mechanisms or, in Polanyian terminology, their capacity for ensuring social protection. A union's capacity for policing transnational labour markets will, *ceteris paribus*, influence its political preference on the EU and its future development.

CONCLUSION

Social scientists have long been critical of the modelling of state–society relations along the lines of neo-classical economics. Society is more than an aggregation of individuals and interest groups engaging in continuous cost–benefit analysis (Polanyi 2001 [1944]). For too long, the question of society has been absent from European integration theories. Neo-Gramscian scholarship has made some positive steps in this regard and a neo-Gramscian perspective is 'open to complementary concepts, more sensitive to the particular national economic and institutional arrangements as well as to the discursive struggles within civil societies' (Bieler and Bieling 2019: 52). The question of labour mobility, an integral aspect of the EU project, especially since the eastern enlargements, remains under-theorised as well as under-investigated. To this end, the concepts of 'embeddedness' and 'double movement', developed by Polanyi (2001 [1944]) are useful for understanding the attendant challenges of labour mobility in an enlarged EU. Embeddedness is a function of industrial relations systems; and should, for whatever reason, this function fail to deliver, we might expect a response from 'organic intellectuals', which could have implications for the consensus upon which the pro-European 'historic bloc' has been constructed.

The free movement of labour is what sets the European integration project apart from other regional free trade initiatives, such as NAFTA. In essence, labour mobility is the human face of European integration and is far more visible than the cross-border movement of goods. Yet, the dynamics and politics of how trade and labour mobility interact have largely been overlooked. We therefore miss what shapes political preferences. Van Apeldoorn cautions that 'if circumstances change, old or new conflicts might again open up' (2002: 163). I would contend that such circumstances have materialised following further episodes of 'deepening' and 'widening' in the 2000s. This has opened up the scope for new conflicts within the EU, which could act as a conduit for politicisation. What form this politicisation might take is unclear and requires empirical investigation.

Chapter Three

Studying European Integration and Preferences across Time

INTRODUCTION

Formulating an EU preference can be particularly difficult, not least because 'every actor has multiple interests, many of which can be engaged by a single issue' (Hall 2005: 132). It is during the process of preference-formation that 'the politics of interest and of identity come together in a single process' (*ibidem*). Yet, what determines this process of aggregation? Do national interests, broadly defined, trump class or sectoral interests? Ideas guide preference-formation and, in a sense, articulate their (material) interests. This articulation not only conveys a preference; it is also relational. In other words, the articulation of a preference is important in a justificatory sense, so as to convince others of the validity of such thinking (Morgan 2005). This, from a methodological standpoint, 'entails the development of "technologies of control", whereby causal relationships within the relevant parts of the social or natural world are posited' (Hall 2005: 135). In simple terms, ideas represent a heuristic that allows actors to make sense of the world. These ideas can be modified through experiences, which, in turn, can inform preference-formation, potentially resulting in a change of heart. This process can be imbued with tension, which could plausibly split a group (*cf.* Lakatos 1970).

Whilst I concur with Hall's contribution to the study of preferences, there is one aspect where we part company. Whereas Hall (2005: 150) feels that 'to urge attentiveness to the role of evolving context in the process of preference formation is to introduce some unpredictability into the analysis', I would argue the contrary. Precisely by engaging with context, which implies descending the ladder of abstraction (Sartori 1970), are we able to better determine how preferences are formed, or how basic preferences are tested against experience. Comparative political economists, such as Hall, typically operate at the macro-level (national) and paint a clear picture; comparative industrial relations scholars, on the other hand, are more concerned with the details at the meso-level (sector) or the micro-level (firm). Whilst the former are often attuned to the changing topography of the (national) industrial relations landscape, not least in the wake of EMU (for example, Hall and Franzese 1998), the latter are more sociological in their bent and therefore better placed to understand context and praxis as well as comparatively contradictory tendencies (for example, Mills 1970; Jackson and Muellenborn 2012).

European integration has been described as a 'broad phenomenon' (Wallace 2000: 39), a 'swiftly moving target' (Marks 2004: 239) and famously by Delors as an *'objet politique non identifié'* ('unidentified political object'). In sum, European integration constitutes an unwieldy concept and studying such an awkward subject over time is not an easy task, which probably explains why there exist 'few comprehensive studies on the simultaneous construction of a market and a polity' (Fligstein and Stone Sweet 2002: 1208). Yet, at the same time, others maintain that the EU and European integration ought to be studied as a 'reciprocal relationship between market construction and polity construction' (McNamara 2010: 130; *see also* Marks 1997; Bartolini 2005; Schmitter 1996, 2009). This inevitably implies an interdisciplinary approach that seeks to overcome the methodological limitations of synchronic comparative research designs. To this end, I deploy a methodological triptych so as to capture the fullest possible picture of the two sides of the EU coin. In short, these are periodisation, which is informed by a neo-Polanyian approach (*see* Chapter Two); the use of the various European treaties as intermittent observation points to determine preferences; and, lastly, a comparative within-case study analysing the most recent phase of European integration through the prism of industrial relations. I will discuss the rationale underpinning these choices in the following sections; suffice to say here that, together, these complement a 'causal narrative' approach (George and Bennett 2005).

Kassim *et al.* (2019: 9) document that EU scholars 'need to recognise the problems in preference formation'. For instance, the preferences of collective actors are often simply deduced from economic theory. This is unfortunate as there are 'multiple factors' that shape preferences (Kassim *et al.* 2019: 1). This chapter explores the question of preferences towards European integration from a methodological vantage point. Competing visions have shaped the European integration process (Haas 1958; van Appeldoorn 2002; Parsons 2003). This aspect is important as '[T]he project of European integration is, at base, a normative project' (Morgan 2005: 94). This normative stance is tied up with what can be termed an actor's 'fundamental preference' (Hall 2005). To date, the vast majority of the research has focused on preference-formation with regard to national governments (for example, Aspinwall 2007; Kassim *et al.* 2019; Moravcsik 1993, 1998, 2018; Schirm 2018). Other studies target the individual level by drawing on Eurobarometer data (for example, Fligstein 2008; Kuhn and Stoeckel 2014; Braun and Tausendpfund 2014). Outside of the preferences of national governments on the one hand, and of individuals on the other, the question of preference-formation on the EU in socio-economic actors remains understudied, with some exceptions (Dimitrakopoulos 2011; Kaiser *et al.* 2008) that inform this study and are discussed below. Understanding the historical aspect is essential if we are to understand the present (*ibidem*: 3). In other words, there is methodological value in determining the changing nature of European integration and the emergence, disappearance and re-emergence of labour Euroscepticism.

This book studies European integration as a macro-political ideal from the perspective of organised labour across three different periods of time. The objective is not only to explain variation across time, that is, between phase one (mid-1950s–mid-1980s) and phase two (mid-1980s–mid-2000s); but also, to investigate why it is that in the most recent phase (mid-2000s–2019) Euroscepticism emerged amongst Irish organised labour but not amongst Italian unions. This requires a two-step research design and draws on the three aforementioned methodological tools or techniques. The development of preferences is an inherently diachronic process and, whilst policy studies regularly incorporate a temporal component into their studies (Howlett and Goetz 2014), EU Studies has a preference for a comparative research design, which, unfortunately, suffers from two substantial shortcomings or biases.

Invariably, definitions of comparative research revolve around the concepts of 'difference' and 'similarity' (Ragin 1987: 6). However, over time, two methodological biases in the social sciences have developed. The first bias has to do with the tendency to privilege similarity over difference (Caramani 2010). In fact, most EU comparative studies 'implicitly apply a M[ost] S[imilar] S[ystems] D[esign]' (Anckar 2007: 390; *see also* Rosamond 2007). The second and perhaps more serious bias has to do with the temporal frame of reference (Bartolini 1993; Pierson 1994, 2004). Researchers tend to opt for a synchronic timeframe, most probably on the grounds that it is more straightforward as well as being grounded in the present. However, this bias has particularly serious consequences that could fuel speculation at the expense of veracity. Certain scholars have critiqued the synchronic design of comparative research and specifically make the case that a limited time horizon 'constitutes a methodological problem for the research on European integration' (Börner and Eigmüller 2015: 3). Similarly, Paul Pierson argues for 'study[ing] European integration as a political process which unfolds over time' (Pierson 1994: 1). Elsewhere, Pierson (2004: 2) writes that

[C]ontemporary social scientists typically take a 'snapshot' view of political life, but there is often a strong case to be made for shifting from snapshot to moving pictures. This means systematically situating particular moments (including the present) in a temporal sequence of events and processes stretching over extended periods.

Synchronic comparisons are, from a methodological standpoint, ahistorical (Bartolini 1993: 134). This implies that such approaches cannot accommodate or control for temporal variance in their schema. To this end, 'one should consider explicitly and systematically the variation over time of independent and dependent variables' (Bartolini 1993: 135). This, of course, is easier said than done. However, if we take European integration as the independent variable, it is possible to identify different temporal frames that display certain characteristics relating to European integration that differentiate it from other temporal frames. This process is of course iterative, accumulative, and overlapping. Yet, from a methodological standpoint there is clear water, so to speak, between the different phases on the road to economic and political integration. Turning to the dependent variable, it is possible to broadly map changing preference-formation on to the different phases of European integration. How this is achieved is a question of operationalisation, which I address below; suffice to say here that there is a deal of variation on the dependent variable.

Studying the EU as a dynamic polity is an objective of this book, albeit from the perspective of organised labour. Schmitter (2009: 59) goes so far as to describe the EU as 'the most complex polity in the world', which, admittedly, makes it a daunting prospect. That said, both periodisation and the European treaties are extremely useful when it comes to analysing the development of the EU as a polity and a market. The different European treaties not only punctuate the constitutionalisation of the EU; they can also be used as yardsticks to gauge actors' preferences on European integration at different points across time. 'Treaty revisions are *the* most significant moments in the integration process' (Armstrong and Bulmer 1998: 286, emphasis added). The treaties are complex documents but a broad church of actors debate the merits of European treaties. Moravcsik (1993, 1997, 1998) used different European treaties in his analysis of national government preferences. Subsequently, some consider Moravcsik's liberal intergovernmentalism as 'the most elaborate theory of preference formation available' (Dimitrakopoulos and Kassim 2004: 221). This may be so: however, there remain serious flaws with the liberal-intergovernmental approach to preference-formation, not least the overriding emphasis on domestic demands for potential national economic benefits over, say, governance-related questions or social costs (*see also* Chapter Two). The EU, with its common currency and labour mobility, differs significantly from other regional trading blocs, such as the North

American Free Trade Agreement and, in this context, political considerations are also important (*see also* De Boissieu and Pisani-Ferry 1998; Hall 2005). These considerations are not only ideational but also relational, particularly where political competition is concerned (Sitter 2001; Bieler 2006). With European integration becoming more and more diffuse over time, the number of actors engaging in debates on the future of the EU and the shape of European integration has increased (Fitzgibbon 2013). This process, which remains under-studied, can lead to new intra-class conflicts that can manifest themselves in different ways but ultimately undermine the pro-European consensus. To this end, looking at EU treaty debates allows us to identify the tensions that arise within different polities. To date, there have been seven European treaties and these provide us with good reference points from which it is possible to capture the position of trade unions on European integration across the three phases.

Tracing the changing preferences of trade unions on the different EU treaties across the three phases of European integration draws on historical narrative methods, but it is nevertheless distinguishable insofar as it aims at identifying causal sequences and explanatory factors (George and Bennett 2005). Furthermore, this approach is particularly useful for 'looking closely at the way a decision was arrived at and the factors that influenced the participants' (Berman 1998: 34). I will return to the question of potential explanatory factors below. The process-tracing in this book is based on qualitative empirical material gathered through visits to national and trade union archives in Dublin and Rome; official trade union documents and press articles on each of the different EU treaties; and over forty semi-structured interviews conducted with high-ranking officials within the national confederations, some of whom had extensive experience at the European level. Research on labour mobility and the construction sector involved an analysis of the grey literature (produced by non-academic and non-commercial sources), various (court) reports, articles in the mainstream print media to determine the salience of incidences of social dumping and semi-structured interviews with construction union officials, some of whom had experience within European trade union structures.

This chapter will be structured as follows. First, I will present the full extent of the research puzzle, including the unions under study and the changing preferences across time. Following that, the methodological triptych is discussed by outlining the diachronic aspect and the utilisation of periodisation; how the operationalisation of political preferences is conducted; and why changing the level of analysis and a comparative within-case is advantageous to deepening our understanding about labour Euroscepticism. I then discuss the qualitative comparative analysis (QCA) method and its potential explanatory power. A final section concludes.

RESEARCH PUZZLE: THE FULLER PICTURE

This book, simply put, traces the preferences of Irish and Italian organised labour on the EU, from the question of the Rome Treaty and membership up to the Fiscal Compact and beyond. More precisely, I study the EU preferences of the three main Italian confederations, CGIL, CISL and UIL, and the Irish confederation, ICTU. The history and subsequent structure of the Irish union system differs from that of its Italian counterparts (Hyman 2001a). Within the three Italian confederations there tends to be greater centralisation, and the different federations have less autonomy, particularly on political questions of a national nature. This differs from ICTU, whose purview is traditionally narrower and whose leadership is more beholden to the views of the individual unions that are represented within the national umbrella organisation (*see* Chapter Four). On account of this difference, I also include three significant unions in the Irish industrial relations and political landscape. These are the Services Industrial Professional and Technical Union (SIPTU),[1] Unite the Union,[2] and Connect (formerly TEEU). SIPTU is a general union and the largest union in Ireland. Unite is also a general union, of British origin, however. Connect is a quintessential 'Irish' union as well as the largest craft union in Ireland. On political questions, ICTU will adopt a formal position provided there is consensus between the constituent members. Individual trade unions, however, are not bound by Congress's position and are free to take up a contrary position on political questions.

Table 3.1 traces the preferences of the Italian and Irish unions on European integration by presenting their positions on membership and the seven European treaties, from the Treaty of Rome in 1957 up to the Fiscal Compact of 2012. I have also included the ETUC's preferences since its creation in 1973, as well as the preferences of the main Italian and Irish social-democratic parties, both of which have close relations with their respective union movements. In total, there are 83 observation points to be explained. In terms of market- and polity-construction, both periodisation, discussed below, and the various European treaties provide useful observation points for tracing unions' changing preferences towards European integration. It is possible to identify three possible preferences that unions can adopt on the question of the EU. They can be pro-EU (protagonists), EU-critical (antagonists) or abstentionist (bystanders). To date, protagonists (Europhiles) and antagonists (Eurosceptics) have received most of the scholarly attention, although there remains room for improvement. Permissive bystanders, on the other hand, have been overlooked. In the following section I will unpack what these preferences entail: after all, as discussed in Chapter One, having a pro-EU attitude can imply different meanings for different political actors.

From Table 3.1 emerge a number of interesting questions that will guide this book. Between phase one and phase two there is variation across time as both Italian and Irish unions followed a common trajectory, namely from an EU-critical to a pro-European position. Two questions arise here. Firstly, what underpinned the EU-critical, or more accurately the EEC-critical, stance? And secondly, did similar logics guide these changing preferences? Establishing the historical origins of the preferences of key unions is important for understanding current views towards the EU (Dimitrakopoulos 2011: 4). Phase two was characterised by a succession of four European treaties, which were underpinned by a pro-European consensus, which was at its most cohesive on the Maastricht Treaty. What explains this pro-European left-wing stance? This requires going beyond mono-causal explanations that identify institutions, interests or ideas as the principal *explanandum* (Moravcsik 1997: 513). Finally, why is it that, in the third phase of European integration, the pro-European consensus unravelled in the Irish case, whilst remaining steadfast in the Italian case? In other words, what explains this variation across space? This is where it is necessary to switch the level of analysis and conduct a comparative within-case study, which is more attuned to the vicissitudes of the contemporary EU. I will return to this aspect below; suffice to say here that this is done in a bid to ascertain whether there is a feedback loop between concrete experience on the grounds and the process of preference-formation. In the following section, I discuss the advantage of periodisation in conceptualising the reciprocal construction of polity and market.

PERIODISATION: TIME IS ON OUR SIDE

Whilst dividing the European integration project into three distinct historical time periods is useful for methodological reasons (Bartolini 1993; Pierson 2004), it also provides a chronological narrative for structuring this book. Rather than focusing on the litany of voluminous developments at the EU level, I focus on significant developments through a neo-Polanyian prism (*see* Chapter Two). In other words, the focus is primarily on important developments that are of broad interest, either positive or negative, from an embedding–disembedding perspective. These include the EU's headline goals – the free movement of goods in phase one; the creation of monetary union in phase two; and the free movement of labour and services in the context of eastern enlargements in phase three – which incrementally, and at times stealthily, reformed economic and social structures. Periodisation is also beneficial in surmounting a significant shortcoming within traditional comparative studies.

Table 3.1 Positions of the Irish and Italian labour movements on European Treaties

	PHASE 1	PHASE 2					PHASE 3		
	Membership (TEEC)	SEA	TEU	Amsterdam	Nice 1	Nice 2	Lisbon 1	Lisbon 2	Fiscal Compact
SIPTU	X[a]	X	Y	Y	Y	Y	O	Y	O
	Y[b]	X							
Unite	X[c]	X	Y	X	X	X	X	X	X
Connect	O	O	O	O	O	O	X	X	X
ICTU	X	O	Y	Y	Y	Y	Y	Y	O
Labour Party	X	O	Y	Y	Y	Y	Y	Y	Y
ETUC		Y	Y	Y	Y	Y	Y	Y	X
CGIL	X	Y	Y	Y	Y		Y		Y
CISL	Y	Y	Y	Y	Y		Y		Y
UIL	Y	Y	Y	Y	Y		Y		Y
PCI/PD	X	Y	Y	Y	Y		Y		Y

Source: various trade union documents and national press clippings X= EU-critical;
Y= pro-EU; O=Abstention

[a] ITGWU; [b] WUI; [c] This position is based on the position of the British TGWU

European integration is a moving target, which presents challenges from a methodological standpoint. Few, however, would disagree that, over time, European integration has become more diffuse. This book is less interested in explaining *why* this is and more interested in the *ex-post* scenario. In other words, *how* is the political 'field' affected, once the economic 'horse' has bolted? I argue that future approximations regarding the EU are informed by concrete experiences relating directly to the nature of economic integration. In order to guide such an assertion, I neatly divide the genesis of European integration into three distinct historical time periods, with each phase speaking to a different, but complementary and overlapping, headline EU goal as well as different Polanyian fixes (*see* Chapter Two). Doing so not only enables us to trace how the EU's problem-solving capacity has changed across time, but it also allows tracing of how national trade unions respond to attendant challenges within a dynamic Euro-polity. Whilst change in the EU's form and content is iterative (that is, events at t^0 feed into the sources of change at t^1) it would, however, be naïve to view this process through a teleological lens as leading to a federal entity. Instead, it is best viewed as open-ended and contentious process whose *finalité* (end point) remains perhaps the greatest puzzle of all.

The first phase is the longest one and stretches from the inception of the project in 1957 through to the mid-1980s. Against the backdrop of the Cold War, this phase was not only critical to the embedding of national economies through welfare state and industrial relations institutions (Ruggie 1982; Milward 2000 [1992]; Crouch 1993; Esping-Andersen 1990); but also it involves the establishment of the EU's supranational institutions, notably, the European Commission (EC) and the European Court of Justice (CJEU), and their nascent forms of governance, much of which failed to feature on the radar of national publics. Whilst the Treaty of Rome established the so-called Four Freedoms, the first phase was mostly about achieving the free movement of goods through the elimination of customs duties and quantitative restrictions (Bartolini 2005: 121). This socio-economic process was accompanied by landmark cases that established a central role for the CJEU as an engine of integration (Burley and Mattli 1993; Patel 2020). I refer in particular to the cases *Van Gend en Loos* and *Costa v ENEL* in 1963 and 1964, which now have a mythological status in the genesis of the EU polity (Vauchez 2010) but, despite their significance, at the time went largely unnoticed (Koch *et al.* 2010).

With the exception of agriculture and competition, common policies were almost non-existent in the first phase of European integration. For instance, the common transport policy envisaged in the Treaty of Rome (Art 70-80 TEC), was, at the start of the 1980s, considered 'the saddest chapter in the history of European integration' on account of the inaction in the sector (Erdmenger 1983: 89). Notwithstanding, the conditions for cross-border trade were established and several different 'national' economic miracles substantiate this (Crafts and Toniolo 1996). Such is especially the case for Italy, more so than Ireland (*see* Chapter Four). In this phase, the political saliency of 'Europe' and its public policies never sufficiently piqued the interest of national publics. Hence, this phase is characterised by the well-worn phrase: 'permissive consensus' (Lindberg and Scheingold 1970). That said, collective interests, particularly employers' associations and organised labour, as well as political parties, made it their business to follow European developments closely (Kirchner 1977).

As Monnet predicted, the EU is adept at turning crisis into opportunity and if '1957' was the response to '1945', then the Single European Act (SEA) of 1986 has to be seen as the response to the stagflation crisis of the 1970s and the EEC's institutional inertia known better as 'Eurosclerosis'. Arguably, the European integration project, as we know it today, only began in earnest with the commencement of the second phase in the mid-1980s and which signifies a qualitative shift in the nature of European integration and the EU's headline goals. Buoyed by a sense of enthusiasm for a renewed integrationist energy, the second phase is characterised by four EU treaties: the Single European Act (1986), Maastricht Treaty (1991), the Amsterdam Treaty (1997) and the Nice Treaty (2000). These developments provide us with valuable information regarding how the EU and European integration is debated, generally, and within the labour movement, in particular. From a research point of view, however, I am interested in explaining the shift in preferences between the first phase and the second one, or, in other words, from a general Euroscepticism to a broad pro-European consensus. Explaining the latter may involve developments that originated outside the EU.

Whereas phase one is characterised by what I term Polanyian fixes at the national level, that is, establishing industrial relations and welfare systems (Esping-Andersen 1990; Crouch 1993), the second phase, closely associated with two-term Commission President Jacques Delors, is defined by complementary Polanyian fixes at the supranational level, such as the Working Time and the European Works Council Directives amongst others. Together, these Polanyian fixes are closely bound up in the concept of a *European social model*, which, albeit ambiguous (Hyman 2005), is important to trade unions' outlook on the EU (*see* Chapter Five). Notwithstanding these Polanyian fixes, which are perhaps more important from a trade union perspective, the second phase of European integration will be remembered primarily for the creation of the common currency, the Euro. The introduction of the Euro not only established the idea of central bank autonomy; it also had implications for national governments' fiscal policies, labour politics and broader macroeconomic concerns. Despite some reservations and dissenting voices, the prospect of a common currency was broadly welcomed by Italian and Irish labour movements: but was there commonality in their motivations?

Establishing the Euro was also critical to creating a European financial market, which, under the Financial Services Action Plan required both 'negative' (removing barriers that impede financial integration) and 'positive' (establishing a common regulatory framework) integration (*see* Quaglia 2007). With regard to the governance of the euro and the European financial market, the European Central Bank (ECB) has a pivotal role. Hence, phase two is characterised by the creation of the common currency, the establishing of independent central banks, the liberalisation of financial capital and the formulation of Polanyian fixes at the supranational level. At the national level, an enhanced governance role transpired for Italian and Irish organised labour so that both countries could satisfy the so-called 'Maastricht criteria' and participate in the common currency. Throughout the second phase, both Irish and Italian confederations were regularly involved in so-called social partnership arrangements at the national level. However, the outcomes of these arrangements, from a neo-Polanyian perspective, vary. This variation would prove telling in the third phase of European integration.

Over the duration of the second phase, European institutions, including the European Council and the European Parliament, became increasingly visible and, particularly the latter, were prepared to play a more important role in shaping the Euro-polity. However, as Schmitter presciently noted 'perhaps [the SEA] went further than its signatories intended or believed possible' (Schmitter 1996: 1). Such a statement could perhaps be applied to all the European treaties signed in the second phase, not least the Maastricht Treaty, which remains the most important development after the Rome Treaty, and which laid the ground for the financialisation of the European economy. This has been an important feature of the European political economy for the past two or so decades. More importantly, the deregulation of financial capital contributed to what is undoubtedly the deepest economic crisis since the Great Depression of the 1930s and the EU is by no means out of the woods. Whilst it is unlikely that the free movement of capital intended by the framers of the Rome Treaty was that of *financial* capital, the same cannot be said of labour mobility, which characterises the third phase of European integration beginning in 2004.

To continue with the analogy of crisis and response: the 2004 enlargement of the EU can be seen as the response to '1989' and the conclusion, in part at least, of the relatively peaceful transition to liberal democracy and capitalism in the former socialist countries of Central and Eastern Europe. This event was not only of enormous symbolical significance for consigning the 'iron curtain' to the historical dustbin; the eastern enlargements are also widely seen as a game-changer in the broader context of the EU (Weiler 2005: 199). Although 'widenings' featured in phases one (Denmark, Greece, Ireland, Spain, Portugal and the UK) and two (Austria, Finland Sweden), none were of the same magnitude nor had the level of concern about social dumping practices ever been so high (*see* Vaughan-Whitehead 2003). In essence, social dumping is a labour market issue: businesses exploit 'new incentives and strategic opportunities to contest or circumvent transnational and national social regulations ... [and] in the short run, social dumping exerts downward pressure on wages and working conditions' (Bernaciack 2015: 2). The phenomenon is inextricably linked to the free movement of labour and services, which, as two sides of the same labour mobility coin, is of immediate concern to trade unions. Rather surprisingly, however, 'social dumping has so far received limited scholarly attention' (Bernaciack 2015: 1). This is where the comparative industrial relations aspect can be instructive; however, unlike traditional industrial relations studies, I link trade union activities on the ground back to their broader preferences on the EU and European integration. I will briefly return to the advantages of this approach below and again more comprehensively in Part III.

Not only was phase three characterised by labour mobility, broadly defined, but we also have the most neo-liberal EU to date. Put simply, the two-term Barroso Commission did more to undermine the political consensus that had come to characterise policy-making at the EU level than any other Commissionership. A liberalising agenda was placed front and centre. The obvious example here is the Services Directive, whose 'country of origin' clause, amongst other things, produced the most visible backlash against the EU (Crespy 2012), and it is in this context that the rejection of the Constitutional Treaty and rising labour Euroscepticism has to be seen (Béthoux, Erne and Golden 2018). To boot, the CJEU, in a raft of controversial cases known as the 'Laval Quartet', ruled in favour of transnational economic freedoms over national social rights. The late Brian Bercusson, a leading European labour law academic, cautioned that the '[N]ineteenth century doctrinal ghosts of the dominance of market freedoms ... have returned to haunt EU labour law of the twenty-first century' (quoted in Bruun *et al.* 2009: 462). As noted earlier, Fritz Scharpf (2010: 235) argues that 'integration through law' 'will have the least effect on the institutions and practices of LMEs'. Yet it is in an LME (liberal market economy), namely Ireland, where resistance to the EU integration process has been more pronounced. Understanding this shift requires shifting the focus to the micro-foundations of European integration.

The third phase sees the buoyed enthusiasm for deeper integration originating in the second phase being utterly dashed, with the rejection of the Constitutional Treaty by two founding member states. This rejection by French and Dutch voters ushered in a 'period of reflection' for the EU (European Council Declaration, 18 June 2005). To what extent there was a true attempt at self-reflection is debateable but, in concrete terms, the repackaged Lisbon Treaty was brought before national parliaments for ratification for a second time. Publics were not to be consulted, with one exception, Ireland, which was constitutionally obliged to hold a referendum (*see* Chapter Five). It is here that we see the pro-European consensus of Irish organised labour come undone. However, more importantly, what explains this shift in preference? And conversely, why is it that Italian unions, which have been exposed to similar challenges in terms of monetary union and labour mobility (OECD 2012), remain steadfastly pro-EU? I will return to how we might respond to these puzzles from a methodological and practical standpoint below.

Of course, the third phase of European integration will be remembered for the financial crisis and it was in this phase that the term 'constraining dissensus' was coined by Hooghe and Marks (2009). Similarly, against the backdrop of the Great Recession, the study of Euroscepticism became a 'true cottage industry' (Mudde 2012) but the focus remained primarily on the extreme right-wing variant. The Brexit decision was certainly the nadir of the EU's history, with some suggesting that 'Brexit will trigger the process of decomposition and reconfiguration' (Gillingham 2016: 251). Although Brexit is not the subject of this book, the pitfalls of comparative analysis also stand for those studying Brexit. In many ways the Brexit vote re-echoes the research puzzle at the centre of this book but, in the absence of a diachronic approach and a disregard for the micro-foundations of European integration, the likelihood of spurious claims increases significantly. One possibility might involve tracing the contours of the debate diachronically. To this end, the various EU treaties could be useful.

EU TREATIES: OPERATIONALISING PREFERENCES

From the European Coal and Steel Community to the European Economic Community to the current day European Union, the nominal description of supranational co-operation leaves observers none the wiser as to the shape, content and extent of European integration. In many ways this is useful, as it allows political entrepreneurs to attribute characteristics to the EU and European integration that are in line with their own visions of the EU. Scholars have focused on either the macro- or the micro-levels in the study of EU preferences. Here, I propose a novel approach to studying EU political preferences, which involves intermittent observations at 'critical junctures' in the genesis of European integration. The objective is to go beyond the pro–anti binary in a bid to determine whether the reality reflects unions' overall vision. This is necessary for, as Parsons (2003: 2) observes, the debates between proponents of community, confederal and intergovernmental preferences consistently 'cut across the main right–left lines.' In this section, I will outline the methodological aspects of studying preferences.

Methodologically speaking, preferences can be specified in two ways: they can either be deduced or observed (Frieden 1999; Katznelson and Weingast 2005; Hall 2005; Hall *et al.* 2014). Deduction is conducted by deriving preferences on the basis of pre-existing theories. Working within a rational choice perspective, Hix (2007) focuses on the preferences of non-state actors.

> An actor (a citizen, political party or interest group) is primarily driven by policy outcomes and will form an opinion about the EU on the basis of whether action at the EU level will produce policies that are closer to his or her preferred policies than existing policy outcomes at the domestic level' (*ibid*: 136).

There are three problems with this approach. First, preferences are seen as exogenous, given and assumed. Critiques of rational choice institutionalism highlight the economic determinism of this approach (*see* Scharpf 1997) and the reification of a singular conception of rationality. Second, the EU is more than just a policy-making venue, it is also the geographical scope within which the multifaceted processes of economic internationalisation are simultaneously, and continually, occurring. Finally, the perspective is static and leaves little scope for processes and social capacities (Pierson 2004: 74).

The second method used to establish what the preferences of actors are is by observation. To this end, actors' preferences are typically gathered from statements that are in the public domain. Such statements are usually contained in either the press media or in official documents, including speeches. By observing preferences across time, it can be determined how actors articulate the EU, as they see it from their position within the European political economy. The various EU treaties are useful not only for tracing how preferences change across time but also for understanding how the politicisation process works. This is because EU treaties generate broad debate and Euroscepticism is best studied 'in the form of public debates involving a mass audience and the media' (Trenz 2016: 83), rather than EU policy debates between experts. By process-tracing the seven European treaties across the three phases of European integration, I will be able 'to identify the intervening causal process – the causal chain and causal mechanism – between an independent variable (or variables) and the outcome of the dependent variable' (George and Bennett 2005: 6). There are, however, no simple causal mechanisms that can account for the formulation of preferences on European integration. Below, I will outline a number of potential explanatory factors that help explain political preferences towards the EU.

Inevitably, however, there are limitations that need to be borne in mind. For instance, there needs to be an awareness that preferences are often calculated (Frieden 1999: 59). In other words, there is a strategic element to preference-formulation. Whilst the formulation of a preference and its public expression are central to the notion of a functioning democracy, the realisation of that preference, is another matter. The terms preference and strategy, as well as other synonyms, are frequently used in the social sciences but they are often invested with separate meanings. 'The essential point is that in any given setting, an actor prefers some outcome to others and pursues a strategy to achieve its most preferred possible outcome' (Frieden 1999: 41). Whereas preferences can, in very simple terms, advocate continuity or change, strategies, derived from preferences, are instruments that the actor employs to get as close to their preference as possible. Whilst the two are analytically distinct, in the real world such a distinction is not so straightforward. Notwithstanding this limitation and considering that 'political science casts too many shadows over the process of preference formation' (Hall 2005: 129), studying EU preferences through observation seeks to divert attention towards crucial factors which can be important in determining political outcomes.

Following van Apeldoorn (2002), who identifies three broad and competing preferences for a European socio-economic order from within the transnational capitalist class, I too seek to unpack broad preferences towards the EU, but from the perspective of organised labour. By refining preferences, it is possible to go beyond the pro- or anti-EU dichotomy. To this end, three possible EU preferences are identifiable. (*see* Table 3.1). Following Hall (2005: 131), I see ideas 'as constitutive of actors' perceptions of even their material interests and as interacting closely with material forces' (*see also* Hall 1989; Blyth 2002). Each European treaty that passes 'inspires a re-evaluation of the beliefs underpinning existing preferences' (Hall 2005: 136). Alone, these treaties are not so meaningful in and of themselves; instead, much depends on how actors interpret them. In that sense, the EU treaties are imperfect, as they are complex legal documents that contain many different provisions. Also, as de Wilde, Michailidou and Trenz (2012: 11) note, 'the legitimacy of the EU is debated in a sphere of multiple and diversified publics, in which rationality and emotion, information and misinformation, justification and denunciation always co-occur.' Notwithstanding, the very requirement that EU treaties be ratified at the national level implies an opportunity for debate not only on the merits of the treaty itself but also on the EU and the direction of European integration more broadly. There is, therefore, a narrative or discursive aspect to how the Irish and Italian unions articulated the EU. It is from such narratives that we can get a clearer picture of whether a union's preference approximates to 'ever closer union' or 'unity in diversity'. What either of these visions consists of will become clearer in later chapters.

With the passing of time and the changing nature of European integration, labour scholars point to a division in organised labour resulting from economic internationalisation and the introduction of EMU (Bieler 2006; Erne 2008). On the one hand, there are unions that are embedded in export-oriented sectors; and on the other hand, there are unions embedded in domestic sectors. Whereas the former mediates economic internationalisation through the free movement of goods; the latter mediates such processes through the free movement of workers and services. In order to empirically assess whether these sectoral differences matter and whether there is an implication regarding preference-formation, it is necessary to shift the level of analysis from the national to the meso- or sectoral level (Bechter, Brandl and Meardi 2012).

COMPARATIVE WITHIN-CASE STUDY: A DEEPER UNDERSTANDING OF EUROPEAN INTEGRATION AND PREFERENCE-FORMATION

Neil Fligstein (2008: 9) notes that 'the EU is like an iceberg: what goes on in Brussels is like the 10 per cent above the waterline' and that 'the really interesting story is the 90 per cent that is harder to see, that is below the surface' (*ibidem*). To what extent it is harder to see depends on the methodological tools at hand as well as the level of analysis. Unfortunately, the micro-foundations of market and polity creation have been overlooked. As Manners and Rosamond (2018: 29) observe, contemporary EU Studies has 'marginalized "integration" as a central guiding *problematique* for the field' (Manners and Rosamond 2018: 29), which 'has had some negative consequences, particularly in relation to how the field deals with the current constellation of crises' (*ibid*: 32). A clear symptom of the EU's existential crisis is the growing phenomenon of Euroscepticism, including a left-wing variant thereof. In order to gain a deeper understanding of this phenomenon, I will outline the merits of adjusting the level of analysis to the sectoral level. This is done so as to determine how European integration, as a substantive process, is filtered through institutions and interacts with the context. I argue that this is important for grasping how the preference-formation process works.

Practically speaking, this involves studying the micro-foundations of European integration (Börner and Eigmüller 2015), which can also represent a form of European socialisation (Beck and Grande 2007; Favell and Guiraudon 2011; Fligstein 2008) and, in some instances, politicisation (della Porta 2015). Both aspects can result in a manifestation of Euroscepticism (Trenz 2016: 82), however, politicisation is more often than not a process which is led by representative groups, including political parties, social movements and trade unions. Politicisation of the EU has been avoided by mainstream parties (Mair 2013) and European Parliament elections are typically of secondary importance. Hence, it is around times of Treaty change that the micro-foundations of European integration are more likely to be discussed in the public sphere. Understanding this dynamic requires more of a bottom-up approach to preference-formation, which is very much an empirical matter rather than an *a priori* assumption (Crespy 2010). Establishing whether there is a link between the effects of the micro-foundations of European integration, such as labour mobility, in a particular social context and the position adopted by trade unions on important stages in the construction of a European market and polity is only realistically possible for the third phase of European integration. Hence, a comparative within case study is conducted only in the most recent phase of European integration.

Traditionally, the discipline of industrial relations engages with questions relating to the governance of the labour market. However, as a sign of the times we live in, the field has become increasingly marginalised from mainstream academia. Colin Crouch (2015: 3), an eminent scholar in the field, laments that '[F]or several decades now the study of labour issues has been a specialized field, rather cut off from the rest of sociology and economics'. To this list, we can add European Studies, with some notable exceptions (Bieler 2006; Erne 2008; Marginson and Sisson 2004; Meardi 2012a). Notwithstanding this marginalisation, the discipline of industrial relations has a lot to offer to European studies generally and Euroscepticism studies in particular. I will return to outline the benefits in detail in Part III; suffice to say here that the question of governance has long been at the centre of the industrial relations discipline (Léonard *et al.* 2007) and that it offers 'the best balance between parsimony and complexity' (Marginson and Sisson 2004: 317).

As noted above, the third phase of European integration is characterised by the free movement of labour and services in the context of a rather unique EU enlargement. Labour mobility is bound up with the concept of EU citizenship, which, in turn, is closely related to the idea of a Euro-polity. However, within the scholarship there is 'a concern with debating the normative philosophical potentials of European citizenship, rather than a focus on evidence about actual participation' (Favell 2010: 193). Arguably, it is the EU citizens' economic rights as wage earners, particularly in the context of eastern enlargement, that can provide a source of tension. This is captured in the term 'social dumping', which rose to prominence in the wake of the 2004 enlargement. Industrial relations scholars are well placed to study this phenomenon, which is not without controversy (for an overview, *see* Bernaciak 2015).

Adopting a comparative industrial relations approach (*see* Hyman 2001b; Almond and Connolly 2019) is fruitful for at least three reasons. Firstly, it allows a change regarding the analytical lens and a change in terms of the level of analysis. To this end, the focus is on a substantive transnational aspect of contemporary European integration, namely, labour mobility, within a specific economic sector: construction. The construction sector is interesting as migrant labourers can be a source of tension and their exploitation can result in social dumping practices (Menz 2005; Krings 2009). This differs from export-oriented sectors, in which 'manufacturing workers are not directly confronted with workers of competing enterprises' (Erne 2008: 6). Secondly, a sectoral approach is a better analytical level for capturing the micro-foundations of transnational socio-economic dynamics (Bechter *et al.* 2012) and it therefore provides a richer context in which we can assess what I term broadly as trade unions' 'coping mechanisms', which have been developed in the face of past, yet persisting, challenges, as well as contemporary ones. Here, unions are treated in their more traditional role

as economic actors and their primary coping mechanisms include industrial relations systems. These institutions, which can be conceptualised as
Polanyian fixes, mediate socio-economic processes of internationalisation.
In addition, however, unions can also deploy a number of diverse strategies
to mitigate against the exploitation of migrant workers and social dumping.
The most obvious example is union organising. To this end, unions' regulatory and non-regulatory coping mechanisms are assessed. The third reason
relates back to the question of political preferences of unions *vis-à-vis* the
EU. Unions internalise transnational socio-economic dynamics (Gajewska
2009) but does this concrete experience, in turn, affect a union's political
preferences towards European integration? In other words, is there a feedback loop between unions' experiences on the ground and their political
preferences? This requires empirical investigation. However, this is only
possible for the third phase of European integration. Regarding the broader
puzzle of variation across time and potential explanatory factors, I draw on
qualitative comparative analysis.

In Part III, I will present an analytical framework that has been devised to
study the micro-foundations of European integration through a broad industrial relations lens. This is done with a view to build a bridge between more
specific accounts of European integration and more general political economy
approaches (Jones and Verdun 2003).

TEMPORAL QCA AND POTENTIAL EXPLANATORY FACTORS

I now return to the macro-political question of determining union preferences towards the EU and European integration across time and space. Here,
in order to devise a set of explanatory factors determining preferences, I
have drawn on insights from cognate disciplines (*see below*) and qualitative
comparative analysis (QCA) which is a synthetic approach between variable-
oriented and case-oriented research (Ragin 1987). In other words, QCA
offers the possibility of a middle road between emphasising relationships
among variables and structural explanations, on the one hand, and emphasising the chronological particularities of cases of agency, on the other (*ibid*:
71). A central aspect of QCA is the treatment of explanatory and outcome
factors with Boolean categorisation. The Boolean approach is simple but useful as it can address configurational complexity, or in the language of QCA,
'multiple conjunctural causation' (*ibid*). This approach can be used to evaluate competing explanations. The dichotomous QCA approach – also known
as crisp-set QCA – provides for two possible results: present (1) and absent
(0) (*ibid*: 88, 141).

This analytical approach is useful for parsimonious explanation and allows the operationalisation of multiple factors across time (*ibid*: 121–3). Where factors are present across the three time periods, we can question their ability to explain variation. This is of particular importance for the final phase of European integration, in which cross-temporal and cross-spatial variation occurs. Drawing on political science as well as political economy and industrial relations contributions on the study of European integration and trade unions, I identify a number of potential explanatory factors that might determine or influence preference decisions (*see*, for example, Teague 1989a, 1989b; Rosamond 1993; Bieler 2006; Erne 2008; Hyman 2001a, 2005; Jabko 2006). I have also drawn on literature that considers political parties' preferences on European integration (such as Featherstone 1988; Gaffney 1996; Geyer 1997; Marks and Wilson 2000; Dunphy 2004; Morgan 2005; Almeida 2012). According to these contributions, preferences are shaped by a mix of historical, international, European, national and organisational factors. Drawing on these literatures, I identify a number of potential explanatory factors. The relevance of some factors might be greater at different stages of European integration. For instance, EMU and the emergence of social pacts were more characteristic of phase two than say phase one, or even phase three for that matter. These factors can only be operationalised for the duration in which they are present and 'active'.

The actor-centred factors include trade union identity and structure; trade union internationalism, including involvement in European-level union structures; and Euro-federalist ideology. Structural or institutional factors include a political opportunity structure that permits politicisation of European integration; Euroscepticism as a left-wing or as a right-wing phenomenon; and the organisation of political economy (LME or CME). The broader processual or contextual factors arising as a (direct) result of E(M)U membership include membership of the euro-currency; social concertation; inflow of intra-EU labour mobility; periphery countries in the euro-crisis. The importance of these contextual factors may vary across the different phases of European integration. Whereas the importance of social concertation was highly important in phase two, associated with establishing the common currency, its importance diminished following the creation of the euro and the onset of the eurocrisis, when both Italy and Ireland were considered peripheral economies in the political economy of the eurozone.

Table 3.2 is a synthesis of the potential factors that can be *excluded*. The evaluation of patterns derived from systemic comparative cross-national analysis (Ragin 1987), is a sound basis for theory falsification (Popper 1959). What Table 3.2 demonstrates is that by holding certain factors constant across time we are able to discount their explanatory potential when it comes to explaining diverging preferences in phase three. For instance, take trade union identity.

Hyman (2001a) identifies three ideal types: business unionism (market); integrative unionism (society); and radical-oppositional unionism (class). However, no type of unionism exists in a pure form. Rather, each type of unionism tends 'to incline towards an often contradictory admixture of two of the three ideal types' (Hyman 2001a: 3). According to Hyman's (2001a) typology, Irish and Italian unions represent two different types of unions. The Italian labour movement, which forms part of Hyman's study, is located on the axis between class and society (2001a: ch. 7). Elsewhere in a later study, Gumbrell-McCormick and Hyman (2013) categorise Irish unions as sharing a number of similarities with British unions. 'Its past colonial status left Ireland with the legal and other institutional features of British industrial relations' (Gumbrell-McCormick and Hyman 2013: 24). Hyman (2001a) locates British unions on the axis between market and class. This seems the logical position for Irish unions, too. Where a union movement's characteristics are prevalently located between class and society, I attribute the value 1. Where such characteristics are absent, I attribute the value 0. The same rule applies for the 'market and society' category. We can see that these characteristics did not fundamentally change across time and can therefore be discounted as having explanatory purchase. Likewise, the same can be said for the Irish and Italian political economies and specific European political economy factors that, over time, and despite some change, have remained constant, or at least constantly different. These national differences could be a basis for arguing as to why we can discern variation between Irish and Italian unions on the question of European integration in phase three; however, pursuing such a line of argument would be ahistorical and therefore, at the end of the day, spurious. Therefore, we need to evaluate the remaining potential explanatory factors. The other factors which can best explain variation between Italian unions in the different phases will feature more prominently in the following chapters, in which their role in explaining outcomes will become clearer.

CONCLUSIONS

At its core, the original objective and subsequent history of the EU is to engender a continental peace by nullifying internecine bellicosity and averting, as much as possible, socio-economic conflict. The genesis of European integration across time has fared relatively well insofar as this ambitious objective is concerned. So much so that the EU managed to convert dissenters who originally opposed their country's membership. That said, there is very little by way of understanding how socio-economic actors' preferences are formulated in the first place and what factors explain its modification subsequently (Dimitrakopoulos 2011). In terms of polity- and market-construction, there are three clearly identifiable phases. In addition, the various European treaties, which are important to establishing market rules as well as constructing an EU polity, also provide useful observation points to assess actors' changing preferences on the direction of European integration.

Although the term appears in its title, this book is not solely about the emergence of Euroscepticism in certain national unions and its absence in others. If anything, the book is more broadly about preference-formation and qualitative change in the EU market and polity across time. As discussed in greater detail in the previous chapter, the traditional theories of European integration – neofunctionalism and liberal intergovernmentalism – cannot explain the disappearance and re-emergence of Euroscepticism. Within the debate, there is a tendency to subsume preferences on European integration into two mutually distinct camps: pro- and anti-European. This is problematic for at least two reasons. First, there is the degree of complex interdependence involved in polity-making and market-building resulting from membership of the EU, which inevitably reorganises state–society relations as well as the social relations of capitalist production. Problematising and studying such a complex and wieldy political phenomenon is challenging, to say the least. Second, shortcomings are the result of two inter-related methodological dilemmas. On the one hand, there is the limited time-horizon of many comparative studies (Börner and Eigmüller 2015: 3; Pierson 1993, 2004). Addressing this implies reassessing the history and historiography of European integration and the actors involved. This requires going beyond the most-similar and most dissimilar dichotomy prevalent in comparative research (Bartolini 1993; Caramani 2010). On the other hand, in an increasingly interconnected world there is a need to go beyond methodological nationalism and macro-institutionalist explanations (Chernilo 2006, 2011). This applies more so to contemporary European integration, whose form has qualitatively changed since its relaunch in the mid-1980s and again in the post-enlargement context of the 2000s. The discipline of EU Studies has largely overlooked the micro-foundations of European integration (Fligstein 2008: 9; Rosamond and Manners 2018: 29), which have the potential to inform preferences on European integration.

Above, I present three rather unique methodological devices that seek to address these methodological issues and help us explain variation, in terms of political preferences, across time and space. These are periodisation; using the EU treaties as a barometer to intermittently gauge preferences; and, in the most recent phase of European integration, a comparative within-case study. By overlooking the diachronic aspect or the transnational socio-economic aspect, one risks overemphasising institutional differences as possible explanations for actors' preferences. Hence, there is a strong argument for broadening the timeframe and switching between levels of analysis. I will return to this aspect in Chapter Seven, when determining the factors that help us explain the re-emergence of labour Euroscepticism in Ireland but not in Italy

Table 3.2 Explanatory Factors Unable to Explain the Puzzle

Changing Union Preferences Across Time				
Presence of Labour Euro-scepticism	**Italian Unions**	**Phase 1**	**Phase 2**	**Phase 3**
		X	O	O
	Irish Unions	X	O	X
Explanatory factors unable to explain variation across time and space				
		Phase 1		**Phase 2**		**Phase 3**	
		Irish Unions	Italian Unions	Irish Unions	Italian Unions	Irish Unions	Italian Unions
Union Identity	Prevalence of Class & Market	1	0	1	0	1	0
	Prevalence of Class & Society	0	1	0	1	0	1
Union Structure	Fragmented Unity	1	0	1	0	1	0
	Centralized Pluralism	0	1	0	1	0	1
Organisation of National Political Economy	Predominantly LME	1	0	1	0	1	0
	Predominantly CME	0	1	0	1	0	1
	Members of EMS/EMU	0.5	0.5	1	1	1	1
	Periphery in Euro crisis	n/a	n/a	1	1	1	1
Contextual Factors	Presence of Social Concertation	0.5	0.5	1	1	0	0
	Influx of (non-)EU Migrant Labour	0	0	0	0.5	1	1
X = Presence of labour Euroscepticism; **O** = No presence of labour Euroscepticism							

Source: Own

Before moving on to Part II, there is a caveat: using only European treaties overlooks 'the lags between decisions and long-term consequences, as well as constraints that emerge from societal adaptations and shifts in policy preferences that occur during the interim'[3] (Pierson 1996: 126). In other words, positions adopted by actors on, say, the Lisbon Treaty, were not taken solely on the narrow scope of the Treaty alone, as this would suggest that the inter-regnum between treaties was of little or no significance. Cognizant that European treaties are not negotiated in a vacuum, and that neither are positions adopted by actors on those European Treaties taken purely on the merits of a single Treaty, I have, following Pierson's advice, taken steps to offset this potential pitfall. To this end, I argue that actors' predictions on the future of the EU have to be made regarding the impact, intended or unintended, that the Treaty will have on national political economies, which is composed of export-oriented and domestic sectors. Such predictions are not only informed by normative preferences towards the EU, but, more importantly perhaps, are shaped by concrete experiences with the integration process in the recent past. Investigation of this supposition, however, requires a different approach and this is where comparative industrial relations comes in. That said. European integration is more than a narrow and sectoral issue. It is also more than an event, it is, in essence, a process of a transnational socio-economic nature and, whilst this might not be reflected in how the EU is typically discussed or debated, it should inform politicisation studies on the subject of the EU.

PART II

CREATING A COMMON MARKET: LABOUR EUROSCEPTICISM AND ITS DISAPPEARANCE

Chapter Four

Italian and Irish Labour on the Supranational Question

INTRODUCTION

The eventual defeat of Nazi-Fascism had come at a high cost and Europe had to be re-imagined, despite the persistence of the underlying political cleavages, enduring class conflicts and continuing economic dilemmas that had marked the post-World-War-I era. This time round, however, policymakers were committed to avoiding repetition of the same mistakes. This required overcoming the morbidities of nationalism and, to some extent, the limits of the nation-state. The 'thirty-year war' (1914–1945) had posed difficult questions regarding the social, political and economic foundations of the nation-state. A serious transformation seemed inevitable if peace and prosperity, necessary preconditions for a stable and prosperous post-war order, were to stand a chance. Achieving these preconditions would require promoting a more co-operative approach to problem-solving. However, the shape and extent of this co-operation still had to be figured out. Would co-operation be confined to non-controversial matters of a humanitarian, social or economic nature? Or would it be cumulative in nature? What institutional form would such a forum take? Would it be intergovernmental and maintain the integrity of the nation-state? Or, instead, a supranational agency, in which case a nation-state's integrity could be challenged or even compromised. These political choices weighed on the minds of many, from individual citizens to interest groups to political parties. Hence, contentious politics, albeit of a high order, were present from the start of the European integration project.

This chapter is concerned with the first phase of European integration, which stretches from the Treaty of Rome in 1957 to the mid-1980s. This three-decade-long phase is very much about setting the foundations of European supranational institutions, growing economies and developing national social institutions. The new European institutions were invested with the supranational authority to oversee the narrow economic integration process; the creating of social institutions was related to trade union strategies to manage class struggles, boost economic performance and facilitate the delivery of the Keynesian welfare state (Crouch 1993; Esping-Andersen 1990; Streeck 1992). These developments are largely symbiotic insofar as they coincided with the 'Golden Age' of European capitalism (Milward 2000[1992]). Remarkably, the European institutions that we are familiar with today – the European Commission, the Council of Ministers, the European Parliament and the Court of Justice – were created at the outset of, and firmly embedded during, this protracted phase.

Hence, this period was characterised by three broad and complementary objectives. The first two were economic integration at the European level and social integration at the national level. The third objective existed on the ideological plane and involved moving beyond the age of political extremes (White 2020a). All three processes were as complex as they were of immediate concern to organised labour. Initially, the scope of European integration was limited to more technical questions concerning the free movements of goods, such as the abolition of quotas and tariffs. To such questions, national publics remained considerably indifferent (Lindberg and Scheingold 1970). This was not the case for organised labour, however, at least not for their leaderships. Regarding the prospect of European integration, individual unions co-ordinated via national confederations, which, in turn, co-ordinated through international channels. Notwithstanding, organised labour's impact on the form of European integration was relatively small (Pasture 2005). This provided an impetus for overcoming ideological divisions within and between confederations at both the national and European levels: a complementary development which, *inter alia*, facilitated the incorporation of the Irish Congress of Trade Unions into the broader European labour movement.

Both the Irish and Italian labour movements have rich and colourful histories, characterised by radical and charismatic leaders and intra-movement fighting, resulting in rival factions with competing visions and worldviews. Each respective labour movement has been subject to different external influences and has had to deal with a broad array of difficult and varied circumstances, from imperialism in the Irish case to fascism in the Italian. Both labour movements played an important role in nation-(re-)building through the creation of social, economic and political rights. To differentiate between Italian and Irish labour, I use the terms *centralised pluralism* and *fragmented unity*, respectively. Understanding these terms requires a more in-depth account of the Italian and Irish labour movements within the broader national historico-political context. This is not possible here; however, there is a rich literature on both (*see* Hyman 2001a; O'Connor 2011; Bruno 2011; Greaves 1982; Turone 1973).

As the Italian unions were the first to be confronted with the prospect of European membership, it makes sense to treat this case first. The prospect of Irish membership was more drawn out but, by the time it finally materialised in 1972, Irish unions were expressing a degree of disquietude. Did the same concerns underpin their reservations as those expressed by the largest Italian union? Before considering that, however, it is necessary to briefly discuss the question of constructing a supranational community. Once this is outlined, I will be returning to the question of how Italian and Irish unions perceived the idea of European integration and how they contributed to the national debate on membership of the European Economic Community (EEC). This discussion is based on archival research at national and trade union archives in Dublin and Rome, as well as access to personal archives.[1] The late 1960s and 1970s were tumultuous years, particularly in Italy, where, following an economic boom, there was a resurgence of class conflict (Crouch and Pizzorno 1978). Ireland, on the other hand, was readying the ground for splendid *non*-isolation, which was the source of much apprehension, not least amongst Irish trade unions.

CONSTRUCTING A SUPRANATIONAL COMMUNITY

Between the conclusion of World War II and the signing of the Treaty of Rome, a number of trans-Atlantic organisations had already been created. These included the Bretton Woods agreement (1944); the General Agreement on Tariffs and Trade (GATT, 1947); and the North Atlantic Treaty Organisation (NATO, 1949). Intergovernmental institutions were also established at the European level: there was the Council of Europe (1949) to oversee human rights and the Organisation of European Economic Co-operation (OEEC), which was responsible for overseeing the distribution of the European Recovery Programme, better known as the Marshall Plan. A central player in all these arrangements was the United States. Hence, the future of European integration was inevitably 'conditioned by the economic and military might of the US' (Carchedi 2001: 10). The Marshall Plan, and its attached conditionality, was central to shaping European politics, creating divisions, and setting the ground for multilateral co-operation in post-war Europe. The Marshall Plan's headline objectives (or conditionalities) included avoiding economic protectionism; integrating the (West) German economy into the broader European context; and containing the rise of socialist and communist parties so as to stem not only the appeal of socialism but also the ideological expansion of the Soviet Union.

Within the OEEC, 'the British exercised decisive influence' (Lindberg and Scheingold 1970: 13). The Italian, Altiero Spinelli (1957: 54), an ardent

Euro-federalist and author of the founding document of Eurofederalism, the *Ventotene Manifesto*, was very critical of the 'false European spirit' of the British and equally, if not more so, of the Americans for being 'duped' by the former into occupying influential roles from trade union internationalism to the North Atlantic Treaty Organisation. Spinelli's concern was that the narrow British post-war vision might materialise, namely, a Hayekian free-trade arrangement pure and simple. This was also of concern to other like-minded individuals, such as Jean Monnet, Robert Schumann and, later, Charles de Gaulle. Monnet was strongly in favour of transcending the nation-state. However, unlike Spinelli, he favoured a more gradual and cautious approach. To this end, the 1950 Schuman Declaration, which created the European Coal and Steel Community (ECSC), was an attempt to thwart the minimalist British vision. The ECSC consisted of six member states, of which Italy, along with France, Germany and the Benelux countries, was one. The nascent body had just enough of a supranational hint to deter the British Labour government of the day, which was in no way prepared to pool sovereignty, not even in just two economic sectors (Diebold 1959).

The next step in Monnet's vision was to drum up further support for extending the scope of supranationalism and for creating a common market. Achieving this vision would require political astuteness, inventiveness and a great deal of secrecy. Monnet was well aware that 'any new impetus toward integration had to come from those who held national power and were willing to use it for supranational ends' (Yondorf 1965: 889). In other words, supranational leaders had to be fashioned out of national political elites. This included leaders in national labour movements. Despite inhabiting a veritably cosmopolitan world, Monnet 'was a forceful advocate of strong organized labour representation' (Milward 2000[1992]: 296). Similarly, Schuman was 'a militant supporter of the Catholic trade union movement and of trade union rights' (*ibid*: 290). Following a setback with the rejection of the European Defence Community by the French parliament in 1954, the following year, Monnet established the Action Committee for the United States of Europe, which comprised 'a highly select group' of political and trade union leaders of the Christian-democrat, liberal and (moderate) socialist tradition' (Yondorf 1965: 889). Parties and unions subscribing to the communist tradition were excluded *a priori*.

Bridging the preferences of national governments was the principal challenge. For instance, the De Gasperi government in Italy was keen to pursue a strategy of European integration, not only economically but also politically.[2] Also, from the Italian perspective, it was important that freedom of movement for workers be included (Moravcsik 1998: 149). This position was supported by the (West) Germans but was a source of anxiety for the French. Whilst support for the idea of political unification was strong, there was a general consensus that the timing was not yet right. The Belgian socialist, Paul-Henri Spaak, was appointed the task of finding a practical solution to the impending impasse.

Spaak is credited with finding the right institutional balance between conflicting national preferences, on the one hand, and a centralised supranational administration, which would have limited freedom, on the other. His masterstroke was 'to give the executive organization scope, which *in time* could develop its prestige and authority' (Laurent 1970: 394, emphasis added). The final result, in concrete terms, was the Treaty of Rome, which represented the widest agreement possible on numerous areas, including commercial policy, agriculture policy and transport. To address concerns surrounding social standards, the French socialist government made the case for the upward harmonisation of social policies (Moravcsik 1998: 108–50). Such an objective was broadly supported by the pro-European trade union movement. In reality, however, the harmonisation of social policies would prove a more complex issue and, consequently, the initiative can be considered to be only partially successful. Although pay parity between men and women was enshrined in the Rome Treaty, much to the subsequent delight of Irish labour, only a mere political commitment was made by national governments to increase social protection at the national level (Milward 2000 [1992]: 188). Once the Treaty of Rome had been agreed upon, all that remained was for the national parliaments of the Six to ratify the Rome Treaty. This was achieved with haste and relative ease. 'But', as Anderson (2009: 16) points out, 'the electorates themselves were never consulted.'

Although the United Kingdom was privy to the collective will of the 'core' European states, there was a clear reluctance to participate. This unwillingness inevitably bore consequences for smaller nations, such as Ireland, Denmark and Norway, whose exports were dependent on the British market. Instead, the UK was instrumental in creating the European Free Trade Agreement in 1960, which was of little interest to the Irish government. The following year, a formal application was made by Tory Prime Minister, Harold Macmillan, to the EEC, only to be unceremoniously vetoed by the French President, General de Gaulle. Perhaps this refusal served to enhance the British commitment to joining the club; UK membership eventually materialised in 1973.

The post-war circumstances were favourable for the creation of cross-border links and transnational political networks, albeit with varying degrees of success. The likes of communism, social-democracy and Christian-democracy sought to influence the incipient integration process, which started at the intergovernmental level but with the objective of subsequently creating something more meaningful on the ideological plane. Of these competing transnational networks, Christian-democracy was 'hegemonic' in western Europe in the first two decades following World War II (*see* Kaiser 2007). 'It dominated the formation of the ECSC/EEC core Europe with fundamental long-term repercussions for the present-day EU' (*ibidem:* 9).

At the European level, Christian-democracy hinges on a Franco-German compromise and 'developed influential conceptions of the supranational *shaped by aversion to ideology*' (White 2020a: 9, emphasis added). Christian-democrats, such as Schuman, Adenauer and de Gasperi, relied on elite-led technocratic and administrative measures (Forlenza 2017; Kaiser 2007). 'Informal circles of the like-minded formed in closed institutions, often aiming for executive and judicial rather than legislative power' (White 2020a: 10). Contemporary literature refers to this as a 'mask for politics' (Burnley and Mattli 1993) or 'integration by stealth' (Majone 2005). Along with Monnet (1978), Christian-democrats believed that no benefit would come from consulting national publics on supranational questions. Instead, 'concrete achievements' (Forlenza 2017: 279) would eventually persuade citizens that European integration was a good thing. Fritz Scharpf (1999) would later term this 'output legitimacy' (*see also* Sternberg 2013); however, at the time, such an approach seemed the most credible response to the dangers of popular sovereignty and to the politics of the piazza, of which Christian-democratic leaders 'would remain particularly wary' (Forlenza 2017: 279).

The dominance of Christian-democracy is due partly to the failure of social-democracy (and communism) to build a transnational constituency. Social-democrats were cognisant of such shortcomings, particularly with regard to the EEC (Steinnes 2009), and belatedly set about establishing such a constituency. A clear indicator that these activities changed perceptions on Europe is the decision of British, Danish and Norwegian social-democrats to seek or support seeking membership of the EEC.[3] For reasons outlined below, the Irish labour movement remained Eurosceptical. However, the prospect of a 'social Europe' with greater social rights gained momentum following the 1973 EC enlargement (Guasconi 2003). Subsequently, the enlarged Commission had only two Christian-democratic Commissioners and, for the first time, the Socialist parties had a larger parliamentary party in the European Parliament than the Christian-democrats.

Early discursive constructions of legitimacy for the new and emerging European order laid emphasis on common objectives, while glossing over controversial issues to the greatest extent possible (Sternberg 2013: ch. 1). The dominant discourses sought to depoliticise European integration, giving rise to the so-called 'permissive consensus' (Lindberg and Scheingold 1970: 39), which most academic accounts take for granted. As demonstrated below, trade union politics in phase one of European integration were not characterised by such a consensus. Preferences towards Europe were amended, in the Italian case, in response to a distinct and transformative capitalist phenomenon, namely, the internationalisation of capital in the 1950s and 1960s

(Petrini 2005). This transnational socio-economic process was complemented by Polanyian fixes at the (sub-) national level (Marshall 1964; Ruggie 1982; Regalia *et al.* 1978), including the construction of social institutions that had the function of embedding the market (Crouch 1993, 1999) and providing what political economists would term 'institutional comparative advantage' (Hall and Soskice, 2001).

As ideas are central to the founding of the EEC, we need to account for its (eventual) endorsement by actors with different world views. 'Having overlooked the role of ideas in the EEC genesis, the dominant accounts are condemned to misinterpret what followed' (Parson 2003: 141). One objective of this chapter is to 'foster dialogue with international, transnational, and national historiographies' (Kaiser and Meyer 2010: 8) from the perspective of Irish and Italian labour; another is to explain the difference in their preferences *vis-à-vis* European integration. In doing so, I address the state-centric bias that exists in the literature, despite the fact that the European project is very much the exception to traditional international relations rather than the rule.

In the following section, I present the positions of Irish and Italian unions within the debate on European integration. Traditionally, organised labour, as political actors, act *vis-à-vis* the state and this is also the case in European matters; although from early on there was an emphasis on transnational co-ordination to mirror the emerging supranational context. The implicit question being asked is why are Italian and Irish organised labour important political actors? The short answer is: legitimacy.

EUROPEAN INTEGRATION: THROUGH THE EYES OF ITALIAN UNIONS

The post-war decade was a unique period in European history in which nationalism was jettisoned and a supranational context slowly emerged. However, 'much of the historiography of European integration has been conceptually underdeveloped and methodologically weak' (Kaiser *et al.* 2008: 2). Much of the emphasis has been on the nation-state as an embodiment of the 'national interest' in the supranational context (*see*, for example, Milward 2000[1992]; Moravcsik 1998). By concentrating on intergovernmental bargaining, which is indubitably crucial, the contested political nature of the European ideal within different national contexts is overlooked. Trade unions contributed to such debates and, whilst their day-to-day energies may well have been focused more on developing an industrial relations system, increasing the wages of their members, pushing for full employment and extending the reach of the welfare state, union leaderships were very keen to shape a supranational project compatible with their world vision. However, unions' world visions differed from country to country and indeed from union to union. Also, how unions engage in the political and industrial arenas can vary and change across time. Trade union systems can condition how a Congress or Confederation acts politically and, to a degree, can shape strategic action with other unions, political parties, employers' organisations and the national government. There are clear differences between the Italian and Irish trade union systems, with the most obvious being that the former is characterised by a troika of centralised confederations, while the latter is set apart due to an incredibly high number of individual unions, many of which are British in origin. For reasons of simplicity, I call these 'centralised pluralism' and 'fragmented unity', respectively. The contours of these descriptions will become clearer in the following paragraphs and throughout subsequent chapters.

The two-decade long brutal fascist offensive in Italy had resulted in the jailing of prominent left-wing activists, most famously, Antonio Gramsci, who died in prison, and Altiero Spinelli, who co-authored a blueprint for Eurofederalism whilst imprisoned. Both Gramsci and Spinelli's writings would influence the 'Europe' policy of the Italian labour movement, which emerged defiantly from the ashes of fascism. On 3 June 1944, the socialists, Christian-democrats and communists signed the 'Pact of Rome' and founded a unitary trade union confederation: the *Confederazione Generale Italiana del Lavoro* (CGIL). The objective of the united CGIL was to unify all the Italian workers in one big union and to consolidate a strong anti-fascist front. Representing over 5 million workers, the CGIL had three General-Secretaries, representing the different political strands, namely, communism, Christian-democracy and social-democracy. In principle, the union was free of political affiliation.

The deterioration of general conditions in Italy was a source of concern to many, not least the Americans, who feared that the *Partito Comunista Italiano* (PCI, the Italian Communist Party) might capitalise on mass unemployment, widespread extreme immiseration and general post-war disillusionment. As Andrew Carew (1987: 25) writes in *Labour Under the Marshall Plan*, 'the key to left-wing strength lay with the trade union movement.' Hence, dividing the communist-led labour movement into factions was a top priority not only of the American administration but also of the American Federation of Labor (AFL), which is described by Romero (1992: 156) as 'one of the earliest and strongest forces advocating clandestine operations', even 'preceding the CIA in secret financing of the anti-communist trade union movement'. The US applied pressure by insisting that participation in the Marshall Plan was conditional upon the exclusion of communists from government. De Gasperi duly obliged in May 1947.

Early the following year, an assassination attempt was made on the life of Palmiro Togliatti, leader of the PCI. The country was plunged into further chaos when the CGIL leadership called a general strike. Matters were further complicated by the fact that fascist anti-strike legislation remained within the Italian penal code. Minister for the Interior, Mario Scelba, declared strike actions 'insurrectionist acts' and called for the arrest and trial of hundreds of trade unionists (Romagnoli and Treu 1977: 24). Giulio Pastore, leader of the Christian-democrat faction of the CGIL, was against the strike. Recognising the opportunity to split the union movement, the AFL 'began to blow on the fires of internal conflict in the CGIL' (Romero 1992: 168). Shortly afterwards, the Christian-democrat faction broke away and established the *Confederazione Italiana Sindacati dei Lavoratori* (CISL). The name was telling, for it emphasised the increased autonomy of its sectoral federations, thereby distinguishing it from the more centralised CGIL. Whilst insisting on being non-confessional, CISL's political future was dependent on the Christian-democrats and Catholic social teaching. Its economic future, on the other hand, depended on securing American funding (Horowitz 1963).

Not all social democrats and republicans joined the newly founded CISL. Instead, another, smaller union, called *Unione Italiana del Lavoro* (UIL), was established, which 'attempted to distinguish itself from CGIL by putting an emphasis on winning immediate material gains for workers, and from CISL by its greater willingness to support militant action which might embarrass the government' (Hyman 2001a: 146). Henceforth, the Italian trade union movement would have the CGIL, CISL and UIL as its primary protagonists. Both CISL and UIL declared themselves to be anti-communist and autonomous trade unions with no formal political ties. All too often, the differences between the three unions are overstated or exaggerated, as is the notion that the CGIL acted as a mouthpiece for the PCI (*see* Ravaglia 2009). On the question of European integration, it was the CGIL's position that influenced the party's and not vice versa (*see below*). In addition, critical interventions and contributions to debates by the unions on a range of welfare- or industrial-relations-related questions have shaped the intellectual landscape.

In the immediate post-war years, Italy, economically speaking, had fallen back to late-nineteenth- or early-twentieth-century levels (Rossi and Toniolo 1996). Legacy effects from the shadow of the fascist period loomed large (Ascoli 1999). Economic changes that mattered had to do with ending the economic policy of autarky, namely, abolishing quotas and tariffs, which had been applied to almost all aspects of economic life. The general election of 1948 was a watershed. The Christian-Democrats emerged as the dominant political force, having expelled the communists the previous year. Whereas De Gasperi would rule Italy for the next decade and a half, the Christian-Democrats played a dominant role in Italian politics for the next four decades or so. While a dominant viewpoint regarding the international order is discernible, '[D]omestic economic policy decisions were nowhere near as clear cut' (Crafts and Toniolo 1996: 440).

Although a universal welfare state was, in principle, envisaged in the newly drafted 1948 Constitution (Casadio 2007), the immediate post-war model of social security was inherited from the fascist regime, including its paternalistic aspects (Ascoli 1999). During the 1950s, the *Istituzione Nazionale di Assistenza Sociale* (INAS) and the *Istituzione Nazionale Confederale di Assistenza* (INCA) were created. Known as *Patronati*, these are bodies created by CGIL and CISL, respectively, to deal with broader social security issues. The remit of INAS and INCA's services ranges from pensions to work-related issues to social rights. Importantly, these social institutions are a unique Italian phenomenon (Saba 1992). This peculiarity is indicative of the classist ideology which underpinned the Italian trade union movement and is encapsulated in a CGIL motto: 'the workers' life is not limited to the factory'. Typical industrial relations indicators, such as union density, which are a proxy for trade union strength, do not accurately reflect the true influence of Italian unions on Italian society. As Hyman (2001a: 147) writes '[D]espite unions' weakness in conventional industrial relations terms, they possessed a significant public status deriving from their role in the post-war structure of the welfare state.'

Between the end of the war and the signing of the Rome Treaty, Italy was a hotbed of politics of all sorts, constitutional, electoral and ideological. While the US might not have determined policies and outcomes, its influence, given Italy's geo-strategic location, was substantial and effective (Faenza and Fini 1976; Carew 1987; Romero 1992). The overriding objective was simple: keep the left – the socialist and communist parties – from playing a role in government. Isolating the communists helped secure victory for *Democrazia Cristiana* in the 1948 election, thereby securing Italy's place in the Western sphere of influence and a place at the European bargaining table. As noted above, De Gasperi was devoted to pursuing a strategy of European integration, both economic and political. The Schuman Plan was welcomed wholeheartedly by the De Gasperi government, despite some reservations from the Italian steel industry (Petrini 2005: 113–17), as was the Spaak Report, which formed the basis of the Treaty of Rome. With the negotiations, not coincidentally, taking place on Italian soil, in Messina (June 1955) and Venice (May 1956), there was undoubtedly pressure to commit to the European vision.

CISL and UIL were clearly in favour of European integration from the outset. However, the CGIL was strongly opposed. The most convincing explanation of the preferences of Italian unions on European integration is trade union internationalism, which, in many ways, mirrors the Italian unions' postwar experience outlined above. Before World War Two had concluded, international trade unionism had begun to re-emerge. The World Federation of

Trade Unions (WFTU) was established in 1945 on an anti-fascist programme of co-operation and pacifism, thereby replacing the International Federation of Trade Unions, much to the regret of the British TUC. The number of unions affiliated to the WFTU was greater than that of any previous labour organisation, with one notable abstention: the American AFL, which refused to associate itself with the Russian union (*see* Carew 1987: ch. 5). Hopes that ideological differences and suspicions could be bridged proved optimistic and the Marshall Plan ensured that the nascent organisation was short-lived.

Although the WFTU never *officially* denounced the Marshall Plan, it was, as Carew (2000: 175) writes, 'the symbolic issue over which communists and non-communists divided'. In January of 1949, the British TUC and American CIO quit the WFTU, despite last-ditch Russian attempts to save the organisation. Over the following year-and-a-half, most Western European federations followed the Anglo-American example. The idea of international trade union unity had collapsed under the pressure of Cold War tensions; and even if such tensions had not transpired, that unity between the communist and anti-communist factions could have continued long-term seems highly unlikely.

Upon exiting the WFTU, trade unions with a social-democratic leaning set up the International Confederation of Free Trade Unions (ICFTU). Meanwhile, the Christian trade unions were organised in a separate international body called the International Confederation of Christian Trade Unions (CISC). By 1950, both the Italian and the international trade union movement were split into three clear camps: the communist unions in the WFTU; the so-called 'free' trade unions in the ICFTU; and the Christian unions in the CISC (later renamed the World Labour Confederation). The CGIL remained affiliated to the WFTU, while the CISL and UIL were affiliated to the newly established ICFTU. Below, I will discuss how the Irish labour movement engaged with trade union internationalism, which contributed to splitting the Irish labour movement into two camps.

CISL (1955a; 1956a) and UIL were clear champions of furthering economic integration beyond the coal and steel sectors. Both unions strongly supported a united and federal Europe. The leadership believed that it was 'necessary to continue the realisation of a united Europe through the development of common institutions, the progressive fusion of the national economies and the creation of a common market and the gradual harmonisation of their social policies' (CISL 1956a [author's translation]). A common market should, however, in their view, consider a number of points, such as: i) a system of safeguarding social clauses; ii) the creation and operation of a development fund; iii) the progressive introduction of the free movement of labour; iv) the development of rules to ensure the operation of free competition in the common market so as to exclude in particular any national discrimination and v) a European investment fund whose goal should be 'the joint development of European economies and the development of less favoured regions of the participating states' (CISL 1956b [author's translation]).

From these progressive propositions we can gather that CISL (and UIL) promoted a grand vision that went well beyond mere economic integration or the creation of a narrowly defined free trade area. As well as an abolition of tariffs, the process should also be complemented with a virtuous upward harmonisation of social policies, especially those governing workers' lives, such as working hours, holidays and wages. In short, broader European interests had to take precedence over narrow national ones. Although the Treaty of Rome was negotiated on Italian soil, CISL and UIL were unable to influence the negotiating position of the Italian government. The unions' dismay was further enhanced when they discovered that the opinions of the industrialists had been invited and considered by the Italian Ministry of External Affairs. Whilst other avenues were explored by the moderate Italian unions to promote their agenda, this necessarily meant transcending national boundaries and creating a European space.

Once established, the ICFTU acknowledged the urgency of the unification of Europe (Carew 2000). A European structure was created to push a moderate trade union agenda, using whatever channels were available, including via Jean Monnet's Action Committee (Haas 1958: 366–7). A labour-oriented conference was organised to coincide with the Messina meeting of foreign ministers. Demands included upward social harmonisation and the creation of an Economic and Social Committee. The election of socialist Guy Mollet in France (also a member of the Action Committee) turned out to be fortuitous for the liberal trade union agenda. The French socialist government pushed for an important trade union demand, namely, the harmonisation of social policies. The proposal caused 'friction and real danger in negotiations' (Laurent 1970: 380) and in the end 'the French settled for a statement of intent by the Six to achieve similar policies' (Moravcsik 1998: 146). A crestfallen Altiero Spinelli, one of Europe's most prominent federalists, felt that the European ideal had been betrayed in favour of an intergovernmental arrangement. Given the underwhelming end product, why did CISL and UIL remain strong supporters of the European project? Was it the potential for gradualism that kept their hopes alive?

As far as the Italian communists were concerned, the European project was capitalist, Atlanticist, imperialistic and anti-communist. The CGIL joined Western communist parties, the Soviet communist party and the communist trade unions 'in condemning the Community as a tool of imperialism that had the two-fold objective of subjugating Western Europe economically and politically to American capital and strengthening imperialism's offensive against the socialist countries led by the Soviet Union' (Dunphy 2004: 72). In other words, hostility towards European integration was based on pro-Soviet and ideological grounds. To this end, the CGIL, and the communist movement more widely, protested against the establishment of NATO bases, the US war in Korea and the creation of the Common Market. However, it is important to bear in mind the hostile environment that communists inhabited.

Once the Rome Treaty was ratified by the parliament, the CGIL were by no means prepared to stand idly on the sidelines. According to the new General Secretary, Agostino Novella, 'the CGIL does not intend to assume a position of passive criticism' (*Rassegna Sindacale*, December 1957 [author's translation]). According to Bruno Trentin (1958) a former *partigiano* (anti-fascist partisan) and now vice-secretary of the powerful CGIL metalworkers' federation, FIOM, Italian unions had a particular international role to play:

> Italian wages are the lowest in the European labour market. This fact gives a precise function to the Italian trade unions as part of an intensification of the movement, to campaign for co-ordination at the European level: to help raise incomes, whose very low level already hinders and will hinder further, any attempts by trade unions in other countries to raise wages. The growing interdependence of national labour markets within Western Europe and the EEC in particular, is a fact to which we must act accordingly [author's translation].

Trentin would rise through the ranks of the CGIL and play an important role as a Gramscian 'organic intellectual' in reorienting FIOM, and later the CGIL, towards Brussels.

ICFTU affiliates from the six EEC member states, including CISL and UIL, established the European Trade Union Secretariat (ETUS) as an independent body in 1958. Despite the WFTU founding a Common Market Action Committee in 1958, the CGIL opened its own office in Brussels in March 1963 and, two years later, established a joint liaison office with its French counterpart, the CGT (*see* Pernot 2001). The WFTU Action Committee was disbanded in 1966. The PCI, however, maintained an anti-EEC stance, which it reiterated at a meeting of the six Communist parties of the EEC countries that took place in Brussels in the same month that the CGIL opened its office. As a consequence the CGIL was now considered by other unions as a 'unitary' or 'classist' trade union representing the common material interest of the workers and not as a purely ideological organisation operating at the behest of the PCI.

Between 1950 and the mid-1960s the Italian economy enjoyed a *miracolo economico* with GDP rising at an average rate of 5.9 per cent (Rossi and Toniolo 1996). CISL, on the advice of the AFL, emphasised company-level collective bargaining. Horowitz (1963: 243) estimates that between 1953 and 1957, out of 748 company agreements, 59 per cent were signed by CISL and UIL. These successful and positive outcomes, particularly in manufacturing, meant that the CGIL, despite initial reservations about betraying broader class ideals, was compelled to follow suit.[4] By 1968, the three confederations had only organised approximately 31 per cent of the industrial workforce. Organising campaigns focused particularly on the metal, steel, automobile and appliance industries, which were leading the economic charge.

Social unrest became synonymous with the final years of the 1960s and culminated with the long *autunno caldo* ['autumn of discontent']of 1968–9, when mass mobilisations were orchestrated by students and workers' movements against a glut of social problems. While the sources of the discontent were many, there was a distinct work-related theme (*see* Franzosi 1995: 263), which the unions were able to harness. This synergy heralded the so-called *stagione del sindacato* ['season of the union'] (Bruno 2011: 169) with the most tangible achievement being the Workers' Statute (1970), which contained the sacrosanct Article 18 on unfair dismissals. 'The act intervenes not to regulate unions at the national level but to promote their presence and action at the plant level' (Treu 1987: 37). Subsequently, membership of the unions increased significantly during the 1970s, as approximately half of the Italian workforce became unionised (Hyman 2001a: 148). This opened a new front for trade unions, but also gave rise to a small but by no means insignificant revolutionary cadre, which can be regarded as Eurosceptic and is dealt with in a separate section below.

During the 1970s, the three confederations achieved a degree of accommodation and in doing so improved labour's bargaining position *vis-à-vis* employers (and the state). At one point there was even talk of the three confederations putting their differences aside and reuniting. This involved weakening the linkages between the confederations and their respective sister parties. Greater autonomy was based on the (fanciful) principle of incompatibility, that is, union officials could not hold simultaneous positions in the union and a political party. Three joint meetings of the CGIL, CISL and UIL (Firenze I, II, III) set the date for the national Congress of each of the confederations to vote for its own dissolution, thereby bringing about the creation of a new united confederation. Ultimately, hesitations, re-evaluations and political considerations demonstrated that the Italian trade union movement was not quite ready to unify. Nevertheless, a number of union federations chose to operate in the spirit of unity at both company and sectoral levels. A compromise emerged in the guise of the *Federazione Unitaria* CGIL-CISL-UIL, despite the best attempts of the Americans (*see* Gumbrell-McCormick 2000: 365). The new union structure was accompanied by the creation of a centre for union research and development, a monthly journal (*l'Unità Operaia*) and a union training centre. This period of trade union détente lasted from 1972 to 1984 and represented an important step in establishing trade union unity at the European level (*see below*).

The developments outlined above were important regarding the realisation of 'centralised pluralism'. Although differences would continue in some areas, henceforth, on many questions, all three unions would typically adopt a common position, with some exceptions particularly in the 1990s. Numerically speaking, the CGIL has remained the most popular union, although the membership gap between the CGIL and the other unions, especially CISL, has diminished. While all three confederations claim to be *formally* independent of political parties, we can still discern a nominal difference between the CGIL and CISL and UIL. Historically, the CGIL is more antagonistic than CISL or UIL, which are more prepared to strike deals with (right-wing) governments (*see* Chapters Five and Six). Another difference has to do with the degree of autonomy regarding the sectoral federations (*see* Chapter Eight). Whereas CISL affords greater autonomy to its regional federations, the CGIL, in communist tradition, is more centralised.

EUROPEAN INTEGRATION: THROUGH THE EYES OF IRISH UNIONS

I use the term 'fragmented unity' to characterise the contradictions of Irish trade unionism. The source of the contradictions can be traced back to the presence of British unions, such as the Amalgamated Transport and General Workers Union (ATGWU), which started organising workers in Ireland towards the end of the nineteenth century. Eventually, Irish trade unionists began to ask questions of the British unions and their ability to deliver for Irish workers. As O'Connor writes, 'there was a niggling sense of neglect [by British unions] on the part of the Irish Labour elite' (O'Connor 2011: 60). Subsequently, the *Irish* Trade Union Congress (ITUC) was established in 1894. Upon establishment, the ITUC was bedevilled by internal rivalries between Irish and British unions. These rivalries were exacerbated following the partition of the island and the creation of what was then called the Free State in 1922. Henceforth, Congress and some of its affiliates 'had to operate under two distinct and mutually hostile regimes' (Henderman-O'Brien 1983: 123).

The largest of the Irish unions, the Irish Trade and General Workers Union (ITGWU), established in 1909, was also bedevilled by rivalries between radical and conservative factions. Its founder, 'Big' Jim Larkin, was a radical firebrand whose name is synonymous with worker militancy. However, the ITGWU's conservative wing, led by William O'Brien, was deeply sceptical of Larkin's brand of 'socialist republicanism' (*see* Grant 2012).[5] Eventually, the Larkinites felt compelled to exit the ITGWU and create a union which advocated a more radical brand of trade unionism. The Workers' Union of

Ireland (WUI) secured a stronghold in Dublin; but outside the capital its presence was practically non-existent and its involvement in the ITUC was successfully thwarted by conservatives until the mid-1940s.

Whereas the division between the conservative and nationalist O'Brienites and radical and classist Larkinites was on ideological grounds, there was yet another division, much uglier, between the 'Irish' unions and the unions headquartered in Britain, the so-called 'amalgamated' unions. McCarthy (1973a: 354–6) writes of 'a heady time', which saw 'the rise of separatism of a strikingly xenophobic kind'.[6] On account of the war effort, the membership of British-based unions grew from 68,000 in 1937 to 108,000 in 1944. This increase translated into greater influence within the ITUC and, for the first time since 1918, the British unions secured a majority within the Congress executive (O'Connor 2011: 166). But now, in an independent Ireland, such a development was more difficult to accept. When a motion came before Congress about an invitation to attend a post-war World Trade Union Conference in Paris, Congress was divided. Delegates of the ATGWU pointed to the Constitution of Congress 'to promote fraternal relations between the workers of Ireland and other countries', while members of the ITGWU argued that the conference was only for the 'allied countries' and, as Ireland was a neutral country, the invitation should be declined (Merrigan 1989: 145). Given the shift in the balance of power in favour of the amalgamated unions, Congress voted in favour of attending and with that the die was cast.

The following year (1945), the ITGWU would end its affiliation with the Labour party and, along with fourteen other conservative unions, leave the ITUC. O'Brien established the Council of Irish Unions (CIU) which was nationalistic, Catholic and anti-communist in its outlook. The CIU took 'a sharp turn to the right' and their annual Congress was typically addressed by a prominent member of the clergy (Hannigan 1981: 41). Eventually, in 1959, the CIU[7] and the ITUC overcame their difference, but not before 'both O'Brien and Larkin had left the trade union scene' (McCarthy 1973a: 381). Once, reunited, however, the Irish Congress of Trade Unions (ICTU) was weak internally. Furthermore, Irish unions were committed to decentralised collective bargaining and a 'voluntaristic' style of industrial relations. Consequently, the bigger unions were reluctant to empower the ICTU.

Despite having gained (partial) independence, Ireland continued to exist in the shadow of its closest neighbour and trading partner, the UK. This meant that the fate of independent Ireland was, all too often, decided in Westminster or Whitehall. The UK's unwillingness to participate in the EEC inevitably bore consequences for Ireland. Although the UK was instrumental in creating EFTA, the Irish government was against joining because it was purely about free trade. In other words, there was no funding for farming subsidies, such as the EEC's Common Agricultural Policy.[8] By 1961,

'British policy toward Europe [had] reversed course' (Moravcsik 1998: 122) and, as the British government prepared an application for membership, the Irish government was compelled to follow suit on economic grounds. The first Irish application was formally submitted in July 1961 and the question of membership 'imposed enormous organizational demands on the Congress and its affiliates' (Merrigan 1989: 194). Ireland's economic prospects did not bear comparison with the existing member states (Garvin 2004: 243) and nor did its foreign policy of neutrality sit well with the West German government (O'Driscoll 2011: 163–86), which suggested instead a lesser, associative membership. Such an outcome would have been closest to the ITGWU's preference.

A second application, despite having been formally initiated, was dealt a massive setback in 1963 when the French President, Charles de Gaulle, vetoed the British application for the second time (Fitzgerald 2001: ch. 4). Nevertheless, full membership of the EEC remained central to Taoiseach Lemass's (and Whitaker's) Second Programme for Economic Expansion (1964–70), which sought 'to adapt, re-equip, extend and reorganise all sectors of the economy to ensure the greater strength and efficiency needed to prosper in a more acutely competitive world' (Irish Government 1963). Meanwhile, the Irish government continued along its path of abandoning protectionism and reducing external tariffs by signing the Anglo-Irish Free Trade Agreement (1965) and the General Agreement on Trade and Tariffs (1968). Following de Gaulle's departure and eighteen months of negotiations in Brussels, the ground was prepared for Ireland's accession to the EEC, along with Britain, Denmark and Norway. Years of 'dignified calm' by Irish policymakers (Keogh 1997: 81) had paid off and all that remained was for the people of Ireland to formally endorse Irish membership. Interestingly, this was the first time in that a national public had been consulted on the question of membership.[9] The campaign is discussed below; however, there emerges a shift in preference by ICTU between Ireland's first application in 1961 and the ratification debate a decade later.

Despite being cautious initially, ICTU developed a more positive stance on the prospect of EEC membership. Yet, by the time of the ratification debate in 1972, ICTU was outright opposed to joining, at least officially. What explains this shift in attitude? Was it the willingness of the Irish government to sacrifice Irish neutrality in return for full membership, as argued by Murphy (2009) and O'Driscoll (2011)? Or was it part of a broader political strategy of the wider labour movement to embrace the progressive 'spirit of 1968', which had enthralled mainland Europe, in an attempt to distinguish themselves from the other mainstream civil war parties? Or is another explanation needed?

The two mainstream parties, Fianna Fáil and Fine Gael, were overwhelmingly in favour of membership. Remarkably, few Irish industrialists displayed misgivings with regard to their ability to compete with their European counterparts. Manufacturing imports had almost doubled since the introduction of the first economic programme (1958), which sought to reorient the Irish economy away from autarky (Jacobsen 1994: 97). Yet, this disheartening trend failed to discourage optimistic industrialists. A government White Paper, *The Accession of Ireland to the European Economic Community*, predicted not only that Irish industry would be competitive but that membership would, within five years, create 50,000 jobs. The prospect of the Common Agricultural Policy was enough to convince interests in the agricultural sector, which, at that time, were 'the most important section of the population' (McCabe 2013: 75). Finally, the prospect of weakening economic dependence on Britain was important, especially from a nationalist standpoint.

At the 1971 ICTU national conference, four motions were presented on the question of EEC membership. The first motion sought safeguards for workers, should membership materialise. The second motion advocated Ireland's entry to the common market. The third motion opposed entry on economic, political and social grounds; and the fourth motion called on Congress to mobilise a campaign of opposition. The first, third and fourth motions were adopted while the second one was defeated, albeit narrowly.

At the conference, the ICTU Executive was reluctant to endorse membership on the grounds that, *inter alia*, sufficient information was not forthcoming from the national government. In concluding his speech to the delegate conference, General Secretary of Congress, Ruadhrì Roberts, stated:

> ... the position at the present time, is we have not enough information to justify an expression of support for EEC membership and such information as does exist, would appear to lead toward the conclusion, that the government of Ireland has not done its job in presenting the special position of Ireland to the EEC; and in making the necessary plans and taking the necessary steps to secure the development of industry in Ireland (ICTU 1971).

This line of argument – insufficient information – is somewhat weak and suggests that the real explanation lay elsewhere. Here, two possible explanations are suggested.

The first reason has to do with the 'fragmented unity' of the Irish trade union system, which meant that the leadership of ICTU was beholden to the opinion of the larger general unions, the ITGWU or the ATGWU. The former was by far the largest union in ICTU, containing a third of the trade union members in the 26 counties (and a much smaller proportion in the North). Usually, the ITGWU's vote within the ICTU was enough to secure the outcome (Derwin 1976). However, with the ATGWU also adopting a negative stance towards membership, the ICTU leadership had little choice but to oppose membership.

The ITGWU produced a six-page pamphlet entitled *No to EEC* (ITGWU 1972). The pamphlet essentially makes a broad economic argument, as opposed to a class-based or ideological argument, for opposing membership. In essence, EEC membership was negative for Ireland's underdeveloped economy, that is, not in the national interest. The ITGWU pamphlet made the argument that the Irish economy is 'far too weak to compete in free trade conditions'. Consequently, there 'will be thousands unemployed as a result of completely free entry of mass-produced foreign goods'. In sum, membership of the EEC would lead to an 'economic catastrophe', which would threaten the standard of living, generate greater emigration where the Irish workforce would 'be forced into the slum labour ghettos of Common Market cities.'

Also, the pamphlet (rightly) criticised the government's White Paper and its arithmetic as well as the European institutions' lack of a regional policy. 'They [the European institutions] have been talking about it for years, but nothing concrete has been done' (ITGWU 1972). The pamphlet also makes an emotional argument on the question of sovereignty and neutrality. This was clearly an attempt to convince cultural nationalists of the risks to these should Ireland join the EEC. Another section of the pamphlet argues that free trade 'does not suit the Irish [Catholic] people'. Here, a quotation from a Bishop is inserted, predicting that the EEC 'would bring ruin to Ireland'! The conservative spirit of O'Brien was alive and well within the ITGWU.

Instead, negotiating a form of association membership was promoted as a better deal for Irish workers and families (*ibidem*). Here, a negative vote, it was believed, would have strengthened the Irish bargaining position in achieving associative membership. Such a strategy would have amounted to a gamble, with the likelihood of a successful outcome, if the recent Brexit negotiations are anything to go by, extremely small.

With regards to relations with the government, the Congress and the ITGWU were dismayed by the lack of engagement between the government and the unions regarding the terms and conditions of the Accession Treaty. Furthermore, the Irish Development Agency and other interests (such as fisheries) had been invited to negotiations in Brussels, whereas the trade unions were excluded. This brings us to the second reason for ICTU adopting a negative, but ambiguous, stance towards EEC membership. In essence, it was due to soured relations with the Fianna Fáil government. Worth noting is that, at the time, the relationship between political parties and trade unions was intrinsic to political competition and socio-economic governance. Whereas the 1960s were characterised as the 'decade of upheaval' (McCarthy 1973c), the 1970s in Ireland were about embracing neo-corporatism, which implied an enhanced role for ICTU. Involvement in the Committee on Industrial Organisation, Employer–Labour Conference and National Industrial and Economic Council enhanced its standing *vis-à-vis* the political class (Roche

1989: 121). Hence, the 'not enough information' assertion was a smokescreen by the ICTU leadership, keen to maintain its influence *vis-à-vis* the government and organised capital. Although, 'the decision to enter the EEC undermined the commitment to planning in any systematic sense' (Girvin 1994: 127), ICTU still envisaged a role in socio-economic planning; and, between 1970 and 1980, nine national collective agreements transpired.[10]

Once ICTU had voiced a negative stance toward EEC membership, the Labour party followed suit in opposing Ireland's accession (*see* Holmes 2006). Few union leaders joined the referendum campaign with any great conviction (Merrigan 1989: 234). Notwithstanding, this was one of the few times, if not the only time, when the fragmented Irish left all sang from the same hymn sheet, albeit reluctantly and with little impact. For historian Emmett O'Connor (2011: 231) the EEC referendum was the Irish labour movement's 'last indulgence with contemporary radicalism' (O'Connor 2011: 231); however, as the following section shows, a Marxist-Leninist brand of radicalism emerged in the 1970s but remained on the fringes of the broader Irish labour movement.

Finally, there's the question of the Workers Union of Ireland (WUI), a relatively small but by no means insignificant union, which was, rather bizarrely, in favour of membership. Under the influence of its leaders, Dennis Larkin (son of 'Big Jim') and, subsequently, Paddy Cardiff, the WUI advocated membership of the EEC. Following de Gaulle's veto of the British application, Dennis Larkin urged the union movement to prepare itself for the inevitability of economic liberalisation. 'The problems which are presented to us by the Common Market, in regard to having to change our system of industrial protection, is a problem which we will face whether there is a Common Market or not ... we have to develop our economy, especially our industries' (D. Larkin (1963), cited in O'Riordan 1994: 63). Hence, the more radically-oriented WUI was the only trade union to endorse membership of the EEC, as pro-European members of its successor union, SIPTU, are often keen to point out.

Another small group emerged, consisting of academics, professionals and artists, called the Common Market Defence Campaign. This group also supported calls for associative membership. Leading members of the group, Anthony Coughlan and Raymond Crotty, would feature again and again in Ireland's relationship with Europe, particularly in relation to the ratification of the Single European Act.

The Irish referendum took place in May of 1972 and 71 per cent of the overall electorate voiced a clear message: 83 per cent voted in favour of Ireland's joining. All 42 constituencies voted overwhelmingly in favour of joining, with the lowest majority in favour being 73 per cent in Dublin, South-West (Keogh 1994: 318). With the farmers' and industrial associations, as well as the two mainstream rival political parties, united on the question, those opposed to membership faced an uphill battle. The prospect of the Common Agricultural Policy and subsidies was a prominent feature of the discourse in favour of joining. As Girvin (2002: 209) notes, the 'Common Agricultural Policy was seen as a way of removing pressure from the government and transferring the subsidisation of agriculture from the Irish state to Brussels.' This signalled the onset of Ireland's so-called 'begging-bowl mentality' (Holmes 2006: 3). It was a position that attracted considerable criticism (*see*, for example, Lee 1984) on account of its instrumental approach to European integration.

EUROCOMMUNISM AND LEFT-WING RADICALISM IN ITALY AND IRELAND

No account of left-wing European politics would be complete without briefly considering the phenomenon of Eurocommunism and left-wing radicalism, both of which emerged in the 1970s. This is not the place to provide a historical account of Eurocommunism or trace the many meetings of the west European communist parties in the 1970s; suffice to say that, within this broad political family, the Italian communist party had a good deal of influence, not only on account of its rich intellectual tradition but also because of the strong electoral performance of the PCI during the 1970s, which almost equalled that of the Christian-Democrats and culminated in the 'historic compromise' of 1976. Whilst studies of Eurocommunism predominantly look at communist parties (*see*, for example, Kindersley 1981), there are also implications for the union–party relationship. Furthermore, I would argue that the origins of Eurocommunism can be traced to the CGIL's reorientation towards Brussels in the 1960s. Although an important member of the WFTU, the CGIL, compared to the PCI, had greater scope for autonomy.

Both national and international developments led to the emergence of Euro-communism. The internal developments can be traced to '1968' and the emergence of a revolutionary style of left-wing thinking, which inspired political violence. The economic boom had created a large, urban working class. Failure in public administration to keep pace with such developments resulted in many social problems manifesting themselves, thereby generating a sort of cultural awakening. The Italian educational system, particularly universities, was, by the late 1960s, at breaking point. Student disillusionment and idealism mixed with a deeper sense of worker alienation and anomie and exacerbated by a lack of urban planning led to *il sessantotto* ('1968') and the '*stagione del sindacato*'. Radicalism found fertile ground in the campuses and the factories. To describe such radicalism as Eurosceptic is perhaps an understatement, as a sizeable minority of left-wing radicals, some of whom belonged to trade unions, were revolutionary in the Marxist-Leninist sense and envisaged ending the 'Imperialist State of the Multinationals' and installing the dictatorship of the proletariat (*see* Meade 1990).

The 1970s in Italy were turbulent years characterised by extremist political violence, which culminated with 'one of the greatest political crimes in recent Italian history and in the history of post-war Europe' (Meade 1990: 141), namely, the kidnapping of Aldo Moro, an important Christian-Democrat politician, and his murder, by the *Brigate Rosse* in 1978. Neo-fascist groups also committed acts of political violence that included the murders of state officials and numerous bombings, many of which remain unsolved. The so-called *anni di piombo* ['years of lead'], had laid bare the curse of ideology to which Italy is susceptible. This susceptibility would place 'Europe' in an appealing light, as a quasi-antidote to competing radicalisms. In response to these developments that had grown out of '1968', the Italian labour movement devised 'Eurocommunism'. However, this strategy must also be seen as a response, particularly by the PCI, to developments outside Italy.

Italian communism started to distance itself from Moscow following the Soviet invasion of Czechoslovakia in August 1968 and of its ideological justification, known as the Brezhnev Doctrine. Eurocommunism proposed a 'third way' between west European social-democracy and Soviet socialism and is synonymous with Enrico Berlinguer, who became PCI leader in 1972. The PCI leadership followed the CGIL in its reappraisal of the EEC. 'The concept of Europe adopted by the PCI increasingly overlapped with that of the main social democratic parties, while remaining distinct from that of the other Communist Parties' (Pons 2010: 47). This repositioning included dropping opposition to NATO, an action taken in 1974. In the 1976 election, the PCI gained more than 34 per cent of the vote, a level that was comparable to that of Europe's major social-democratic parties. Eurocommunism, for the PCI, 'was a movement aimed at gradual reform. indicating a new model of socialism and *a positive idea of Europe*' (Pons 2010: 59, emphasis added) and although Berlinguer declared that it 'was not an ephemeral phenomenon' (*ibid*: 59), Pons argues that it 'ended without any lasting political achievement'[11] (*ibid.*: 63). This is not necessarily the case, as the intellectual legacy of Eurocommunism lives on in Eurofederalism.

There was a great deal of compatibility between Eurocommunism and Eurofederalism and were this not the case then the chance of Altiero Spinelli running on a communist ticket in the first European Parliament elections in 1979 would have been next to impossible. In an interview, Spinelli (1978) stated 'I do not think I am boasting when I say that the Party [PCI] has, in fact, adopted the line which I had sought and supported for many years, especially the need to transcend economic unification and move towards a European political union.' Spinelli also notes that 'the most fervent supporters of European unification are the workers' (*ibidem*; *see also* Napolitano 2008: 313–15).[12] Since the 1960s, the CGIL had actively sought to establish links with other national unions, regardless of their ideological orientation. This process sought to replicate 'centralised pluralism' in the Italian context, but at the European level. This orientation culminated with the admission of the CGIL to the nascent ETUC in 1974, which, in no small part, was down to strong linkages with CISL and UIL developed through the unions' collective struggle in the *autunno caldo*, and the attendant achievements, such as the *Statuto dei diritti dei lavoratori* [Workers' Rights Charter] (1972) and the *scala mobile* [wage indexation] (1975).

Turning now to the Irish case, the draw of Marxist-Leninist ideology was increasing not only in the mainstream Labour party, which rallied around the claim that the 'seventies will be socialist', but also within the republican nationalist movement and Sinn Féin in particular. At its 1971 *Ard Fheis* [national congress] a prominent member denounced 'the New Empire of Monopoly Capital, the Common Market'. At the 1973 *Ard Fheis*, 'total opposition to the EEC was reiterated' (Hanley and Millar 2010: 270). Unsurprisingly, the slogans alone proclaimed both the Labour Party and Sinn Féin were opposed to Irish membership of the EEC.

Following the civil rights movement in Northern Ireland in the 1960s, Sinn Féin (and its military wing, the IRA) eventually split in 1970. The minority faction became known as Provisional Sinn Féin while the larger faction is called Official Sinn Féin, which changed its name to Sinn Féin-Workers' Party, and eventually became the Workers' Party in 1982. Whereas the Official branch of Sinn Féin had greater influence in the Republic, the Provisional branch remained more relevant in the North. The former declared itself a Marxist-Leninist party and, although Sinn Féin was of no great electoral significance in Irish 1970's politics, a report from the American ambassador noted that 'communism has made more progress in Ireland in the last two or three years than it made in the last thirty of forty years' (cited in Hanley and Millar 2010: 235). This was most probably an alarmist exaggeration but, nevertheless, there was at an ideological level a shift 'from the form of a nationalist popular front to a Marxist class-based front, with people power rather than armed struggle at its cutting edge' (O Broin 2009: 219). The merits of Eurocommunism ('democratic socialism') were discussed in left-wing circles as 'activists also began to read Gramsci and looked to Milan and Bologna rather than Moscow for ideological guidance' (Hanley and Millar 2010: 362).

A lengthy Official Sinn Féin (Workers' Party) (1977) publication – *Irish Industrial Revolution* – underlined the changing class structure of Irish society and its implications for the republican struggle.

For us, the national question can only be formulated as peace among the divided working class in the two states in Ireland so as to allow a united Irish working class to conduct democratic and militant struggle for the creation of an industrial revolution in all Ireland and the overthrow of Anglo-American imperialism, and ultimately the construction of an Irish Workers' Republic (Sinn Féin 1977: 8).

The ultimate objective was a planned economy and full employment. Notably, however, 'withdrawal from the EEC' was not a prerequisite for achieving these (*ibidem*). Instead, Sinn Féin 'will force the EEC to assist in the aim of Full Employment within the territory of Ireland' (*ibid.*: 134). This position is closer to that of the PCI and, although Eurocommunism is a term that has never really featured in Irish political discourse, the Sinn Féin position can be described as critical engagement with the EEC. This aspect will become of greater importance when labour Euroscepticism re-emerges in the third phase of European integration (*see* Chapter Eight). Suffice to say here that Sinn Féin's reorientation involved intensifying their involvement with the trade unions (Hanley and Millar 2010: 244).

CONCLUSION

What is evident from the previous discussion is that opposition to EEC membership is present within both Irish and Italian trade union politics, albeit with varying strengths and degrees of commitment. Following Pasquinucci (2016: 297), it is important that the term Euroscepticism be 'adapted to the specificity and complexity of historical occurrences'. In Italy, trade union identity is important in explaining both support and opposition to the EEC. In the aftermath of World War Two, the sense of identity was strengthened (Crouch 1993: 176). The best demonstration of how identity shaped Italian trade unions' positions on European integration is through the prism of trade union internationalism, which became more complex as a result of an emerging Cold War in 1947–8. Here, regional integration only served to consolidate divisions in the domestic sphere, which were mirrored in the international trade union movement. For the WFTU, the Marshall Plan was '*the* divisive issue' (Carew 1987: 302, emphasis added). Aided and abetted by their respective governments, British and American organised labour conspired to create the anti-communist ICFTU and its European sister-organisation, the European Regional Organisation (ERO), to which the CISL and UIL affiliated.

CISL promoted 'the direct participation of representatives of the working class in all the negotiations regarding collaboration plans and European integration within the administrative bodies and the relative consultative bodies' (CISL 1955b) [author's translation]. These energies were seized upon by

Monnet and resulted in the European Economic and Social Committee being created. However, the Committee only had a consultative role, and its members had to be nominated by national governments. Hence, as 'a transnational political pressure group at the European level, the trade union movement largely failed' (Pasture 2005: 121). Also at the national level, the CISL leadership subscribed to Christian-democracy (Ciampani 2000) and accepted its 'top-down culture of public administration' (Forlenza 2017: 278). Similarly, CISL claimed to be apolitical, 'basically accept[ing] the broad economic and social goals of the government' (Weitz 1975: 229). Influenced in its development by the ideas and resources of the US labour movement and the ICFTU, CISL, established a CIA-funded union school in Florence to train a new generation of officials in collective bargaining and organising techniques. Rejecting the pro-business attitude of Christian-democracy, a new generation of officials, principally in the metalworkers' federation, promoted a more decentralised collective bargaining strategy, particularly in the industrialised north. The success of this strategy also influenced the CGIL's bargaining strategy as well as its ideological outlook. I will return to this latter point in the following chapter and again in Chapter Eight.

Whereas the identity factor is useful in the Italian case, it is less useful in the Irish case because an 'irredentist obsession' (Lane 2008: 32) prevented ICTU (and the Labour Party) from affiliating to any international labour organisations. Despite geographical and ideological distance from 'Continental' Europe, the year 1957 is also considered to be of significance in Irish political history, albeit for reasons other than the Treaty of Rome. As Garvin (1982: 37) notes, '1957 is conventionally thought of as the end of an era, marking the final exhaustion of the ideas of the first generation of political leaders.' Abandoning economic protectionism was, naturally, a source of concern for the union movement but, as Ó Gráda (1997: 114) notes, 'it is the lack of protest at the shift to a more outward looking policy that is significant'. The first Irish application for membership of the EEC was made in 1961 and whilst membership did not materialise until 1973, the question of EEC membership generated debate within Irish left-wing circles. As noted above, ICTU's (1971) *official* reason for opposing membership was not having 'enough information'. Whilst there might have been cause for opposition on economic grounds – increased foreign competition would have had (and did have) serious implications for indigenous industries (Jacobsen 1994) – the ICTU leadership opposed entry on political grounds, and weak political grounds at that. This, I argue, was so as to appease the larger general unions within Congress and maintain good relations with the political class, particularly Fianna Fáil. However, once ICTU adopted a negative position, this pushed the Labour party into adopting a similar stance (Holmes 2006).

The ATGWU and ITGWU were sceptical of membership, albeit to varying degrees and for different reasons. Whereas the former followed the British anti-European line (*see* Teague 1989a, 1989b), factions within the latter advocated associative membership of the EEC. Others adopted a more nationalist orientation. An ITGWU official argued that Ireland 'would be relegated to the minor role of a county council [within the EEC]' and that '[Irish] independence would be a sham and those that achieved it stabbed in the back' (*Irish Times*, 7 April 1972). Whereas such an overt nationalist stance is not unusual in trade union circles, it is not the norm, and many on the Irish left sought to distance themselves from the likes of Sinn Féin, which was extremely hostile to membership on sovereignty grounds.

Interestingly, the WUI, despite being disposed to a classist ideology, advocated accession. Whilst this position remains to be fully researched, it is at odds with that of the CGIL, a bastion of communist thought in Western Europe. Two possible explanations are ventured here. First, that the WUI was playing politics and sought to distance itself from its rival the ITGWU. Second, the reformist stance of its deputy leader, Paddy Cardiff, abhorred ideological stances (*Irish Times*, 11 June 2005).

For Italian unions, the transformative aspect of economic integration changed trade union mindsets, both in terms of industrial relations and how to engage with supranational institutions and processes. In other words, this was a time of social learning for Italian organised labour, whose power resources increased in tandem with economic growth. Until the 1960s, 'management was able to dominate labor largely because of political factors' and 'was able to dismiss any worker it wanted to' (Regalia *et al.* 1978: 102). Also, 'demands and demonstrations of dissent were dealt with by government action' and 'police repression' (*ibidem*). Strong economic growth raised the spectre of distributional conflicts between social classes, which resulted in the resurgence of class struggle (*ibid.*). Here, the three confederations learned from one another. For instance, the largely communist-socialist idea of the union as the general representative of the entire working class was also adopted by CISL and UIL (*ibid.* 1978: 103, 138). Strict adherence to ideology was, particularly by the CGIL, forfeited in the name of a broader inter-confederal solidarity that could be mobilised for political ends. Also, the emphasis on articulation mechanisms as the social basis of power was central to union strategy. We will return again to this point in Chapter Five and in Part III.

The three Italian confederations, particularly CISL (Ciampani 2000), were key players in overcoming ideological divisions in the European context and in establishing the ETUC. Bridging union ideological divisions also resolved a potential dilemma for ICTU, which might not have been able to affiliate to one or other of the factions for fear of reigniting historical tensions that had previously split the union movement. If anything, ICTU's involvement in the

ETUC strengthened its role *vis-à-vis* the affiliates. Europeanism was also a strategy of other confederations and their leaders to enhance their authority in the domestic sphere (*see* Pernot 2001: 35–7). The progressive aspect of the EEC, particular for women, would become more apparent in the years following accession and put membership in a better light.

Whilst material factors are important in determining political preferences, so too are ideas, which were of utmost importance to the launching of European integration (Parsons 2003; Morgan 2005). However, there is a tension therein. As White (2020a: 2) notes, 'the EU has been built on ideology, and also against it.' Peace and prosperity, two Kantian ideals, are the cornerstones of trade union support for European integration. However, the politics of socioeconomic governance plays out at various spatial levels. This includes not only the (sub-)national and supranational levels but also the transnational level. Just as CISL sought to distance itself from *Democrazia Cristiana* (Weitz 1975), so too did CGIL from its ideological roots. Whilst the strategy of Eurocommunism is more synonymous with the PCI, its roots can be found in the CGIL's reorientation. Also, at the national level, the communist union underwent a reorientation in terms of basic trade union industrial relations functions and the importance of unified labour political action. Such an approach is also reflected at the European level. Hence, the transformative nature of post-war capitalism, to which the cross-border free movement of goods was a critical factor (Cohen and Federico 2001, ch. 7), elicits a reaction and a response from Italian organised labour. The economic 'boom' had marked a point of no return. As 'dislocation' theorists of nationalism have argued (*see*, for example, Gellner 1983), the advance of the class structures of post-war capitalism, accentuated by internal migration and urbanisation as well as technological advancement and industrialisation, exposed groups to new schemes of understanding

Eurocommunism is distinguishable in both theoretical and programmatic terms from Christian-democratic and social-democratic ideas of Europe. This point will be developed further in the following chapter and in the concluding chapter. For now, the objective of Eurocommunism, at its simplest, was the democratisation of market relations *within* the institutional framework of the EEC and its constituent members. This includes the development of vertical and horizontal articulation mechanisms (Crouch 1993), so to ensure a robust form of industrial democracy. Eurocommunism must also be seen as a response to an internal threat to Italian democracy. Giorgio Napolitano (1978), a stalwart of the post-war Italian left, writing in *Foreign Affairs*, warned of the risks that political violence posed to Italian democracy:

> If the workers, the left-wing forces [including unions], and the Communist Party did not put forward their own constructive proposals – both short-term and medium-term – aimed at preventing a deterioration of the conditions in

which Italy is struggling today, if they did not contribute to a united effort of all democratic forces, the crisis might come to a head, with catastrophic results for Italian democracy. Progress towards socialism would be hopelessly delayed; there might be a very grave political and social slide backward (Napolitano 1978: 790).

Elsewhere, Napolitano describes Eurocommunism as giving 'ever newer and richer content to democracy – promoting an effective mass participation in the management of economic, social and political life, transforming economic and social structures, carrying out substantial changes in the power relationship between the classes' (cited in Miliband 1978: 160). In other words, a multilevel, post-revolutionary politics for a transnational economy, with a socialist foundation. In Gramscian terms, this implies developing a hegemony from the bottom up and translating it into an effective presence in the repositories of power that exist at the national and European levels. 'Eurocommunism has no illusions about the nature of the capitalist state' (Miliband 1978: 169) and is therefore open to forging horizontal and vertical linkages with other representatives of the working class in the name of a social(ist) Europe.

Chapter Five

Constructing a
Pro-European Consensus

INTRODUCTION

The second phase of European integration spans the period from the mid-1980s to just after the start of the 2000s. Four European Treaties punctuated this phase. Undoubtedly, the two most impactful were the Single European Act (SEA) and the Maastricht Treaty, which are the focus of this chapter; the Amsterdam and Nice Treaties will be dealt with in the following chapter. The 1970s had presented multifaceted crises – the collapse of the Bretton Woods system and the two OPEC oil crises – which challenged national social democracy and the Keynesian welfare state. Furthermore, the Empty Chair Crisis[1] had exposed the limitations of the European Community's capacity to solve collective action problems. Overcoming 'Eurosclerosis' would require brinksmanship and vision, a task which fell to Jacques Delors, who served almost three terms as President of the Commission. His impact on European integration and trade union politics was such that few would dispute that Delors 'did more than any individual since Jean Monnet to advance the cause of a united Europe' (Grant 1994: 285). With Delors at the helm of the European Commission, the prospect of a Social Europe was placed firmly on the European agenda. For starters, Delors envisioned an enhanced role for the 'social partners' at both European and national levels as a means for navigating crises, constructing consensus and, not least, lending legitimacy to difficult challenges ahead.

In 1979, the same year of the first elections to the European Parliament, occurred an event of historic proportions, the significance of which would cast a long shadow, not least for organised labour. I am, of course, referring to the election of Margaret Thatcher's Conservative Party in the UK. Hence, this period is also synonymous with a paradigm-shift from demand-oriented Keynesianism to a more supply-oriented neo-liberalism. Thatcher's vision for the EU was a 'loose trading area, devoid of political ambition and stripped of all supranational power' (Watson 1996: 267). In other words, a single market *tout court*. The accession of the UK and Denmark, at the European level, upset the Christian-democratic apple cart, which, in anticipation of elections to the European Parliament, had established the European People's Party (EPP) grouping in 1976. Its election manifesto clearly articulated federalist ambitions (Kaiser 2007). The conservative parties of Britain and Denmark, on the other hand, established a separate political grouping within the European Parliament called the European Democrats, whose European programme was at odds with the EPP's federalist views. Subsequently, relations between Helmut Kohl, leader of the German Christian-democrats, and Thatcher, were considerably tetchy and characterised by a mutual suspicion (Watson 1996). Also, at the national level, Christian-democrats were losing ground following the social transformations that accompanied the 'Golden Age' of European capitalism from the end of the Second World War in 1945 to the early 1970s, when the Bretton Woods monetary system collapsed. These transformations challenged traditional values, such as religion and family. Together, these developments meant that Christian-democrats 'lost their original hegemonic political position' (*ibid.*: 311).

In France, the 1981 elections produced the first post-war victory for the French Left, inspiring 'dancing in the streets' (Sassoon 1996: 545). Its victor, the socialist François Mitterrand, promised to implement a radical *projet socialiste*. Based on a 371-page programme, '[a]uthority in all its forms – not just capitalist authority – was being challenged' (*ibid.*: 544). The *Projet Socialiste pour la France des années 80* summoned the spirit of '1968' and the following excerpt is a flavour of its revolutionary tone, which goes beyond French borders.

> The realization in France of a socialist project will be a shock within our European environment, which will cause it to be less marked by liberalism and Atlanticism. Engaged in the construction of a socialist society, *France will contribute to the democratization of the Community*, she will utilize the institutions to favour the convergence of the social struggles against unemployment, for the reduction of the working time, for the control of multinational companies, for the defence of liberties and for the extension of democracy (*Partie Socialiste* 1980, cited in Miró 2017: 5, emphasis added).

Following Mitterrand's election, 'the French economy was subjected to an extensive programme of nationalization, a *dirigiste* industrial policy and planning, industrial relations legislation that favoured the trade unions, redistributive reforms of social programmes and Keynesian economic stimulation, including public-sector job creation' (Bailey 2005: 27; *see also* Hall 1986, 1989). However, 'France was squeezed between a *dirigiste* domestic economic strategy and a *neoliberal* foreign economic policy, [with] the latter rapidly overwhelming the former and dictating the realignment of the country' (Sassoon 1996: 557, emphasis in original). Consequently, Mitterrand was, by 1983, forced into a U-turn, in which austerity was deemed necessary so as to ensure the prestige of the *franc fort* ('strong franc': the policy of tying the currency to the German Deutschmark, as a low-inflation anchor). What had started with dancing in the streets and the promise of a socialist, democratised EEC ended with a commitment to market discipline and Euro-modernisation. For Anderson (2009: 158), this U-turn had 'finally made the country a normal democratic society, purged of radical doctrines and theatrical conflicts'.

Mitterrand's failed socialist experiment in France is significant for two reasons. Firstly, it led to the relaunch of European integration and the first major revisions of the Treaty of Rome. Speaking in the German Bundestag, Mitterrand (1983) stated: 'It is not a question of forgetting each actor's legitimate interests, but of transcending them in the re-found dynamism of the construction of Europe' (cited in Parsons 2003: 177). During the French presidency of the EEC, Mitterrand, the following year, 'surprised everyone' by calling for supranational reforms (*ibid.:* 180). He found an unlikely ally in Chancellor Kohl, with whom he shared a disdain for Thatcherism. For both intergovernmental conferences leading to the Single European Act (SEA) and Maastricht Treaty, Franco-German co-operation succeeded in isolating Thatcher from the debates, thereby ensuring that considerable institutional reform was possible (Johansson 2002a, 2002b). The 'British press consequently proclaimed that the British Prime Minister had been "ambushed" by the Christian Democrats' (Hix and Lord 1997: 170). This move would not go unforgiven, especially by the British tabloids.

Secondly, Mitterrand's U-turn hastened the Europeanisation of social democracy (Abse 2000; Dunphy 1992, 2004; Bailey 2005). By the turn of the 1990s, even the 'ultra-stable' Swedish Social Democratic Party, from a country then outside the EC, responded to 'economic and electoral realities by reversing its economic and social policy in favor of fiscal austerity and opening the Swedish economy to more international competition' (Kitschelt 1994: 170, 172). European social democracy found an ally in Mitterrand's former finance minister, namely, Jacques Delors. A former Christian trade unionist, Delors had also served as a member of the European Parliament from 1979 to 1981. A devout European federalist and, more importantly, an ideational polyglot, Delors could 'combine conversing in the Catholic political language of federalism, subsidiarity and a Europe of the Regions' (Kaiser 2007: 325). Delors' biographer, Charles Grant (1994: 287) writes, 'many of Delors' most important principles – federalism, subsidiarity, opposition to Anglo-Saxon capitalism, belief in a "European model of society" and support for a communitarian version of socialism – derive at least indirectly from personalism.' A philosophy of Christian communitarianism developed by Emmanuel Mounier, a Catholic philosopher, personalism, whose ideals are bound up closely with the Christian-democratic vision of 'Europe' (Burgess 1991: 96), had a profound effect on Delors. These were the ideals that shaped and informed his vision for European society, for which Delors identified three components, the last of which entailed an enhanced role for organised labour. These components were as follows:

> First, a social and economic system founded on the role of the market. Second, we have a state which intervenes, regulates and fills lacunae left by the market. The third element is the role of professional bodies and trade unions, the 'social partners', which help to make people more responsible. There are no longer enough of such intermediary groups between the state and the individual, with the result that political leaders are often unduly guided by opinion polls. These three elements have to, on the one hand, produce enough competitiveness to maintain the standard of living and to prevent unemployment from rising, and, on the other, provide citizens with cover against the risks of sickness, old age and so on (Delors, cited in Grant 1994: 288).

Even while still President-Designate, Delors set about 'visiting the capital cities of the member states, consulting with Heads of State and government and the leaders of organised interests' (Drake 2000: 90). Unlike previous Commission Presidents on such whistle-stop tours, Delors was less interested in the appointment of Commissioners; instead, his primary objective was to construct a political consensus for radical reform.

In his first speech to the European Parliament, Delors (1985) presented his bold vision to relaunch European integration: completion of the single market, the creation of a 'European social space' and a common currency. Whilst Delors will be remembered best for the creation of the single market and for launching monetary union, the adoption of the 1989 Community Charter of the Fundamental Social Rights of Workers, together with a Social Action Plan for its implementation, were of considerable importance for European trade unions. Together, these endeavours initiated a new era of economic integration and European social policy and, in academic circles, Delors' endeavours produced both optimism and pessimism. Firmly placed in the latter camp, Fritz Scharpf (1999, 2002) cogently argued that the institutional configuration of the EU had created a 'constitutional asymmetry' between European policies promoting market efficiencies, on the one hand, and national policies promoting social protection and equality, on the other:

> National welfare states are legally and economically constrained by European rules of economic integration, liberalization, and competition law, whereas

efforts to adopt European social policies are politically impeded by the diversity
of national welfare states, differing not only in levels of economic development
and hence in their ability to pay for social transfers and services but, even more
significantly, in their normative aspirations and institutional structures (Scharpf
2002: 645).

Wolfgang Streeck (1998) also questioned the decoupling of social policy
and economic governance and shared Scharpf's pessimism about the plausi-
bility of shifting socio-economic regulation from the national to the European
level. In such a 'multilevel political economy', Streeck notes (1998: 431),
'politics is decentralised in national institutions located in and constrained by
integrated competitive markets extending far beyond their territorial reach,
and where supranationally centralized institutions are primarily dedicated
to implementing and maintaining those markets'. Whereas solutions 'must
have the character of European law in order to establish constitutional parity
with the rules of European economic integration, ... [solutions] also must be
sufficiently differentiated to accommodate the existing diversity of national
welfare regimes' (Scharpf 2002: 645). For Scharpf and Streeck, such an outcome was unlikely:

> [I]t seems misleading to conceive of the multilevel polity of integrated Europe
> as a federal system-in-waiting; that is, of an institutional superstructure that
> will ultimately develop a unified capacity to suspend internal competition in
> the service of social cohesion. In reality, the multilevel political system of the
> European Union seems by now to have firmly established itself as a *liberaliza-*
> *tion regime* dedicated to enhancing competition and freeing market forces from
> political interference, and indeed one that has become sufficiently settled to be
> largely self-reproductive and capable of conditioning its own further evolution
> (Streeck 1998: 432, emphasis in original).

Given such a pessimistic academic vista, there is a paradox which is central
to this chapter: if the prospect of a social-market economy, a cornerstone of
European social-democracy, and re-regulation of the economy at the European
level, was fanciful, how is it that national trade unions were in favour of
endorsing such a scenario? Could it be that, in light of Mitterrand's failed
socialist experiment and the ascendancy of a Thatcherite neo-liberal creed,
that the promise of Delorism was seen as a better option for organised labour?

This chapter deals with the relaunch of European integration and an emerging pro-European consensus that was evident against the backdrop of the
SEA and the Maastricht Treaty. The development of these two key treaties
is outlined in the following section. Following that, I turn to how the genesis
of European integration was represented in the debates of Irish and Italian
unions. Here, the year 1988 is pinpointed as an important year in terms of

how European integration was framed. The following year saw the Berlin Wall come down, resulting in a crisis of faith for left-wing forces. Enter Delors anew, with a bold vision, namely, monetary union. Once again, the charismatic talisman was able to rally trade union support, which is discussed in the fourth section before the final, concluding section.

THE TWO ACTS OF THE SECOND PHASE OF EUROPEAN INTEGRATION

No sooner were the first direct elections to the European Parliament held than the German and Italian foreign ministers, Hans-Dietrich Genscher and Emilio Colombo, presented a proposal to enhance the political character of the European Community. This involved increasing the powers of the European Parliament, reforming the decision-making process and limiting the use of the national veto. Although the proposal was not embraced by all national governments, it did place the need for reform of the European project at the heart of debate. Speaking in 1982, on the occasion of the twenty-fifth anniversary of the Treaty of Rome, the President of the Commission, Gaston Thorn, called for another Messina conference to break the institutional deadlock and put an end to the defeatist terminology of Eurosclerosis. Finally, in 1984, through sheer single-mindedness and determination, Altiero Spinelli presented the European Parliament with a 'Draft Treaty Establishing the European Union.'

> Spinelli had the purpose, the energy, the strategy, and the breadth of vision necessary to push the Parliament towards a new treaty, via the various resolutions required to achieve it during 1981–1983. His own personal charisma, influence and reputation both within and without the Parliament enabled him to gather widespread support for the project which initially did not look promising in the prevailing circumstances of the early 1980s. This particular role which he played was vital and cannot be exaggerated. And in this sense his contribution to the movement for European Union was more important than the actual imprint which he stamped upon the content of the E[uropean] U[nion] T[reaty] itself (Burgess 1991: 103).

Although Spinelli's gesture was largely symbolic in nature – as only member state governments could draft and approve such a process – it highlighted the desire and the need for institutional reform. Whilst the 'Spinelli Treaty' was broadly federalist in nature, it also contained the concept of subsidiarity so as to assuage those harbouring concerns about the possible emergence of a centralised, federal superstate.

The responsibility for rebooting the European project fell to the new European Commission President, Jacques Delors. The shape of this reboot, however, would not be to everybody's liking. Notwithstanding, Delors's

stateman-like proclivity for building and maintaining cross-class heteroge-
nous coalitions ensured that his vision contained aspects that were appealing
to different political predilections. As Jabko (2006:7) notes, 'the promoters
of Europe consistently exploited the fact that "the market" meant rather
different things in different contexts and for different actors.' The promise
of Delors's drive and the activism of the Commission differed greatly from
the 'inertia of the Community institutions' of the previous decade, which
had resulted in the disheartening of most national trade unions (Teague and
Grahl 1992: 197).

During Italy's presidency of the European Community in 1985, the primary
objective of the Italian government, led by the socialist Bettino Craxi, was the
rilancio (relaunch) of the economic *and* political integration process. Having
outwitted Thatcher, as well as the Danes and the Greeks, such a relaunch was
endorsed and the process formally set in motion. Following this, Delors made
drafting a White Paper the Commission's priority. Based on his predecessor's
report to the European Council in 1982, the Commission's seminal White
Paper, *Completing the Internal Market* (EC 1985), outlined the most considerable obstacles to the free movement of goods, services and financial capital
in the European market. The UK Commissioner for the Internal Market, Lord
Cockburn, ensured that the White Paper contained no hint whatsoever of
idealism. As Drake (2000: 93) notes, the White Paper 'employed a rational
discourse of pragmatic, if not technical, policy initiative. The focus on the
internal market was strong, but not exclusive, in that it was placed in its broader
socio-economic context'. In other words, the political dimension was, to a
degree, left sleeping. The blueprint for the single market, as Ross (1995: 31)
observed, contained 'little Europeanist rhetoric, no prophetic visions, and
no high phrases hinting at spillovers. It eschewed anything likely to inflame
anyone's particular passions'.

The defining characteristics of the Single European Act was the removal of
the national veto and its replacement with qualified majority voting (QMV)
in matters relating to 'the establishment and functioning of the internal market' (Article 100a); and the earmarking of the end of 1992 as the completion
date. Other changes included the formal recognition of the European Council,
the creation of a Court of First Instance, and an enhanced consultative role
for the European Parliament, known as the 'co-operation procedure'. With
restrictions on the use of the national veto, the legislative output of the EU
increased significantly as the liberalisation drive intensified. In anticipation
of monetary union, financial capital markets were completely deregulated
(Directive 88/361/EEC). Importantly, the principle of 'mutual recognition'
was 'a politically un-invasive but substantively demanding form of liberalization' (Moravcsik 1998: 315). In other words, simple but at the same time
nothing short of revolutionary.

Many were surprised by the speed and the extent of the reforms that were coming out of Brussels. Commenting on the SEA, Schmitter remarks (1996: 45), 'perhaps it went further than its signatories in 1985 intended or believed possible'. Geoffrey Howe, Thatcher's longest serving minister, admitted that '[T]here was one consequence of the Single European Act that I had certainly not fully anticipated, namely the impact on the so-called 1966 Luxembourg Compromise' (which ended the abovementioned Empty Chair Crisis) (Howe 1994: 458, cited in Endo 1999: 148). In the absence of national vetoes, institutional and market reforms were now possible and the speed at which market-making legislation was passed was impressive (*see* Wessels, Maurer and Mittag 2003).

For Delors and other Euro-enthusiasts, such as the Italian government, the SEA did not go far enough (Burgess 1991: 130; Drake 2000: 91). In particular, social aspects of the 1984 Draft Treaty on European Union, such as the European Social Charter, had been omitted. That said, the inclusion of Article 118(a/b), which related to health and safety issues as well as social dialogue, was seen as a positive step towards creating a European system of industrial relations.[2] Henceforth, '[T]he Commission shall endeavour to develop the dialogue between management and labour at European level which could, if the two sides consider it desirable, lead to relations based on agreement' (Art 118[b]). Its inclusion is all the more important when one considers that some years previously, Delors's attempts to engender social dialogue had failed. In 1985, at Val Duchesse, outside Brussels, Delors convened a meeting between the European social partners but, as Martin and Ross (1999: 324) observe, '[N]either ETUC nor UNICE had mandates to negotiate' and discussions 'broke down quickly'.[3] Such an outcome particularly suited the latter, but Delors was keen to construct a scenario that would entice UNICE into constructive social dialogue (*see below*).

In addition to 'engaging important unionists privately' (Martin and Ross 1999: 324), Delors made his presence felt by speaking at different trade union conferences, notably the 1988 ETUC and TUC general conferences, where he urged organised labour to reconceptualise its strategic interests by endorsing European social dialogue and the integration project. The charm offensive struck a particular chord not only with the Swedish unions, which subsequently established a Brussels office, but also more famously with the British unions, with whom Delors' speech resonated to such an extent that the leader of the TGWU, a staunch Eurosceptic, proclaimed:

> The only card game in town at the moment is in a town called Brussels, and it is a game of poker where we have got to learn the rules and learn them fast. We do not fancy that we are slow on the uptake in industrial negotiations, but this is a new kind of negotiating and now is the time for us to learn some new rules,

to learn some new languages, to learn who is who and what is what among our trade union counterparts in the other European countries, to learn how to make the best of Community committees (R. Todd, cited in Mitchell 2012: 30).

Until late 1987, the British TUC pursued a strategy of 'naïve Keynesianism' and officially opposed British membership of the European Community (Teague 1989a). Securing the support of the influential TUC was central to Delors's vision. Urging the British unions to play a key role, Delors outlined the prospect of a social Europe, in which statutory labour rights would counterbalance the liberalising thrust of the single market project. 'In response, Congress gave him a standing ovation!' (Mitchell 2012: 30). Upon learning of Delors's overture, Thatcher was beyond livid and only days later responded with a legendary Eurosceptical speech in Bruges: 'We have not embarked on the business of throwing back the frontiers of the state at home, only to see a European super-state getting ready to exercise a new dominance from Brussels.' The battle lines were now clearly drawn.

Convincing the TUC would, in turn, strengthen the ETUC, which was of fundamental strategic importance to Delors's vision. 'A more effective ETUC', as Martin and Ross (1999: 324) wrote, 'might then cause the UNICE to reconsider its nay-saying posture. Moreover, a stronger ETUC, partly dependent upon Commission resources, could also be an ally for the Commission in broader political matters'. At the time, however, there was no guarantee of such an ambitious prospect materialising. As Burgess (2002: 183) notes:

> It was not possible at the historical juncture of 1985–88 to know if the SEA and 1992 would lead logically to further movement toward European integration, or if they were simply a set of specific historical events with no necessary implications for the future. But it was already clear in 1988 that there were several state and non-state actors which were determined that they would have far-reaching consequences.

The 'state and non-state actors' to which Burgess refers include Mitterrand, Kohl, Delors, the Commission, the majority of the European Parliament as well as 'a veritable ant hill of federalist elites' from across the Community which 'acted with purpose to ensure that the Single Market would be implemented, that EMU would be relentlessly pursued' and, importantly from the perspective of organised labour, 'the foundations for a "social Europe" would be firmly put in place' (*ibidem*). It is no coincidence that it was around this time that the Irish Prime Minister, Charlie Haughey, decided to engage in tripartism at the political level (*see below*).

The actions of the ETUC substantiate the uncertainties of the period. In December 1988, the ETUC adopted a Community Charter on Social Rights, 'in the hope of spurring the Commission into action' (Silvia 1991: 633). If

Delors wanted the support of the ETUC (and its affiliates) he would have to deliver on his promises. The following year, despite the opposition of the Thatcher government, the Social Charter[4] was adopted; it covered, *inter alia*, employment and remuneration; improvement of living and working conditions; freedom of association and collective bargaining; information, consultation and participation rights; gender equality; health and safety in the workplace; and vocational training. The Charter was accompanied by an ambitious Social Action Programme,[5] which was endorsed by the European Council. The Commission even reinforced the wording of the preamble, adding a new statement that 'the same importance must be attached to the social aspects as to the economic aspects' of the internal market. However, the 47 initiatives included in the Social Action Programme were not binding and each of them would be subject to Council approval. Nevertheless, both the Charter and the Action Programme were 'an important impetus' for the Community social-policy field in the early 1990s, which laid the ground for the Social Protocol attached to the Maastricht Treaty (Welz 2008: 257).

Having created a network of close supporters, the 'Delors mafia' – a term used by his detractors – was strengthened for Delors's second term as Commission President, starting in 1989. Before turning to that, however, it is necessary to consider the historic cataclysm resulting from the fall of the Berlin Wall and the imminent dissolution of the Soviet Union. Albeit ultimately to prove hollow, the self-congratulatory, 'end of history' triumphalism of this time was palpable and left-wing political forces were plunged into a deep crisis of faith. As expressed by Sassoon:

> ... when the Berlin Wall collapsed, the conventional reformist idea that it was necessary to possess a large public sector to countervail the negative tendencies of the private sector had evaporated from the programmes of all socialist parties. The privatization of the public sector, previously unthinkable even among most conservatives, came to be accepted by many socialists. *The world of socialists had irrevocably changed* (Sassoon 1996: 649, emphasis added).

Speaking at the Collège d'Europe in Bruges, Delors (1989a) stressed 'the need for a European power, commensurate with the problems of our times' and the desire 'to explicitly reconcile necessity and ideal'. It is neither improbable nor coincidental that the Frenchman chose Bruges to underline his vision. Delors warned:

> History does not wait ... Economic and Monetary Union turns out to be the only way to reinforce European construction and to ensure its political dynamism ... History is accelerating ... We need a commitment to results. Such is the lesson of events ... A new political impetus is required (*ibidem*).

With the reunification of Germany imminent, the French push for EMU and social integration 'accelerated' (Parsons 2003: 205). Having a reunited Germany anchored at the centre of the EC is 'the *sine qua non* of the Community's future' (Ross 1995: 49) and Mitterrand recognised this.

If the SEA was about market-building, then the Maastricht Treaty was about state- and polity-building. This meant closing the democratic deficit; strengthening subsidiarity; improving decision-making procedures; institutional reform; and developing a common foreign and security policy (CFSP). These endeavours, however, were subject to a complex, twelve-way intergovernmental process. Even within member states, as Parsons (2003: 210–11) notes, '[e]lites fought over variants of what they called European Monetary Union and its institutional trappings', which 'cut across right and left'. Once again, Thatcher was ambushed and, in November 1990, she was 'compelled to resign over her resolute refusal to moderate her intolerable obsession with Delors and his federalist intentions' (Burgess 1991: 204). Even if Delorism was merely the straw that broke the Iron Lady's metaphorical back, his esteem amongst trade unionists can only have improved. In any case, EMU, regardless of its institutional shape, remained 'a gamble' (Moravcsik 1998: 440), leaving open the prospect that Thatcher, and her supporters, could well have the last laugh.

European treaties are complex documents by their very nature and the Maastricht Treaty was no different. The objectives of the treaty included: the creation of a common currency and an independent European central bank; an increase in policy areas covered by QMV; an extension of the powers of the European parliament; the principle of subsidiarity; and the creation of European citizenship. Developing a social dimension to European integration was an additional aspiration and, to this end, the Social Protocol was of great import. Almost all of these objectives were of interest to the European trade union movement. Of particular and enduring significance was the creation of the common currency and the so-called 'convergence criteria', which implies significant fiscal discipline and constraints on public spending. The same can be said of the Social Protocol, particularly, but not uniquely, from the perspective of organised labour; it is worth briefly outlining how it materialised.

Undeterred by the 'strategic silence' of the employers (Streeck and Schimtter 1991), Delors sought to unblock UNICE's hesitancy to discuss European social policy. The objective of engaging the social partners was twofold. First, 'to strengthen the role of trade unions' (Grant 1994: 289); and, second, Delors hoped to 'neutraliz[e] opposition from some Member States to a social dimension of the interior market by activating the national and European interest organizations for the common European cause' (Welz 2008: 251). Hence, the objective was not solely the institutionalisation of European social dialogue but also 'a revised definition of interests and preferences' (*ibidem*; *see also* Falkner 1998).

The long and winding discussions between UNICE and ETUC rather unexpectedly produced an agreement on how to strengthen the role of the social partners in the Maastricht Treaty. Working from Article 118(b), the social partners changed the wording from 'developing social dialogue' to 'promoting consultation' thereby 'downsizing the Commission's influence' and 'stressing the autonomy' of the social partners in the social dialogue process (Welz 2008: 274). This wording has endured in the Treaties of Amsterdam, Nice, and Lisbon. That said, the Social Agreement and Maastricht Social Protocol would never have come about had the General Secretary of the British employers, Dick Price, not rescinded his opposition to the agreement with the ETUC. 'The importance', for Delors and many others, 'of this agreement ... cannot be overstated' (cited in Welz 2008: 267), but it did cost Price his job! In the run up to the Maastricht IGC, there was growing resistance to the wording of the Social Agreement being adopted for the draft Treaty. In response, 'the ETUC threatened EU-level industrial action ... [and] was willing to use the national parliaments and their capacity of having to ratify the Maastricht Treaty' (Welz 2008: 272).

Although Thatcher was no longer on the scene, her replacement, John Major, continued to resist negotiation on social policy. Unsurprisingly, the social policy dossier was, according to Irish Prime Minister, Charles Haughey, 'certainly the most protracted and possibly most difficult' in the TEU negotiations (cited in Falkner 1998: 88). Resolving entrenched differences required 'quick action from the [Dutch] support team and smart politics from Delors himself' (Ross 1995: 191). The deadlock was ended by removing social policy articles from the body of the main text and instead compiling them in a separate Social Protocol that is attached to the Treaty. This solution permitted the EU and the eleven member states to pursue a European social policy agenda, whilst exempting Britain from any social legislation. Notwithstanding this last-minute compromise, some scholars (for example, Lange 1993; Streeck 1994; Jabko 2006) deemed the Social Protocol unimportant, or at best a sideshow to EMU. In any case, the ratification of the Maastricht Treaty was the source of prolonged and acrimonious debate, particularly in France and, especially, Denmark. But how was the SEA and its successor, the Maastricht Treaty, debated in Irish and Italian trade union circles?

Before turning to the responses of Irish and Italian organised labour to furthering economic integration and monetary union, it is necessary to outline another initiative of Delors, namely, the Structural Funds, which were delivered in two different *paquets*, known as Delors I (1987) and Delors II (1993). Delors designed these so as to soften the opposition of national governments to the Commission's broader political objectives – the single market, EMU and social Europe (Johnston 1994: 94–7). As Drake (2000: 104) notes, the first Delors *paquet* 'became instrumental to the success of the implementation of the "1992" programme'. Here, Delors pushed his luck by promising some national governments more than he could actually deliver (Watson 1996: 298)! Both packages had a socio-developmental component that sought to tackle Europe's economic divergences and social malaise. Delors II, to which I return in the following chapter, involved increased funding for the peripheral and underdeveloped countries through the Structural Funds[6] and the newly created Cohesion Funds. The latter were specifically created for Ireland, Greece, Spain, Portugal and southern Italy (Laffan, O'Donnell and Smith 2000; Della Porta and Caiani 2006). One of Delors' concerns, however, was that the focus on these funds would overshadow the bigger picture, which still remained open to a degree of interpretation. Here, I turn to Irish and Italian organised labour's interpretations, by assessing their preferences towards the SEA and the Maastricht Treaty.

IRISH AND ITALIAN ORGANISED LABOUR: RESPONDING TO THE SEA AND MAASTRICHT

Throughout the 1980s, the standing of organised labour *vis-à-vis* the state deteriorated significantly (Jacobi *et al.* 1986). The Italian and Irish domestic contexts in the 1980s and early 1990s were both characterised by profound crises, albeit of different orders. For the Irish there was a dire economic crisis to which the political class appeared at a loss to respond. In Italy, decades of political patronage had come home to roost, resulting in a deep political crisis that ultimately led to an unceremonious ending for the first Italian Republic. In both cases, the Italian and Irish governments followed similar exit strategies from the crises, which can be summarised as an intergovernmental collective solution at the European level and an enhanced role for organised labour at the national level. In this section, I will discuss the attitudes of Irish and Italian unions to European integration and Delorsism; suffice to say here that whatever apprehension towards Europe existed in the mid-1980s was all but dispensed with by the early 1990s.

Upon Ireland joining the EEC, Irish indigenous industries were devastated. This devastation exacerbated the unemployment crisis of the 1980s and, although foreign direct investment (FDI) made a modest impact, it did little to stem mass emigration. Fianna Fáil's electorally popular expansionary macroeconomic policies and promises of full employment, in an international context of a deteriorating economy, exacerbated Ireland's economic imbalances (OECD 1982: 12). Hell-bent on attracting FDI, national governments offered a range of incentives, including export tax holidays; cash grants;

duty-free import of capital equipment; training grants; guaranteed loans and subsidisation of interest; provision of ready-made factories in industrial parks; and research and development (Jacobsen 1994: 28). These incentives were offered so as to alleviate a growing unemployment problem, which, by the mid-1980s, stood at almost 17 per cent. To make matters worse, by 1986, Irish national debt was almost 120 per cent of GDP and the Irish currency underwent a devaluation. Engaging with the social partners was not considered an option by the four governments that held power between 1981 and 1987 (Roche 2009). Although, tripartism, between the government, employers and unions, was attempted in the preceding decade, partly in response to the ERM, it had failed, partly because ICTU was insufficiently capable of disciplining its affiliates (Hardiman 1988). The decade's fifth election would signify a new departure for Irish organised labour.

Subsequent to the signing of the Single European Act in February 1986, the Irish Fine Gael–Labour government set about obtaining ratification through the parliament (Gallagher 1988). However, the constitutionality of the Single European Act was challenged and brought before the Supreme Court by a long-standing Eurosceptic, and academic, Raymond Crotty. According to the Irish Constitution, *Búnreacht na hÉireann*, any amendments that substantially alter the complexion of the Constitution must be offered for public endorsement. In a landmark case, the Irish Supreme Court held that the Single European Act did exactly that, with one of the Supreme Court judges seeing the SEA as a 'fundamental transformation in the relations between the member states' and as 'the threshold leading from what has hitherto been essentially an economic Community to what will now also be a political Community' (cited in Keatinge 1989: 167). Therefore, the SEA had to be put before the Irish people. The ruling was an unexpected one and neither political party nor interest group was prepared for a referendum. Adding insult to injury, the Fine Gael-Labour coalition government had, in the meantime, collapsed under the pressure of prolonged austerity. The 1987 general election returned a Fianna Fáil minority government, under the leadership of the indefatigable Charlie Haughey, who had promised that, if elected, he would bring the social partners together in an attempt to collectively resolve the ever-deepening problems facing the country.

Following months of negotiations, the Programme for National Recovery (PNR) was signed in October of 1987. The agreement sought to address the twin crises of mass emigration and chronic fiscal imbalances by introducing wage restraint, an hour reduction in working hours and tax reform. Interestingly, the agreement's opening chapter was dedicated to the European dimension and stated: 'The Programme is based on the fullest participation by Ireland in the international economy and in the European Community.' What is a little surprising about such an unequivocal statement is that both Fianna

Fáil and the trade union movement had previously voiced serious misgivings about the SEA, particularly with regard to Title III on security issues. Whilst in opposition, Fianna Fáil had raised concerns regarding the potential implications of political integration for Irish neutrality.[7] The party also feared that, in light of recent enlargements (Spain and Portugal), Ireland's quota of regional aid would be diminished. Once in government, however, Fianna Fáil endorsed the ratification of the SEA.

The maintenance of Common Agricultural Policy (CAP) subsidies ensured farmers' support for the Treaty. Fine Gael, along with Fianna Fáil, set a trend by campaigning mainly on the platform of potential job losses in case of non-ratification (Gallagher 1988). Left-wing opposition came from the more marginal Workers' Party, which countered the Fine Gael- Fianna Fáil narrative by highlighting that unemployment at the time was much higher than when Ireland first joined. Also, the Green Party and Sinn Féin opposed the SEA on the grounds that sovereignty would be further eroded and Irish neutrality endangered. So too did Raymond Crotty's Irish Sovereignty Movement. There was also a hotchpotch of other groupings that campaigned on moral grounds. For instance, a conservative Catholic group, Family Solidarity, argued that acceptance of the SEA would result in abortion being imposed on Ireland by Brussels. This threatened to undo the theo-conservative victory in the 1983 referendum, the so-called Eighth Amendment, which outlawed abortion in Ireland for the next three-and-a-half decades (until 2018). Despite having already endorsed the SEA as a government party, Labour, once in opposition, simply 'fudged the issue' (Holmes 2006: 131) by failing to adopt an official position! Labour members, however, were free to campaign in support, abstain or reject the treaty. The Labour party, however, was not alone in its abstention: it was joined by the ICTU leadership. What is somewhat puzzling about this stance is that the latter could have defended deepening integration along social policy lines.

Following accession in 1973, socially-oriented Directives on equal pay and equal treatment had to be transposed into Irish law. The Irish government of the day had sought a derogation on the Directive for Equal Pay on the grounds that pay parity would cause financial difficulties for certain economic sectors. The government was, of course, referring to the public sector, where women were paid much less than their male counterparts and upon getting married were forced to retire and take up their 'natural' place in the home. Buoyed by the social legislation, ICTU (and feminist groups) lobbied the European Commission, opposing the granting of this dispensation to the Irish government. As a result of this pressure, no such derogation was allowed to the Irish state. Hence, in social policy circles, this legislation was seen as being significant and progressive; however, to what extent this was successfully communicated to the wider trade union movement is an open question.

At the annual ICTU conference in July 1988, William Wallace, ICTU President, remained pessimistic about the prospects of the Irish economy and indigenous firms and insisted instead on a special arrangement for Ireland.

> The impact of this unlimited free competition will change the present industrial structure of Europe beyond recognition. It will create a situation where only the very large, more successful companies can survive. Irish firms with less resources could go to the wall ... This will have a particularly detrimental effect on the Irish economies ... The Single European Act would be disastrous for both economies in Ireland [and Northern Ireland] unless some agreement is reached beforehand about phasing it in more gradually (Wallace 1988).

Both the ITGWU and the WUI were against the SEA, mainly on sovereignty grounds and regarding neutrality. There was also concern that the introduction of QMV would diminish the influence of smaller member states. The ATGWU, under the leadership of Mick O'Reilly, also advocated a 'No' vote. Paradoxically, many trade unionists were more critical of Fianna Fáil's 'Damascus road' conversion (*Irish Times*, 12 May 1987), rather than Labour's ambiguous position. Another significant concern within the general debate had to do with foreign policy: 'the debate on the Single European Act ... centre[d] more and more on the provisions relating to European Political Co-operation and their alleged implications for Irish neutrality' (Brown 1998: 21). Labour members, such as Emmett Stagg and Michael D. Higgins (President of Ireland at the time of writing), formed a group called the Labour Campaign for Peace and Neutrality, advocating a 'No' vote on the grounds that Ireland would be co-opted into NATO, thereby undermining Irish neutrality. Similarly, the ITGWU was particularly concerned about neutrality and, in response, ran a low-visibility campaign under an emotively charged slogan: 'We serve neither King nor Kaiser' (*Irish Times*, 12 May 1987). This Irish Citizens' Army motto was on a banner famously draped from the original Liberty Hall in 1914 and was a precursor to the formal declaration of neutrality by the Irish state. The President of the ITGWU, John Carroll, feared that the SEA would 'seriously compromise our traditional independence in foreign policy matters; it will undermine our military neutrality by drawing us into closer cooperation with NATO members, and it will erode our freedom to determine our own economic and social policies' (quoted in *Irish Times*, 12 May 1987).

Given the renewed relationship with the Fianna Fáil government, ICTU might well have chosen to support ratification of the SEA. As noted above, the ICTU leadership did not have any qualms about committing to the European project in the PNR. According to ICTU official, Patricia O'Donovan, the Irish confederation's stance was taken to demonstrate discontent with the inability of the EEC to deal with the economic crises:

> Trade unions ... pointed to the lack of European policies and instruments to deal with unemployment, social disadvantage, industrial restructuring and social dumping. The period of the late 1970s through to the late 1980s was characterised by a sense of frustration at the apparent inability of the EEC to come to terms with the major challenges of poverty and unemployment. The disproportionate influence during this period of the policies of free trade, unfettered competition and deregulation, pursued in particular by the British Conservative government under Margaret Thatcher, threatened to collapse the EEC into a free-trade zone without any civic, social or political dimension. The general sense of alienation from the European project that this generated among trade unions during this period, is best illustrated by the fact that Congress did not participate in the referendum campaign on the Single European Act in 1987 (O'Donovan 1999: 50).

Remaining taciturn as a strategic response to 'alienation from the European project' appears bizarre and was a smokescreen for the real reason, which had more to do with the weakness of ICTU. Since the ITGWU, ATGWU and WUI had come out in opposition to the Treaty, the ICTU leadership has very little choice but to abstain. Adopting an oppositional stance might have jeopardised relations with government. In the end, with its hands somewhat tied, the leadership decided that no official position would be adopted.

The Irish referendum, held on 26 May 1987, passed overwhelmingly, with 69 per cent voting in favour. That said, only 44.1 per cent of the electorate turned out to vote. Voter apathy and general confusion are the most likely reasons for the low turnout. Tony Brown, an official of the Labour Party was very critical of the quality of the debate. 'People were confused about issues that had never been explained and politicians were struggling with concepts that had never been tackled with any degree of seriousness ... Much of what passed for debate at the time of the Referendum was nothing more than national inferiority complexes being given an unwarranted airing.' Following the result, Raymond Crotty penned *A Radical's Response*, in which he lamented that

> The Tánaiste, Mr Lenihan, admitted in the Dáil that the government had spent from taxpayers' money £1,700,000 on leaflets and £16,000 on media advertisements to influence in the best banana republic fashion, the people's choice. That was about fifty times more money than the anti-SEA movement was able to mobilise by voluntary subscription. In addition, the Government Information Service was used to issue a constant stream of propaganda in favour of the SEA (Crotty 1988: 156).

This issue of government spending in European referendums would resurface a decade or so later. In any case, by the time of the next European treaty, the ITGWU and WUI had merged. Before turning to that, however, the question of the Italian unions and their preferences towards the SEA will be explored.

Having an open economy engaged in international trade and having been bailed out by the IMF in 1976 to the tune of $530 million, the Italian economy was, by the turn of the 1980s, suffering from low growth and investment, a weak currency, high inflation rates and balance of payment difficulties. Now integrated into an international economic system, Italy 'could no longer rely on low wages' (Sassoon 1986: 70). To address Italy's loss of competitiveness, a number of initiatives, including a devaluation, were pursued. In 1984, the Italian unions and employers agreed to the revision of the wage indexation machinery, the *scala mobile*, and the deregulation of the labour market, in exchange for subsidies for social security taxes to the employers and an increase in family allowances to the workers (Regini and Regalia 1997: 201). The following year, attempts were made to renegotiate a social pact, but political divisions had re-emerged between the three confederations. On account of the sister parties of the CISL (DC) and the UIL (PSI) being in government, both unions were reluctant to refuse government proposals, as the CGIL had done. Instead, the socialist Prime Minister, Bettino Craxi, attempted to introduce the reforms to the *scala mobile* by decree. The PCI and CGIL managed to collect enough signatures to force the government to hold a referendum *abrogativo* (which, if carried, can force the government to rescind legislation) on the law. The PCI and CGIL urged Italians to vote against the proposed legislation, but CISL and UIL remained faithful to the position assumed by the sister parties. The referendum was passed with 54.3 per cent voting in favour, but the net effect of the result was to split left-wing forces in Italy, with the PSI being accused of having conceded its values to business interests.

The CGIL's repositioning *vis-à-vis* European integration began in earnest when it affiliated to the ETUC. Along with CISL and UIL, the Italian unions' position had 'a significant political role and could now benefit from being an operator in the union structure in Brussels' (Ciampiani 2013: 76). Should political energies align between the three confederations, there was scope for developing considerable influence within the ETUC. Almost immediately, the three confederations began to submit documents as a unitary federation. CGIL reformists, such as Bruno Trentin, leader of the metalworkers' federation (FIOM), and Aldo Bonaccini, official responsible for international policy, and CISL reformist, Emilio Gabaglio, also of the international office, repeatedly placed the question of the unions' international relationships at the centre of debates. These debates often related to either a western-ETUC dimension, or had an eastern European flavour. Following CGIL's official departure from the WFTU in 1978, criticism of the socialist regimes of the East and their overly bureaucratic system of economic planning on political liberty, civil rights and trade union autonomy grounds (*see*, for example, Cuozzo 1979) began. In particular, the embattled Polish union, *Solidarność*, was the source of much concern and served to emphasise the notion that trade unions were the only institution with an ability to transform not only the socialist system but also, by extension, the liberal-democratic setting and the supranational arena. The term '*Eurosyndicalismo*' entered the trade union lexicon; although the term is mentioned in different union debates and trade union outlets, such as *Rassegna Sindacale* articles, it never really gained traction, at least not in the same way as its 'sister' term, *Eurocommunismo*. Nevertheless, its introduction, and use, underlines an earlier made point about Eurocommunism and its origin lying within trade union theory and praxis. In any case, the holding of elections to the European Parliament in 1979 is seen as being of importance for *Eurosyndicalismo* (Magnani 1979), with many trade unionists running on a socialist, Christian-democratic or a communist ticket, such as Aldo Bonaccini, who was a CGIL official elected to the European Parliament on the PCI list.

In an interview with a French paper *Libération*, and reproduced in the Italian left-wing paper, *Unitá* (26 October 1982), Bruno Trentin and Jacques Delors, then Finance Minister in Mitterrand's government, expressed their firm belief that the only viable solution for the French and Italian trade unions was deeper political integration and the creation of an industrial relations system at the European level to complement the pre-existing system at the national level. The piece clearly highlights the extent of both men's ideological commitment to the European ideal. When Delors, some years later, became President of the European Commission, their shared vision, albeit grandiose and incredibly ambitious, appeared to be within touching distance or at least much more obtainable. Within this grand vision, simply termed here as Delorsism, organised labour, as noted above, would have an important role to play.

All three Italian confederations were supportive of the SEA, which was seen as a product of the Colombo-Genscher proposal (see above) but, more specifically, of the singlemindedness and devotion of Spinelli to the federalist ideal. In particular, Article 118, which introduced European social dialogue and enhanced the role of the ETUC, was a welcome development, not least because CISL's Carlo Savoini (2000) played a central role in drafting its wording. The following year 1987, CISL established a specific Department for Community Policies, distinct from its international department which was headed by future ETUC leader, Emilio Gabaglio. The idea of 'social Europe' had begun to germinate and, in the following years, there was a sense of optimism regarding its realisation (Ciampani and Gabaglio 2010). Whilst this sense of optimism goes beyond trade union circles, there was, at the same time, a general disappointment that the Single European Act did not go further. Secretly, there were hopes that its rejection by the Danish parliament[8] might result in the reopening of negotiations. However, the other member states refused to even await the result of the Danish referendum, which was held so as to overcome the Danish parliament's ratification difficulties. Only following ratification by the Danish public did the Italian government sign the Act. Most political forces in Italy, including the PCI, saw the European treaty as a lifeline for an ailing economy (Cavatorto and Verzichelli 2008: 219). By now, the PCI was a strong advocate of European integration and their vision of Europe was in line with that of Spinelli: a supranational federal entity. Hence, the *'fede Europea'* successfully unified all three confederations as well as mainstream political forces. There was, however, the exception of the *Lega Nord*, which was only a marginal political force at the time.

In June 1988, the Italian section of the European federalist movement sent a proposition with 114,000 signatures to the Italian Parliament (Uleri 1996: 107). The proposition called for a referendum on conferring a mandate on the European Parliament to create a European Constitution. In November 1988, the two chambers of Parliament backed this proposition by means of an *ad hoc* constitutional amendment. The *ad hoc* referendum[9] took place in parallel with the European elections on 18 June 1989, and attained a high turnout (81per cent) and an 88 per cent yes vote.[10] This overwhelming result was an indication of the support for the European (federal) project by the political class and the masses. A further example of Italy's broad-based commitment to European integration was visible in the steps taken in order to ensure that Italy joined the Euro a decade later (*see* Chapter Six).

FRAMING EUROPE: BETWEEN PRAGMATISM AND IDEALISM

With the SEA ratified, Delors turned his attention to the Community's most ambitious project, a common currency. Here, I identify 1988 as a pivotal year. Above, I have already outlined how Delors's charm offensives towards the ETUC and the British TUC were relatively successful. The very same year, both the CGIL and ICTU organised conferences to deal specifically with the completion of the single market and the daunting prospect of foregoing the Lira and the Punt. Both conferences placed an emphasis on economic convergence and social cohesion. The need for a growth strategy to address unemployment and offset negative effects from the creation of the single market was underlined, not least for underdeveloped regions such as southern Italy and the west of Ireland. To this end, the Delors's *paquets* were important, particularly in the Irish case. Whereas 'Make Europe Work for Us' was the theme of the ICTU conference, the theme of the CGIL conference, on the other hand, was *Per un Programma Europeo della CGIL* ['For a European Programme of the CGIL']. From these slogans, we can gain an insight as to how the Irish and Italian confederations interpreted the European project, a point I will return to.

Whilst differences can be discerned from the respective conference slogans, there was also a degree of commonality between the two conferences. For instance, both the leaderships of the CGIL and ICTU emphasised the social dimension of the internal market. Also, the European level was identified as the ideal level at which to regain the initiative and address the emerging neo-liberal ideology. As the ICTU General Secretary, Peter Cassells, stated,

> [I]t [the EU level] offers the prospect that trade unions can confront the power of transnational capital, backed up by a system of Community law and acquired negotiating rights ... it is clear that the struggle by trade unions for a firm social basis to the Internal Market is only beginning (Cassells 1988).

The preferred mechanism for devising pro-labour policies was European social dialogue provided meaningful results could be achieved. To this end, the EU's sectoral level is identified as the optimal level to conduct social dialogue (*ibidem*).

Bruno Trentin, leader of the powerful metalworkers' federation, was, in 1988, elected General Secretary of the CGIL. Trentin's influence over the Italian trade union movement in general, and the CGIL in particular, cannot be overstated. As already stated, the CGIL's conference slogan was *Per un Programma Europeo della CGIL*, which immediately conveyed an explicit commitment by the CGIL to the European project. The CGIL committed wholeheartedly to the implementation process of the SEA and promoted the logic that there must be equilibrium between competition, technological development and social justice. Only a Europe united politically could address the differences between Northern and Southern Europe and diffuse the tensions between Eastern Europe and Western Europe. Two excerpts from Trentin's speeches highlight the CGIL's preference for parallelism between economic and political integration and the challenges in articulating such a vision. Speaking at the 1988 conference Trentin (1988) stressed the need to

> ... outline the characteristics of a European CGIL programme, which means defining a policy [*una politica revindicativa*] which acknowledges the creation of the European community as a fundamental option and which outlines clearly the implications and the new constraints that arise from this policy for the Italian

trade union, the CGIL, in its everyday operations at the national level as well as at the company level [author's translation].

A few years later, speaking at the 1991 XII CGIL Congress, Trentin high-lighted the limitations of the nation-state in an integrated Europe and empha-sised the responsibility of organised labour to overcome national differences in a *Confederazione della Grande Europa:*

> It is the European unions and the European left that today must overcome old national divisions or myopic electoral calculations to become the driving forces of a great European Confederation, which is able to bring with it, together with the existing political unity of the Twelve, new regional federations and single states, to create the first representative institutions and political organ of co-ordination for social policy, for the management of large projects (in the areas of transport, environment, telecommunications, energy and culture), a permanent forum for consultation on crucial issues such as foreign policy and of European security, in order to configure, in the words of Jacques Delors, 'a new form of political entity' in which the nation-state does not vanish, but instead delegates to its internal (the Region) and its external (the Community) certain attributes of sovereignty which can no longer be focused on one level [author's translation].

These extracts reveal the Euro-idealism of the Italian trade union move-ment, which went beyond working within the framework of the ETUC. Instead, the vision was extended to the entire project and the creation of a federal Europe.

The ICTU conference, on the other hand, was more cautious in tone and borderline pessimistic. The conference title, Make Europe Work for Us, is revealing when compared against that of the Italian unions. However, the promises of Ireland's membership of the EEC – economic growth and increased employment – had, as yet, proven elusive. Hence, an unbridled optimism would have been misplaced.[11] Therefore, ICTU's position, at this stage, can be seen as pro-European but Euro-pragmatic. Concerns remained with regards to the completion of the single market and the restructuring of the Irish economy. While receipt of the structural funds, which were to be doubled for Ireland, was acknowledged, an ICTU policy paper, written by General Secretary, Peter Cassells (1988), argued that more funds were neces-sary to grow an indigenous industrial base, so as to exploit the economies of scale potential, provide for urban renewal and allow infrastructure projects to improve the competitiveness of the economy. Within the policy paper there was what might be termed a 'peripheral' logic, which was tinged with pes-simism both from an economies-of-scale and a regional-disparity perspective. Regarding the former, 'Ireland would appear to be at a considerable disad-vantage … unless adequate countervailing policies are put in place' (Cassells

1988: 7). Such 'countervailing policies' included, first and foremost, regional funds but, despite an increase from £350 million to £700 million, 'it seems unlikely that a doubling of structural funds which will be available to Ireland will be sufficient to promote convergence with the European economy' (*ibid.*: 6). Hence, 'more assistance will be required than is at present on offer from the Community's regional policy and national programmes' (*ibid.*: 7). Also, Cassells envisaged that 'moves towards harmonising company taxation may adversely affect the [manufacturing export] sector' (*ibid.*: 11). Furthermore, Cassells expected the Irish state to continue playing an interventionist role:

> Congress wishes to emphasise that it will resist strongly any initiative at Community level which seeks to dilute the appropriate role of the State in industrial policy in Ireland. In any proposals which emerge on competition policy or State aids to industry, due account must be taken of the essential need for State involvement in promoting industry in a small, late-developing economy (*ibid.*: 12).

Regarding the prospect of a social Europe, Cassells (*ibid.*: 19) added, 'that it is clear that Congress has a responsibility to seek support in Ireland for the measures already proposed in the Commission's social dimension'. Here, access to government on account of tripartism could prove useful. Notwithstanding, convincing the Irish trade union community of the potentialities of tripartism, as well as the social and economic virtues of European integration, was never going to be easy, for there remained a considerable degree of scepticism both *vis-à-vis* tripartism and, as the SEA referendum result attested, towards European integration. Might the persuasion and magnetism of Delors help in this regard?

The address by Delors, entitled '1992: The Human Dimension', to the delegates was an exercise in optimism and persuasion; however, his bent for federalism was toned down considerably. For Delors (1988b: 1), because of 'all the controversy that surrounded the challenge to the Irish government's right to ratify the Act ... sight may have been lost of some important aspects'. Delors referred here to Article 118, which provided for social dialogue and was therefore the sole provision of the SEA that spoke directly to organised labour. The Frenchman was keen to point out that European integration was about more than structural funds:

> Member States [cannot] give importance only to specific elements of the whole Community programme which seem to be of direct and immediate interest to a particular part of the Community, or to a particular section of society ... The challenge that faces us all is to participate fully, and not sectionally, in the creation of a new economic and social environment, in which prosperity is no contradiction of solidarity, and in which every part of the Community has an essentially equal interest.

Interestingly, on the Irish model of industrial relations, that is, decentralised collective bargaining, Delors praised the voluntaristic approach as it 'fits squarely with the spirit of 1992' (*ibid.*: 9). He also underlined the importance of social dialogue as an 'indispensable tool in the building of the European society' and concluded by exclaiming '[Y]our movement has a great contribution to make. Europe needs you' (*ibid.*: 10). From such language, it is clear that Delors' was no King nor Kaiser! Could his promise of a social Europe convince the more sceptical quarters of the Irish trade union movement? The referendum on the Maastricht Treaty would answer this question.

THE TREATY ON EUROPEAN UNION: A NEW DAWN

The fall of the Berlin Wall in October 1989 expedited a political response from Europe's elite to deepen European integration. At its simplest, the Maastricht Treaty was, first and foremost, about monetary union. That said, the rationale underpinning the decision to pursue monetary integration varied from member state to member state. For Ireland, EMU signified the continuance of a dual political-economy strategy. On the one hand, there was the prospect of monetary independence from the UK, a process which had started with participation in the EMS in the late 1970s; on the other hand, participation in the common currency was important for promoting external investor confidence in Ireland. Once again, the Italians 'sought a maximalist agreement' on EMU, 'but its negotiating hand was weak' (Dyson and Featherstone 1999: 531–2).

There is little doubt that the Maastricht Treaty 'constituted one of the most important treaty changes in the history of European integration' (Laursen 2012: 122). In terms of ambition, the Maastricht Treaty is equally as significant as the Rome Treaty, if not more so. The objectives of the Treaty on European Union, to call it by its official name, have already been outlined above. Certainly, the inclusion of the Social Chapter was, for organised labour, an important development, as was the creation of European citizenship, at least on normative grounds. Of immediate concern, however, was the creation of a common currency. By the time the Maastricht Treaty was being negotiated, policymakers had accepted that the fundamental task of governments was to struggle against inflation. Unemployment was therefore of secondary importance. This rationale was first adopted by the German Bundesbank in 1973. Just as 'the decision to set up the EMS was viewed with skepticism by many market operators, economists and experts, and even by some officials' (Padoa Schioppa 1985: 349), so too was the more serious prospect of monetary integration, which went a step further and involved the sacrificing of monetary autonomy. 'In no other policy domain has there been such a centralization of power in a supranational EU institution' (Martin and Ross 2004: ix). Although EMU leaves fiscal policy in the hands of the member states, it significantly limits their discretion over its use.

The Treaty also envisaged the creation of an independent central bank dedicated to price stability, which, so the argument went, would bring about stability and allow economies to grow. Also, national central banks were obliged by the Treaty to be independent. Neither the European Central Bank (ECB) nor the national central banks were to 'seek or take instructions' from EU institutions or national governments (Article 108, TEU). Although it is virtually impossible for a central bank, European or national, to completely ignore the political context in which it operates, the ECB is, comparatively speaking, well insulated from criticism and democratic accountability. As Tooze (2018: 98) writes, '[T]he ECB's constitution provided plenty of safeguards. Its deliberations were shielded from public scrutiny by minimal transparency requirements.' 'To call it apolitical', however, 'would be a misnomer, because it, in fact, entrenched a conservative bias against inflation as the unquestionable doxa of Europe' (*ibidem*). Henceforth, the overriding emphasis for national governments would be the promotion of productivity and competitiveness through the control of inflation. The decision to drive ahead with monetary integration was a brave and ambitious move, especially if one believes that political union should precede monetary union.

From the outset, numerous scholars and practitioners have pointed to the design flaws in monetary union (for example, Verdun 1996; Bieler 2006). Certainly, it seems clear now, as it did then, that the eurozone did not meet all the criteria of an Optimum Currency Area, which, according to the theory of that name, requires a great deal of labour mobility and the ability for fiscal transfers (Baldwin and Wyplosz 2006). Nevertheless, policymakers were willing to take a chance with the hope that, with time, the eurozone would satisfy the criteria of the OCA theory. This process is termed endogenisation (Baldwin and Wyplosz 2006: 367–8) and was a gradual one to be achieved through, on the one hand, the implementation of the prescribed Maastricht criteria and, on the other, the transnational integration of markets. According to this argument, a process of 'coaxing by markets' would ultimately result in the convergence of national economies. Member states that failed to fulfil the Maastricht convergence criteria after this process *should be* deemed unfit to join EMU. Regardless of design flaws, the prospect of a common currency was enough for governments, mainstream political parties, and the vast majority of employers' associations and trade unions to lend their support. How Irish and Italian organised labour justified deeper economic integration is the question to which I now turn.

The conclusion of the Cold War was of greater significance for the Italian Left than it was for the Irish. This goes for both the PCI and CGIL. If the 1987

Irish election was significant for ushering in the last-ever single-party government and reintroducing social partnership, the Italian 1987 election was of equal significance, albeit for different reasons. Firstly, the 1987 campaign was the PCI's last one as the *Partito Comunista Italiano*. By the time of the next election, the PCI, which had 'created a mass political culture without counterpart on the European Left' (Anderson 2009: 284) would be no more, or at least unrecognisable. Following the fall of the Berlin Wall, we had the so-called *svolta della Bolognina* ('Bologna turning point'), which gave rise to the PCI's successor, the *Partito Democratico* (PD), which subsequently sought to distance itself from its predecessor by repudiating its past. For many admirers of the PCI, the newly established PD 'no longer seemed to represent any distinctive Italian tradition' (Anderson 2009: 285). The second reason the 1987 election was significant had to do with the arrival of a new (regional) political force, the *Lega Nord* (Northern League), which would grow in popularity and shape national politics as well as the European debate. Today, the *Lega*, as it is now called, is a national party and is the oldest party in the Italian parliament. Furthermore, it has been campaigning on a Eurosceptic platform since the 1990s.

The XII Congress of the CGIL in October of 1991 responded to the *svolta* in a way that signified a considerable reorientation, which, in many ways, had already commenced following Trentin's election as General Secretary. From Trentin's lengthy speech, an excerpt from which is presented above, it is clear that he was under no illusion as to the scale of the challenge facing post-Cold War trade unionism: 'the decline of the general union, of class and its replacement with the proliferation of hostile corporations, with the devastating risks that this prospect represents, not only for the unity of the trade union movement, but for the stability and progress of democracy' (Trentin 1991 [author's translation]). Of the reforms envisaged by Trentin, the most significant is the confederation's break with the PCI. Following the announcement, a headline in *La Repubblica* (18 October 1990) simply read '*La CGIL "Cancella" il PCI* [The CGIL "Denies" the PCI]'. Those remaining loyal to the 'old' ideals of the CGIL formed a minority group, called *Essere Sindacato* ['Essence of Union'], under the leadership of Bertinotti, future leader of *Rifondazione Comunista* (*see* Andruccioli 2008). The main bone of contention became the question of tripartism, or, to use the Italian term, *concertazione*. This issue was later resolved by introducing democratic norms which went a considerable way to legitimising the union's stance (*see* Baccaro 2003). Upon becoming leader of *Rifondazione Comunista*, Bertinotti was replaced at *Essere Sindacato* by Elenora Leone. *Essere Sindacato* was eventually dissolved at the 1996 congress; however, a splinter group called *Alternativa Sindacale* was created, led by Gian Paolo Patta. Albeit an important faction, it remained at the fringes of the CGIL.

Trentin, however, was keen to emphasise the need for greater unity amongst the Italian confederations and within the broader European trade union movement:

> We propose, with this Congress, that the three Italian trade union confederations define, in a unitary convention, a new platform for initiatives on international issues of greatest urgency. A platform that the Italian trade union movement could compare with the democratic political forces, in Italy and in Europe, with all the forces of the European trade union movement and, of course, with the trade union and political organizations of the various nations, most directly concerned. It is necessary, first of all, to define a common line of conduct on the issues of international co-operation and European co-operation (Trentin 1991 [author's translation])

Concertazione was identified as the best instrument to tackle Italy's growing national debt. This resulted in the historic agreement signed in July 1993 with the Ciampi Government, which is identified as a decisive factor for Italy's entry into EMU (*see* Chapter Six). The 1991 CGIL congress also addressed the question of European integration in a post-Cold War setting: 'The political unity of Europe, today a European Community, tomorrow a great European Confederation, which establishes new cultural, civil and institutional relations with the Eastern societies that have freed themselves from totalitarianism, constitutes the first test bed of the international trade union policy of the CGIL' (Trentin 1991 [author's translation]). Change of historic proportions was at hand and Trentin highlighted the importance of trade unions in shaping the following decade:

> Over the next ten years, the industrial geography and the division of labour will change. And the social geography will also change in the great Europe that will be built *with us or against us*. Transformations of these dimensions will inevitably affect the firm, its organisation, employment levels and the distribution of employment, with the increasingly significant weight of small business and the tertiary sector, working conditions and social composition and of the working classes, as well as labour markets and the extent of migratory flows. The CGIL, the Italian and European trade union movement cannot deceive themselves to face these transformations – whose outcomes are not predefined, but remain open to the impact of decisions, projects and, also, of the union's conflicting initiative – with defensive tactics of the Eighties, undergoing a new 'passive revolution' which this time risks really overwhelming the very idea of 'general union'. These are the real and great stakes of the coming years (Trentin 1991, emphasis added [author's translation]).

The Treaty on European Union (TEU), signed in February 1992, was swiftly ratified by the Italian parliament. The three confederations – CGIL, CISL and UIL – were strong supporters of the Treaty and, as we shall see in the following chapter, were prepared to go to considerable lengths to ensure Italy's participation in EMU. In particular, the Social Protocol, which was attached to the Treaty, was important for explaining trade union support. However, a deep political crisis resulting from decades of corruption, coupled with a degree of political disorientation on the Left following the dissolution of the Soviet Union, engendered considerable turmoil in Italian politics. During this period of turmoil, it was the three union confederations that stepped into the breach to secure the transition to the second Italian Republic and Italy's participation in the common currency.

Turning to Ireland: could labour Euroscepticism, outlined above, be overcome to create a pro-European consensus?

Both the Labour party and ICTU campaigned in favour of the Treaty, marking the first time that both party and confederation formally approved of further European integration, albeit 'a somewhat reserved approval' (Keatinge 1993: 72). Not all members of ICTU were in favour: for example, the (British) union Manufacturing Science Finance remained sceptical. Elements within ICTU were critical of the government and accused it of hiding behind Britain on questions of European social policy (De Bréadún 1992a, 1992b). Had Ireland followed the British and opted-out of the Social Charter, in the name of FDI, it is unlikely that Irish trade unions could have supported the Treaty's ratification and social partnership would most likely have ended prematurely. In the interest of tripartism, Fianna Fáil was keen to create a cohesive and hierarchical trade union movement capable of enforcing central agreements. This means rationalising the union movement. To this end, state support was made available to unions, encouraging them to merge. In 1989, the Irish state paid out £290,000 in grants to facilitate union mergers (Allen 2000: 115). While an important merger was that of the three public sector unions to create IMPACT (today called Fórsa), the most significant was the merger between the ITGWU and the WUI to create the Services, Industry, Professional, Technical Union (SIPTU). SIPTU received a grant of £700,000 and claimed a membership of 155,000 workers. 'The sheer size of this union, comprising 40 per cent of all union members, gave its leadership a huge influence on the direction of the official labour movement' (*ibidem*).

Yet again, Labour TDs Emmett Stagg and Michael D. Higgins broke with the official Labour party line and voted against the Treaty on neutrality grounds. Although broadly in favour of European integration, the Workers' Party and the newly formed breakaway group Democratic Left, also argued that the Maastricht Treaty was ultimately flawed, with the former disseminating a pamphlet entitled *Europe Deserves Better* (Dunphy 1992). Also, longstanding anti-EC activists Raymond Crotty and Anthony Coughlan launched their campaign under the aegis of a new umbrella group called the National Platform for Employment, Democracy and Neutrality. Those opposing the

Maastricht Treaty were buoyed by its (slim) rejection by the Danish public on 2 June 1992.

Despite some reservations, SIPTU and the ATGWU, Ireland's two largest unions, advised their memberships to vote in favour of the Treaty in a joint statement. However, a number of SIPTU union activists at regional executive, branch and trades council levels expressed concerns over the lack of debate within the union and criticised the executive's recommendation. Such concerns would characterise further European Treaty debates (*see* Chapter Six). Also, the ATGWU, for the first and only time, followed its British affiliate, the TGWU, by abandoning its Eurosceptic stance and endorsing the Treaty. As noted above, the TGWU leadership described Brussels as 'the only card game in town'. Both unions were critical of the government's handling of the referendum with reference to the confusion surrounding the question of free travel and abortion, as well as the 'one-sided presentation of the arguments', which 'is engendering widespread cynicism and suspicion' (cited in the *Irish Times*, 2 May 1992).

Unfortunately, during the course of the referendum, much of the debate hinged not on the economic and political implications of monetary union but instead on moral issues, particularly the question of abortion. Despite the government's having negotiated Protocol 17, which exempted Ireland from giving more progressive abortion rights, the waters were muddied during the course of the referendum campaign when the Irish Supreme Court ruled on a highly controversial and divisive case involving a 14-year-old girl who became pregnant after being raped. The Court refused the girl's right to travel to the UK to obtain an abortion that, at the time, was illegal in Ireland. The case, known as the X-case so as to protect the identity of the girl involved, was considered an assault on the freedom to travel. The government sought to amend Protocol 17 but the European Council refused to reopen negotiations on the Treaty and instead made a Solemn Declaration to assuage concerns. Notwithstanding, pro-life groups such as Irish Right to Life, Support Life Group and Family Solidarity campaigned for a 'No' vote. Pro-choice groups, such as the Repeal the Eighth Amendment Campaign, the Women's Coalition and the Coalition for Freedom and Women's Rights campaigned in favour of the Treaty.

The Irish referendum was held on 18 June 1992; with the £6 billion in transfers from EC funds being 'the main element in the government's case' (Keatinge 1993: 74), a considerable majority (69 per cent), compared to the French (51 per cent) and the (second) Danish results (57 per cent), voted in favour. To what extent this can be put down to trade union support is difficult to know; however, over time, supporting European integration had become politically acceptable in Irish trade union circles. That is not to deny that a deep-seated Euroscepticism remained amongst more radical left-wing elements. However, the emerging 'Celtic Tiger' period of economic growth kept most of these in the proverbial corner – until the shock result of the referendum on the Nice Treaty, which is discussed in the next chapter.

The Maastricht Treaty and the introduction of EMU was the defining feature of the second phase of European integration and, for good reason, received considerable attention from national union centres. For instance, the German confederation (DGB) 'was leading discussion on EMU within the German labour movement from the early 1990s onwards' (Bieler 2006: 106). Similarly, the social dimension of the EU was 'absolutely essential' in harnessing support for EMU (*ibid.*: 104). This does not imply that there were not serious reservations about the design of the common currency. Concerns abounded regarding the emphasis on price stability at the expense of employment; the insulation of the ECB from democratic norms; the lack of flexibility within the 1997 Stability and Growth Pact; and its limiting effect on public investment in key public goods such as education. Nevertheless, in both Ireland and Italy, there was a general consensus that monetary union was a positive step forward. In both countries, as discussed in the next chapter, tripartism was important in legitimising the process of EMU.

CONCLUSION: DELORS AND EU-PHORIA

The 1980s represented a challenging time for European capitalism. Causes of continuing economic crisis were supposedly linked to increased trade union power, which, so the argument goes, inhibited the operation of market mechanisms (Breen *et al.* 1990: 162). Macro-structural trends in this period, such as technological advancements and the burgeoning service economic sectors; greater participation of women in the workforces; and increases in atypical employment were common challenges for Irish and Italian unions as well as national policymakers. Henceforth, the search for employment flexibility and restructuring of the welfare state would become calling cards for the New Right, in an undisguised bid to undermine trade union power. The rise of neo-liberal Thatcherism was seen as a direct threat to trade unionism, which was 'driven into retreat' (Baglioni 1990: 8). Italian unions went from being 'undoubtedly the most militant and adversarial of all the unions in the advanced industrial countries' of the 1970s, to being 'among the most receptive in Europe to consensus solutions to the problem of industrial adjustment' (Regini 1996: 66). Despite union density being at its highest ever, with 55 per cent of the workforce unionised (Roche 2008), the Irish unions' fears of a Thatcherite assault were probably more acute than the Italians', on account of geographical proximity to the UK. Isolated in a terribly conservative country, ICTU perceived the prospect of social partnership with considerable hope.

The Single European Act and the Maastricht Treaty constitute a veritable paradigm shift in the relationship between European governance and the member states. Notwithstanding the significance of these agreements, the treaties were subjected to relatively little debate in national parliaments, particularly the Italian parliament. With negotiations already having been concluded, there was a sense that debate was futile and all that remained was for the parliaments to ratify the agreement without more ado. This was very much the case with the SEA, which was considered by many in Italy as *Spinelliana* and therefore positively Italian in provenance. Whereas the SEA was presented as a *fait accompli*, the opposite was the case for the Maastricht Treaty, which was seen more as a first stage on the bumpy road to EMU. The degree of bumpiness would, however vary from member state to member state and, in that regard, from Ireland to Italy. Notwithstanding its future significance, the Maastricht Treaty, much like the SEA, was the subject of little fuss or debate, at least in Italy. In fact, only a small number of Italian parliamentarians attended the debates and fewer again actually knew what it was they were speaking about (*La Stampa*, 30 October 1992). For Italians of almost all political creeds, the main priority was inclusion in the common currency. Such discussions were very lively in Italy, where 'entry into EMU [is an] imperative; anything else would be punished domestically as failure' (Dyson and Featherstone 1999: 509). This peculiar brand of Europeanism would contribute to opening a new dialectic between technocracy and politics. This was an ongoing process throughout the 1990s and will be discussed further in the next chapter.

In Ireland, it is likely that European politics would have met a similar fate were it not for the actions of Raymond Crotty. Obliging the government to hold a referendum on European treaties meant that political parties and interest groups had to embark on internal debates on the pros and cons of the individual treaty, as well as the merits of European integration more generally, before adopting an official position. Ireland was unique in this regard. The Regional Secretary of the ATGWU (now Unite the Union), underscored the importance of Crotty's actions, which facilitated a more democratic process, though often grudgingly:

> ... democracy is absent [in the EU] ... who else holds a referendum? ... The democracy that exists here isn't the Irish government saying 'we have to have a democratic way of dealing with this', it's because Raymond Crotty stood out against the system and said that when that impact on the Constitution was being decided, the people had to be given a vote ... and that's how we won this democracy ... The Irish government doesn't want to know about referenda ... So, it was to his ever-lasting credit that he fought and got us that right (Interview, 9 June 2013).

This 'right', however, by no means guaranteed a quality debate, nor did it ensure that engagement would be on the merits or the demerits of the question at hand. All too often, 'distractions' diverted attention away from the immediate socio-economic implications of deeper European integration. For instance, Proinsias De Rossa, leader of the socialist Workers Party, was also critical of the quality of debate and argued that 'there is a need for the Irish trade union movement to have a higher profile in debating these issues both at home and in the EC' (Brown and De Rossa 1988: 34).

Both ICTU and the CGIL held pivotal 'Europe' conferences in 1988. The pro-European sentiment expressed at these respective conferences was consolidated following the fall of the Berlin Wall the following year. Whilst both conferences had a pro-European theme, there was a distinct difference in how 'Europe' was perceived. The completion of the single market and the prospect of economic and monetary union and political co-operation were identified as being integral to maintaining Ireland's competitiveness. The PNR acknowledged the European dimension but there was very little by way of vision, other than ensuring continued access to the CAP and structural funds. The only input of a social-democratic flavour, clearly suggesting a trade union involvement, is the following:

> We are anxious that Ireland should play the fullest part possible in the completion of the internal market, subject to full account being taken of the possible serious difficulties for our economy from an insensitive application of some of the proposals involved and, also, of course, to market-opening measures being matched by more effective Community action to achieve greater economic and social cohesion (Irish Government [PNR] 1987: 7).

From the above extract, and the general gist of the PNR's Europe chapter, there is a sense that there was no great appetite for exploring fully the political implications of deeper economic integration or that the EEC and European integration existed as more than a *fait accompli* rather than an open-ended process that could and should be shaped through direct trade union engagement. A similar appraisal was made by Patrick Keatinge regarding the Irish political class.

> The failure to evolve a strategic approach towards economic integration ... is part of a more general characteristic of [Irish] political life. Politicians prefer not to justify policy positions in terms of overarching concepts or grand designs so far as 'Europe' is concerned (Keatinge 1989: 173).

For Keatinge,

> ... this [partly] may be a manifestation of a political culture which eschews conceptualisation in general, in favour of responding to parochial demands; partly it may be a shrewd refusal to offer hostages to fortune. Whatever the reason, the concept of European Union is rarely approached directly' (*ibidem*).

This reluctance to be drawn on the bigger picture would come back to haunt the Irish political class.

As far as ICTU was concerned, European social policy was an intergovernmental process and therefore pressure should be applied via the Irish government. To this end, Congress sought meetings with the government to discuss its attitude to the social dimension programme. Following the UK's opt-out from the EU's social policy, ICTU's analysis arrived at a curious conclusion: 'the ambivalence of the UK on the Social Charter may discourage some investors' (ICTU 1991). Hence, opt-outs were seen as negative only from a narrow, FDI perspective! This was in keeping with the logic of Irish social partnership, which O'Donnell (2000: 72) describes as 'a new shared understanding that competitiveness [is] the precondition for achievement of all other economic and social goals, [and this is] the central motivation for the partnership experiment'.

The conclusion of the Cold War acted as an accelerator both of European integration and the transformation of the Italian Left, which involved a reconfiguration of union–party relations. Instead, a greater emphasis was placed on trade union unity among the three confederations, so as to strengthen their hand *vis-à-vis* national governments and employers, and also within the workings of the ETUC. Here, the significance of the election of Bruno Trentin to General Secretary of the CGIL cannot be overstated. Following his election as General Secretary, he was keen to reorientate the CGIL and the EU was central to this reorientation. To this end, Trentin envisaged 'a multi-ethnic European social area, governed by fundamental universal rights of citizenship' (Trentin 1988 [author's translation]). In other words, Europe, like Italy, must be *'fondato sul lavoro'* ['founded on labour']. This, in concrete terms, puts workers at the heart of the European project and underlines the need for *multilevel* economic democracy within the EU. Developing the European level would require strengthening the role of the ETUC. Here, the three Italian confederations frequently acted in unison, speaking with one voice (Ciampiani 2013). A convinced 'European', Trentin would find a boon companion in Jacques Delors. There was great mutual respect between Trentin and Delors, with the latter writing the Preface to the French edition of Trentin's book *Città del Lavoro* [*City of Work/La Ville du Travail*] (Delors1998). Delors paid tribute to Trentin's character:

... a strong man, intransigent but of great sensitivity, and also an intellectual and a researcher in social sciences, capable of combining thought with action ... Bruno Trentin's intuition, his applied research, its formalization in the battle of ideas and in the political struggle, remain our compass (*ibidem*) [author's translation].

The ideals of Delorism are key in explaining the construction of a pro-European consensus amongst national trade union centres. Delors' speech at the ETUC Stockholm Congress made a particular impact on the Italian and Irish confederations (Galantini 1988; Cassells 1988) and put the prospect of 'social dialogue' on the agenda. Furthermore, the European Council had decided to double the Structural Funds budget by the time of the completion of the internal market in 1992. The 1988 ETUC Congress is also of significance for the European trade unions' relationship with European integration as a strategic response to Thatcherite neo-liberalism. As Ernst Breit, President of the ETUC noted, 'they [neo-liberals] are trying to make workers and their trade unions take responsibility for the rise in unemployment. It's unacceptable and is nothing more than an attempt to paint the victims as the perpetrators'; and if unions did not reorient their actions towards the European level 'the structures of the internal market will be turned against workers and their trade unions' (cited in Degryse and Tilly: 2013: 41). This reiterates the 'with us or against us' sentiment of Trentin's speech cited above. Henceforth, campaigning for a social Europe, which would ensure economic and social cohesion, would be a clarion call for the European trade union movement. 'The ETUC, which had found itself isolated, was now back in the game' (*ibid.*: 115). ETUC had evolved from a 'veto organisation' to a 'voting organisation' (Dølvik 1997: 414–5) and a new General Secretary of Italian origin was elected, Emilio Gabaglio.

Whereas the Italian confederations, exemplified by Trentin, sought to transform the ETUC into a protagonist for the political unification of Europe, ICTU, on the other hand, were ambivalent about their role within the European trade union movement. This ambivalence is evident in the questions posed in an ICTU (1988b) position paper presented at the 1988 conference, in which a number of 'issues' were raised. These include, *inter alia*, '[W]hat should our priorities be in the "social programme" field?' and '[D]o we need to develop international trade union machinery to deal with developments such as European companies, negotiations on working hours, worker-participation, minimum wage rates, etc.?' Might the answers to such questions become apparent over the course of the 1990s?

Chapter Six

Constructing a Social Europe: From Amsterdam to Nice

INTRODUCTION

The Single European Act (SEA) and the Maastricht Treaty were fundamental to the EU's dual headline goals, namely, the single market and European Monetary Union (EMU). The introduction of the latter was by no means a *fait accompli*; rather, it was an almost decade-long process that officially occurred in three stages. The first stage began in 1990 and entailed the elimination of exchange controls and restrictions on moving capital between member states. Steps towards achieving this had already been taken with the passing of the SEA. Stage II began in 1994 and involved greater co-ordination of national economic policies as well as programmes to control inflation and reduce budget deficits. The process of creating independent central banks was also set in train, with the European Monetary Institute (forerunner to the European Central Bank) being created to encourage co-operation between central banks. Stage III was *the* critical stage, which introduced the so-called convergence criteria for the economies of member states seeking admittance to EMU, with the two most important (and closely observed) criteria being a budget deficit of less than 3 per cent of GDP and a public debt ratio not exceeding 60 per cent of GDP (Savage 2005). On 1 January 1999, eleven[1] member states joined the Eurozone, thereby foregoing monetary autonomy and the possibility of future devaluations of national currencies. Both Ireland and Italy were amongst the first group joining the common currency: but what did EMU imply for the Irish and Italian unions and labour market governance?

Although the Maastricht Treaty 'was not a triumph for Thatcherite neo-liberalism', it 'was biased in favour of the neo-liberal project due to the neo-liberal orthodoxy underpinning EMU' (van Apeldoorn 2001: 81). For Delors, and the European trade union movement, the EU level provided an opportunity to address the neo-liberal imbalance in the EU's constitution. To this end, three developments had important implications for actors' preferences and strategies (Falkner 1998; Erne 2008). These were: first, the formulation of a European social policy, which became 'a major issue' (Falkner 1998: 78) throughout the 1990s; second, the introduction of European social dialogue, which enhanced the role of the ETUC (Dølvik 1997); and, third, the rollout of regional funds designed to offset some of the negative effects of sacrificing monetary autonomy. Against the backdrop of EMU and further enlargements, commitments to deepening European integration and fine-tuning the EU's institutional balance continued, notably with the adoption of two further European Treaties. These were the Amsterdam (1997) and Nice (2001) Treaties. Of the two, the former is of greater significance for organised labour. Whilst my primary analysis of Irish and Italian unions' preferences *vis-à-vis* European integration is made using trade union debates on these two 'grand bargains', there were other developments at the European level that are also worthy of attention, not least because one of these developments constituted Delors's departing salvo and its significance lives on nearly two decades later.

Following the SEA and Maastricht Treaty, European integration was, politically speaking, more complex and problematic. In the absence of the possibility of currency devaluations, and on account of EMU not meeting the labour market mobility criterion of an optimum currency area (Mundell 1961), member states' industrial relations–welfare state nexuses were brought into sharp focus. Furthermore, the situation was exacerbated by the level of unemployment and 'jobless growth' (Overbeek 2003) in the EU member states, which was an obstinate and worrisome socio-economic trend despite an emerging technological revolution. Albeit an EU-level concern, from the perspective of economic and monetary governance employment-related policies remained a national prerogative. There was, nevertheless, within the EU, a growing consensus that something on the labour governance front had to be done, resulting in Delors's mandate to analyse the causes of Europe's unemployment problem and propose possible solutions. In response, the Commission published an enduring White Paper entitled *Growth, Competitiveness and Employment* (*GCE*) (CEC 1993). The document was relatively well received and smacks very significantly of Delorism. As Ross wrote:

> No one who read the White Paper could fail to be impressed, in particular when the Commission's effort was contrasted with other programmatic contenders on the field. Moreover, no one familiar with Europe's recent history could overlook that its vertebrae were trademark ideas of Jacques Delors (Ross 1995: 225).

Written so as 'to appeal to a broad spectrum of interests' (Drake 2000: 132), *GCE* 'attempted to combine contradictory elements' (Goetschy 1999:

120; Bieling 2003: 67) and is therefore best construed and understood in the spirit of 'constructive ambiguity' (*see* Chapter Two), as the following excerpt from the Preamble attests:

> ... we are faced with the immense responsibility, while remaining faithful to the ideals which have come to characterize and represent Europe, of finding a new synthesis of the aims pursued by society (work as a factor of social integration, equality of opportunity) and the requirements of the economy (competitiveness and job creation) (*CEC* 1993).

In reality, finding a 'new synthesis' was more about reimagining the relationship between economy and society and less about 'remaining faithful to the ideals' of national social models. Yet were the repositories of such ideals, namely, organised labour, prepared to endorse such a reimagining? And if so, what was the justification?

Precisely because labour market governance was a national competence, there was within the *GCE* a 'discourse of limited responsibility' (Drake 2000: 128). To this end, the EU's role in this reimagining was only 'to *assist* this movement which reconciles our historical loyalties with our wish to take our place in this new world that is now emerging' (*ibidem*, emphasis added). Typically of Delors, tripartism 'wherever possible' was promoted so as to engender a broad consensus on questions relating to EMU and labour market governance (*CEC* 1993: 67). Tripartism was a feature throughout the 1990s and early 2000s: it was used to address political crisis, in the case of Italy; to ensure that Ireland and Italy both made the cut for Stage III of EMU; and as a means for internalising the evolving European Employment Strategy, an important component in 'Europe's emerging multi-tiered system of social policy' (Leibfried and Pierson 2000: 288). Following the publication of *GCE*, various European Council summits (for example, Essen, in 1994) acknowledged the document's contents and objectives by 'linking Keynesian and supply-side measures' (Goetschy 1999: 120). Whereas a central aim of the business lobby was to have competitiveness upgraded to the status of 'objective', thereby putting it on a par with 'economic and social progress' (Mazey and Richardson 1997: 123), organised labour had the objective of putting the question of employment on the IGC agenda. Against the backdrop of an emerging transnational social movement (Mathers 2007) and transnational industrial action occurring (Erne 2008), the question of employment took priority, culminating in a Title on Employment in the Treaty of Amsterdam. The so-called European Employment Strategy (EES) became the cornerstone of the EU's employment policy and, such was the heightened sense of crisis, it was launched before official ratification of the Treaty by the member states. Henceforth, the overarching objective was to 'modernize the European social model', which 'represent[s] [an] acceptance of the need to redesign welfare systems and labour market regulations' (Adnett 2001: 35).

In particular, the Italian social model underwent a deal of 'modernisation' (Graziano 2007; Ferrera and Gualmini 2004). Here, the emphasis was on a range of 'third way' measures, which included, amongst other things, increasing working time flexibility and the introduction, for the first time, of temporary work agencies (Talani and Cerviño 2003). Such developments gave rise to what is termed the 'new' politics of the welfare state, which has generated a large and diverse literature (*see*, for example, Bermeo 2001; Comptson 1997; Scharpf 2000; Pierson 2001; Ferrera and Rhodes 2000). Notwithstanding this burgeoning literature on welfare state and industrial relations reforms, 'very few contributions analyse in detail the role played by the EU in the changes' (Graziano, Jacquot and Palier 2011: 1).

On an ideological plane, the 'competitiveness' discourse was closely associated with hegemonic neo-liberalism, but it permeated the ideological orientation of both European Christian-democrats and social-democrats (van Apeldoorn 2001, 2003). As part of this transcending discourse, employment creation was promoted in parallel with the need to improve competitiveness. This discourse has its own lexicon, which merges neo-liberal concepts with Christian- or social-democratic ones. Here, the oxymoronic term 'flexicurity' is perhaps the most emblematic and noteworthy. Hans-Jürgen Bieling (2003) uses the term 'communitarian neoliberalism' to describe this fusion of ideas, which served three functions:

> First, it provided a modest but very popular criticism of the devastating social effects of a disembedded economy. Second, its criticism of excessively deregulated markets had no profound impact on the prevailing socio-economic order. Third, by stressing the importance and the productive potential of community networks, it allegedly opened up a new perspective in order to correct and mitigate some of the most painful social effects of neo-liberal restructuring without relapsing into an allegedly old-fashioned style of Keynesian state intervention.

Following the ratification difficulties with the Maastricht Treaty, an enhanced role was envisaged for the social partners, drawing an explicit link between the crisis of political legitimacy of the EU and the ensuing social crisis (Mazey and Richardson 1997: 121; Bieling 2003: 53). In these two-level games (Putnam 1993; Marks and McAdam 1996), trade unions played an important transmissive role, not only vertically, between the domestic and the supranational levels, but also horizontally, *vis-à-vis* political groupings and EU institutions (Johansson 1999). As Greenwood (1997: 175) notes: 'Labour interests now play an institutionalised role in the development of social Europe and have demonstrated their ability to set issues on its agenda.'

To this end, European social-democracy received a double boost in the mid-1990s: first, from the accession of Sweden, Finland, and Austria to the EU; and second, from social-democratic parties' 'neo-revisionism' (Sassoon 1996: 730–54) which paid dividends at the polls in a number of member states and was interpreted not so much as an out-and-out critique of neoliberalism but more as an accommodation with it. 'Thus, *even in Sweden* the intellectual climate had shifted somewhat towards neoliberal positions' (*ibid.*: 743, emphasis added). In other words, social-democracy had adjusted to this new phase of capitalism and the so-called knowledge-based economy. To this, we can add an enhanced role for the ETUC.

The political philosophy of 'communitarian neoliberalism' provides a new lens through which social problems can be analysed. The advantages of adopting the ideas and discourse of 'communitarian neoliberalism' is that they 'are very appealing within the public sphere' and 'provide an effective rhetoric to transform the relations of civil society and to assure public support for the necessities of neo-liberal competition' (Bieling 2003: 69). In doing so, attempts were made to establish a collaborative and consensual environment wherein pre-existing divisions between political and social forces could be overcome. All too often, however, reality had the habit of exposing rhetoric and providing crystallisation points around which a counter-narrative could be constructed.

This chapter switches between the European level and the national levels at different points. Having assessed European social policy in the 1990s, I will turn to the question of EMU and the engagement of Irish and Italian organised labour with tripartism. Such arrangements saw the influence of organised labour increase in both the Irish and Italian contexts, but with different outcomes. These diverging outcomes could have implications for trade union influence in the future. Following this section, I return to the European level, where the process of treaty formulation is briefly assessed. Unlike previous European treaties, the Amsterdam Treaty was quite politicised, with transnational mobilisations occurring (Mathers 2007). Such developments piqued the interest not only of social movement scholars (for example, Imig and Tarrow 2001; della Porta and Tarrow 2005) but also labour scholars (for example, Bieler 2006; Erne 2008). At the same time, Euroscepticism scholarship began seriously studying the initial rise of Eurosceptic and populist parties. Albeit generating a 'true cottage industry' (Mudde 2012), the scholarly focus was primarily on right-wing Euroscepticism, whose objective was not the politicisation of the EU for democratic ends but rather the defence of national sovereignty. Before concluding the chapter, and the second phase of European integration, I assess the preferences of Irish and Italian trade unions on a changing Europe by analysing trade union debates on the Amsterdam and Nice Treaties. The negative Irish referendum on the latter sent shockwaves throughout the EU; but to what extent did Irish unions influence this result?

EUROPEAN COPING MECHANISMS:
EMBEDDING A TRANSNATIONAL MARKET

Upon relaunching European integration with the SEA, Delors was eager not to reanimate politics: 'a factor itself contributing to [its] success' (Drake 2000: 106). Yet, Delors is renowned, at least in trade union and leftist circles, for having quipped that 'nobody can fall in love with the single market'. In other words, the market alone will not suffice. Having recognised this, Delors sought to create an *espace sociale* by imbuing the integration process with a social dimension, whose absence was 'increasingly being politicised' by labour-friendly actors (Falkner 1998: 73). Creating an *espace sociale* amounted to an attempt to 'embed' the emerging transnational market at the European level, *à la* Polanyi (*see* Chapter 2). Delors embodied this vision to such an extent that we can speak of a veritable 'Delors effect'. Under his stewardship and beyond, numerous important steps were taken towards establishing a European social model. These included the introduction of 'two distinct and innovative paradigms' (Welz 2008: 255), namely, social dialogue and the formulation of social Directives. An additional instrument with a social and redistributive hue was the Cohesion funds, which were of particular relevance in Ireland.

As documented in the previous chapter, Delors went to considerable lengths to reorient the social partners towards social dialogue, whose introduction in the 1990s 'brought an extension of the Community competence in a wide range of social policy issues' (Falkner 1998: 81) and was of particular significance for the trade union movement. Following the important 1988 ETUC Congress, serious efforts were undertaken to rethink the role of the ETUC. The Italian confederations, along with the German *Deutsche Gewerkschaftsbund* (DGB), were the flag-bearers of these initiatives. A 1991 ETUC Report advocated that it 'should become a genuine confederation with appropriate competences and tasks. That would imply the transfer of some competences from the national to the European level, and that decisions taken on trade union action by the ETUC instances should be respected' (ETUC 1991: 11, cited in Gorges 1996: 101). An enhanced role was envisaged for the larger confederations within the ETUC and majority voting was introduced, while the rights of the smaller organisations were also protected. The 1991 Congress ratified the Report's proposals; in doing so, the ETUC became 'the *first* major Euro-group to reform its internal structure with a view to enhancing its negotiating capacity at the European level' (Falkner 1998: 157, emphasis added). The Congress also elected a new General Secretary: an Italian trade unionist by the name of Emilio Gabaglio. The appointment of Gabaglio was made in recognition of the energies Italian unions' had invested in the renewal process (interview with J. E. Dølvik, FAFO, Oslo, 7 February 2014).

Following the long and winding discussions between UNICE and ETUC, which unexpectedly produced the Social Agreement, Delors was keen to exert 'the shadow of law' (Bercusson 1992), which meant compelling the social partners, and UNICE in particular, to establish a framework of labour rights by threatening to enact hard EU social laws where social partnership agreements were not forthcoming. Contrary to some scholars (for example, Lange 1993; Streeck 1994; Jabko 2006), the Social Protocol was of considerable justificatory importance to supporters of European integration occupying a position on the left of the political spectrum. The introduction of social dialogue 'brought an extension of the Community competence in a wide range of social policy issues' (Falkner 1998: 81). However, in order for social dialogue to have any meaning, a fundamental requirement needs to be satisfied: the presence of a cohesive trade union movement and an equally cohesive suitor. The European social partners could now formally conclude bipartite agreements. There is not the space here to detail the twists and turns in this newly established process: suffice to say that, despite its slowness, there was now the possibility for the social partners to conclude framework agreements, thereby unblocking issues, such as parental leave (1995), which had remained deadlocked for over a decade. In subsequent years, agreements on part-time work (1997); fixed-term work (1999); and telework (2002) were concluded. All of these were transposed into Directives. The effectiveness of social dialogue, however, really depended on what labour lawyer, Brian Bercusson (1992), terms the 'shadow of the law'. This 'shadow' was cast by the Commission, and therefore required the *real* threat of legislative action should an agreement between workers' and employers' representatives not be forthcoming.

The Social Protocol attached to the Maastricht Treaty also extended Community competence to a wide range of social policy areas, including the information and consultation of workers. Here, the European Works Council Directive was held up as an example of provisions of the Maastricht Treaty that had 'the potential to unblock even issues which previously had failed to be adopted for *more than twenty years*' (Falkner 1998: 186, emphasis added). However, the true key to unblocking the enduring deadlock was the whipsawing actions of an American multinational, Hoover, playing its French workforce off against its Scottish workforce. According to an insider's account, the so-called Hoover affair was 'a true eye-opener' and 'served as a trigger for relaunching discussions on the information and consultation of workers in multinational companies' (Lapeyre 2018: 134). This event raised the awareness of the member states and paved the way for the adoption of the Directive on European Works Councils. No longer could employers rely on the quasi-automatic British veto to protect them from labour-rights governance. Also, there was agreement on the Posted Workers Directive (1996) which was important in offsetting social dumping practices in the construction sector. This provision will be discussed in greater detail in Part III.

The creation of social dialogue and the development of a body of social legislation, known as the social *acquis*, represents a supranational regulatory response to the creation of the single market and EMU, albeit an eclectic one. However, Delors was keen to complement the regulatory aspect with a redistributive one. The introduction of the Cohesion Funds was important against the backdrop of the Maastricht convergence criteria and the battle against mass unemployment, which remained stubbornly present across Europe (Blanchard *et al.* 2006). For Delors, a redistributive policy was required so as to ensure the success of both economic convergence and social cohesion. Furthermore, Delors considered redistribution an integral component of federalism, not least when we speak of unemployment:

> ... in all federations the different combinations of federal budgetary mechanisms have powerful 'shock-absorber' effects, dampening the amplitude either of economic difficulties or of surges in prosperity of individual states. This is both the product of, and source of the sense of national solidarity which all relevant economic and monetary unions share (Delors 1989: 89).

Albeit significantly limited in terms of budget, Delors was keen to construct a similar solidarity-based mechanism between the EU member states. Of course, a concern of Delors was that these rather limited Cohesion funds would become the primary focus and ultimately distract from the overarching goal of creating an optimum currency area (*see below*).

Delors (*ibid.*: 85) singled out the Irish case for 'experiencing a politically uncomfortable rate of emigration'. On account of this, and the weaker and more peripheral characteristics of Ireland, the Irish government achieved a small political victory, namely, that Ireland would be recognised as a single region. Delors's *paquets* I and II had a socio-developmental component and not only sought to tackle Europe's economic divergences and social malaise but also to engender a sense of solidarity between member states. The so-called *Piano Delors*, as it was termed in Italy, can be seen as a 'critical juncture' in the evolution of European integration and yet again required serious brinksmanship from Delors (*see* Grant 1994: 241–2). With monetary union in mind, the primary and overarching objective of the *paquets* was economic convergence and social cohesion and they can be seen as

> ... *the first substantial European level attempt to confront regional inequalities* by planned redistribution among member states ... [A]nd, most important, sought to consecrate a long-term commitment to the kinds of interregional transfers found in federal systems (Ross 1995: 365, emphasis added).

Whilst the setting of EU social standards through social dialogue and the formulation of labour-friendly social Directives and the redistribution of EU funds constitute important features of the emerging *European* social model, a concept which was beginning to take on a more concrete meaning, there were also important developments at the national level that were of immediate relevance for organised labour. It is to this aspect that I now turn.

IRISH AND ITALIAN TRIPARTISM: FROM EMU CONVERGENCE TO EMPLOYMENT AND COMPETITIVENESS

The prospect of monetary integration only reached the agenda of the EU once the single market project was well under way and German concerns had been catered to (Martin and Ross 2004: 8). All aspiring entrants faced significant challenges in meeting the Maastricht criteria and were exposed to an enhanced level of surveillance from the Commission (Savage 2005). Inevitably, EMU required significant macroeconomic restructuring, thereby 'alter[ing] the configuration of strategic constraints and opportunities within which actors behave, [and] privileging certain actors and certain courses of action. It also changes the way in which domestic actors define their interests and form their identities' (Dyson 2002: 2). The restructuring pressures, however, were not symmetrically distributed across the eleven or so prospective EMU members (Pochet and Fajertag 1997 2000). This was especially the case with regards to Italy and Ireland, where the emergence of tripartism 'is both most evident and most surprising' (Baccaro 2011: 376).

The emergence of tripartism enhanced the *political* role of Irish and Italian organised labour and went a significant way towards legitimising the macroeconomic sacrifices that were to be made in the name of EMU. Having already outlined the origins of Irish tripartism in the previous chapter, I will, in this section, briefly identify the origins of the Italian equivalent.

Throughout the 1980s, the Italian economy performed relatively well, remaining above the G7 average (Rossi and Toniolo 1996: 445). Despite this strong performance, a profound political crisis was brewing. Designed 'to disperse power rather than concentrate it' (Hine 1993:2), the Italian political system had created multiparty coalitions which were weak and rather ineffectual. The net effect of this flawed political system was a decades-long political culture of clientelism and corruption, the extent of which became gradually exposed as the findings of a national judicial investigation unfolded slowly in the early years of the 1990s. The *mani pulite* ['clean hands'] movement uncovered endemic political corruption, known as *Tangentopoli*, in the ruling Christian-democratic and socialist parties.

The 1992 election is described by historian Paul Ginsborg as 'the most significant elections in Italy since 1948' (Ginsborg 2003: 255) and, against the backdrop of alarming revelations of enduring corrupt practices, the *Democrazia Cristiana*'s share of the vote fell to its lowest ever, from 34.3 to 29.7 per cent. Similarly, the vote of the newly established *Partito Democratico* sank to a new low of 16.5 per cent. Comparatively, the *Partito Socialista Italiano* fared better, securing 13.6 per cent of the vote, down from 14.3 per cent. The unquestionable winner was *Lega Nord*, which increased its share of the votes from 0.5 per cent to 8.7 per cent. The arrival of *Lega Nord* on the national political scene was particularly worrisome for many on the Italian left, for, if *Lega Nord* was to follow its *Roma ladrona* ['thieving Rome'] logic to its full conclusion, the political integrity of the Italian state would be severely threatened.

After the elections, a coalition government was cobbled together under the leadership of 'one of the most brilliant and most enigmatic figures in Italian politics' (Ginsborg 2003: 264), the socialist Giuliano Amato, who was facing immediate crises of immense proportions. The *Observer* wrote on 26 July 1992: 'The country is in a state of chaos, a state of war. It is fast becoming the banana republic of Europe. It has the highest murder rate in the European Community, the most rampant and blatant corruption, an ailing economy, a floundering government, and an anguished and embarrassed population' (cited in Ginsborg 2003: 263). The historian Paul Ginsborg (2003: 263) terms these crises, which were engulfing the Italian peninsula, as a 'single, dangerous whole'.

National currencies, including the Italian Lira and the Irish Punt, were the subject of speculative attacks and both governments devalued their respective currencies, with the Italians being forced to temporarily exit the ERM. As noted in the previous chapter, inter-unions relations had become strained since the mid-1980s, following the revision of the *scala mobile* (Regini and Regalia 1997: 201). The CGIL, under the leadership of Bruno Trentin, pursued a strategy to improve relations between unions. Undoubtedly, the CGIL's overtures were in response to the existentialist crisis of the Italian left and the 'dangerous whole' crisis as described by Ginsborg (2003). Also, with the employers' association, Confindustria, becoming a more politically oriented interest group (*see* Mattia 1993), the CGIL was keen to raise its national *political* profile (Mershon 1993). To this end, tripartism was seen as a viable strategy for addressing the root causes of the Italian crises.

The technocratic government of Amato called on the unions and employers to engage in tripartism. The government was keen to abandon wage indexation, the *scala mobile*, and exact a one-year wage freeze at company level, in a bid to address Italy's inflationary issues. Initially, Bruno Trentin was reluctant to abandon the wage index mechanism in fear of a grass roots backlash. However, with the financial crisis not abating and mounting political pressure,

Trentin was left with little choice but to endorse the business-friendly proposal. As anticipated, the 1992 tripartite agreement, *Protocollo sulla politica dei redditi*, was unpopular among factions of the CGIL and a number of wildcat strikes were called in protest. Consequently, Trentin (1992a, 1992b), outlined three reasons why he signed the tripartite agreement with Confindustria and the government: first, so as to avoid a new crisis of government and fresh elections; second, in order to maintain unity between the three confederations; and, last, to prevent a split between the socialist and ex-communist factions in the CGIL. Trentin resigned shortly after signing the 1992 pact but, in accordance with Italian tradition, his resignation was not accepted.

The following year, another round of *concertazione* took place between the government, organised labour and capital, but not before Amato was replaced by another technocratic administration. The President's appointee, Carlo Azeglio Ciampi, had served as Governor of the Bank of Italy since 1979. The unions were keen on tripartism so as to reverse the relative defeat of the year before. The 1993 'July pact' aligned sectoral wage increases to the government's macroeconomic targets, set by the Maastricht criteria, and introduced a two-tier structure of co-ordinated bargaining, at the sectoral and company level. Two aspects are of interest here. Firstly, the period between the pacts of 1992 and 1993 also saw 'greater efforts by the confederations to forge trade union unity' (Regini and Colombo 2011: 128). Organised labour, unlike Confindustria and the political class, had not been implicated in the *mani pulite* investigations, and therefore enjoyed a reputation of moral integrity – at the time, a resource in short supply. Hence, a show of unity was important. Secondly, from an industrial relations perspective, the establishment of two-level bargaining was 'an important victory for the union movement, since the employers had pushed for a single locus of collective bargaining' (Baccaro, Carrieri and Damiano 2003: 50). In other words, by strengthening the articulation mechanisms between different levels of collective bargaining, the unions strengthened what I term their coping mechanisms. This accomplishment contrasts with that of the Irish unions and will prove telling in the third phase of European integration, which is discussed in the following two chapters.

The unions put the second tripartite agreement to an internal referendum, in order to forestall any criticism that the agreement was the result of undemocratic elitist action. Also, in doing so, a degree of democratic legitimacy was afforded to the implementation of difficult measures. Approximately 1.5 million workers voted, with 68 per cent approving the content of the accord. 'The social peace which resulted from this far-sighted reform was to be of *fundamental importance* for Italy's economic recovery' (Ginsborg 2003: 277, emphasis added). By now, the unions wielded a considerable degree of influence and governments that chose to overlook the unions paid a high price. In

1993, a popular referendum in Italy was held to amend the electoral system, in a bid to reconfigure the relationship between society and the state along centre-left and centre-right lines. Henceforth, political competition would be characterised by 'polarised bi-polarism' (Ierachi 2006). This change would symbolise the passage from the First to the Second Republic and was put to the test the following year. With the Christian-democrats and socialists utterly discredited, the 'Left looked poised for its first victory since the war. Instead, a thief came in the night' (Anderson 2009: 285). The 'thief', to which Anderson refers is none other than media mogul, Silvio Berlusconi, and his *Forza Italia* party. Elected on the promise of a new Italian miracle, Berlusconi's centre-right coalitian government included the regionalist and xenophobic *Lega Nord* and the neo-fascist *Alleanza Nazionale*. Even within Berlusconi's party there were Eurosceptic voices, with the 'most prominent detractor' (Quaglia 2005: 283) being the Foreign Minister, Antonio Martino, chief economist of *Forza Italia* and member of the Thatcher-inspired Bruges Group, a UK-based Eurosceptic thinktank. Critical of the design of EMU, Martino believed that 'convergence [is] neither a necessary nor a sufficient condition for monetary unification' (cited in *ibidem*).

Berlusconi would fall foul of the unions' renewed sway when he attempted to unilaterally drive through unpopular pension reforms, thereby sparking the largest demonstrations by trade unions since the *autunno caldo*. As a testament to the unions' power, Berlusconi was forced into a U-turn on the reforms. As Braun (1996: 212) notes, the unions 'used the conflict in the name of *concertazione*: they acted in defence of their right to decide reform'. After the fall of the Berlusconi government, in December 1994, it became clear that antagonistic politics would not prevail. The post-Berlusconi governments were of a social-democratic orientation and pursued different strategies, as Ferrera and Gualmini (2004: 136) note:

> ... on the one hand, they stressed all the medium-term advantages of the entry into the Euro, and particularly the advantages for trade unions and employers; on the other, they elaborated a new discourse in support of financial adjustment, in order to further delegitimise the status quo, and make the reform more acceptable to the trade unions at the symbolic level.

The involvement of organised labour in macroeconomic-governance-related questions was, by the mid-1990s, a constant fixture in both the Italian and the Irish political landscapes. In Ireland, despite changes of government involving all the major parties, the practice of tripartism continued at regular intervals throughout the decade and, as Hardiman (2002: 7) attests, 'the European context of the 1990s played a vital role in maintaining its stability'. The 1986 NESC[2] report *A Strategy for Development 1986–90* had played a 'major role' in 1987's tripartite agreement by 'pinpoint[ing] the key requirement for an urgent action plan to tackle the unsolved problem of public expenditure' (Hastings, Sheehan and Yeates 2007: 19). Hence, in many ways, NESC had anticipated the strictures of the Maastricht criteria, thereby setting the tone for successive tripartite agreements. As Dermot McCarthy, vice-chair of NESC (and Secretary-General to the government) comments, 'NESC developed the debt/GNP ratio as a performance measure long before Maastricht' (cited in Hardiman 2002: 8). This, however, is more a case of good fortune than of good strategy. Perhaps we can call it the luck of the Irish.

As the process of Irish tripartism 'gained in problem-solving capacity' (Hardiman 2002: 10), the foundations of the Irish economic miracle, known more affectionately by advocates of tripartism as the 'Celtic Tiger', were laid. By the mid-1990s, concerns about 'jobless growth' were a distant memory, as the Irish economy grew at an average annual rate of 8.5 per cent per annum between 1994 and 1999, almost four times that of the EU15. Notwithstanding, the strictures of the Maastricht criteria remained integral. For instance, the tripartite agreement of 1997, Partnership 2000, explicitly states: 'Fundamental to [this agreement's] successful implementation ... is the management of our public finances in accordance with the Maastricht criteria and the EU Stability and Growth Pact' (Dept of Taoiseach 1997: 6). Within a tightening labour market, ICTU's influence on the government increased, and this increase was evident both in terms of the pay deal and the scope of the issues up for negotiation. In the 2000 Programme for Prosperity and Fairness (PPF 2000–2003), the pay terms were 'a good deal higher than in any previous agreement' (Hardiman 2002: 11). Also, by 2000 Irish industrial relations had undergone a considerable transformation. As Bill Roche observes:

> Much that had seemed fixed and immutable is now changed or in the melting pot, especially in the areas of the alignment of employment relations with business imperatives, the role of the State, the conduct of collective bargaining, the circumstances of trade unions and the implications of the increased openness of the Irish labour market (Roche 2007: 75).

Irish tripartism, following Irish entry to the EMU, played 'an even more important role in economic management than hitherto' (Hardiman 2002: 11) but, by the turn of the millennium, a number of tensions had come to the fore. There was, for industrial relations scholars, the paradox of participation, in which 'unions have been invited to become social partners in the macroeconomy but appear increasingly unwelcome partners in the workplace' (*ibid*: 76). Notwithstanding this participation paradox, there is no disputing the trade unions' tripartite role in legitimising Ireland's participation in EMU and securing its relatively smooth entry to the Eurozone. Certainly, compared to the Italian experience, Ireland's journey was a less convoluted one.

The Maastricht criteria set strict limits on the aspiring national governments; however, as Savage (2005: 33) notes, the 'Treaty [also] create[s] incentives for governments to engage in creati[ve] accounting and gimmickry.' At the behest of the German central bank, the Stability and Growth Pact[3] strengthened the threat of financial penalties and Treaty violators now 'suddenly faced much more daunting prospects' (*ibidem*), including the prospect of being denied entry to EMU.[4] This ultimate sanction invested the EU with considerable coercive power, which is translated into the Italian lexicon as the *vincolo esterno* ['external constraint'], a term whose use became quotidian and took on a particular significance with regards to Italy's rightful place in the EU.

In Italy, the second stage of EMU was complemented by a more institutionalised political exchange. The question of the *vincolo esterno* was turned into 'a manifestation of the politics of collective identity' (Radaelli 2002: 226) by the social-democratic governments of Prodi and D'Alema. Re-entering the ERM in 1996 was a positive step in this direction but the Italian administration still had a considerable way to go: achieving EMU membership would require not only tripartite agreements in 1996 and 1998 but also a degree of 'budgetary gimmickry', to use Savage's terminology.

With the deadline for Stage III drawing ever-closer, the European Parliament's Task Force on Economic and Monetary Union reported it 'unlikely that Italy will meet the criteria' (cited in Savage 2005: 129). The so-called *Ulivo* [Olive Tree] coalition, under Romano Prodi, was undoubtedly facing an arduous task and, if joining EMU was to happen, then a degree of fiscal inventiveness would be required. Undeterred by the negative forecasts, the centre-left government embarked on an ambitious, austerity-driven budgetary programme which involved budget cuts and privatisations, described here by Savage:

> The cuts were generated primarily by a 5 percent across-the-board reduction in ministerial accounts, a hiring freeze, closing hospitals, trimming the length of military service by two months, and limiting railroad subsidies. Italy's privatization efforts included the sale of *Autostrade*, the toll system, and a 41 percent share in the Rome airport (*ibid.*: 129).

As though this was not enough, the government also launched an 'extraordinary fiscal manoeuvre' (Ferrera and Gualmini 2004: 69), namely, a 'tax for Europe', which was levied on all incomes and was to be refunded provided membership was secured.[5] Fortunately, Eurostat, on this occasion, accepted Prodi's fiscal chicanery, partly in acknowledgement of the extent of the Italian reforms, albeit not without some bewilderment from particularly the Germans and the financial press. *Lega Nord* was the sole party to explicitly oppose the tax, with even *Rifondazione Comunista* supporting the initiative, albeit in return for a 35-hour working week from 2001.[6]

There were three Italian tripartite agreements between 1996 and 2002. The 1996 agreement, *Patto per Lavoro* ['Pact for Employment'] makes plenty of references to Italy's membership of the EU and the Euro but, as the following excerpt demonstrates, particular emphasis was also placed on modernising the Italian labour market under the aegis of the European Employment Strategy(EES).

> With regard to labour market policies, the Government and the social partners confirm the priorities of the European Union set at Essen and the contents of the Protocol of 23 July 1993 ... It is also necessary to achieve the convergence objectives set out in the Maastricht Treaty by implementing a tight fiscal policy ... The guidelines of the employment policy are inspired by the content of the Delors White Paper on *Growth, Competitiveness and Employment*, where the emphasis is on the needs of infrastructure, training and research on the provision of services for local systems of small and medium enterprises (*Patto per Lavoro* 1996 [author's translation]).

Also, albeit largely symbolic, the second tripartite agreement in 1998, known as the Christmas Pact, was 'specifically devoted to the institutionalisation of social concertation, from central to local level, in line with the Amsterdam Treaty' (Negrelli and Pulignano 2010: 148). The space is not available here to fully document the extent of the measures undertaken to modernise the Italian labour market; suffice to say that, in terms of employment reforms, the second half of the 1990s was 'eventful' and that 'significant policy changes progressively opened up the Italian labour market, making it more flexible and more workfare-oriented.' (Graziano 2007: 550, 555). Whilst the Treu (1997) and Biagi (2003) reforms of the Prodi and Berlusconi governments were not examples of tripartism, they were important in that they went a considerable way towards restructuring the Italian labour market by increasing the participation of women and young workers. Important provisions of the *Pacchetto Treu* include the introduction of new flexible contracts and part-time work. Also, temporary agency work, a practice hitherto outlawed, was made permissible, resulting in its proliferation 'all over the country' (Ferrera and Gualmini 2004: 102). Notably, these reforms were all 'in line with the European flexibility imperative' (Graziano 2007: 552), central to Delors's White Paper.

In 2001, Berlusconi was returned to government with a strong parliamentary majority. As advisor, Marco Biagi, a well-respected labour law expert, had a big role in drafting a White Paper on labour market reform. Inspired by the EES and continuing in a similar vein to the Treu reforms, the White Paper contains a number of controversial proposals. Firstly, *concertazione* is criticised for its 'low effectiveness and innovation potential' (cited in Ferrera and Gualmini 2004: 156). Instead, the practice of 'social dialogue' was promoted, wherein consultations with the social partners would take place but the ultimate decision remained with the government. Secondly, Article 18 of the *Statuto dei Lavoratori*, which, as outlined in Chapter Four, was the product of struggle and therefore quasi-sacrosanct, was earmarked for reform. Mindful of 1994, the unions were on the defensive and wary of Berlusconi, particularly the CGIL. Few, however, could have anticipated the assassination of Biagi by the *Brigate Rosse* in March 2002. In response, the CGIL called a general strike, and three million workers were mobilised in Rome but, if Berlusconi's objective was *divide et impera*, as suggested by Ferrera and Gualmini (2004: 157), then he was ultimately successful. CISL and UIL, in the absence of the CGIL, negotiated the third *Patto per l'Italia* ['Pact for Italy'] in July 2002. 'In general, the Pact [is] characterized by a welfare-to-work approach, in line with the policy objectives set at the European level' (Graziano 2007: 561).

Whereas the Italian system was more prone to adopting European norms (Graziano 2007; Ferrera and Gualmini 2004; Negrelli and Pulignano 2010; Arrigo 2004), in many ways the Irish system second-guessed aspects of the Maastricht criteria, as well as the 'neoliberal communitarianism' of the EES. As noted above, the 1987 PNR agreement was mainly about fiscal correction and employment creation. Whereas the former pre-empted the Maastricht convergence criteria (Hardiman 2002), active labour market policies, associated with the EES, were also adopted early on, in a bid to address the significant unemployment problem (O'Donnell, Cahill and Thomas 2010). Implementing the EES in Ireland was less about its more transformative aspects, such as increasing labour market flexibility, and more about its 'softer' aspects, such as life-long learning.

Tripartism played an important role in both Ireland and Italy, not only in securing both countries' entry to the common currency but also in ensuring there was a pro-European consensus on the Amsterdam and Nice Treaties (*see below*). This pro-European consensus amongst trade unions lent considerable legitimacy to the necessary reforms for entry to EMU. Whereas Savage (2005: 130) and others might see Italy's Euro-tax 'as one of the most cynical fiscal policy schemes undertaken by any EU member state to comply with the Maastricht criteria', that is to misunderstand the genuine attachment there was to the EU in Italy, which went beyond simple economic calculation.

AMSTERDAM AND LEFTOVER NICETIES

During the 1990s, unemployment was high in Europe (*see* Blanchard *et al.* 2006 for an overview) and this unemployment provided the backdrop to the formulation of the Amsterdam Treaty. Having 'waned in the absence of concerted political will' (Drake 2000: 135), Delors' White Paper on *Growth, Competitiveness and Employment* was revived by his brief successor. Jacques Santer's inaugural speech to the European Parliament was entitled 'For a European Confidence Pact for Employment' and the first chapter of the Commission's 1996 Work Programme – 'Action for Employment and Solidarity' – was emphatically endorsed by the Italian Presidency of the European Council. Also, the discourse of 'competitiveness' came to the fore in this period, which implied a number of things. Firstly, a shift in the mode of taxation from employment and investment to consumption; secondly, increasing labour market flexibility, reducing the risks of hiring faced by employers; thirdly, austere fiscal policies; and, fourthly, wage restraint (CEC 1993: 65–7). In addition, but always in the name of competitiveness, the Commission also developed rules on state aid that were also designed to boost employment. The Commission argued that 'the negative effects of such aid outweigh the possible short-term benefits in terms of maintaining a certain level of employment' (CEC 1995: 78).

Other developments at the European level, which cannot be covered in detail here but were central to the single market programme, include public procurement liberalisation and piecemeal sectoral liberalisation drives. Whereas the former ensured that public contracts were awarded strictly on economic, rather than social, criteria, the latter entailed far-reaching consequences for hitherto sheltered sectors (such as telecommunications, postal, energy and rail services). Both of these liberalisation processes took place against the backdrop of the implementation of the Maastricht convergence criteria at the national level.

In June 1996, the Italian Presidency of the European Council convened a Tripartite Conference on growth and employment, focusing on improving job growth and broadening the scope of social dialogue, but it failed to deliver anything other than platitudes. European trade unions threatened the withdrawal of their support, should there be no substantial reference to employment in the Amsterdam Treaty. The year 1997 will be remembered as a year that gave rise to transnational social movements and industrial action. Mather's (2007) *Struggling for a Social Europe* traces the so-called Euro-Marches movement across different EU summits between 1997 and 2000. Following a dispersed series of 'Euro-Marches Against Unemployment, Precarity and Social Exclusion', movements from all corners of Europe converged on Amsterdam, culminating in a 50,000 strong demonstration demanding that the EU and its constituent members tackle the problems of rising unemployment, job insecurity and social exclusion. The Euro-Marches 'made credible the idea of pan-European political mobilisation' and also advanced 'the struggle for "a different Europe"' (Aguiton and Cremieux 1997, cited in Mathers 2007: 2). Also, in 1997, the closure of the Renault plant at Vilvoorde produced the first Euro-strike, which 'became a paradigm for transnational collective action' (Erne 2008: 35). Following the closure, the ETUC organised mobilisations that included over 100,000 trade unionists taking to Brussels' streets under the banner 'European Action Day for Full Employment'. Similarly themed demonstrations were also organised for the extraordinary Jobs Summit of the European Council, with 20,000 trade unionists assembling to highlight the scourge of rising unemployment (*La Repubblica*, 20 November 1997). Whilst, initially at least, there was a mutual suspicion between the Euro-Marches movement and the ETUC, the EU and national governments could not ignore their demands.

The EU accession of Austria, Finland and Sweden in 1995 added weight to a proposed Employment Chapter to the Amsterdam Treaty. The German Kohl government constituted the main opponent to the inclusion of an Employment Chapter; however, the German government found itself isolated following the election of centre-left parties in France and the UK. Thirteen out of the fifteen member states were now governed by social-democratic parties. This provided a unique opportunity to shape the EU in accordance with a social-democratic vision; however, at a meeting of national social-democrats in Malmö, Sweden, it became apparent that clear divisions remained on the Treaty. These competing visions prevented a cohesive front forming and characterised intergovernmental negotiations. Whereas the French socialist prime minister, Lional Jospin, was critical of the neo-liberal and monetarist approach of the EU, the newly elected British prime minister, Tony Blair, was strongly opposed to 'hard law' and European intervention in employment policy (*see* Pollack 2000). He did, however, end the British opt-out on EU social policy.

The Amsterdam Treaty went a considerable way towards the vision outlined by Delors's GCE. Recognition was given to the need to balance the Stability and Growth Pacts with a stronger commitment to supporting employment. Here, the new Chapter on Employment was important, as it had a provision that a high level of employment was now an objective of the EU. With this in mind, Community activities were to include 'the promotion of coordination between employment policies of the Member States with a view to enhancing their effectiveness by developing a coordinated strategy for employment' (Art. 2 (3)). Also, the member states 'shall regard promoting employment as a matter of common concern and shall coordinate their action in this respect within the Council' (Art. 2(19)). Henceforth, the 'objective of a high level of employment shall be taken into consideration in the formulation and implementation of Community policies' (*ibidem*). Finally, the Amsterdam Treaty also included a Protocol on Public Services, strongholds of organised labour, which was 'intended to impede zealous liberalization efforts by the Commission in public services' (Smith 2005 [1999]: 39).

Such was the immediacy of the employment question that an extraordinary Jobs Summit was called in Luxembourg to authorise the initiation of the new employment process prior to the formal adoption of the Treaty. Subsequently, the so-called Luxembourg Process was set in motion, which provides specific obligations for member states, such as: the annual drafting of a National Action Plan (NAP) based on specific European guidelines; promoting employability, adaptability, entrepreneurship and equal opportunities; and providing substantive information on the evaluation of national policies with respect to the goals set at the EU level. For Moravcsik and Nicolaïdis (1998: 36) 'Amsterdam represents the beginning of a new phase of flexible, pragmatic constitution-building in order to accommodate the diversity of a continent-wide polity.' Here, they are referring to the inclusion of the Employment Chapter and the introduction of a new policymaking tool, formally named the Open Method of Coordination (OMC), which was introduced under the aegis of the Lisbon Agenda. Launched under Romano Prodi, ex-Prime Minister of Italy, who replaced Jacques Santer after his unceremonious resignation from the Presidency, the objective of the Lisbon Agenda was to strengthen the European economy *vis-à-vis* other established and emerging economies. The overarching goal, however, was, once again bound up in 'constructive ambiguity': 'to become the most competitive and dynamic knowledge-based economy in the world, capable of sustainable economic growth with more and better jobs and greater social cohesion' (European Council 2000). Achieving 'greater social cohesion', according to the EU's new social policy agenda, involved 'the modernisation and improvement of the European social model' (*ibidem*: 7). Here, the desired outcome was a European capitalism that resembled the Anglo-American variant, a capitalism in which the 'invisible hand' redistributed the wealth and ensured societal wellbeing, thereby subordinating the labour force to the exigencies of competitiveness (van Apeldoorn 2002). The OMC was part of this formula and was essentially an intergovernmental process identifying indicators; allowing surveillance and benchmarking, with a view to establishing 'best practices'; and proposing detailed guidelines for national policymakers. The 'soft law' approach was promoted in particular by the British and Swedish governments, as a 'third way' for EU social policy between regulatory competition and harmonisation and as an alternative to both intergovernmentalism and supranationalism.

For the vast majority of social-democrats, the inclusion of the Employment Chapter was a considerable achievement. For others, it amounts merely to 'a symbolic move' (Moravcsik and Nicolaïdis 1999: 63; *see also* Blanpain 1998). For others again, the Amsterdam Treaty represented a missed opportunity for European social-democratic forces to leave a more durable imprint on the EU. As Dini (1997: xxvii), Italy's Foreign Minister, stated '[T]he long night of Amsterdam closed on a note of bitter disappointment.' Not only was the Amsterdam debate 'striking in its vagueness' (Movavcsik and Nicolaïdis 1998: 33), but it failed to cater for forthcoming developments, namely, the imminent eastern enlargement. 'Euro-manifestations [demonstrations] have now become a normal feature of ETUC action' (ETUC 2003: 91) and mobilisations were organised at the two European Council summits at Porto and Nice in June and December 2000. The latter mobilisation involves a 70,000 strong contingent marching for a social Europe and the adoption of the Community Charter of Fundamental Social Rights of Workers.

The Nice Treaty was mostly about streamlining the existing institutional structures in time for the EU's eastern enlargement. By now, the Treaty-drafting process was a less secretive affair (Svendrup 2002: 129). However, the objective of the Treaty was mainly to deal with the so-called 'Amsterdam leftovers', namely, the composition of the Commission and weighting of member states' votes in the legislative processes where QMV was permissible. Also, enhanced co-operation was incorporated into the Treaty framework. The final stages of the Nice Council are described as being 'a shambles', so just as well 'the questions that they addressed remain relatively unimportant' (Ludlow 2001: 1). The treaty was neither a triumph nor a disaster: the Italian Prime Minister described the situation aptly: 'it's not a Ferrari, but a car that works ... Elsewhere they would call it Fix It Again Tony' (*La Repubblica*, 13 December 2000). There were, however, two additional developments at the Nice Council that are noteworthy from the perspective of organised labour and therefore worth mentioning.

Firstly, following a report from a European Commission's expert group (*Comité des Sages*) advocating that a basic set of fundamental civil and social rights be enshrined in the EU's *acquis*, and the publication of a *Manifesto for Social Europe* by prominent legal scholars (Bercusson *et al.* 1997), the European Council decided to draft a Charter of Fundamental Workers' Rights in the European Union. This decision was 'a consolidating and not a creative step, designed to garner a degree of public of popular legitimacy at a relatively low constitutional cost' (de Bùrca 2001: 16). The draft Charter was published in July 2000, with the final draft being signed at the Nice Summit in December 2000. Secondly, annexed to the Nice Treaty was a Declaration on the Future of the Union, calling for a greater debate on the future of the EU. This led to the creation of a European Constitutional Convention, which we will return to in Chapter Eight. The Nice Treaty entered into force on 1

February 2003, more than three years after the Treaty was agreed. The delay was due to the Irish electorate voting against the Treaty, which is discussed below.

IRISH AND ITALIAN ORGANISED LABOUR ON THE AMSTERDAM AND NICE TREATIES

Trade union positions on the Amsterdam and Nice Treaties have to be seen against the backdrop not only of monetary union and the Maastricht criteria but also consider the question of unemployment and the emerging EES. By now, the motto of 'social Europe' was part and parcel of trade union vernacular when debating EU questions. To boot, trade union mobilisations, co-ordinated by a restructured ETUC, served as a reminder to governments that cross-border mobilisations were possible and that the trade union agenda could not be entirely ignored. That said, there was very little by way of substantive provisions in the Treaties of Amsterdam or Nice that furthered the idea of a 'social Europe'. Notwithstanding, the promise of a more social Europe remains on the agenda, with the clearest example being the Charter of Fundamental Rights, agreed at the Nice IGC but only to be incorporated into the *acquis communautaire* during the next round of grand bargaining.

At both the CGIL and UIL Congresses in 1996 and 1998, respectively, the question of unemployment and European integration was central. For Sergio Cofferati (1996: 25), Trentin's replacement as General Secretary, 'economic growth alone ... is not enough to generate the necessary work ..., to guarantee social cohesion ... This makes the construction of a European Union, with a federal political character, even more necessary'. At the UIL Congress in Bologna, its General Secretary, Pietro Larizza, unveiled the union's newly rebranded flag. The traditional colour red was abandoned for blue, evoking the colour of the EU's flag. The EU's twelve stars were also emblazoned on the UIL flag. Whilst the Italian unions were somewhat content with the Amsterdam Treaty, there was a general sense that its provisions did not go far enough. The Foreign Minister, Lamberto Dini wrote,

> ... the Treaty, as often in the history of European integration, does not fully correspond to the expectations of the most far-sighted governments. But it creates the minimum conditions for initiating the negotiations that will make it possible to recover an alternative Europe [*l'altra Europa*] and bring a historic plan to completion ... However, there has not been the institutional acceleration that we would have liked ... The Treaty of Amsterdam is a transit station towards a future which is still partly to be defined (*La Repubblica*, 20 October 1997 [author's translation]).

The Italian Chamber of Deputies easily ratified the Treaty on 25 March 1998, with 428 voting in favour, one vote against and 44 abstentions. The Senate followed suit on June 3.

In Ireland, all mainstream political forces were in favour of the Amsterdam Treaty. However, the circumstances under which Irish referendums are held were subject to change on account of two legal cases being brought by individuals against the Irish state. In 1995, the Supreme Court ruled that the then Fine Gael-Labour government had acted unconstitutionally by spending public money to support a particular position in Ireland's second divorce referendum. The case was brought by Patricia McKenna, former Green Party MEP, and, as a result, a Referendum Commission must now be established each time a referendum is held, so as to ensure a balanced argument is presented to the electorate. The first Referendum Commission was set up for the plebiscite on the Amsterdam Treaty. The second case was brought by an academic, Anthony Coughlan, another longstanding Eurosceptic and colleague of Raymond Crotty, against the national broadcasting service. Coughlan made the argument that, during the same referendum, the allocation of time to each side during debates was unequal and therefore constitutionally unfair. The Supreme Court found that the national broadcaster had failed to allocate equal time. Henceforth, the political context changed, with both sides in the political debate being allotted equal airtime to voice their respective opinions.

The vast majority of Irish trade unions, including SIPTU and ICTU, were supportive of the Treaty, as was the Labour Party. Writing on behalf of ICTU in the *Irish Times*, the deputy General Secretary, Patricia O'Donovan (1998) stated:

> ... while the Amsterdam Treaty is not going to radically change the direction in which Europe is going, it contains important *new commitments* in the areas of employment and social rights. These have the *potential* to impact significantly on the lives of workers and the citizens of Europe. If these provisions *can be activated* and developed in a meaningful way, then the Amsterdam Treaty *could* come to be regarded as an important milestone on the way to building a citizens' Europe [emphasis added].

The tone is lukewarm at best, and it was more the promise of the Amsterdam Treaty for a more social Europe that secured ICTU's support. Whereas the Irish trade union movement, along with their European colleagues in the ETUC, would have preferred if the report of the high-level reflection group, *Comité des Sages* entitled 'For a Europe of Civic and Social Rights' had been taken on board and the Community Charter of Fundamental Social Workers' Rights incorporated into the *acquis communautaire*, but they were prepared to wait. The Irish National Organisation of the Unemployed, which had attempted to travel to Amsterdam to join the demonstrations, was critical of the Treaty. Its leader, Mike Allen, argued that '[N]o serious commentator on Europe believes that the Amsterdam Treaty is an adequate response ... Those who advocate a Yes vote do so out of habit, and the hope that something better will come along in time' (*Irish Times*, 21 May 1997).

On the day the Amsterdam Treaty was put before the Irish people, 56.2 per cent of the electorate turned out to vote, with 61.7 per cent voting in favour of the Treaty. The glow resulting from popular ratification was overshadowed by another, more historic vote, namely, the referendum on the Good Friday Agreement, which effectively brought sectarian hostilities to an end on the island of Ireland. Justifiably, it was this topic that captivated the hearts and minds of the electorate and not the EU Treaty.

The Nice Treaty, in general, and the prospect of the Charter, in particular, created divisions in the Italian centre-right, *Casa delle Libertà*, with *Lega Nord* referring to the latter as a communist document and threatening to descend on Nice with 250,000 *leghisti incazzati* ['angry Lega supporters'] (*La Repubblica*, 26 October 2000). Members of the CGIL,[7] principally from Tuscany, did travel to Nice, however, to demonstrate under the banner '*l'Europa dell' occupazione e dei diritti e non solo della moneta*' ['A Europe of employment and rights and not just a currency']. Nevertheless, there was a sense that trade union demands were not reflected in the final draft of the Treaty. For instance, questions concerning social security, amongst others, were still subject to the unanimity rule. 'This', for UIL,

> ... was the highest stake on the table at the Nice summit: the affirmation of the basic principle for any democracy, the majority vote. The definitive abandonment of the unanimous vote would have meant overcoming the Europe of Nations and archived [*mandato in soffitta*] the right of veto of a single state, which is a real brake on the integration process and on European democracy (Cedrone 2001[author's translation]).

Also, whilst agreement on the Charter of Fundamental Rights was welcome, its deferral was considered a missed opportunity. On a more positive note, CISL pointed to the Social Agenda decided at Nice as a means for increasing trade unions' influence. Called for by the French government to strengthen and modernise social Europe, the Agenda set specific priority objectives to promote employment and social protection over a five-year period and 'national trade unions will be called upon to intervene in the implementation of this Agenda' (Cal 2001[author's translation]). For the three confederations, all eyes were now on the 2004 IGC and hopes were pinned on the Constitutional Treaty. As the International Secretary of the CGIL, Giacomo Barbieri (2001), notes '[T]he new appointment [IGC], driven by a further mobilisation of trade unions and associations, should be an opportunity to draw up a real European Constitution [author's translation]'.

As noted above, the Nice Treaty failed to capture the imaginations of scholars and practitioners alike. 'Rarely', as Dinan (2004: 288) notes, 'did an intergovernmental conference devote so much time to so few issues with so few consequential results'. Once again, this European Treaty was easily ratified in the Italian Parliament, with 298 deputies voting in favour, seven voting against and six abstaining. The ratification process was expected to progress smoothly; however, it was dealt a setback when the Irish electorate, in an act that stunned Europe, voted against its ratification.

On the Nice Treaty, both ICTU and Labour advocated a Yes vote in the referendum. The latter used the opportunity to 'embrace the opportunity to place the party as a leading proponent of the EU in Ireland' (Homes 2006: 172). SIPTU also supported the Treaty, as the former General Secretary stated in an interview: 'we went along with Nice here, but we were not unanimous about it' (interview with ex-Gen. Sec. SIPTU, 3 December 2012). This not only suggests that the pro-European consensus of the Irish labour movement, which was very much elite-driven, was beginning to jar with an emerging social reality. Similarly, the popularity of the decade-long practice of tripartism was beginning to look frayed, as the Celtic Tiger showed it had a darker side. For instance, 'there was a substantial widening in earnings dispersion in terms of hourly wages among all employees' (Barrett, Fitzgerald and Nolan 2000: 130). Also, by 1997, as O'Rian and O'Connell (2000: 331) note, 'Irish government spending had fallen to 35 per cent of GDP, marginally higher than the US, and 13 percentage points below the European average'. Critiquing the success of the Irish economy, however, was, as far as the mainstream political class was concerned, unpatriotic and unwelcome. This point will become clearer in Chapter Eight.

The ATGWU refused to lend its support to either the 'co-option' of ICTU in competitive tripartism or the Nice Treaty. On the latter, its General Secretary, Mick O'Reilly, writing in the *Irish Times* (31 May 2001), stated that the 'ATGWU believes, there is a need for nations to reclaim democratic powers from multinational corporations, that are increasingly dictating the terms of world economic relations, in defiance of labour rights, environmental concerns and the public interest.' Implicitly critical of the leadership of the Irish labour movement, O'Reilly believed that 'the referendum on the Nice Treaty has been marred by unsubstantiated rhetoric, indifference to fact and an ostrich-like approach to European issues' (*ibidem*). Concerns were also raised about the possibility of enhanced co-operation and a multi-speed Europe, which could have implications for Northern Ireland, should Ireland opt-in and the UK opt-out (or *vice versa*). The following day, ICTU General Secretary, Peter Cassells, in the pages of the same broadsheet, made the case as to why the Nice Treaty was good for Irish workers by referring directly to the emerging social *acquis*. 'Europe has given us equal pay, reductions in working time, improved rights for part-time and temporary workers, parental leave' (*Irish Times*, 1 June 2001). ICTU's sole lament is that it 'would have preferred if the Government had fought harder to retain a commissioner for each country' (*ibidem*)! Perhaps this regret is based on the fact that the recent two-term European Commission for Social Affairs, Pádraig Flynn of Fianna Fáil, had provided Irish organised labour with a direct point of contact within the Brussels executive. Rather surprisingly, Flynn, a conservative on Irish social questions, sang from the same hymn-sheet as the more traditional European social-democrats during his tenure in Brussels.[8] Notwithstanding, the function of a European Commissioner is to serve the broader European interest and not further the national interest.

Much of the debate on the Nice Treaty was misleading and hinged less on the contents of the Treaty and more on the pending eastern enlargement. Here, the official message was that there was a moral obligation on the electorate not to stand in the way of Europe's thwarted destiny, namely, the reunification of East and West Europe. Also, access to new markets was seen as beneficial for Irish exports. The majority of Irish unions supported ratification, despite the fact that there were no plans to place restrictions on the free movement of workers from the new member states. The implications of this decision will become clearer when they are discussed in Part III of this book.

The Yes campaign was 'lacklustre and indifferent' as well as lacking 'energy, passion, intensity, and crucially, a visible campaigning presence on the ground in individual constituencies' (O'Brennan 2003: 7). The No campaign, by contrast, was 'charged with conviction, well organized and gained in confidence as the campaign went on' (*ibidem*). Hitherto, high levels of support for European integration had unquestionably been related to the visible insignia of EU branding on the side of new roads, public buildings, and trains and so on, which were benefits from EU funds. Also, official discourse regularly linked the success of the Celtic Tiger to membership of the EU. This narrative, however, lost its purchase and appeal in 'the new context' (Hayward 2002: 169). On 7 June, the Irish electorate voted 'No' to the Nice Treaty by 53.87 per cent to 46.13 per cent. Voter turnout was alarmingly low, at just 34.8 per cent. This low turnout was used to explain away the 'negative' result (Sinnott and Thomsen 2001); but the more important question is what explains this low turnout and why was the No campaign more successful in mobilising the vote?

With a general election the following year, there was reluctance on behalf of the pro-European political parties to spend much money on the Yes campaign. This decision was based on a presumption that the Irish electorate would simply vote in favour. However, as Peadar Kirby notes, one possible reason why a majority voted against the Treaty is precisely because of

> ... the urgings of all the major political parties, business and farmers' leaders, the Catholic bishops and the trade union movement. For it [the Treaty] offered an increasingly rare opportunity to voice an effective protest against the concentration of power and the erosion of the bonds of solidarity which characterise society today (Kirby 2002: 32).

In other words, second-order voting won the day.

As noted above, the No campaign was more organised and critical of the EU. For instance, Green Party MEP, Patricia McKenna (MEP), argued that the Treaty would lead to 'an authoritarian and totalitarian' EU (*Irish Times*, 23 May 2001). The Republican Left, including Sinn Féin, argued that Irish neutrality would be undermined. A telling account of the lacklustre campaign fought by the official pro-Nice side, namely, the government, is that of the then-Prime Minister, Bertie Ahern, who refused to be drawn on the future of the EU, despite such a question being of considerable relevance. Rather, for Ahern (2001), '[T]he Treaty of Nice is about enlarging and extending the European Union, and about giving to others the same chance to develop that was given to us thirty years ago ... That is the view of the Nice Treaty held throughout Europe, and a view I share.' Fundamentally, however, 'the central tenet of the government's referendum campaign (the necessity of Nice for enlargement) was undermined by the key tactic of its campaign (an emphasis on rhetoric)' (Hayward 2002: 174).

Following defeat at the ballot-box, a number of guarantees were sought by the Irish government from the EU so as to address the concerns of the Irish electorate. The Seville Declaration secured assurances that Irish neutrality would not be affected though these were more reassuring promises than binding guarantees. It was also agreed, much to the delight of ICTU, that each member state would retain a Commissioner. These were the two key changes following the first referendum. Also, within the national framework, greater powers of scrutiny were afforded to Irish parliamentarians on EU-related questions. Finally, there was a concerted effort to co-ordinate a more effective Yes campaign; civil society was not prepared to leave it to the political class to carry the day.

In the run-up to the second referendum, the Labour Party advised voters not to treat the referendum as an opportunity to inflict damage on the Fianna-Fáil-led government and to wait until the impending election. The slogan read: 'Hold Your Fire. The Government [Fianna Fáil] Can Wait. Europe Can't'. Left-wing opposition to the Treaty coalesced around the Alliance Against Nice and included members of the Green Party, Sinn Féin, Socialist Party and People Before Profit. Mick O'Reilly, a self-declared republican socialist and former Regional Secretary of the ATGWU,[9] formed a grouping called Trade Unionists Against Nice and argued that 'Nice is in effect a framework for a massive privatisation programme, which will result in Irish workers paying more for run-down public services. Is it any wonder that the business community have never before spent so much money advocating a Yes vote?' (*Irish Times*, 9 October 2002). As with the first referendum, O'Reilly argued that the Treaty 'serves the selfish and profiteering interests of large international corporations which is why trade unionists will vigorously campaign for its defeat – again' (*ibidem*). Neither was the ICTU leadership spared criticism: 'They are undemocratically urging a Yes vote, without any mandate or consultation with members of constituent unions on an issue whose potential importance far exceeds that of any social partnership agreement' (*ibid.*). Similarly, Sinn Féin (with Irish neutrality off the agenda) underlined the privatisation agenda. At an Alliance Against Nice protest, held outside the offices of the employers' association, Sinn Féin argued that

> ... the reasons IBEC are backing the Nice Treaty have a lot more to do with the privatisation agenda Nice advances than with concern for Irish jobs and workers. Their recent statements calling for cutbacks in wage increases shows how hollow those concerns are (Sinn Féin 2002).

Their argument rested on Article 133 of the Treaty, a rather obscure Article which deals with the Commission and EU trade deals with other trading blocs or countries.

Shortly after the first referendum, SIPTU used their support of the Treaty as a bargaining chip to ensure the survival of the national airline, Aer Lingus, which, like airlines in the rest of Europe and beyond, was facing significant difficulties in the wake of the terrorist attack on New York's Twin Towers (*Irish Examiner*, 12 October 2001). To what extent this strategy succeeded is unclear; however, for the second referendum, the union was firmly on board and making a moral argument as to why the Treaty should be supported. SIPTU President, Des Geraghty, argued that 'the trade union spirit of solidarity and fairness' must prevail and be extended to workers from the candidate member states, whose 'pay and conditions can be secured most effectively through EU membership' (*Irish Times*, 16 October 2002). On the question of labour mobility and social dumping, Geraghty argued that 'this is less likely to materialise in an expanded EU' and that the opposite was the likely outcome: 'the truth is that foreign citizens do not want to emigrate for work, they want to work in well-paid jobs in their own countries. EU membership will help to make this possible' (*ibidem*). Hence, 'ratification of the Nice Treaty would ... encour[age] workers to remain at home' (*ibid.*). Here, to support his argument, Geraghty used the examples of Greece, Spain and Portugal, whose accession to the EU 'indicate no tendency towards significantly greater emigration' (*ibid.*). As will be seen in the following chapter, this was not entirely true and social dumping was a feature, producing some important ECJ case law, known as the Laval Quartet. In any case, Geraghty assured that 'SIPTU has a proven track record in organising immigrant workers and securing their full entitlements in terms of wages and working conditions' (*ibid.*). A week after SIPTU's national Executive Council endorsed the Treaty, it was upstaged when delegates at a Dublin regional conference voted to oppose it because 'it opens the way to greater military intervention and further economic liberalism' (*Irish Times*, 12 October 2002). This vote was used by the anti-Nice campaigners to harangue the trade union leadership and accuse them of being 'out of step' with the workers (*ibidem*). Hence, as noted by the SIPTU leadership above, a Eurosceptic contingent within SIPTU was emerging.

Fianna Fáil, second time round, was better organised, having established a dedicated campaign office and press centre. The party committed €500,000 (compared to the €60,000 allocated in Nice I) to the campaign (*Irish Times*, 8 October 2002). Pro-EU organisations, such as Alliance for Europe, brought together a wide range of interests specifically for the campaign. Founded by Professor Brigid Laffan, a prominent pro-European academic, the alliance had a strong pro-business bias.[10] Overseeing the pro-Alliance's launch was Professor of International Business, Colm Kearney, who rejected speculation that a Yes vote would result in Ireland being flooded with cheap labour. He argued that recent studies had concluded that a maximum of three million people would move from candidate states in Eastern and Central Europe to current EU member states over the next 15 to 20 years. And 80 per cent of these would move to Germany and Austria, which are close to their homelands and where they already have strong migrant networks (*Irish Times*, 10 October 2002). One such report was that by a state advisory agency, Forfás, which sought to allay concerns by claiming that

> ... Ireland is highly unlikely to witness large migration flows from the new CEE entrants. On the contrary, in a situation in which Ireland is expected to need migrant labour in the medium to long term, some movement of labour from the accession countries to Ireland will be of benefit (Forfás 2002: 49).

This, we now know, was a gross miscalculation, the extent of which will be discussed in Part III. In any case, the Yes campaign had an estimated €1.68 million to convince the Irish public, almost ten times that of the No campaign (*Irish Times*, 8 October 2002). The second referendum was held on 19 October 2002, with 62.9 per cent of 49.5 per cent of the electorate voting in favour. The EU was back on track, or so it seemed.

CONCLUSIONS: EUROPE HITTING HOME

Phase two of European integration involved considerable 'adaptational pressures' (Börzel and Risse 2000) for its constituent members, not least Ireland and Italy, which, against the backdrop of economic and political crises, and in the name of EMU, underwent significant transformations. Although Delors' ten-year reign concluded in 1995, his influence on European integration continued throughout the second half of the 1990s, and beyond. Nowhere was this more evident than with EMU; but Delors's keenness to imbue the EU with a social component was achieved in three ways – social dialogue, EU labour laws, and redistributive policies – which were tantamount to embedding the transnational market. Albeit to varying degrees, all three European developments were significant for Irish and Italian unions and went a considerable way towards underpinning the pro-European consensus.

In the second phase, Ireland experienced nothing short of a socio-economic and cultural transformation. 'Over the space of just six years in the 1990s, the country saw phenomenal growth in jobs, output and incomes as well as significant changes in consumption, lifestyles, values and patterns of political and social organisation' (Daly 2005: 133). There was also a transformation in politics, but more so in format rather than in content. The Irish political landscape was now shaped by 'competitive' tripartism (Rhodes 1998) and the proliferation of foreign multinationals. The former created a macroeconomic framework that was appealing to the latter, namely, international competitiveness. This was achieved by maintaining competitive wage levels, ensuring macroeconomic stability by keeping inflation low and taking corporate tax rates out of political competition and by promoting employment creation in allowing a degree of flexibility. These objectives also happened to be complementary to the EES and the requirements of the Maastricht criteria, which also included control over public expenditure. Both of these aspects were catered to under the rubric of Irish tripartism, which was not without its critics, both in academia and beyond.

Academic critics of Irish tripartism, most notably, Kieran Allen, pointed to the failure of Irish organised labour to strengthen its industrial-relations arm. Allen (2009: 59) went as far as to say that it 'demobilises workplace unionism by ensnaring it in a web of procedural agreements and detailed productivity concessions that have been dictated from above'. D'Art and Turner (2006) were also critical of ICTU's failure to ameliorate the landscape for unions and for not securing legislation on trade union bargaining. Writing on Irish tripartism, Regan (2012a, 2012b) speaks of 'an Irish third way', which, for ICTU, had less to do with wage restraint and more to do with access to political power. Also, within trade union circles, criticism on similar grounds came principally from Unite the Union, which was a rather unusual union in that it operated in two jurisdictions. A British-based union, Unite was a vociferous critic of the Irish socio-economic model and the co-opting of ICTU by government elites into what it considers as neo-liberal tripartism (Hastings, Sheehan and Yeates 2007: 47). Considered the 'old left' within the Irish labour movement, its leader, Mick O'Reilly, was equally critical of the EU, which, to his mind, served the interests of international capital at the expense of the working classes (interview with former Regional Secretary, 9 January 2012). In the long tradition of British trade unionism (Hyman 2001a: ch. 5), Unite believes that class conflict was best fought (and perpetuated) on the shop floor and that any political bidding was to be conducted through the Labour Party, to which it was officially affiliated. Ironically, the latter was becoming increasingly pro-EU and was keen to present itself as *the* pro-European party (Holmes 2006).

The Italian experience was also characterised by 'third way' ideas (Negrelli and Pulignano 2008; Negrelli 2005), this was more so in the late 1990s and early 2000s and was not to the liking of all three confederations. Rather than access to power, the Italian confederations, certainly in the case of the CGIL, were more interested in rebuilding trade union power by strengthening the articulation mechanisms between the different levels of collective bargaining. Baccaro and Howell (2017: 121) correctly observe that comparing Italian industrial relations in the 1970s and 1980s, on the one hand, and the 1990s, on the other hand, is like 'is like looking at pictures from two different geological eras'. Certainly, by comparison with Ireland, Italy's political economy was subjected to greater restructuring pressures so as to ensure entry to EMU. The most significant sacrifice, in addition to reforming the pension system, privatisations, labour market reforms and the once-off Euro-tax, was the abolition of the *scala mobile*, which had been considered 'a fundamental right which workers could not sacrifice' (Amyot 2004: 171). When, in the mid-1980s, the economist Ezio Tarantelli suggested amending the mechanism, he was assassinated by the *Brigate Rosse* (*see* Chapter Four). However, once the egalitarian mechanism was seen to be 'standing in the way of Italy's entry into the EMU' (*ibid.*: 172), the three confederations were prepared to overcome rivalry and let '*the* symbol' of Italian union power go (Baccaro and Howell 2017: 128, emphasis in original). This sacrifice and others were made so as to secure Italy's entry to EMU, which became a project of the centre-left more so than of the parties of the right (Quaglia 2005). Rather than *la moneta unica*, the Italian term for the common currency, EMU – for the Italian left-wing political forces in general and the three union confederations in particular – was *l'unica moneta* ['the only currency'].

In any case, the Italian unions, by comparison to their Irish counterparts, fared better in industrial-relations terms, with particular thanks to the 1993 agreement, which recognised union structures within firms. The

Rappresentanze Sindacali Unitarie was significant, as this 'reinstitutionalized the balance of power between Italian social partners' (Talani and Cerviño 2003: 210). By comparison, the Irish unions had little to show in terms of industrial relations strength and the union leadership was quite content just to have seen off the threat of Thatcherism. In regards to this, social policies that irked the British Tories put the EU in a relatively good light from the perspective of organised labour in general and Irish organised labour in particular.[11] Tripartism was promoted as a factor underpinning the emergence of the Celtic Tiger, resulting in a newfound optimism, which was shared by trade unionists whose governance role was key in having 'shaped Ireland's economic success' (Hastings, Sheehan and Yeates 2007). Whereas in Italy the agenda of the EES was internalised through the tripartite arrangement (Ferrera and Gualmini 2004; Graziano 2007), this was less the case in Ireland, where its 'positive flexibility' had 'yet to be grasped' (Cassells 2000: 71, 73). Despite the government setting-up tripartite working groups, very few succeed in developing concrete EES policy initiatives (Donaghey 2008; Hardiman 2006). Rather than Ireland learning from Europe, ICTU General Secretary, Peter Cassells, was of the opinion that 'Ireland could play a leading role in modernising the European Social Model' (Cassels 2000: 74). On the crest of an economic wave and with delegates from all over the world visiting the Irish capital to meet trade unionists and understand the ingredients of economic success, their aggregate ego, if we can speak of such a thing, was inflated.

Both the Italian and Irish confederations sought to shape the Amsterdam and Nice Treaties either by lobbying their national governments or through the ETUC (O'Donovan 1999). The results in both instances were disappointing but provided scope for constructing a more social Europe in future. In the greater scheme of things, the Chapter on Employment and the signing of the Charter of Fundamental Rights were, for the ETUC and the Irish and Italian confederations, considered steps in the right direction, thereby consolidating a pro-European consensus amongst organised labour. This support, however, was not without conditions and has been described as a 'yes ... but' (Hyman 2005; Bieler 2006). What remained a puzzle, or at least a missing piece, was what exactly did the 'but' look like? UIL's International Secretary, Carmelo Cedrone, was critical of the EU's lip-service and procrastination on the question of social Europe but provided an insight as to how the 'but' might be overcome.

> The most negative aspect, for the trade union, is that once again social policy is the one that has paid the price, remaining entangled in the trap [*reti*] of unanimous voting. All this happened while everyone was striving, including the governments, to praise the much vaunted 'European social model' (Cedrone 2001).

On the European level, once again, there was no shortage of academic criticism, which was levelled first and foremost at the ETUC for having 'gone native' and being in an 'elite embrace' (Hyman 2005) with the EU institutions, whose ambition, particularly the Commission, was to 'cajole and seduce' the peak European association (Martin and Ross 1999; Hyman 2005; *see also* Gobin 1997; Goetschy 1999). However, following the Vilvoorde episode (Moreno and Gabaglio 2007: 161–3; Erne 2008: 34–5) and upon the realisation that national governments were dragging their feet, the ETUC did eventually complement its favoured technocratic strategy with mobilisations, particularly surrounding inter-governmental conferences, that sought to politicise the social dimension of European integration. Following these mobilisations, there was a degree of hope that the ETUC had come of age as a political organisation and was now 'a supranational trade union organisation that can aspire to become an autonomous and relevant social and political actor on the European scene' (Barbieri 2001). That said, for Barbieri and the CGIL, there remained scope for the ETUC and its national affiliates to '[*S*] *indacalizzare di più*' [be more militant] (*ibidem*).

PART III

LABOUR MOBILITY AND
IONS: COPING MECHANISMS
AND POLITICISATION

Chapter Seven

Labour Mobility: A Defining Characteristic

INTRODUCTION

Part III of this book is divided into two chapters. This chapter presents the findings from a comparative study, which takes place at the sectoral level. By focusing on the construction sector, we are better able to determine the effects of labour mobility and its attendant challenges and to assess whether or not Irish and Italian trade unions' coping mechanisms are fit for purpose (Bechter *et al.* 2012). The following chapter focuses on determining whether or not there is a feedback loop between unions' experience with labour mobility, as a defining characteristic of the third phase of European integration, and their broader preferences towards the EU. The third phase of European integration can be neatly divided into two distinct periods, namely pre-financial crisis up to 2008 and the crisis period itself. Although the Barroso Commission (2004–14), which launched three EU treaties, bridged both timeframes, this chapter is very much rooted in the pre-financial crisis period and is concerned with labour mobility in the context of EU enlargement.

The Eastern enlargements of the EU set in train a number of dynamics that qualitatively altered the nature of European integration, giving rise to a growing academic interest in the politicisation of the EU (*see*, for example, Zürn 2016; De Wilde, Leupold and Schmidtke 2016; Statham and Trenz 2013). De Wilde and Zürn (2012) define such politicisation as consisting of three components: i) increasing the EU's salience; ii) polarisation of views in relation to the EU and its political and economic direction; and iii) increasing the number of actors engaging in political interest with the EU. Do we see an increase in the EU's saliency and polarisation of views within the trade union movement? And if so, can these developments be traced back to labour mobility and its attendant challenges?

On account of the unbridgeable gap in labour costs and incomes between the 'old' and 'new' member states, combined with the flexible labour market regimes embraced by most of the 'new' states, the 'old' states feared that movement of capital eastwards in search of lower labour costs (Marginson 2006). The prospect of labour mobility, namely, the free movement of goods and services from east to west, also proved a source of concern for unions in the 'old' member states. This aspect was central to the first Barroso Commission's neo-liberal agenda, which can be termed a 'deepening through widening' strategy. This strategy rested on the wholesale liberalisation of services and the 'country-of-origin principle' (*see* below).

Fears surrounding social dumping in the 'old' member states, either through capital flight from west to east or through labour mobility from east to west, became heightened and increasingly commonplace in political discourse and debates (Vaughan-Whitehead 2003; Bernaciak 2015). In terms of deterring the social dumping associated with labour mobility, the unions sought to protect their labour markets by lobbying their respective governments to place restrictions on the free movement of labour (but not services) from the 'new' member states. The vast majority of 'old' member states, often at the behest of unions, implemented restrictions on the free movement of labour originating from the 'new' member states. However, these restrictions did not extend to the 'posting' of workers, which was exempted from restrictions on migration because the (temporary) 'posting' of workers from one member state to another is governed under the free movement of services.

A critical development was the draft Services Directive of January 2004, which hinged on the controversial 'country-of-origin' principle, defined as 'a radical version of mutual recognition whereby service providers could trade services in any EU country while abiding only by the regulations of the country where the company has its headquarters' (Crespy, 2016: 82). The Services Directive was the brainchild of Commissioner Bolkestein, who embodied the 'deepening through widening' approach and saw the 'big bang' enlargement as an opportunity to radically alter the EU's services market. Bolkestein jettisoned the traditional supranational liberalisation approach, which involved sectoral liberalisation, for example in the energy, telecommunications and aviation sectors. Instead, a wholesale cross-sectoral liberalisation, including public services (Crespy 2016), was attempted by Bolkestein.

In the context of enlargement, the prospect of cross-sectoral liberalisation and the inclusion of the country-of-origin principle only served to generate significant politicisation and resistance, led by trade unions. Following two years of politicisation and public mobilisations, the likes of which the EU had hitherto never seen, the Directive was 'substantially amended' (*ibid*: 83) by the European Parliament. That said, it was not long before the 'country of origin' principle was back on the agenda and pitting EU economic rights against national social rights.

The country-of-origin principle was shelved only to be reintroduced through the backdoor via the European Court of Justice's (CJEU) so-called 'Laval Quartet' rulings. These rulings, were, to say the least, very controversial; and generated considerable debate both within unions and more broadly in academia (*see*, for example, Woolfson and Sommers 2006; Dølvik and Visser, 2009; Scharpf 2010). The ECJ was first called upon to adjudicate a dispute in Sweden's construction sector involving Latvian workers. The dispute demonstrates in a microcosm the major challenges facing trade unions in the enlarged EU and 'exposes the fragile nature of hard-won labour standards in the face of economic liberalization, deregulation and European enlargement' (Woolfson and Sommers 2006: 49). The infamous Laval case produced a rather clear division between 'old' and 'new' member states, reflecting a broader conflict of rights and interests within the EU (Bercusson 2007; Lindstrom 2010). In its ruling, the CJEU clearly favoured the former and promoted EU economic rights over national social rights. In doing so the CJEU 'seemed singularly unconcerned, and uninformed, about the niceties of labour law and industrial relations' (Dølvik and Visser 2009: 515).

Or, in Polanyian terms, the CJEU favoured the disembedding of markets over embedded markets (*see* Chapter Two). Following this, and to continue the Polanyian analogy, we might expect to see a counter-movement. As Dølvik and Visser note, the ruling is 'unacceptable to trade unions' (*ibidem*), but what shape might a counter-movement take? Put differently, does labour mobility generate a politicisation of the EU and European integration and might this affect political preferences? These questions will be tackled more concretely in the following chapter; however, the empirical evidence presented below is important when it comes to the formulation of trade unions' political preferences on the changing nature of European integration and the governance thereof. In short, lax regulatory environments that permit frequent social dumping will generate 'losers' and, should the trend go unchecked, the likelihood of politicisation increases. In other words, we see a polarisation of views and, when permitted, mobilisations against the EU. Although as we shall see, how this mobilisation materialises depends largely on political factors (*see* Mair 2007, ch. 8).

This chapter is structured as follows. First, it outlines the uniqueness of the EU's eastern enlargement in the 2000s and describes how the creation of a transnational labour market affected trade union strategies, not least in the construction sector, which was particularly impacted. Following that, migration, generally, and intra-EU migration, particularly, is discussed in more detail with regard to Ireland and Italy. Situated in an emerging field of study, which can be termed transnational labour studies, an analytical framework for understanding trade unions' coping mechanisms is presented. Then the regulatory and non-regulatory coping mechanisms of Irish and Italian construction unions are assessed in two separate sections. The frequency of social dumping incidents is telling, and, in the Conclusion, the political consequences of frequent social dumping episodes and inadequate coping mechanisms are discussed.

AN ENLARGEMENT WITH A DIFFERENCE

The eastern enlargement of the EU in 2004 differed from previous ones in which the magic number of new entrants was three. The first decade of the new millennium saw the membership almost double, from 15 to 27 member states. Intra-European migratory flows are greatly influenced by conditions in the receiving country, that is, the pull factors determine the size of the migration (*see* Böhning 1972: 72–5; Stan and Erne 2014). With regards to the Eastern enlargement, both the push and the pull factors – high unemployment and low wages in one country and high wages in another country – were particularly strong and so stimulated labour mobility. By 2007, it is estimated that almost 2.3 million Poles had migrated to western Europe (White 2011). Of course, labour mobility was facilitated by the availability of low-cost travel and improved infrastructural linkages. Social networks, established during the 1990s, were important in explaining who went where (Perrotta 2011). This was especially the case between Italy and Romania (Anghel 2008); migratory trends between these two not only had a circular pattern (Stan and Erne 2014; Perrotta 2011) but were also, prior to Romania's accession, often clandestine in nature (Ban 2009). These trends met Italian employers' demands for flexible, short-term, insecure migrant labourers, many of whom found work in the construction sector (*see below*). The 'transition' and 'patchwork' regulatory framework also shaped who went where (Donaghey and Teague 2006).

Unsurprisingly, given its uniqueness, the prospect of Eastern enlargement received no shortage of academic attention from welfare state scholars (Vaughan-Whitehead 2003; Kvist 2004); industrial relations scholars (Meardi 2012a, 2012b); immigration scholars (Pries 2003); and trade union revitalisation scholars (Dundon *et al.* 2007; Gall 2009). Unfortunately, there has been very little cross-fertilisation between these disciplines as well as a distinct lack of cross-national research. A recent strand of transnational labour literature has gone some way to address this lacuna (*see*, for example, Lillie and Greer 2007; Wagner 2014); however, nowhere has there been any attempt to determine the political consequences resulting from the changing socio-economic dynamics associated with European integration. A comparative within-case study is well-placed to research the affects of these contemporary dynamics and can situated in this emerging discipline of transnational labour studies; however, it goes that little bit further by relating it back to (changing) trade union preferences on European integration (across time). In other words, it allows us to establish whether there is a feedback loop between experiences on the ground and changing political preferences on the EU and European integration. In doing so, I hope to offer a bridge between more specific accounts of European integration and more general political economy approaches (Jones and Verdun 2003). Certainly, the question of labour mobility featured in the Brexit debate and EU migrants were often scapegoated for the real problems in the UK, namely, a deregulated labour market that favours individualism over collectivism.

CONSTRUCTING TRANSNATIONAL LABOUR MARKETS, SOCIAL DUMPING AND TRADE UNION STRATEGIES

The creation of a flexible transnational labour market is one of the more understated objectives of the EU. Labour markets lie at the intersection of the single market and monetary union. Labour market mobility and labour market deregulation are considered two sides of the same single-market–monetary-union coin. The concept of EU citizenship, introduced with the Maastricht Treaty, is closely linked with the idea of mobility. Some academics (for example, Recchi 2008; Recchi and Favell 2009) see citizenship and mobility as a positive driving force behind European integration, the creation of a European identity and the creation of a pan-European labour market. In the context of EMU, labour mobility has an important role in offsetting asymmetric economic shocks. Mundell (1961) is famously noted for his exaltation of labour mobility as a precondition for an optimal currency area. Transnational labour markets play an important role when it comes to *national* industrial relations and trade union strategies. There is evidence of industrial relations systems diverging within national contexts while converging internationally at the same time (Bechter, Brandl and Meardi 2012). At the same time, 'supranational politics, transnational production, and transnational labor markets are supplanting and undermining national institutions as influences on employer and union strategies' (Lillie and Greer 2007: 552).

The creation of a transnational labour market carries particular implications for the construction sector. That said, important institutional differences remain at the (sub-)national level (Balch *et al.* 2004: 181). Overall, the European construction sector is an important economic sector. Often, activity in the sector is used as a barometer to measure the health of the general economy.

In 2008, the construction sector represented an activity worth €1,305 billion, that is, 10.4 per cent of the EU's GDP; the sector employs 16.3 million workers (without taking into account the jobs generated in other related sectors), that is, 7.6 per cent of total employment within the EU; and there are nearly 3 million enterprises, most of which are small or medium-sized. Many of the workers are self-employed (about 22 per cent) (Cordeel 2009; EC 2011). Other structural characteristics include project-based work; male domination and a long-standing relationship with migrant labour. Also, subcontracting is synonymous with construction and, as a result, a large number of small and medium-sized enterprises compete for jobs and tenders. Typically, savings are made not on materials but on labour costs, unlike other sectors such as manufacturing. Also, the option of delocalisation is not possible. Writing on the changes in the construction sector Cremers (2009: 201) notes:

> The process of diversification, combined with a Europeanization of the territory in the late 1980s, led to the emergence of giant conglomerates in a broad field of economic sectors … At the same time, a clear divergence developed on the operational side, with, at the top of the production chain, a concentration on core business and externalization of the execution to dependent subcontractors.

Research has found that on the back of deregulation there has been an increase in subcontracting practices, with the number of tiers increasing in the subcontracting chain (Houwerzijl and Peters 2008). There has also been a qualitative change regarding the employment relationship, with a growth in atypical types of work. Drucker *et al.* (2000) conducted a survey of 200 large construction employers in nine EU states. The research found that more than half of the companies had increased their use of fixed-term, temporary and casual contracts.

Complex subcontracting chains and the use of atypical forms of employment reinforce labour market segmentation, with migrant workers typically occupying the lower tier (Lillie 2012). Moreover, outsourcing places competitive pressures on subcontractors, who, in order to win a contract, may resort to underhanded tactics. For starters, outsourcing can discourage workers from taking industrial action because blame is often passed up or down the subcontracting chain (Grimshaw *et al.* 2005). The issue of bogus self-employment is also a worrisome phenomenon in the sector (Harvey and Behling 2008). Also, the practice of 'posting' workers has become more controversial in recent years (Woolfson and Somers 2006; Cremers, Dølvik and Bosch 2007; Cremers 2009; Dølvik and Eldring 2006; Lillie and Greer 2007; Dølvik and Visser 2009; Wagner 2014), an aspect I will return to below.

The term 'social dumping' is an ambiguous one and is often used arbitrarily (*see* Bernaciak 2015). By and large the term is used by protagonists on the left of the political spectrum and, in particular, by trade unions. Employers' associations appear more reluctant to employ the term, in discourse that is. Surprisingly, the European institutions have not offered a definition of the term. 'There is a total absence, in terms of statistics and studies that may help in assessing the phenomenon of social dumping' (Vaughan-Whitehead 2003: 358). The practice is perceived as having negative effects, which are all too often to the detriment of industrial relations systems and employment standards. While there are those who dismiss social dumping as a myth,[1] it could also be argued that the European Commission attempted to legalise social dumping via the 'country of origin' clause in the original Services Directive. I would argue that the concept, which is defined more clearly below, is contrary to the spirit of European integration, which sought to eliminate competition on social standards by harmonising such standards upwards. This is reflected in Article 117 of the Treaty of Rome.[2]

Vaughan-Whitehead (2003: 325) defines social dumping as:

> Any practice pursued by an enterprise that deliberately violates or circumvents legislation in the social field or takes advantages of differentials in practice and/or legislation in the social field, in order to gain an economic advantage in terms of competitiveness, the state also *playing a determinant role in this process* (emphasis added).

As can be seen from Vaughan-Whitehead's definition, social dumping can have an illegal[3] or a legal character. We are more interested in the 'legal' or 'quasi-legal' forms of social dumping, wherein employers seek to exploit legal loopholes and, in doing so, gain competitive advantage. This can lead to 'reverse discrimination', whereby national firms (or workers) are bound by collective agreements and foreign service-providers are not. Consequently, the latter gain a competitive advantage over national enterprises. Such a development could, in the long-term, undermine collective bargaining systems; but also, if left unchecked, manifest a reaction which could be interpreted as Eurosceptic.

Vaughan-Whitehead (*ibidem*: 344) clearly emphasises the role of the state in facilitating the practice of social dumping: 'by allowing particular practices to develop, providing the appropriate legal framework, or failing to combat unfair competition based on much poorer working conditions, they [the state] encourage enterprises to base their operations on social dumping'. Similarly, the ETUC points to the role of the state.

> Social dumping can occur because of weak enforcement. When workers are hired in a different member state from where the work is performed, and when the host member state does not, or is not allowed to, have proper inspections, it is difficult to check that employment standards are met (ETUC 2015b).

Labour law depends on national enforcement, 'but member states do not invest enough in labour inspection' (ETUC 2015b). Here, trade unions can play an important role, but this is often a learning experience and an inferior substitute for regulation.

There are three types of intra-EU labour mobility and each could potentially lead to a form of social dumping. A detailed examination of these is not possible here; suffice to say that each raises convoluted legal, economic and social issues. A synthesis of these is displayed in Table 7.1, which lays out the type of mobility, the social dumping threat and the law applied..

Table 7.1 Types of EU mobility in construction

Type of mobility	EU freedom	Social dumping threat	Law applied	Principle
Individual migrant	Free movement of workers	Under-paid and general exploitation	National labour law	Territorial
Self-employed	Freedom of establishment	Bogus self-employment	National labour law	Territorial
Posted worker (through TWA)	Free movement of services	Circumvention of collective agreement	EU competition law	De-territorial

Source: Adapted from Bosch and Weinkopf (2013)

Each aspect of this intra-EU mobility has generated a significant body of literature (*see* Bosch and Weinkopf 2013; Bernaciak 2015). How the posting of workers, which corresponds with the freedom to provide services, can be used as an instrument to increase flexibility and competitiveness is particularly interesting and it has given rise to a number of controversial CJEU cases. For instance, the *Rush Portuguesa* (1990) ruling held that obligatory work permits were restrictive to the freedom to provide services. Following this ruling, and similar issues in the German construction sector (*see* Menz 2005), there was sufficient political will under Delors (Drucker and Dupre 1998) to regulate the practice through a European Directive. Eventually, the Posted Workers Directive (1996/71/EC) was agreed on, without the controversial 'country of origin' clause. Following a brief discussion on 'posted' workers, the resurfacing of the 'country of origin' will be dealt with.

The 'country of origin' principle permits service providers from one member state to operate in another while having only to adhere to domestic laws governing those activities, instead of those of the country in which the services are being provided. In other words, it amounts to the deterritorialisation of (labour) law; deterritorialisation facilitates social dumping and would inevitably lead to a 'race to the bottom'. The so-called Bolkestein Directive sought to reintroduce the 'country of origin' principle on a grand scale; however, in light of the Eastern enlargement, such a prospect was of immense concern to unions, particularly regarding the posting of workers. An anti-Bolkestein campaign signalled that national unions, rather than the confederations, were paying more attention to the European level. This is particularly the case in the construction sector, which, as previously mentioned, is particularly vulnerable to the 'country of origin' principle. Here, the EFBWW lobbied the Commission to make it aware of the legal chaos that would ensue, not least in regard to employment rights. The principle was eventually dropped from the Services Directive: but not before a wave of transnational trade union mobilisations the likes of which the EU had hitherto never witnessed (Crespy 2016; Parks 2015).

Soon, however, the construction sector was at the centre of a 'transnational political conflict' (Lindstrom 2010), which reintroduced the 'country of origin' principle. I refer here to the Laval Quartet judgments of the CJEU. These cases, three of which were situated in the construction sector, have generated not only significant academic literature but also trade union literature. Due to space constraints, I will deal only with the Laval case. In 2005, Laval un Partneri, a Latvian construction firm, won a contract worth €2.8 million to refurbish a school at Vaxholm, a suburb of Stockholm. To carry out the work, the firm posted 35 workers to the site. The workers were paid half of what a Swedish worker would have received. The firm was not a signatory of the collective agreement governing the Stockholm construction sector and refused to sign an 'application agreement', a problem which was becoming more frequent amongst foreign firms (*see* Woolfson and Sommers 2006). On the day before the fourth meeting, Laval claimed that they had signed a collective agreement with the Latvian construction union, making another agreement unnecessary. Unhappy with this response, the Swedish union initiated a picket on the construction site, followed by protests outside the Parliament. Secondary industrial action (which is legal in Sweden) by the electricians' union strengthened the hand of the unions. Laval made an application to the Swedish Labour Court, claiming that the grounds for industrial action were illegal. The Swedish court referred the case to the European Court of Justice.

Prior to joining the EU, organised labour in Sweden had voiced concerns regarding the compatibility between Sweden's system of autonomous collective bargaining and the transposition of Community law. According to a provision of Swedish law, known as *Lex Britannia*, it is possible for Swedish unions to resort to industrial action with the aim of putting aside (inferior) foreign collective agreements and replacing these with Swedish collective agreements. Hence, this law permits the use of strike action by unions against foreign employers with a view to establishing a collective agreement and deterring the practice of social dumping. This action is legitimate under Swedish law, regardless of whether the employees of the enterprise are union members or not and regardless of whether the foreign employer has already signed a collective agreement in another country.

By now, the case was the focus of international attention, with fifteen member states submitting observations to the CJEU. The case divided the EU into two clear camps: according to observations submitted by the member states, wherein a) the 'old' member states' were sympathetic to the Swedish unions' position, a notable, yet unsurprising, exception being the UK; and b) the 'new' member states were supportive of the Latvian employers' position (Lindstrom 2010). The Court found that collective action was permissible, *provided* the action was in the general public interest. In this case, the CJEU found the trade unions' actions to be excessive and not in the public's general interest. Also, the Court ruled that the Posted Workers Directive range of protections – working time, holidays, minimum rates of pay, health and safety, non-discrimination and so on – established a *maximum*, as opposed to a minimum range of entitlements which the employer must honour. Moreover, trade unions in the host member state could not engage in collective action, even where the collective agreement was being undermined by foreign service-providers, as to do so would obstruct the *fundamental* freedom to provide services. This, in a perverse way, results in 'reverse discrimination', whereby firms registered and operating in the host state are legally bound to respect the entire collage of benefits and entitlements that have been achieved by workers' representatives over the years, while foreign service-providers can circumvent these 'constraints' by simply posting workers. As the industrial action was judged to be illegal, the unions involved were ordered by the Swedish court to pay damages of €54,000 to Laval un Partneri, which had, meanwhile, filed for bankruptcy. This was welcomed by Swedish employers' association and deplored by the Swedish unions.

According to the ETUC (2008b) the Laval judgment created 'intolerable uncertainty for unions involved in virtually any case of industrial action over migration and free movement, a naturally growing area for disputes as Europe integrates its labour and services market'. The European construction federation, EFBWW, stated (2008a), 'it is clear that the judgments may create very serious legal precedents at European level as to what Member States and trade unions are entitled to do to combat social dumping.' Labour lawyer Hepple (2010) expressed concern that the Laval, and other judgments, 'have the potential to reintroduce into common law systems, such as the Irish system, the Taff Vale principle,[4] whereby unions can be held liable for unlimited damages (and ultimately liquidation) for collective action which is found to be in breach of EU law'. In light of the *Rüffert* case, the ETUC (2008a) called the ruling 'destructive and damaging' and which equated to 'an open invitation for social dumping.' Mario Monti (2010) submitted a Report to the Commission President, Manuel Barroso, in which he noted that the debate surrounding the CJEU's rulings 'has the potential to alienate from the Single Market and the EU a segment of public opinion, workers' movements and trade unions, which has been over time a key supporter of economic integration'. Monti (2010) further noted that 'the Court's cases have exposed the fault lines that run between the single market and the social dimension at national level.'

Although the Laval case represents a worst-case scenario from a trade union perspective, it is nevertheless instructive as to the challenges faced by unions in the face of increased transnational pressures. Although one might recognise the strict legal interpretation adopted by the CJEU, the ruling did little to assuage concerns that traditional union strategies were insufficient and perhaps outdated when it came to dealing with unscrupulous employers who used cross-border practices to out-manoeuvre trade unions, side-step national legislation and under-bid (national) competition. Such fears were only accentuated in light of enlargement, on account of the wage- and social-gaps that existed between East and West in terms of labour costs and workers' rights (Vaughan-Whitehead, 2003; Marginson, 2006). The Laval Quartet served to highlight the limitations of the Posted Workers Directive and placed 'social dumping' and the 'country of origin' principle centre stage (again) (*see* Dølvik and Visser 2009). What quickly became clear is that national systems of industrial relations were no longer beyond the reach of the logic of the single market.

TRADE UNION COPING MECHANISMS: AN ANALYTICAL FRAMEWORK

Industrial relations systems and trade unions have come under increased pressure from challenges of a transnational nature (Baccaro and Howell 2017). These challenges intensified in the context of enlargement, with the free movement of labour and services, thereby posing difficult questions for trade unions. The term 'coping mechanism' is purposefully broad. This is because 'the characteristics of an industrial relations system are usually multi-dimensional' (Crouch 1993: 60). All too often, this complexity is not captured in a varieties of (welfare) capitalism approach, whose level of analysis remains at the national level. A study of industrial relations across 27 EU countries and nine sectors identifies a great degree of variation regarding *within* national models of industrial relations (Bechter, Brandl and Meardi 2012). Sectors that display most similarity across countries are those that are characterised by a transnational dynamic and EU regulations (*ibidem*). Hence, the term 'coping mechanism' is coined in the transnational context of intense labour mobility. Such mechanisms are contingent on history and are the product of concrete (class) struggles.

Two broad types of coping mechanisms can be identified: national, on the one hand, and European (or transnational) on the other. Table 7.2 provides a non-exhaustive overview. In no particular order, unions can pursue strategies through a) established collective bargaining mechanisms; b) autonomous action; c) the state; d) the EU; and e) transnational collective action (Menz 2005; Erne 2008; Bieler 2006). These can be sub-divided into two further categories: those that are regulatory or institutional in nature and those that are non-regulatory in nature. Here, the primary interest is in *regulatory* and *non-regulatory* coping mechanisms in the *national* context. In a multilevel governance context, coping mechanisms can also originate outside the context of the nation-state (such as the Posted Workers Directive). Such mechanisms, however, are incorporated into the national set of regulatory coping mechanisms and are therefore incorporated into the analysis. There are also transnational non-regulatory coping mechanisms, such as the mobilisations against the Services Directive; however, these are beyond the scope of this study.

Regulatory coping mechanisms include, first and foremost, systems of industrial relations, which, in the Irish and Italian cases, exist at the sectoral level and whose collective agreements are (*de facto*) legally binding. Whether unions availed themselves of EU transition agreements is also considered a regulatory coping mechanism (Donaghey and Teague 2006), as are protective measures extended to posted workers. Non-regulatory coping mechanisms place an emphasis on trade union agency. Such strategies are designed to address challenges arising from labour mobility and might require unions to think outside the box. Non-regulatory coping mechanisms include, above all, the unionisation of migrant workers. Ancillary strategies include conducting information campaigns on rights and so on to improve the living and working conditions of migrant workers; and even mass mobilisations to raise awareness and/or bring pressure on the government to enact regulatory provisions.

This part of the book is based on an extensive reading of general industrial relations literature as well as literature relevant to the construction sector, including trade union documentation and grey literature, which includes various reports by national and international organisations. Also, articles in the mainstream print media are used to determine the salience of incidences of social dumping. Finally, more than 25 semi-structured interviews were conducted with Irish and Italian construction union officials, some of whom have experience within the EFBWW.

INTRA-EU MIGRATION TO IRELAND AND ITALY

According to data from the Irish 2006 Census, new member state nationals constituted the largest group of migrant workers in Ireland. Between May and December 2004, 54,000 migrants from new member states arrived. Between

2004 and 2010, over half a million Personal Public Service Numbers (PPSNs) were issued to national citizens from the new member states (Doyle, Hughes and Wadensjö 2006; Barrell *et al.* 2007). Relatively speaking, this number is quite significant and unprecedented in Ireland's past. Of the total of EU10 citizens to whom PPSNs were issued, it is estimated that at least 70 per cent ended up in some form of formal employment (Hughes 2011: 12). In Italy, on the other hand, migrant labour constituted 9 per cent of total employment in 2005 and by 2008 this number had risen to 13 per cent (ISTAT 2008). The major increase, in recent years, is mainly due to the number of Romanians arriving in Italy (20.5 per cent of the total official population of foreigners in 2008), many of whom were, following accession in 2007, taken out of illegality (Caritas/Migrantes 2009: 86; ISTAT 2009: 5). With the Irish construction sector grinding to a halt due to the onset of the economic crisis in 2008–9, migrant workers were the first to lose their jobs as migration trends were reversed. This was not the case in Italy, where migration levels continued to increase in the years from 2007 to 2012. According to the OECD (2013b: 11) 'free circulation within European OECD countries rose in 2011 and is four times more common in relative terms than migration from elsewhere.' This suggests that the challenges associated with labour mobility remained longer and were more constant in the case of Italy; and, by 2012, EU27 migrant workers constituted the largest migrant group in Italy, at 27.4 per cent, within which Romanians were the largest sub-group (Caritas/Migrante 2012).

Ethnicity and gender can determine the sector and occupational role taken-up by migrants (Näre 2011). Unsurprisingly, given the labour-intensive nature of the work, male migrant workers tend to be concentrated in the construction sector. As described in greater detail in the following chapter, Ireland was experiencing strong economic growth and a considerable number of EU migrant workers found employment in the construction sector (OECD 2006). Addressing these shortages was fundamental to ensuring continued economic growth, which, of course, was considered to be in the 'national interest'. The construction sector was an important sector in the overall economy, and it was considered important that high levels of productivity be maintained (DKM, various years). In other words, the Celtic Tiger must be fed.

Increased access to cheap credit transformed Ireland's residential mortgage market, with the total level of mortgage debt growing from over €47.2 billion in 2002 to over €139.8 billion in 2007, an increase of almost 200 per cent (Kelly 2009). Lax planning laws coupled with cheap credit fuelled an unprecedented construction boom. Construction accounted for 5.5 per cent of GNP in 1996 and by 2006 this had risen to 10.3 per cent (DKM, various years). The number of new houses granted planning permission increased by over 133 per cent from 1997 to 2004. In the same period, planning permissions granted for new apartments more than quadrupled. Also, public capital expenditure on housing more than trebled. Regarding non-residential construction, activity also increased significantly on the previous year: roads, an increase of 18 per cent; airport development, an increase of 115 per cent; and energy, an increase of 51 per cent (DKM, various years).

Table 7.2 Trade unions' coping mechanisms

	Regulatory	**Non-regulatory**
National	▪ Institutionalised industrial relations system ▪ Use of EU (temporary) transitional agreements ▪ Co-operating with labour law enforcement agencies ▪ Extending protective measures to posted workers ▪ Addressing migrant workers' needs in collective bargaining	▪ Unionisation of migrant workers ▪ Information campaigns on rights, etc. for migrant workers ▪ Integration of migrant workers into the union structure ▪ Creation of external organisation to deal with migrants' specific needs ▪ Lobbying national government ▪ Mass mobilisations
Transnational	▪ Joint mutual assistance funds. ▪ Secondary EU legislation (e.g. Posted Workers Directive) ▪ Collective bargaining at sectoral level	▪ Co-operation with unions in sending country ▪ EU information campaigns (e.g., www.posted-workers.eu) ▪ creation of cross-border unions (e.g., European Migrant Workers Union) ▪ Co-ordinated mobilisations

Source: author's own

The number of construction firms with 20 or more employees almost doubled between 1997 and 2002. Activity in the sector increased year on year from 2002 to 2008 and employment in construction rose by 40 per cent over the same period. The sector accounted for 13 per cent of total employment in 2007. This compares to an EU average of 8 per cent. One of the greatest challenges facing the construction sector was meeting the demand for labour. The enlargement of the EU was seen as an opportunity to address labour shortages in the construction sector (DKM various years; Forfás 2005). The relatively higher wages in the sector – the average hourly earnings increased from €16.70 in March 2004 to €18.61 in September 2005 – were, 'expected to attract migrant workers *and* to moderate earnings growth' (NESC 2006: 40, emphasis added). Thus, the 2004 enlargement and decision not to impose restrictions not only provided the Irish employers with access to a massive supply of labour but also provided a market-oriented solution to wage growth, which is key to 'competitive corporatism' and (more importantly) competitiveness (OECD 2006: 110). In 2008, migrants comprised 17 per cent of the Irish construction workforce, which constituted almost one in seven of the total workforce (CSO 2007a). While the majority occupied positions in the lower tiers of the construction sector, it is worth mentioning that not all migrants ended up in low-skill jobs. A number of skilled and high-skilled positions such as carpenters and plumbers, engineers, architects and quantity surveyors were also filled by migrants (Bobek *et al.* 2008).

Although activity in the Italian construction sector never quite reached the heady heights of the Irish sector, the picture is similar, in many ways. A migrant workforce was the lifeblood of a strong construction sector. Similarly to Ireland, the majority of migrant workers were to be found in the low-skilled tiers of the sector (Galossi 2011). Even prior to eastern enlargement, European migrant labour was an integral component of the Italian construction sector (Strozza 2004). Reports by *Camera di Commercio di Verona* (2003) and *Camera di Commercio di Roma* (2004) highlight the significant presence of Romanian businesses (c.a. 65 per cent) operating in the construction sector. By the end of 2007, there were about 16,000 Romanian constructions business and self-employed workers in Italy (Caritas/Migrantes 2008). A number of insightful ethnographic studies highlight how these developments placed greater demand on undeclared labour from Romania, as employers sought to circumvent Italian regulations such as in regard to contributions. (Anghel 2008: 794). As Ban (2009: 140) notes, 'the most lucrative headhunting business was in the recruiting of skilled and semi-skilled construction workers (such as master masons, concrete structure engineers, or licensed truck mechanics and drivers), because in the Italian construction sector the skilled and especially the semi-skilled were in high demand.'

As can be seen from Figure 7.1, the Italian and Irish construction sectors were healthy in the 2000s. The spectacular rise and equally spectacular decline of the Irish construction sector illustrates the dangers of boom–bust cycles, while, on the other hand, the Italian share of construction remained constant *vis-à-vis* economic performance (IMF 2013). Ireland's unprecedented experience with migration was followed by another development that was unprecedented not only in Ireland's history but also in the history of post-war Europe. I am referring to the global financial crisis, whose impact on Ireland was compounded by a dysfunctional banking system and a housing bubble. Between 2007 and 2009, Ireland's GNP declined by nearly 20 per cent: an unparalleled decline in the post-war order. Initially, the large migrant workforce acted as quasi-buffer against the crisis, as EU migrants lost their jobs at a much faster rate than Irish workers. Many of these lost jobs were in construction (Hughes 2011: 15). Notwithstanding this dramatic fall, Irish construction unions faced challenges on different fronts. In Italy, the challenges never really went away, despite the financial crisis. Furthermore, the Italian sector was more integrated into the European market. In other words, the transnational dynamic is more visible in Italy. Following on from this, one could surmise that the potential for social dumping remains greater in Italy as the transnational element is more persistent across time.

Figure 7.1 Advanced economies: construction's share (as per cent of GDP)

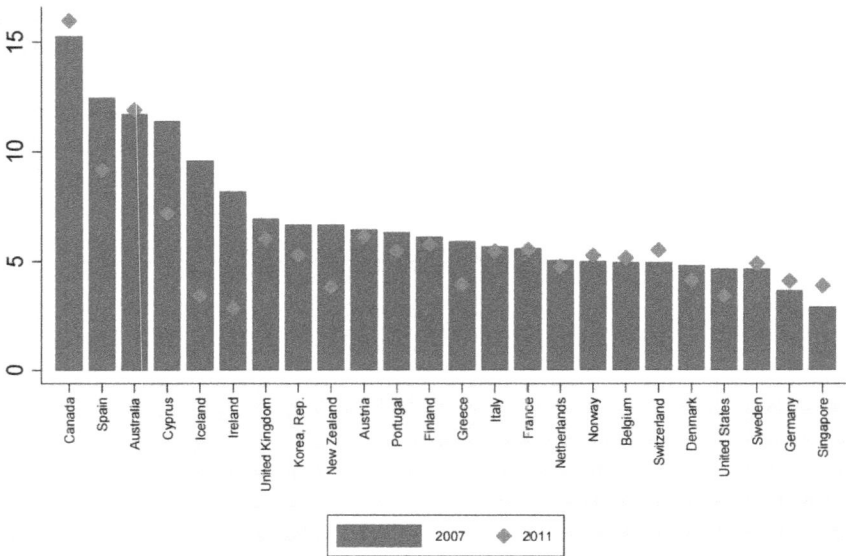

Source: IMF (2013)

REGULATORY COPING MECHANISMS OF ITALIAN AND IRISH UNIONS: FIT FOR PURPOSE?

How do trade unions engage with intra-EU transnational labour migration in a post-enlargement context and what is the scope for strategic intervention? Penninx and Roosblad (2000) identify a number of dilemmas facing unions, such as the question of whether immigration should be resisted, that is, whether to lobby the government for greater restriction. This can also be conceptualised as a regulatory coping mechanism (*see* Table 7.2), albeit a temporary one in an EU context. Upon the arrival of migrant workers, a second dilemma arises. Here, unions can either include or exclude migrant workers. This is an example of a non-regulatory coping mechanism and refers primarily to organising, which I discuss in the following section. Here, I am primarily concerned with the formal embedding institutions, namely, industrial relations systems.

The question of 'immigration is strangely neglected by industrial relations scholars' (McGovern 2007: 218) in favour of broader questions such as economic internationalisation. Consequently, there is very little literature on the question of industrial relations and migration. By comparison, there is a burgeoning literature on the question of organising and union 'revitalisation' (Gall 2009). The objective here has less to do with explaining why it is that certain unions adopted particular responses and more to do with the effectiveness of union strategies in offsetting potential negative effects associated with labour mobility. To this end, I assess how Irish and Italian unions, generally, and construction unions, specifically, retained control over the labour market with reference to social dumping practices. Unlike Lillie and Greer (2007), who use wage developments as an indicator to determine the degree of control, I use the frequency of social dumping, which is a better and more reliable indicator. The greater the frequency of reported social dumping incidences, the less capacity to police local labour markets.

As in Italy, there is a long tradition of collective bargaining in the Irish construction sector. The 'centralised pluralism' and 'fragmented unity' of the Irish and Italian trade union systems respectively is also mirrored at the sectoral level. In other words, whilst the Italian unions are divided along different lines, these divisions are (most of the time) bridgeable. This in itself strengthens the unions' capacity to police the labour market. The Irish unions, on the other hand, cohere under one entity, in the construction sector. It is an ICTU body called the Construction Industry Committee;[5] however, inter-union rivalry prevails. Notwithstanding this difference, the 'functional equivalence' (Ragin 1987: 48; *see also* Hyman 2001c: 214–17) between Irish and Italian unions facilitates comparison. Based on an extensive reading of general industrial relations literature and that relevant to the construction sector, including trade union documentation and grey literature, eight criteria have been selected against which it is possible to determine the robustness of unions' regulatory coping mechanisms in a transnational context. The criteria are i) collective bargaining extension mechanisms; ii) liability in the subcontracting chain; iii) measures regarding social payments; iv) vertical articulation mechanisms; v) presence of posted workers; vi) incorporation of migrant workers' demands into the collective bargaining framework; and vii) additional regulatory measures. The eighth criterion is restricting the free movement of labour. I will discuss this first before turning my attention to the others; however, due to space constraints, I will focus only on the most important factors,[6] which are critical to ensuring a union's capacity to police local labour markets.

Although the possibility of state control over borders has, in the context of the EU, diminished considerably, there is, during periods of enlargement, a temporary regulatory measure available.[7] Hence, trade unions could pressurise their governments to avail themselves of these measures (*see* Donaghey and Teague 2006). While this can be seen as an example of a regulatory coping strategy by unions, there are perverse results, because such measures only preclude the free movement of labour and not the free movement of services! In other words, the scope for social dumping remains, as the posting of workers is still possible (*see below*). As per Figure 7.2, the incidences of posting are greater in Italy than in Ireland. If, as much of the research demonstrates, the posting of workers has become synonymous with an employers' strategy to circumvent restrictive measures and social dumping (Dølvik and Visser 2009; Wagner 2014), then we would expect to see more instances of social dumping in Italy.

For the 2004 enlargement, Italy, with the support of construction unions, placed restrictions on the free movement of labour (not services) and continued with a permit system based on employers' predictions. In 2006, there was an additional increase in the number of permits issued but, seeing that the number of applications was lower than those allocated, the Prodi government applied the free movement rules at the end of 2006 (Barbagli 2007). The Irish government, along with the UK and Sweden, placed no restrictions on labour mobility in 2004. Here, the decision was a unilateral one taken by the government and the unions were not even consulted. What is striking is that this unilateral decision was taken by the government against the backdrop of almost two decades of social concertation. However, for the 2007 enlargement, the Irish government did impose restrictions on labour mobility. ICTU (2006) were formally in favour of this (temporary) national re-regulation strategy, although there were some internal dissenting voices. The Italian government, on the other hand, adopted a quasi-liberal approach (OECD 2012). In other words, a quota system was maintained; however, the system was streamlined for certain 'strategic sectors', such as construction, domestic and personal care and agriculture (Makovec 2009). Therefore, Romanians were indirectly shown preferential treatment as, traditionally, Romanian workers were concentrated particularly in construction and domestic care. By January of 2012, both Italy and Ireland had applied free movement rules.

Whilst state-led restrictions are considered a regulatory coping mechanism to counter potential ill-effects resulting from economic internationalisation, these can only ever be temporary. Typically, unions' primary coping mechanism is the industrial relations systems, which are the product of national struggles and were created, *inter alia*, to ensure industrial and social peace (Crouch 1993; McCarthy 1973c). Typically, Ireland is considered to have a voluntaristic industrial relations system (Roche 1989) and therefore does not have a strong system of sectoral bargaining. However, following a 'decade of upheaval' in the 1960s (McCarthy 1973c), a collective bargaining structure emerged in the construction sector, establishing the Registered Employment Agreement[8] (REA); the REAs were legally binding. Hence, the Irish construction sector is the exception which qualifies the voluntaristic rule. The Construction Industry Committee (CIC) of ICTU represents the construction unions, of which there are six in total (SIPTU, Connect, Unite, UCATT,[9] OPATSI, BATU) while the Construction Industry Federation (CIF) and Irish Business and Employers Confederation (IBEC) represents the employers. The number of unions has hindered their effectiveness in industrial relations[10] and in 2002 tensions came to a head when three[11] of the six unions in the CIC refused to participate in the collective bargaining round.

Collective bargaining in the Italian construction sector is rather unusual in that it takes place at both the national level *and* the regional level. The logic for this two-level structure is a) the large number of SMEs in the sector; and b) the geographical diversity of Italy and different building traditions. Territorial-level bargaining can cater for these regional idiosyncrasies. The actors involved in the collective bargaining process are the National Association of Construction Industries (ANCE), on the employers' side; on the trade unions' side, there are the respective construction federations of the CGIL, CISL and UIL. In the same order, these are FILLEA,[12] FILCA[13] and FENEAL.[14]

As can be seen from Figure 7.2, the number of posted workers, as expected, is clearly higher in Italy, where restrictions were imposed. Contrary to expectations, however, the level of social dumping compared to Ireland is significantly lower (*see below*). This can, partly at least, be explained by the capacity of Italian unions to relocalise, embed or domesticate transnational socioeconomic processes. As can be seen from Table 7.3 there are important differences between the Italian and the Irish coping mechanisms. A blow-by-blow account is not possible here; instead, I will focus on key differences between the Irish and Italian industrial relations context. Here, I contend that an initiative introduced by the Italian unions to combat illegal social dumping by organised crime in the construction sector (interview with union officials) has rather unwittingly had a broader impact on operations in the sector, and it has effectively rendered social dumping practices associated with labour mobility all the more difficult for duplicitous firms.

Figure 7.2 Postings by destination country, 2007–9 (in thousands)

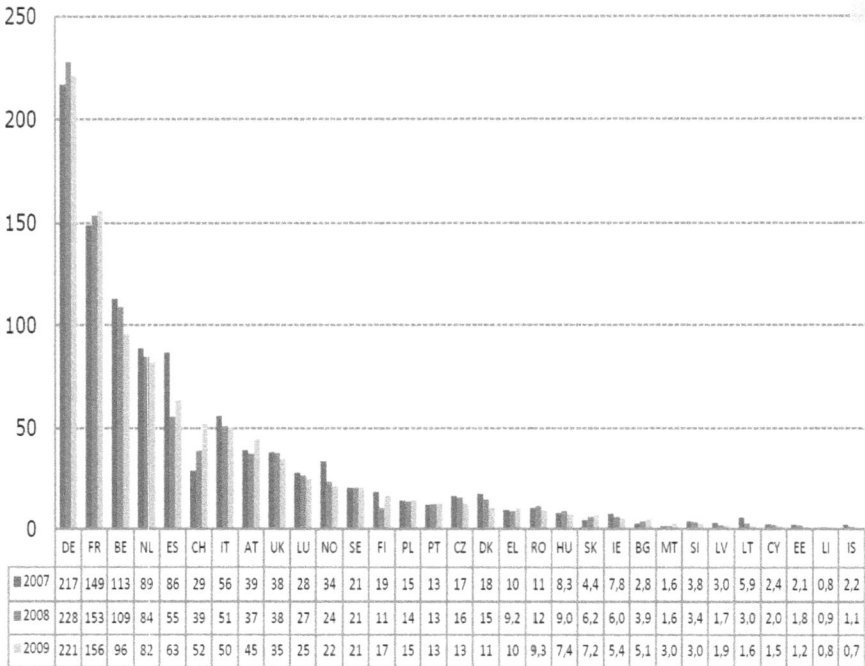

	DE	FR	BE	NL	ES	CH	IT	AT	UK	LU	NO	SE	FI	PL	PT	CZ	DK	EL	RO	HU	SK	IE	BG	MT	SI	LV	LT	CY	EE	LI	IS
2007	217	149	113	89	86	29	56	39	38	28	34	21	19	15	13	17	18	10	11	8,3	4,4	7,8	2,8	1,6	3,8	3,0	5,9	2,4	2,1	0,8	2,2
2008	228	153	109	84	55	39	51	37	38	27	24	21	11	14	13	16	15	9,2	12	9,0	6,2	6,0	3,9	1,6	3,4	1,7	3,0	2,0	1,8	0,9	1,1
2009	221	156	96	82	63	52	50	45	35	25	22	21	17	15	13	13	11	10	9,3	7,4	7,2	5,4	5,1	3,0	3,0	1,9	1,6	1,5	1,2	0,8	0,7

Source: EC (2011)

Italy is only one of five[15] member states that implements measures regarding social fund payments (Jorens, Peters and Houwerzijl 2012). In the 2000s, the Italian rules governing the awarding of contracts, public *and* private, were made stricter. The contractor (and subcontractor) must produce a *Documento Unico di Regolarità Contributiva* ['single insurance contribution payment certificate'] or DURC as it is more commonly referred to. The DURC is a certificate that demonstrates that a construction company is tax compliant and that all social contributions have been paid in full. In other words, the terms and conditions of the collective bargaining agreements in Italy have been honoured. Otherwise, companies are excluded from participating in calls for (public) tenders. The DURC is issued once the *Istituto Nazionale Previdenza Sociale* [National Social Security Institute] (INPS), the *Istituto Nazionale per l'Assicurazione Contro gli Infortuni sul Lavoro* [Italian Workers' Compensation Authority] (INAIL) and the *Casse Edili* [a special construction workers' fund] are satisfied that a construction firm's affairs are all in order. The latter is a bipartite organisation set up by the sectoral trade unions and employer organisations and it is this body that officially releases the DURC. Here, the competent *Cassa Edile* checks the regular contributory position of the company; the inspection covers all of the company's operational building sites and the workers employed in the region. If the company is in compliance and not included in the national database of irregular companies, the *Cassa Edile* then issues the DURC.

Where a negative assessment prevails, the DURC will indicate that the company has a status of contributory irregularity with INPS, INAIL and *Casse Edili*. Consequently, the company will then lose any public contracts awarded, will not be allowed to enter into contracting or subcontracting contracts (on account of joint responsibility), and will not be entitled to payment or final payment. Regarding private works, the qualification linked to the building license will be suspended. Hence, the DURC system prevents unfair competition resulting from the use of non-registered (migrant) workers; enables contractors to certify their regular status for the assignment of public and private works by submitting a single document; and rewards companies that have been complying with the rules.

The DURC also applies to foreign companies, which must provide equivalent documentation from their relevant national body responsible for social contribution payments. Where there are no such funds or obligations on firms in the country of origin, the foreign undertakings must pay contributions to the *Cassa Edile*. Hence, foreign firms cannot be exempted on the grounds that there is no equivalent construction fund in their country of origin.

The certificate was originally introduced in the early 2000s to tackle the level of undeclared work in the sector as well as the problem of organised crime, which had infiltrated the industry (CNEL 2008). While initially introduced at the regional level, the DURC was subsequently applied nationwide. Between 2002 and 2007, the DURC was continuously tweaked and updated. Following a joint statement signed by the Italian social partners in October 2010, the requirements for a DURC became more stringent for works with a value equal to or greater than €70,000. From 2012 on, in order to acquire a DURC, employers have also had to demonstrate that the proportion of the total value of the work constituted by labour costs is not less than a 'fairness index' (*indice di congruità*). Regarding public contracts, there are even more stringent rules. The fairness index represents an opportunity to counteract social dumping by companies and to award contracts to more virtuous companies. This contrasts with Ireland, which has a liberal procurement regime in which tenders are generally awarded on the basis of the most economic advantage, with little or no consideration given to employment-based social indicators (Kunzlik 2013). Similarly, the subcontracting chain is weak, insofar as the main contractor can turn a blind eye to unscrupulous practices further down. In short, there is no joint responsibility in Ireland (Jorens, Peters and Houwerzijl 2012). Together, the DURC and the joint liability strengthens the regulatory coping mechanisms of the Italian unions, which goes towards curbing the incidences of social dumping. However, these alone are insufficient and are best accompanied by non-regulatory coping mechanisms.

NON-REGULATORY COPING MECHANISMS OF ITALIAN AND IRISH UNIONS: A BRAVE NEW WORLD

A non-exhaustive list of non-regulatory coping mechanisms includes: information campaigns on rights and so on for migrant workers; integration of migrant workers into the union structure; creation of external organisation to deal with migrants' specific needs; mass mobilisations and/or strikes; and, of course, unionisation of migrant workers. As membership-based organisations, it is widely argued that investing in organising can result in achieving three interrelated objectives for unions: union renewal; politicisation of the rank and file; and enhanced labour market control (*see* Frege and Kelly 2004). It is the enhanced labour market control aspect that is of primary interest here, although I will return to the politicisation of rank and file in the following chapter. The organising model is associated more with liberally oriented economies, in which the 'curse of institutional security' (Hassel 2007) is absent. According to this logic, we would expect to find a greater emphasis on organising migrant labour in Ireland than in Italy. Again, the objective of this analysis is not to identify whether social, political or economic conditions facilitate, or constrain, migrant unionisation (*see* Milkman 2000: 2–3). Nor is it to explain why unions pursue the particular strategies they do towards migrant labour (*see* Marino 2012). Instead, the emphasis is on capacity to police local labour markets and prevent social dumping.

Table 7.3 Synthetic overview of Italian and Irish construction unions' regulatory coping mechanisms

	Ireland	Italy
Level of sectoral agreement	National (REA) 1960s – 2013 Struck out *McGowan and Others v Labour Court*	National and territorial 1960s – Present day
Legal extension (*erga omnes*)	Yes	*de facto erga omnes* (Treu, 2011)
Liability in subcontracting chain	'approved subcontractors' (section 10 REA) No liability extended (Jorens et al., 2012) Soft law	DURC (2004) – INPS, INAIL, Casse Edili Joint responsibility (Jorens et al., 2012), extended to foreign service providers Hard law
Vertical articulation mechanisms	No (Geary, 2007)	Yes, *Rappresentanze Sindacali Unitarie*
Transposition of PWD	Broad (van Hoek and Houwerzijl, 2011; CLR, 2011)	Broad (van Hoek and Houwerzijl, 2011; CLR, 2011)
Other	Minimum wage; Safe Pass	Bilateral agreements with French, German and Austrian social funds; Incorporation of migrant workers' interests into collective bargaining framework

Source: Own

Some migration scholars speak of migratory regimes and their qualitative characteristics (*see* Pott *et al.* 2016). By tracing the migration regimes relevant to Ireland and Italy, it is possible to determine that they have changed over the years. Different migratory regimes generate different challenges with regards to the terms and conditions of the employment relationship. In other words, the challenges associated with clandestine migration differ from those of a permit system regime, which differs again from issues accompanying a more liberal or quasi-liberal regime. Hence, different migratory regimes necessitate different responses from the trade union movement. Naturally, there are pros and cons to each migratory regime and different regimes can also coexist and overlap. Here, unions' prior experience of previous migration regimes might be beneficial in tackling questions associated with successive regimes.

Union strategies can be divided into top-down and bottom-up strategies. Whereas top-down approaches come from the confederal level and are high-profile, with the objective of raising public awareness and, in particular, migrants' awareness of their rights and entitlements, bottom-up strategies have to do primarily with organising migrant labour and are led more by individual unions. Despite their reputation for being inimical to trade unionism (Castles and Kosack 1973), there is little empirical evidence to support the idea that immigrants are 'unorganisable' (*see* Turner *et al.* 2008). The objective here is not to explain why differences emerged between Irish and Italian unions; instead, it is to set out how historical contingencies shaped the context in which unions found themselves. Whilst there are contextual similarities between Ireland and Italy, insofar as both countries experienced post-enlargement labour mobility, there are historical differences regarding migratory regimes. A number of scholars (for example, Perrett *et al.* 2012; Kjeldstadli 2015) have described the relationship between trade unions and migrant workers as a learning experience and one of trial and error in terms of strategies. As can be seen from Table 7.4, the key difference between Ireland and Italy is that, since the late 1980s, Italy has experienced (clandestine) migration, which originates from outside the EU. Clearly, this is still an issue today. The origins of this trend can be traced back to the late 1980s and early 1990s, with the collapse of communism in Eastern Europe and the conflicts in the Balkans. Together, these led to anomalous movements of people to Italy (Fassmann and Münz 1994). Although the numbers of these later levelled off, the migratory flow of Romanians to Italy remained constant and circular (Perrotta 2011; Ban 2009).

Table 7.4 Overview of Italian and Irish migratory regimes

	Italy	Ireland
Decade	**Type of migration regime**	
1980s	Clandestine migration	Net emigration
1990s	Permit system, clandestine migration	Permit system, return migration
2000s	(Quasi-)liberal regime (intra-EU)	Liberal regime (intra-EU)

Source: author's own

Since the late 1980s, migration has become a more structural phenomenon in Italy. The CGIL, and later CISL and UIL, have been particularly active in engaging with migrants, regardless of their origin. Initiatives vary from providing advice to migrant communities on a broad array of issues to pressuring governments to undertake regularisations as a strategy to combat irregular employment. The first *centro lavoratori stranieri* [centre for foreign workers] was established in Bologna by the CGIL in 1987. In an interview, its founder described to the author the poor conditions that clandestine migrants had to endure. Many lived in tented communities, existing on the fringes of the economy and often being exploited in the (informal) labour market. Since, CISL and UIL have created similar bodies (ANOLF[16] and UNITI[17,] respectively), which offer social and legal services. Essentially, these structures carry out the work of public offices while, at the same time, putting unions face-to-face with what are often the most vulnerable people on the labour market and in society. Furthermore, this meant that the Italian unions already had structures in place to meet the challenges associated with intra-EU liberal migration, which initially had a clandestine element. That said, Italy's migratory regime can better be described as quasi-liberal, albeit temporarily: during the 2004 enlargement, the Italian government, at the behest of unions and employers, availed themselves of the Transitory Agreements, which limited the free movement of workers *but not services.*

Once the liberal migratory regime was unilaterally introduced by the Irish government in 2004, the Irish unions were like rabbits caught in the headlights of enlargement. Prior to 2004, little effort was made by trade unions to actively recruit new migrant workers (Arqueros-Fernández 2011). If anything, ICTU adopted an instrumental stance on migrant labour, whereby 'exploitation of a vulnerable group undermines pay and conditions of indigenous workers and is unfair and uncompetitive towards decent employers who comply with the law' (ICTU 2005: 7). This stance, coupled with a good deal of complacency, drew criticism from civil society groups, such as the Migrant Rights Centre (MRC). As an ex-MRC official, and current SIPTU official stated in an interview.

> In the early 2000s, MRC was dealing with a lot of immigration specific matters, processing of permits, etc., however, the more significant problems were around exploitation and the workplace, so the MRC adapted itself to deal with that and tried to talk to the trade unions about it but there wasn't much engagement, very minimal at best ...We [MRC] started to campaign for some sectors that had some potential for unionisation, so the first big success was in the mushroom sector ... and then we brought SIPTU in (MRC 2004).

Eventually, in 2005, ICTU launched an 'outreach' programme with the objective of addressing the question of declining trade union density by recruiting new members, especially in occupations in which the number of migrant workers was disproportionately large, such as construction. Unions, at the biennial Delegates' Conference, decided to reconcile ongoing turf wars and work in co-ordination to pool resources. The Conference report was especially optimistic: 'Congress has put a strategic shape on its activities and this should equip us to deal with whatever challenges emerge in the future' (ICTU

2007). This new 'strategic shape' referred to a new union 'outreach' service, which was publicised through a top-down media advertising campaign, providing information, advice and support to workers through the use of a free phone number, e-mail and call-in centres. Five unions, including SIPTU and Connect, were to participate in the initiative, which was seen as being complementary to the existing recruitment strategies of the individual unions.

In the Irish case, the bottom-up approach came from the individual unions with greater resources, such as SIPTU. The smaller unions, such as Connect, did not have such resources at hand (Krings 2007). With the exception of Unite, unions in Ireland and Italy hired migrant workers to work within the union, in an attempt to reach out to migrant workers. Unite's exception is at odds with the union's legacy, which advocated an organising model over a servicing model prior to SIPTU's change of direction in the mid-2000s. Furthermore, this jars with the strategy adopted by Unite in the UK (*see* Simms 2010). With regard to the Italian unions, progress in relation to migrant workers was more advanced, particularly at the confederal level. One of the Italian interviewees even went from '[clandestine] babysitter to confederal secretary'.

Between 2006 and 2008, SIPTU invested considerable resources in adapting the union to the challenges of a modern and dynamic labour market. A *Guide for Shop Stewards* placed emphasis on the importance of recruiting migrant workers as 'the first step to protecting workers' rights' (SIPTU 2006: 18). The services of Mike Crosby, known for strategic organising campaigns in the US and Australia, were recruited to conduct an internal review of the union. Crosby advocated those increased resources be used for organising. SIPTU went about becoming an organising union instead of a servicing union and targeted specific sectors where there was a concentration of migrant workers: namely, contract cleaning, construction and hotel and catering. The union also set up an organising and campaigning unit and recruited individuals who had previous experience working on migration-related issues (for example, the MRC). With regards to progress, an official commented when interviewed that 'SIPTU as a union is going through a transition.'

Finally, at the European level there is the European Federation of Building and Woodworkers (EFBWW); however, not all unions are 'plugged in' at the European level. Those that are, however, used these opportunities to either anticipate future challenges and prepare or even forge stronger linkages with trade unions in migrants' countries of origin. For instance, SIPTU, in 2006, signed a co-operation deal of mutual support with Polish union, NSZZ Solidarność, which involved mutual recognition of union membership. This would not have materialised were SIPTU and Solidarność officials not engaging with each other at the European level. Connect and Unite, on the other hand and rather tellingly, did not engage at the European level. This contrasts with the Italian construction unions, which are very integrated into the European trade union structures generally and the EFBWW in particular. At the time of this research, Domenico Pesenti of FILCA was General Secretary of the EFBWW. From Table 7.5, the involvement of the Italian unions in all European trade union structures at the European level is very clear. This involvement alone would be insufficient in confronting contemporary challenges and in combating social dumping threats; however, the Italian unions' engagement at the European level is, as demonstrated above, buttressed by robust regulatory and non-regulatory coping mechanisms at the national level. In the Irish case, the presence of unions, other than SIPTU (and public sector unions) and the level of engagement in European trade union federations by Irish unions generally, and Connect and Unite in particular, is non-existent. This lack of involvement is noteworthy and can partly be explained by the historical legacy of parochialism and lack of internationalism that pervaded Irish trade unionism throughout much of the twentieth century.

Table 7.5 Engagement of union officials in European federal structures

Federation	Italy	Ireland
EFBWW (Construction)	FILCA-CISL, FeNEAL-UIL, FILLEA-CGIL	SIPTU
EFFAT (Food, Agriculture, and Tourism)	FAI-CISL, FLAI-CGIL, FISASCAT-CISL, FILCAMS-CGIL, UGC-CISL, UILA-UIL, UIMEC-UIL	SIPTU
INDUSTRIALL (Manufacturing and Energy)	FILCTEM-CGIL, FIOM-CGIL, FEMCA-CISL, FIM-CISL, M-UIL, TEC-UIL	SIPTU
EPSU (Public Services)	FPS-CISL, FEMCA-CISL, FILCTEM-CGIL, FLAEI-CISL, FP-CGIL, PA-UIL	CPSU, ESU, FÓRSA, INMO, PSEU, SIPTU, AHCPS,
ETF (Transport)	FAI-CISL, FIT-CISL, FILT-CGIL, FLAI-CGIL, UIL-TRASPORTI	SIPTU, FÓRSA
ETUCE (Education)	SCUOLA-CISL, FLC-CGIL, SCUOLA-UIL	ASTI, IFUT, INTO, TUI

Source: author's own

From the above, it should be clear that the Italian industrial relations system is more robust than the Irish equivalent. Here, the DURC has been critical in combating social dumping and illicit work practices in the construction sector, which is characterised by a strong transnational dimension. Also, Italian unions are more experienced with the phenomenon of (clandestine) migration and have a stronger presence within the EFBWW. Together, the Italian unions are better equipped to deal with challenges arising from transnational labour markets.

INCIDENCES OF SOCIAL DUMPING POST-2004

Incidents of social dumping were experienced in Italy and Ireland post-2004. However, the extent and frequency of such cases in Ireland was alarming. A number of high-profile social dumping cases came to light in the post-2004 period. Two in particular captured the public imagination, namely, the GAMA and the Irish Ferries cases. In February 2005, Socialist Party TD Joe Higgins told the Irish Parliament that GAMA construction company was 'importing' Turkish workers and only paid them about €2–€3 per hour, in breach of the minimum wage law. The workers were required to work 'grotesque' hours, were accommodated in company barracks and their situation was a modern version of 'bonded labour'. The case highlighted the sophisticated means that multinationals used to dupe workers out of their wages and engage in social dumping.

In November 2005, a 'deeply entrenched dispute' developed between Irish Ferries and SIPTU, which 'threatened to derail the national social partnership process' (Eurofound 2005). Irish Ferries sought to replace 543 workers with eastern European agency crew, and to reflag its vessels to Cyprus. SIPTU mobilised: as a result, Irish Ferries vessels were laid up in Welsh and Irish ports for almost three weeks. In December 2005, on the back of the Irish Ferries debacle, ICTU organised the largest national demonstration seen in almost thirty years. The day of protest saw mobilisations in Cork, Galway, Limerick, Waterford, Sligo, Athlone and Rosslare. The demonstrations also had a transnational dimension, as a number of British unions, at the request of the International Transport Workers Federation, also demonstrated in Holyhead, Wales. Keen not to demonise either the EU or the migrant workers, ICTU's leading banner simply read 'Equal Rights for Equal Workers'. The class-based solidarisitic logic expressed here differs greatly from the logic of 'enlightened self-interest' that ICTU (2005) had previously adopted (*see also* Krings 2008).

Whilst the GAMA and Irish Ferries cases captured the public imagination, a plethora of micro-level social dumping cases escaped public attention. One in particular is briefly worth mentioning, as it concerns the union Connect. In 2004, Lentjes, a German contractor, won a €380 million contract to refurbish an ESB power plant in Moneypoint, Co. Clare. Polish firm ZRE Katowice (ZRE) had an Irish subsidiary (ZRE) which was subcontracted to carry out scaffolding work at the site. ZRE employed 200 workers, all of whom were from Poland. The workers were earning one-third the minimum hourly rate for the construction sector. In addition, for a number of weeks, the workers had not received any pay. Once aware of these malpractices, the German firm terminated its contract with ZRE, on the grounds that the company was not complying with Irish law. Upon learning of these grievances, Connect balloted its members, who voted in favour of industrial action. Despite the threat of an injunction by the power plant company, Connect issued a strike notice to Lentjes and ZRE; however, the Irish subsidiarity had rather cynically gone into liquidation, leaving the workers high and dry.

The union demanded the workers, many of whom were not union members, be paid wages owed and additional entitlements such as holiday pay. In addition, the union insisted the workers be re-employed by the new subcontractor. With the parties unable to resolve the dispute, discussions were brought before the Labour Relations Commission. The main point of contention was who would pay the workers what was due to them. Both the semi-state ESB and Lentjes argued that they were not responsible for paying the workers, while ZRE declared they were financially incapable of paying. After four days of deliberation, agreement was reached. Lentjes was to pay €600,000 towards the amount owed and the remainder was to come from the Irish Insolvency Fund. The workers received a letter from the Chairman of ZRE, offering flights home and a job with ZRE in Poland. Whilst the outcome was a positive one, the union's decision to call a strike was a risky one. As we saw in the Laval case, the CJEU condemned strike action seeking to prevent social dumping on the grounds that it inhibited the efficient functioning of the market. Also, it is not plausible to call a strike every time there is an episode of social dumping.

There have also been incidences of social dumping in Italy; however, by comparison, these are at a much lower level and less frequent. There is not the space here to detail the minutiae of these incidents (*see* Golden 2016), other than to say that the Irish construction sector has been disproportionately affected by social dumping. Unfortunately, this is especially the case in Ireland. One corroboration of this point is the case load of the Labour Court (2006), which, in the post-enlargement context, increased by 64 per cent, with a large number of the cases alleging breaches of the REA in construction. According to a Labour Relations Commission (2005) report:

> The positive increase in our population has not always been accompanied by a seamless introduction to a positive and encouraging employment situation. For some employees, it has been a difficult transition resulting in very unacceptable working environments. Such experiences reflect in a negative way upon our treatment of vulnerable migrant workers and are unacceptable in a society that aspires and legislates for equity of treatment for all.

The non-regulatory coping mechanisms of Irish and Italian unions are synthetically displayed in Table 7.6. Fundamentally, the Italian non-regulatory coping mechanisms provided unions with an enhanced capacity to police the labour market. Here, the experiences of the late 1980s and 1990s stood the unions in good stead and ensured a stronger presence on the ground. This differs significantly from the Irish experience. Unfortunately, there is no reliable data on the unionisation rate of migrant workers in the Irish and Italian construction unions; however, if we take sectoral union density as an indicator, it suggests that more migrant workers are represented by unions in Italy than in Ireland. Perhaps this is on account of the Italian bi-partite *cassa edile* system (a special construction workers' fund), which ensures that employers are unaware of whether (migrant) workers are members of a union or not. Hence, the fear factor is removed. From the 'plus' signs, we can see that the Italian unions, whether at the confederal or sectoral level, are stronger when it comes to what I term non-regulatory coping mechanisms. A crude indicator is the level of integration of migrant workers into trade union structures. This is greater in Italy (*see* Golden 2016); however, SIPTU is developing this capacity.

Table 7.6 Synthetic overview of construction unions' non-regulatory coping mechanisms

Non-regulatory coping mechanisms	Italian unions			Irish unions		
	Sectoral union density 56% (2009)[a]			Sectoral union density 22% (2007)[b]		
	FILLEA	FILCA	FENEAL	SIPTU	Connect	Unite
Information campaigns on rights	++	++	++	++	++	+
Creation of external migrant body	++	++	++	–	–	–
Unionisation of migrants	++	++	++	+–	+	+
Integration of migrants into union structure	++	++	++	++	+	+
Engagement at European level	++	++	++	++	–	–
Mass mobilisations	–	–	–	+	+	+

Source: own [a] Zucchetti (2009); [b] CSO (2012)

CONCLUSION

Transnational labour mobility is a cornerstone of European integration. From a scholarly perspective it is interesting as 'it exposes ... the influence of the nation state, processes of labour market segmentation, and the role of trade union policy and practice' (McGovern 2007: 218–9). The Celtic Tiger brought with it a number of challenges for trade unions, not least those in the construction sector, which, as one interviewee put it, had become an 'exploiters' paradise'. Another described the sixth floor of SIPTU's Liberty Hall, where the construction branch is housed, as an 'accident and emergency room', such was the number of aggrieved migrant workers. While the level of activity was lower in Italian construction, the phenomenon of posting was more prevalent (EC 2011); also, unlike Ireland, which followed a boom–bust cycle, Italian construction remained relatively constant throughout the financial crisis (IMF 2013). *Ceteris paribus*, the level of social dumping was significantly lower in the Italian context. This is on account of the complementary relationship between Italian unions' regulatory and non-regulatory coping mechanisms.

In both Ireland and Italy, steps were taken to strengthen collective agreements with a view to preventing social dumping. However, in the Italian case, these steps were taken *ex-ante* enlargement, whereas in the Irish case steps were taken *ex-post* enlargement. Although it is likely that the Italian social partners had their eye on undocumented labour and criminality rather than enlargement, the introduction of the DURC has nevertheless been widely viewed as a positive development with regard to protecting (migrant) workers. The DURC was requested and strongly promoted by the unions (*see also* Ales and Faioli 2008) and is considered an example of 'best practice' in European construction (EFBWW 2008b). Between 2005 and 2008, the certificate has facilitated the regularisation of 125,000 workers. Also, the DURC 'functions as a preventative tool for the general liability arrangement' (Jorens *et al.* 2012: 94), which means that social dumping is more difficult even in cases where work is being carried out further down the subcontracting chain.

The migrant workers' centres created by the Italian unions, particularly the CGIL's *centro lavoratori stranieri* [centre for migrant workers], fulfil the functions of a public body by providing a range of services. This puts unions face to face with migrant workers and builds trust, as well as facilitating unionisation, even though Italian unions do not *per se* follow an organising model (Marino 2012). Not by any stretch of the imagination are things perfect in Italian construction: all sorts of challenges remain. For instance, Italian construction workers, initially, questioned whether migrant workers should get the same rates even though they had not participated in the struggle to achieve them. An official informed the author that engaging with such questions required explanation and education.

The Irish unions, on the other hand, not only had weaker regulatory cop-ing mechanisms that were designed for another time, but they also they were slow off the mark in responding to enlargement. Much of the exploitation of migrant workers occurred on public construction works, such as the GAMA and Moneypoint cases described above, which certainly helped the unions in framing the deleterious effects of social dumping and its human costs. This echoes Vaughan-Whitehead's (2003: 344) argument highlighting the role of the state in facilitating social dumping. FÁS, a state agency, were advertis-ing on their website dozens of construction jobs offering well under the minimum wage (*Irish Times*, 6 February 2006). Also, in the mid-2000s, there were almost twice as many full-time dog wardens (41) than labour inspec-tors (21) to police the labour market and sniff out exploitation! The extent of the exploitation presented Ireland's social partnership model with its most difficult test since its inception, two decades prior. I will return to this in the following chapter.

The Irish unions, unlike the state, were more than aware of their collec-tive failings (*see also* Geary and Gamwell 2019). Once Irish unions realised the challenges associated with transnational mobility and perceived migrant workers as a strategic opportunity, a great deal of progress was made. This was particularly the case with SIPTU, which was also active at the European level. However, SIPTU alone cannot organise the entire labour market. Here, improved relations with the Migrant Rights Centre are a welcome develop-ment. All things considered, the Irish experience is best seen as a learning cycle (Kjeldstadli 2015). As one union official put it, 'we were feeling our way' and 'if we had to do it again we'd do it differently … we've learned a lot from our mistakes' (interview with SIPTU official).

It should now be clear why the construction sector represents a good test case for analysing European integration in the third phase, as a disaggregated (but characteristic) form thereof. Whilst labour mobility is not problematic *per se*, it does present challenges for trade unions. However, in accordance with Lillie and Greer (2007: 552), 'many scholars continue to assign over-riding influence to national institutions on shaping the interactions of unions and employers and treat transnational political arenas as apolitical and exog-enous to policymaking, downplaying the neoliberal orientation of elites'. It is important, however, to link this chapter back to the overall focus of the book, that is, unions' changing preferences towards European integration. In the fol-lowing chapter, I will discuss the debates surrounding the Lisbon Treaty and the Fiscal Compact. It is in these debates that Euro-critical arguments come to the fore in the Irish case, but not the Italian. The Italian unions were not only supporters of the EU but also strong advocates of a federalised Europe. This is also reflected at sectoral level, where the promotion of European collective bargaining is seen as part of a wider state-building strategy, and which resembles the creation of industrial relations mechanisms at the national level.

That said, engaging with other unions at the European level can be an important resource. As an ICTU official noted:

> [B]y the sheer fact that I was on Committees in Europe ... I knew what was coming down the track probably more than most people in Irish society, certainly more than the politicians. So, you were in a situation where a) you could influence things at an early stage, and b) you knew better than most people what was coming down the line (interview with ICTU Industrial Officer).

The analytical focus of this chapter has been on European integration as a socio-economic process, rather than seeing the EU as simply an artefact designed to serve a (trans)national elite. Whilst there are scholars who study the consequences of post-enlargement labour mobility for trade unions and industrial relations (Woolfson and Sommers 2006; Lillie and Greer 2007; Dølvik and Visser 2009; Meardi 2012a, 2012b; Marino 2012; Lillie 2012; Bosch and Weinkopf 2013; Greer *et al.* 2013; Wagner 2014, 2018) the link is rarely, if ever, made to (changing) political preferences. The objective of this chapter has been to demonstrate that political preferences have sociological roots; and, should European integration be determined to be a disembedding and disruptive process by 'organic intellectuals', then we can expect these developments to make an impact on political preferences. The social purpose of European integration (and EMU) is to improve the living and working conditions of EU workers and where this, for whatever reason, is not forthcoming then we can expect resistance to manifest itself. In other words, European integration is as much about politics as it is about economics. Certainly, market pressures are difficult to politicise but, as Erne (2018: 240) notes, '[I]ndividual attitudes become a social force *only if they are mobilised*' (emphasis added). This brings us back to what social movement scholars (for example, Tarrow 1994) term the political opportunity structure (POS), which, in the EU system, operates on two levels (Marks and McAdam 1996). Within national systems, POSs can differ and, as noted in Chapter Two, it is possible to discern a difference between the Irish and Italian POS, namely, the holding of referendums on EU Treaties. This provides actors with an additional avenue for politicising European integration, as we shall see in the following chapter, which focuses mostly on discourses. However, it is equally important, particularly when it comes to organised labour, to focus also on activities (Erne 2008: 21): hence the focus of this chapter.

The *modus operandi* of organised labour and their coping mechanisms came under increasing pressure in the wake of European enlargement. This is particularly evident when viewed through the prism of labour mobility, the so-called human face of European integration. Labour mobility high-lighted not only both the economic and political struggles involved but also the difficulties in politicising the 'negative externalities' associated with the phenomenon. Where unions' coping mechanisms are found to be ineffective, the first port of call is the government, not least when there is a framework for concertation in place. This is because the governance of the labour market remains primarily at the national level; however, there are strong pressures within the EU context, but also particularly in Ireland for different reasons, for their deregulation. Consequently, unions began to question not only the concept of concertation (*see* Chapter Eight) but also the further constitution-alisation of the EU. This is the subject of the following chapter.

Chapter Eight

Lisbon and the Re-emergence of Labour Euroscepticism

INTRODUCTION

This chapter brings us back to our research puzzle: why did the pro-European consensus of Irish and Italian unions, established in the second phase of European integration, eventually unravel in the Irish but not in the Italian case? While this chapter can be read alone, it will make more sense if read in conjunction with the previous chapter, which acts as an important backdrop to the Lisbon Treaty debates. The third phase of European integration was from the mid-2000s to the present day. There were a number of significant developments from a labour politics perspective, including rulings by Irish and EU courts, episodes of social concertation in both Italy and Ireland, three EU Treaties and difficult ratification referendums not only in Ireland but also in two of the EU's founding member states. As noted in the previous chapter, this phase can be neatly divided into two separate and quite distinguishable phases, namely, the pre-financial-crisis period and the post-2008-crisis period. The former period is more about the single market and labour mobility in the context of enlargement and its attendant labour market challenges, culminating with ratification difficulties for the Constitutional Treaty and the Lisbon Treaty. The latter period has to do with the financial-cum-sovereign-debt crisis, which is more concerned with EMU, and presented the EU with its most serious test to date. EU executives responded by devising a more a more 'vertical' style of EU economic governance (Erne 2015), which included the Fiscal Compact. This new economic governance regime would carry severe consequences for labour politics (Erne *et al.* 2024). Of course, we also have the nadir for the EU project, namely Brexit in 2016, which had direct implications for the EU, generally, but Ireland in particular (see chapter 9).

In the previous chapter we discussed the neo-liberal orientation of the Barroso Commission and its 'deepening through widening' strategy, which was given a boost by the CJEU with the 'Laval Quartet' rulings. The latter confirmed the 'deepening through widening' strategy by reintroducing the 'country of origin' principle, while promoting EU economic rights over national social rights. These rulings, discussed at greater length in the previous chapter, were, to say the least, very controversial; and generated considerable debate both within unions and more broadly in academia. The highly regarded political scientist, Fritz Scharpf (2010), argued that the controversial Laval Quartet rulings, by the CJEU, were of lesser consequence for the more liberally-oriented, Anglo-American form of deregulated capitalism rather than the more coordinated variety of capitalism.

Baccaro and Howell (2017) make a similar point when they argue that 'the liberalizing impact' of the EU's endeavours — single market programme and liberalisations, monetary union or CJEU rulings — have 'affected most those countries that had the hardest work to do in remaking their political economies' (2017: 188). Referring implicitly to the Laval Quartet and explicitly to the argumentation by Scharpf (and Streeck 2014), Baccaro and Howell (2017) make the case that EU integration and market-creation has had 'little effect on the institutions and practices of liberal market economies [such as Ireland and the UK], but far more upon coordinated and social market economies' (*ibidem*). Here, the case of Italy 'stands out' (*ibid.*).

By singling out Italy as one of the member states having gone the furthest in restructuring its political economy, particularly in the name of monetary union, which included mass privatisations and other 'restrictive measures' (*ibid.*: 140–1; *see also* Rutherford and Frangi 2018), including the abolition of wage-indexation in the 1990s, Baccaro and Howell (2017: ch. 7) make the argument that it 'is like looking at pictures from two different geological eras' (*ibid.*: 121). Given this scenario, is it not paradoxical that Italian unions remain staunch supporters of the European project, which is to their detriment? Ireland, on the other hand, is considered to have benefited greatly from the membership of the EU (Hardiman 2002; Laffan and O'Mahony 2008; Regan 2012a; O'Riain 2004, 2014), not only in economic terms, 'becoming one of the most open economies in the world' (O'Riain 2014: 39), but also in terms of social legislation originating at the EU level. As Baccaro and Howell note, 'European-level social protection ... has had the most impact upon those countries with already weakly regulated labor markets' (2017: 191). Here, Ireland is a case in point. Yet, an expanding cohort of unions adopted increasingly Eurosceptic positions precisely at a time when Irish economic eyes were still smiling. So, what explains the changing preferences of Irish unions and the enduring preferences Italian unions towards the EU?

The rejection of the Constitutional Treaty by French and Dutch voters, and the initial rejection by Irish voters of the Lisbon Treaty generated a significant literature on EU politicisation, which has been conceptualised by De Wilde and Zürn (2012; *see also* Zürn 2016; De Wilde, Leupold and Schmidtke 2016; Statham and Trenz 2013) as consisting of three components: i) increasing the EU's saliency; ii) polarisation of views in relation to the EU and its political and economic direction; and iii) a widening of the number of actors engaging in political interest with the EU. Pre-eminent EU scholars, Hooghe and Marks, coined the term 'constraining dissensus' (2007) to describe the phenomenon of increased EU politicisation and posited a 'post-functionalist' theory of integration (2009), which places an emphasis on the cultural dimension of the politicisation process of the EU (*see also* McLaren 2006; Inglehart and Welzel 2005; Inglehart and Norris 2016; Fligstein 2008; Fligstein, Polyakova and Sandholtz 2012).

Although unions have been involved historically in developing democratic mass politics (Bartolini 2000) and more recently in the EU polity-building process (*see* Chapters Four and Five), the lion's share of politicisation scholarship has focused either on public opinion, that is, the individual level, or political parties at the national level (for example, Hooghe and Marks 2005, 2007; McLaren 2006; Brinegar and Jolly 2005; Gabel and Scheve 2007). Social actors or civil society organisations, such as unions, which operate at the organisational or meso-level, have so far been overlooked. This oversight becomes all the more apparent when considering their increasingly important role in debates on EU-related questions (Fitzgibbon 2013; Béthoux, Erne and Golden 2018).

EU-related questions have traditionally been the preserve of trade union elites, particularly in Ireland. As to how politicisation of the EU evolved in Italy and Ireland, we can detect differences, which can, to a certain extent, be explained by a number of factors including: how the challenges associated with contemporary economic integration, in the context of enlargement, were offset; the political opportunity structure; and how the EU has been internalised by the political system. As detailed in the previous chapter, the implications resulting from post-enlargement labour mobility were of greater significance for Ireland; but how these issues manifest themselves politically is also important. Would the framework provided through social concertation be sufficient? Or would an alternative strategy be pursued by unions? In other words, did challenges, outlined in the previous chapter, put EU integration in a different light and effectively challenge the conventional wisdom espoused by the pre-existing pro-European consensus, which, as discussed in Chapter Six, had prevailed since the late 1980s? The re-emergence of labour Euroscepticism still requires an adequate explanation (Fitzgibbon, Leruth and Startin 2017; Mathers, Milner and Taylor 2017) as does the continuance of a pro-European consensus in the face of the EU's post-2010 new economic governance regime, which sought to commodify employment relations and public services (*see* Erne *et al.*, 2024).

The next section sets the scene and analyses the debates surrounding the Constitutional Treaty and its successor the Lisbon Treaty generally, and in the Irish and Italian labour movements, in particular. These developments must be seen against the backdrop of the 'Laval Quartet' rulings and national developments, with a transnational dimension, highted in Chapter Seven. Having averted a quasi-constitutional crisis following Treaty ratification success in 2009, the EU was then plunged into a financial-cum-sovereign debt crisis, which constituted the project's greatest challenge to date. An important component of the EU's response was the Fiscal Compact, which is discussed in the third section. The fourth section focuses on the debates within Irish and Italian organised labour and their changing preferences on the EU's constitutional and economic evolution. There is then a final, concluding section.

THE CONSTITUTIONAL TREATY AND LISBON TREATY DEBATES IN ITALY AND IRELAND

There was, having achieved the Euro, a strong desire to create a European Constitution, although calling it such was always going to be risky. The declaration at the Nice summit (*see* Chapter Six) led to the European Convention on the Future of Europe and compared to the traditional intergovernmental Conference (IGC)[1] approach, the Convention was more open and transparent, providing observation status to the European social partners and inviting submissions. In short, 'it conducted its musings in a far more open and participative manner' (Holmes and Roder 2012: 8) and EU executives decided on naming it the Treaty establishing a Constitution for Europe, which was abbreviated to the Magritte-esque Constitutional Treaty (CT), a term many considered contradictory (Fossum and Menéndez 2011). Pro-Europeans felt the CT would surely be a step towards a Eurofederalist vision, even though the term 'federal' was removed from Article 1 of the final draft and replaced with 'a union of European States'.

Once the draft Treaty was completed by the Convention it was passed over to the IGC, where a number of provisions were watered down (*see* Holmes and Roder 2012). In addition to extended QMV, the CT finally gave legal status to the Charter of Fundamental Rights (henceforth the Charter). The latter, originally an initiative of the Delors' Commission and a commitment to 'the social dimension' of the single market, was a long time in the making (*see* Chapter Six). The CT was signed in Rome on 29 October 2004 in an attempt to resurrect the synergy and willingness of the original signatories to the Treaty of Rome.

The Italian left, particularly the *Partito Democratico* (then called *Democratici di Sinistra*), were very supportive of a federalist treaty, which meant a greater use of QMV, social policy as a shared competence and a bigger redistributive budget for structural and cohesion policies. Former CGIL leader Bruno Trentin, now a left-wing MEP and a member of the 'Spinelli Group', was still an influential personality within the Italian trade union movement and beyond. In 2003, Trentin, within the *Partito Democratico*, presided over a working group whose function was to elaborate the party's political ambition for Europe. The future of the EU and Italy was articulated in a document entitled *Manifesto per l'Italia* (2003),[2] which highlighted the importance of obstructing the right-wing parties – *Lega Nord* and *Polo delle Libertà* – and their vision of Europe, namely a *Federazione di stati nazione* [federation of nation states]. To celebrate the anniversary of the seminal *Venotene Manifesto*, Trentin and others launched a *Manifesto per l'Europa* on the same small island where Spinelli and Rossi had penned the original document whilst in a fascist prison. The sub-heading of the manifesto read: *Più Europa per una nuova Europa* ['More Europe for a new Europe'].

With former Italian prime minister, Giuliano Amato, as vice-President of the Convention, and with Italy due to hold the EU presidency in 2003, there was a deal of optimism and a sense that this was Europe's moment. The Party of European Socialists tapped into this optimism by holding a seminar in Florence in 2003, so as to establish common positions amongst national social-democratic parties on the EU's future. However, the optimism of the Italian left was short-lived and somewhat dented by the fact that Berlusconi was in government at the time. Matters were only worsened when, in a speech to the European Parliament, the Italian leader compared the German socialist MEP, Martin Schulz, to a concentration camp guard!

In 2005, a critical year for the CT, the Italian government set about its ratification in parliament. Once again, the parliamentary debate was 'low key, and did not elicit much public attention or media coverage' (Quaglia 2012: 126). In Ireland, the centre-right government, in preparation for a referendum, published an *Explanatory Guide to the Constitutional Treaty*, which was widely distributed. However, referendum preparations were slow, most probably to avoid a repeat of the (first) Nice Treaty referendum.

While welcoming the Charter, generally, and the right to collective bargaining, in particular, ICTU was critical of the Irish government for threatening to follow the UK government's lead and opt-out from it. 'This was done despite 20 years of social partnership and clearly at the behest of groups like the American Chamber of Commerce' (ICTU no date). For ICTU an opt-out from the Charter 'does not square with any reasonable definition of the common good' (*ibidem*). As to whether ICTU would have supported the CT's ratification is unclear, however, it would appear unlikely on account of the government's reluctance to opt in to what ICTU considered a milestone on the road towards social Europe. Developments elsewhere meant that no Irish referendum was held.

The fate of the CT was effectively dealt a fatal blow by the negative French and Dutch votes. 'For the first time in the history of European integration, the people's verdict in a referendum brought an end to a treaty' (Hobolt 2009: 204). The trope of the 'Polish plumber' became a defining characteristic of the French debate on the CT and was an embodiment of the country-of-origin principle, albeit a fabricated ploy for political ends. Supposedly instrumental-ised by nationalistic, xenophobic 'Eurosceptics' to scare voters into rejecting the treaty (Favell, 2008; Etzioni, 2007; Nicolaïdis and Schmidt 2007), the spectre of the 'Polish plumber' entered the referendum debate at a late stage, following a controversial press conference with EU Commissioner, Fritz Bolkestein, the author of the Services Directive (Béthoux, Erne and Golden 2018). Although the country-of-origin principle was dropped from the final draft of the Services Directive, this was not until the following year. In any case, the controversial principle was reintroduced through the backdoor via the CJEU's Laval Quartet rulings (*see* Chapter Seven), just in time for the ratification of the CT's successor, the Lisbon Treaty.

In response to the EU's constitutional crisis, the European Council launched a 'period of reflection', which concluded in March 2007 with the Berlin Declaration's call for a new treaty. The bones of the CT were resur-rected, but without the trappings of statehood, following much deliberation, debate and political brinkmanship, not least by the German leader, Angela Merkel. As noted by the *Financial Times* (24 June 2007):

> Angela Merkel … emerged with her reputation enhanced, as a clear-sighted leader and a persuasive negotiator. She looked after the interests of big and small alike, essential in an enlarged EU. Against the odds, she produced a detailed road map for a 'reform treaty' that manages to preserve most of the substance, but watered it down enough to satisfy the 'minimalists' in France, the Nether-lands and the UK. Those governments were desperate to have a deal that would not require them to call referendums, and risk another No vote. Ms. Merkel persuaded the 'maximalists' [such as Italy] to shelve their ambitions and accept a second-best deal.

Other than the omission of the trappings of statehood, the Lisbon Treaty did not differ substantively from the CT. The 'new' Treaty introduced a num-ber of provisions, most of which had to do with improving the functioning of the EU's institutions in an enlarged EU. For example, the number of MEPs was adjusted and a new post, the President of the European Council, was cre-ated. Positive provisions from a trade union perspective included a European Citizens' Initiative[3] and the aforementioned Charter. Also, the 'co-decision' procedure was extended to more policy areas, which translates into an increased role for the European Parliament. Another significant development was the ability of the Commission to sign binding international agreements on behalf of the EU. This provision would become more controversial in the future (for example, the EU–Canada Comprehensive Economic and Trade Agreement better known as CETA). Finally, what at the time seemed an innocuous provision in the Treaty turned out to be of considerable significance; I refer here to Article 50, which enabled the UK to leave the EU.

In the meantime, not only was the final draft of the Service Directive agreed but, more controversially, two of the Laval Quartet rulings had been made, which were extremely contentious and generated considerable debate within unions and academia alike. As noted above, some scholars, including Scharpf (2010), Streeck (2014) and Baccaro and Howell (2017), make the argument that these rulings, as well as membership of the E(M)U, more generally, are of little or at least less consequence for the more liberally oriented forms of deregulated capitalism, such as Ireland's. Yet Irish labour Euroscepticism emerged during debates on the Lisbon Treaty and, were it not for the ensuing economic crisis, exposing the fragility of such a variety of capitalism, there is a distinct possibility that the EU's constitutional crisis would only have been deepened. Referendum fear gripped national governments, following the French and Dutch rejections, and only Ireland held a referendum on the so-called Reform Treaty.

The ETUC supported the ratification of the Lisbon Treaty and, having wholeheartedly supported the CT, so too did the three Italian confederations. The Italian political class in general and the unions in particular were strong supporters of a 'political' and 'social' Europe. National congresses of Italian unions regularly make numerous references to Europe and, typically, the call is for *more* 'Europe'. For instance, the following extract is a speech from Epifani, the ex-General Secretary of CGIL, in 2006 and is indicative of the level of support for the idea of Europe and the need for greater integration that exists within the Italian union movement.

> Europe has to be a true political and institutional construct, a regulated market with shared norms, common institutions and full reciprocity, a process of participation and democracy, a social model, an idea of responsibility based on human rights, a common space for many values and idealisms … A Europe, which is like a house where everybody can feel like a citizen and not just a producer or a consumer. *It is necessary that we ask ourselves what can we do to overcome an inertia that could bring us backwards* (Epifani 2006, emphasis added).

Most member states' parliaments had ratified the Treaty by the end of 2008. The newly elected Italian government, which for the first time in Italy's post-war history contained no communists, ratified the Treaty overwhelmingly with *all* 551 deputies voting in favour, including the *Lega* or as it was known then *Lega Nord*, despite their having opposed the CT.

As the Lisbon Treaty was being concluded, rumours circulated that once again the Irish government was considering following the Blair government's line by opting-out of the Charter. As the news broke, there was consternation and alarm within Irish trade union circles and officials warned that 'the trade union movement in Ireland would never support a treaty with an opt out, which would be doomed to failure in a referendum' (*Irish Times* 26 June 2007). The 'period of reflection' was used by Irish unions to warn the Irish government of the price of an opt-out. At an ICTU conference, with then Prime Minister, Bertie Ahern, present, it was made patently clear that 'support for a European Union Treaty *will be conditional* on the Charter remaining as an integral part of any proposed Treaty' (ICTU 2007: 54, emphasis added).

Within the Executive Council of ICTU, there was some debate over the Treaty and the merits of the Charter. Whereas those in favour of the Treaty pointed to the Charter, 'which assumes a new importance in an Irish context in the aftermath of the Ryanair Supreme Court Judgement' (ICTU 2007: 136). This case involved Ryanair and the pilots' union IALPA,, which had sought to negotiate with Ryanair over various work-related issues. Ryanair refused to recognise or negotiate with the union. Both the Labour Court[4] and the High Court ruled against Ryanair, but the latter appealed to the Supreme Court. The judge ruled in favour of the longstanding anti-union aviation company and, in doing so, effectively emasculated the 2004 Industrial Relations Act (Eurofound 2007; O'Sullivan and Gunnigle 2009). Hence, advocates of the Treaty argued that the Charter would serve to reverse, partially at least, this anti-union ruling.

The Irish employers' association, IBEC, sought to put business jitters to rest by offering the reassurance that 'the notion that the Charter creates an obligation to introduce compulsory collective bargaining is incorrect', and that that there was nothing in the Lisbon Treaty which would require Ireland to make any provision for mandatory union recognition (cited in Ewing 2010). In other words, the *status quo ex ante* prevailed. Detractors within the trade union movement also questioned the merits and concrete effect of the Charter, which they argued subjected the right to strike to national legislation.

The unions questioning the merits of the Charter, and the Treaty more broadly, were SIPTU, Unite and Connect (formerly TEEU). Whereas the Unite position might have been anticipated, Connect's stance came as a surprise, as hitherto the union leadership had largely remained taciturn on European debates and merely followed ICTU's lead on previous EU questions. Having campaigned for the Nice Treaty (*see* Chapter Six), SIPTU felt aggrieved that unions were overlooked by government on the question of labour mobility in the context of enlargement, despite social partnership being in place. This, according to the former General Secretary, 'facilitated a "race to the bottom", the large scale casualisation of jobs and an explosion of employment agencies … without enhancing our employment protection legislation by one syllable' (cited in the *Irish Times*, 30 May 2008). The previous chapter corroborates this view.

SIPTU was also sceptical of the capacity of the Charter to deliver and made their support of the Lisbon Treaty conditional upon a governmental guarantee that robust legislation for collective bargaining be introduced. A leaked confidential paper submitted to social concertation negotiations shows that trade union recognition was being sought by the unions; however, this request was rebuffed out of hand by the employers and the government (*Irish Times, ibid.*).

The Executive Council of ICTU voted by 14 votes to 5 in favour of supporting the Treaty. SIPTU, rather surprisingly, abstained from casting a vote and consequently did not adopt a formal stance in the referendum. Inevitably the silence of Ireland's largest union was interpreted widely as a rejection of the Treaty. This strained relations with the Labour Party, which supported the Treaty. The latter accused SIPTU of playing politics, when the union should be judging the Treaty on its merits alone rather than using the referendum as an opportunity to achieve what was customary in all other member states, namely, legislation on trade union recognition. Arguably, SIPTU's decision not to adopt a formal stance was a compromise with its 'sister' party.

Connect (formerly TEEU) operates in the construction sector and is a quintessential *Irish* trade union (Dineen 2022), which affiliated to the nationalist CIU in 1945 (*see* Chapter Four). The union is less well known, primarily because it strictly attends to industrial relations matters, where it is no shrinking violet (*see* Chapter Seven). The decision of Connect to join the debate on the Lisbon Treaty set a precedent for the union. It was 'the first time the union adopted a political stance' (interview, former-General President, Connect). On previous EU treaties, the union's stance was 'indifferent' and there was 'no debate' (*ibidem*). Adopting an explicitly critical position, as opposed to SIPTU's fudge, was unpopular with the pro-European cohort within the Irish labour movement and the wider political class; however, there were no complaints from its members (*ibid.*) whose experience of economic integration differed from the typical narratives.

Similar to SIPTU, Connect would have supported the Treaty had the government strengthened trade union rights. During the campaign, Connect constantly drew attention to the Laval Quartet cases, as the following quotation demonstrates:

The TEEU [Connect] favours a social Europe but unfortunately recent key judgements by the European Court of Justice show that the pendulum has swung against workers' rights and in favour of big business. In the circumstances, it would be foolish to provide the institutions with more power (TEEU 2008a).

Despite the government not seeking an opt-out from the Charter, the Lisbon Treaty was rejected in a referendum by a margin of 53.4 per cent to 46.6 per cent and, unlike the first Nice Treaty referendum, the turnout was high, at 53 per cent. The oppositional stance of Connect and Unite, and the silence of SIPTU, played an important role if we consider that 'elites have a central role in shaping public discourse and mobilizing opposition to international integration' (Baccaro, Bremer and Neimanns 2021: 406). The mainstream parties were complacent in launching a campaign and reliant on what we might term the EU's 'output legitimacy' (Scharpf 1999). This complacency was exacerbated by a contemptuous political class, including the new Prime Minister, Brian Cowen, and his party colleague, Charlie McCreevy, then EU Commissioner for the Internal Market, who admitted not having read the Treaty. Such confessions were rather damaging, with Eamon Gilmore (2016: 26), the Labour leader, describing the 'yes' campaign as nothing other than 'a fiasco'.

The 'no' vote increased by ten percentage points from what it was at the time of the second Nice Treaty referendum. Post-referendum analysis indicated that voting was 'heavily class-correlated' (Storey 2008: 77). Furthermore, the single most important issue that exercised people was working conditions (Milward Browne IMS 2008). Of those who voted for the Treaty, 42 per cent were concerned about working conditions as were 55 per cent of those who voted against it (*ibidem*). This fact has been overlooked by a number of post-referendum analyses (such as Quinlan 2009; Barrett 2012). Also, 61 per cent of Labour supporters voted against the Treaty, suggesting that its leadership was out of step with the grass roots. In response, Gilmore declared that 'Lisbon is dead'! However, unlike France or the Netherlands, the Irish voters were deemed for the second time to have suffered from a momentary lapse of pragmatic wherewithal and were therefore offered a chance of forgiveness and redemption.

Jean Claude Piris, head of the EU legal service, had a track record in salvaging EU treaties, and was called upon to design a roadmap that could prevent an EU constitutional crisis. Several concessions were secured by the Irish government, including the retention of a Commissioner,[5] legally binding guarantees that Irish abortion, tax or neutrality policy would not be affected. However, only a 'solemn declaration' on workers' rights was secured. Anecdotally, this is down to the Blair government's blocking of a legal provision on workers' rights, which is a position that would also have suited the Irish government of the day.

On the back of these guarantees, a date in October 2009 was set for a second referendum. 'For the Lisbon II referendum, the Yes side changed dramatically in formation and tactics' (Fitzgibbon 2013: 26). Pro-Lisbon supporters, within organised labour and organised capital[6] concentrated their energies and engaged more forthrightly in the debate. 'Ireland for Europe', spearheaded by academic Brigid Laffan 'cultivated a broad network of supporters throughout the country, fighting a visible media campaign with high-profile figures' (Quinlan 2009: 144). The yes-side was heavily funded in the second vote, with an estimated €10,206,000 versus €780,000 on the no-side.[7]

A group of public sector unions established the so-called Charter Group (2009), which, as the name suggests, underlined the importance of the Charter of Fundamental Rights by disseminating a pamphlet entitled, *Lisbon and Your Rights at Work: Why the Lisbon Treaty is Good for Workers and their Unions*. Both the General Secretary of ICTU, David Begg, and Labour Party leader, Eamon Gilmore, were present at its launch. Within the pamphlet, the severity of the Laval Quartet judgements is dismissed with arguments that the judgements came about as a result of inadequate transposition of EU Directives into national law.

The leader of the ETUC, John Monks, addressed the 2009 ICTU biennial conference. In what could be interpreted as a dig at Unite, SIPTU and Connect for using the Treaty as an opportunity to extract concessions from the government, Monks (2009) pointed out that '[T]here is no conditionality in the ETUC's support for Lisbon.' By the time of the follow-up referendum, the Labour leadership had cajoled the SIPTU leadership into revising its position but, more importantly, by now the socio-economic context had changed dramatically following the collapse of American and British banks. Second time round, SIPTU re-joined the chorus of pro-Lisbon unions. The semi-*volte-face* came about after 'leader of the Labour Party [E. Gilmore] promised ... in the event of Labour getting back into government ... they would commit to legislate for collective bargaining rights' (interview with ex-General Secretary, SIPTU). On the basis of this promise, SIPTU campaigned for the ratification of the Treaty.

Unite and Connect both maintained their critical stance against the Treaty, the Charter and the 'solemn declaration'. Scepticism was also expressed about the prospect of Labour being able to fulfil their promises. 'Irish workers', the Unite leader highlighted,

> ... are alone in Europe as having no legal right to representation by a union ... [T]here was a singular failure to secure the clause that would prevent social dumping and second-class treatment of workers. For that reason, we are recommending to all of our members that they should reject Lisbon once again (*Union Post* 2009: 22).

Connect's leadership called on its members to 'reject Lisbon yet again and ensure that in any renegotiation, a social protocol is attached ... Then, the TEEU [Connect] will reconsider its position' (TEEU 2009a). The likelihood of workers' rights being given primacy over the interests of the market was slim.

Second time round, the Irish electorate voted by 67.1 per cent to 32.9 per cent in favour and the Labour leader 'got a congratulatory telephone call from Commission President José Manuel Barroso' (Gilmore 2016: 34). Having avoided a constitutional crisis, the EU was back on track, or so it seemed.

THE FISCAL COMPACT: PACTA SUNT SERVANDA[8]

The onset of the financial crisis resulted in what, at the time, seemed like a slow and tortuous muddling through from EU executives and national governments. Presented with its deepest crisis to date, EU executives eventually responded with the Fiscal Compact and a raft of emergency legislation — 6 Pack and 2 Pack — thereby signalling the advent of a new economic governance regime (Erne 2015). In essence, national governments, now without recourse to monetary tools such as currency devaluation, had to pursue an 'internal devaluation' and implement 'structural reforms', often at the behest of EU executives, so as to secure bailout funds with a view to restoring competitiveness and economic growth. Both Ireland and Italy found themselves in the eye of the economic storm, with the former receiving formal visitations from the so-called Troika, which consisted of officials representing the European Commission, European Central Bank (ECB) and International Monetary Fund (IMF). Although Italy did not receive any formal visitations from the Troika, neo-liberal prescriptions were nonetheless delivered, albeit in a more surreptitious fashion via (not so) secret letters from the ECB.

Along with Greece, Portugal and Spain, both Ireland and Italy were categorised as belonging to the 'periphery' and their problematic collective status was embodied in the disparaging moniker 'PIIGS'. Ireland was facing economic ruination unless the government blanket-guaranteed the banking system, covering customer deposits and *all* the banks' own borrowings to the tune of €440 billion. Described as 'biggest financial gamble', the move 'forced billions in losses ... on Irish taxpayers [and] ... socialised the cost of decade-long misadventures of runaway banks whose managers and private shareholders enjoyed the spoils of bumper profits through the boom' (*Irish Times*, 25 September 2010). In short, the banking crisis was magically transformed into a sovereign debt crisis.

The Italian banking system, by comparison, was relatively secure (Di Quirico 2010); however, Italy's economic woes involved its public finances.

The fall in economic activity reduced the amount of revenue collected, and anti-crisis policies combatting rising (youth) unemployment increased expenditure. Consequently, the budget deficit and public debt increased significantly, which meant breaching the parameters of the Growth and Stability Pact. 'Consequently, the crisis has empowered the [Eurosceptic] League and weakened Berlusconi's government at the same time' (*ibid.:* 14). Rather than elections, Berlusconi, in 2011, was replaced by a quintessential technocrat, Mario Monti (*see below*).

It was against the backdrop of a financial-cum-sovereign-debt crisis that the Fiscal Compact was debated in Italy and Ireland. The Irish Fine Gael–Labour government felt that 'another referendum could be avoided', but the Attorney General advised that 'on balance, a referendum would be required' (Gilmore 2016: 174). Evidently, there was a fear of a legal case being brought if a referendum was not held. Hence, yet again, Ireland was the only EU country to hold a referendum on the latest EU Treaty. In Italy, by contrast, it was the absence of resistance by the unions that was bizarre (Castellani and Queirolo Palmas 2018; Gago 2018).

In comparison to previous EU treaties, the Fiscal Compact was negotiated relatively quickly, thanks in large part to the so-called 'Merkozy' combination, and was signed in March 2012, by all member states save the UK and the Czech Republic. Originally, the EU and 'Merkozy' were keen on member states 'adopt[ing] the debt brake as a provision in their own constitutions' (Gilmore 2016: 173), just as the German government had done of its own volition in 2009. This aspect unnerved the Irish government, which managed to have it 'watered down' in negotiations (*ibidem*). Now a debt brake was 'preferably' enshrined constitutionally (*ibid.*). The Irish government felt that this minor, but critical, change would get it out of holding a referendum; but, as noted above, this was not to be. However, the government did have 'the advantage of surprise' (*ibid.*).

The context under which the Fiscal Treaty referendum was held left Irish unions with very little wriggle room (Geary 2016). Nevertheless, the Labour leader, Gilmore (2016: 175), was fearful that Ireland would fail to ratify a third EU treaty (at first attempt) in twelve years: 'there was little positive that could be said about this treaty. Indeed, if we got into arguments about the structural deficit and the complexities of the debt brake ... we would probably lose.' To boot, the ETUC set a historical precedent by disapproving of the Treaty.

> EU leaders are wrong to believe that a new Treaty will restore growth and resolve the sovereign debt crisis. The ETUC opposes this new Treaty. We are convinced that the proposal before us will weaken Europe instead of reinforcing it. The new Treaty will undermine the support of the population for

European integration, and it will stifle growth and increase unemployment (ETUC 2012).

In the run-up to the referendum, the majority of the trade union leadership was very critical of the Fiscal Treaty and in the absence of the constraints associated with social concertation (Culpepper and Regan 2014), which was collapsed by the government and the employers, ICTU could speak more freely compared to previous campaigns. Speaking at the Labour Party conference in April, 2012, ICTU General Secretary, Begg, berated the European financial elite.

> The decision to conflate banking and sovereign debt was a policy failure of epic proportions. The fact that the ECB was complicit in that decision and will not now take its boot off our necks to allow us to ameliorate that debt is reprehensible ... Europe is currently under the control of neoliberal ideologues who are quite willing to press their austerity dogma to destruction – our destruction. We are too small to matter. We are no more than an economic laboratory in which they can try out ever more extreme versions of policies that have already failed (Begg 2012a).

ICTU's chief economist, Paul Sweeney (2012), argued that economic governance was being used as a means to dismantle social Europe by arguing that the new rules of economic governance were means of a) restricting negotiating mechanisms; b) attacking industrial relations systems; c) putting downward pressure on collectively agreed wage levels; d) weakening social protection and the right to strike; and e) facilitating the privatisation of public services. For those reasons, he recommended the Treaty 'should be rejected' (*ibidem*).

The Fiscal Treaty presented the Irish trade unions with a dilemma. This sentiment was expressed by the former General Secretary of ICTU during an interview with the author.

> Nobody saw any merit in the Fiscal Treaty, as such ... All the arguments that were deployed in favour of it were highly disingenuous. However, there was a poisoned pill in it ... no access to E[uropean] S[tability] M[echanism] if you needed it, unless you signed up to the Fiscal Treaty. And that was what decided it insofar as people decided on it. The problem for us [ICTU], and why we didn't come out with a collective position on it was we just didn't feel that you could advocate in favour of something which you knew was wrong, but you were only doing because there was a gun to your head.

ICTU's Executive Council were slow in arriving at a decision; however, no formal vote was ever taken. Arguably this was so as to not enflame tensions stemming from the Lisbon Treaty debate and not make an already bad situation worse. Despite headlines from pro-business broadsheets such as 'A decision by ICTU to stay neutral, or to recommend a No vote, would be a huge blow to the Yes campaign' (*Sunday Business Post* 2012a), ICTU announced that it would *not* be making a recommendation as to how workers should vote on the Fiscal Treaty. The *Irish Independent* (26 April 2012), Ireland's most popular paper, ran with the headline 'ICTU's silence failed members'. The editorial wrote that 'the ICTU leadership took the easy course' and 'closed their eyes' (*ibidem*).

Instead, a synthesis paper was prepared by the General Secretary. The following excerpt is taken from that paper:

> Deeper European integration is unavoidable if the Euro is to survive … But … social Europe is being dismantled via austerity … Anyway, what is now proposed goes much further than anything seen up to now in Europe … Acceptance of the Fiscal Compact Treaty would tie us to even more exacting standards of fiscal discipline indefinitely … For the future we can expect wage rises to be low in line with low inflation and the machinery of the Fiscal Treaty will seek to keep unit labour costs within strict limits … While the treaty is wrong from our economic and social perspective it becomes hard to oppose it unless a satisfactory alternative to the ESM can be advanced (ICTU 2012).

This paper was distributed to the wider trade union community and highlighted the 'troubling dilemma' of Ireland being a programme country. A small conciliation, or perhaps even a minor victory, was the fact that a debt brake was not inserted in the Irish Constitution. This differed from Italy; a point I return to below.

The Charter Group[9] (2012a, 2012b) formally endorsed the Fiscal Treaty, which they argued would help stabilise the Euro, a necessary condition to relaunch economic growth and create jobs. Furthermore, the group, drawing on research by an investment bank(!), adopted scaremongering tactics by warning that failure to ratify the Fiscal Treaty would cost €11,500 per person in Ireland.

SIPTU's position could be described as being ambiguous and a formal position was, once again, not taken by the union leadership. According to a policy document '[U]nless we can come up with a viable alternative to ESM funding, it would be illogical to vote No on the grounds that it is an "Austerity Treaty", because rejection would mean even greater austerity' (SIPTU 2012a). Here, SIPTU advanced a (Euro-)Keynesian response based on two options. Firstly, the creation of Eurobonds by the ECB. Secondly, a stimulus plan for the construction sector. Here, the government could, over a three-year period, access the state pension funds (about €5 to €10 billion) and engage in large-scale capital investment projects. The proposal argued that for every infrastructural investment of €1 billion it would generate 10,000 jobs.[10] Only if the government agreed to this plan would SIPTU support the Treaty. With no interest from government, SIPTU did not take a formal position and was accused by the business-friendly media of 'sitting on the fence' (*Sunday Business Post* 2012b).

Unite was the most vocal opponent of the Fiscal Treaty, with the Regional Secretary (Unite the Union 2012a), arguing that, if it was ratified, Ireland 'will be facing into a decade of high unemployment and emigration'. Three broad arguments were made as to why workers should reject the Treaty. First, it would inhibit growth across the Eurozone and the EU as a whole. Second, the European institutions were pursuing a wage deflationary strategy. Third, 'austerity measures will mean even more cuts in investment, public services and social protection' (Unite the Union 2012a). Taken together, these developments would only perpetuate the economic crisis and create greater instability. Unite also questioned the arithmetical basis of the formula used to calculate the structural deficit. According to a Michael Taft, a (former) Unite economist the structural deficit 'is hypothetical' (Unite the Union 2012b).

Inter-union tensions inevitably came to the fore. Whereas Unite rebuffed the 'gun to the head' position by arguing that external funding was possible, SIPTU likened this approach to 'playing Russian roulette with potentially awesome consequences' (SIPTU 2012a). Connect was less visible this time round. Nevertheless, continued resistance to the direction of European integration was adopted. Urging its members to vote against the Fiscal Treaty, a press release declared '[I]t is becoming increasingly obvious that austerity is not working' (TEEU 2012). Similarly, there was the absolute rejection of enshrining 'the draconian Fiscal Compact Treaty in *our* Constitution' (emphasis added), as well as a reiteration of the Keynesian stimulus package 'to generate growth and jobs' (*ibidem*).

On referendum day, 60.3 per cent voted in favour. Clearly, the context of the financial crisis played an important role as did the framing of the Fiscal Compact as the 'Stability Treaty' (Gilmore 2016).

Turning now to the Italian context, this period saw Berlusconi being replaced by a character who *Time* magazine hailed as 'the man who can save Europe'. Mario Monti, who became *Presidente del Consiglio* in 2011, had, as Rector of Bocconi University in Milan and as a former Commissioner, contributed to the diffusion of the doctrine of 'expansionary austerity' (Helgadóttir 2015). Dubbed 'Super Mario', he introduced grand policies such as the 'Save Italy' and 'Grow Italy' decrees and was keen to reform Italy's employment protection legislation (*Financial Times* 2011a, 2011b). These reforms put Monti on a collision course with the unions, which were united in their opposition to the technocratic government's austerity measures and in particular the *Salva Italia* emergency budget of December 2011.

On 2 February 2012, the three confederal leaders, Camusso, Bonanni and Angeletti, sent a letter to Monti, expressing their concern about the proposed contents of the Fiscal Treaty and the lack of a social component promoting economic growth and jobs. The letter expressed 'opposition and perplexity with regards to the Fiscal Treaty as the only response to the economic crisis' and argued that the budgetary rules contained in the Treaty were too rigid (Camusso, Bonanni and Angeletti 2012). In particular, the unions expressed concern, along with the ETUC, with the intergovernmental approach being pursued by the national governments of the member states. The letter was followed by a co-ordinated European day of action on 29 February, with the objective of sending a message to national governments *before* they signed the Fiscal Treaty, highlighting the lack of provisions in the Treaty to tackle unemployment and economic growth. Unlike the mobilisations on the Amsterdam Treaty (*see* Chapter Six), this action was decentralised and largely ineffective.

During the negotiation of the Fiscal Compact, the Monti government pursued a two-fold strategy: defend the national interest while safeguarding the EU integration project (Moschella 2017). The Italian delegation was strongly in favour of counterbalancing fiscal consolidation with provisions designed to foster economic growth. This latter aspect never materialised; however, there was little choice but to accept the outcome: as Monti stated, 'it is necessary to project the image of a mature country that accepts a necessary and reasonable discipline, in reality and in appearances' (cited in Moschella 2017: 217).

The reaction of the Italian unions to the Fiscal Treaty could be best described as lukewarm or even 'excessively moderate' (Leonardi 2018: 112). For the first time in the history of the CISL and UIL, a critical position was adopted towards a European Treaty. The Fiscal Compact also brought about a change of position for the CGIL. Although the opposition did not amount to much, the criticism was significant, although ultimately in line with the ETUC's position.

The Italian Parliament ratified the Fiscal Compact on 14 September 2012, but the technocratic Monti government even went beyond what was required by introducing enshrining the German-inspired *Schuldenbremse* (debt brake), which was also contained in the 'secret' Triochet-Draghi letter to Berlusconi. In one of his last acts as Prime Minister, Monti enacted legislation, Law 243, close to Christmas, with no parliamentary debate whatsoever!

On Christmas Day 2012, Monti announced his intention to compete in the February election of 2013. Despite strong backing from Merkel and Sarkozy, things for the technocrat-turned-politician did not go so well, with his party list, *Scelta Civica* (Civil Choice), scoring a modest 10.6 per cent. After months of negotiations, the PDs, along with the centre-right, managed to form a grand coalition government; although the government lasted until

2018, the office of prime minister changed hands three times. The most controversial prime minister was Matteo Renzi, especially from the perspective of organised labour.

Where Monti (and Fornero) had failed, the centre-left Renzi government took up the mantle by declaring war on the *vecchia guardia* ['old guard'] of the Italian left, which inevitably included the CGIL (Golden 2013). With the prospect of Italy holding the presidency of the EU, Renzi was eager to demonstrate his zeal for reform and his political brinksmanship by introducing the Jobs Act, which 'deliberately attacked one of the most important symbols of the postwar Italian union movement' (Rutherford and Frangi 2018: 452), namely, Article 18. This earned Renzi the sobriquet of *il rottamatore*, 'the wrecker'!

The *Federazione Impiegati Operari Metallurgici* (FIOM), representing metalworkers, is an important federation within the CGIL. FIOM mobilised its workers and launched a movement aptly called UNIONS[11] in support of a referendum on the Jobs Act, putting its leader, Landini, on a collision course with the Renzi government, which had 'formed its social coalition with Confindustria and the ECB' (Landini, cited in *La Repubblica* 28 March 2015). In 2016, the CGIL managed to collect 1.1 million signatures for three abrogative referendums on three so-called *quisiti*. These were Article 18; a voucher system (as an alternative form of payment for temporary work); and the subcontracting chain. In January 2017, the Constitutional Court decided that whereas the *quisiti* on vouchers and subcontracting were admissible, a referendum on Article 18 would not be admissible. In any case, the new Gentiloni-led government announced that it would abolish the voucher system and reintroduce full joint responsibility into the subcontracting chain. But in another twist, the government reintroduced the voucher scheme, albeit in a more limited form.

A group of economists (such as Riccardo Realfonzo and Laura Pennacchi) with close links to the CGIL launched a campaign to amend the Fiscal Compact's 'golden rule' once it entered legislation in 2014. 'Citizens are disoriented', according to Pennacchi, and are 'faced with an increasingly serious crisis. There is a need for an awakening not only on an economic level, but also on a democratic level, and a battle like this can contribute to change'.

The group of left-wing economists launched a campaign for what they considered a strongly pro-European referendum. Four different amendments were envisaged and each one required the gathering of 500,000 signatures. Hence, four separate campaigns were necessary (*see* www.referedumstopausterita.it). The overriding objective was to generate 'an open and democratic debate on the reasons for the obtuse austerity that the Fiscal Compact imposes', not just in Italy but 'throughout the European continent' (*ibidem*). In total, 1,500,000 signatures were gathered but none of the four *quesiti* reached the necessary quorum.

As noted above, the Lisbon Treaty and the Fiscal Compact were debated in very different contexts. The pro-European consensus had already begun to unravel in the Irish labour movement with the former, partly by way of politicising the shortcomings of a weak regulatory environment is an increasingly transnational labour market. The Fiscal Compact, on the other hand, was related to EMU, but also meant consequences for industrial relations, especially in Italy (Jordan, Maccarrone and Erne 2021). Notwithstanding the inclusion of debt brake, the Italian unions remained reluctant to criticise the EU and this is discussed in the following section.

DISCUSSION: EMERGENT LABOUR EUROSCEPTICISM AND WAINING PRO-EUROPEAN CONSENSUS

All too often, trade unions are either treated cursorily or in an overly simplified way by EU scholarship, as the two following examples on the Lisbon Treaty demonstrate. Firstly, '[T]he Technical, Engineering and Electrical Union and the Unite trade unions opposed the Treaty on the same issue of workers' rights' (Quinlan 2009: 144). Secondly, 'TEEU's [Connect's] shift against the Lisbon Treaty followed the controversial ECJ rulings' (Leconte 2010: 228). Whilst the statements themselves are *per se* not incorrect, they shed little light on the question of *why* such stances are adopted and instead focus on *how* opposition was articulated. However, unions are astute political actors. They have to be as, all too often, they have to operate in hostile environments *vis-à-vis* employers, governments and, more recently, EU executives. To this end, and to avoid public contempt, the framing of issues by unions is of utmost importance.

Understanding labour Euroscepticism requires assessing the socio-economic conditions in which unions and their members find themselves. These conditions can be influenced by membership of the EU in two ways: either by the single market and its attendant dynamics or by the fiscal constraints of EMU. The latter has been less problematic, that is until the onset of 'Great Recession' and the EU's new economic governance regime. Both aspects, for different reasons, are difficult to politicise (Szabò, Golden and Erne 2021). Regarding the single market aspect, unions, as labour market actors, use their various coping mechanisms to police an increasingly transnational space. This can mean a steep learning curve (Kjeldstadli 2015) and the job of union leaderships is to interpret these conditions as best they can and, where possible, mitigate their impact – for their members, first and foremost, but also for broader society, including migrant workers. The controversial Laval Quartet judgements revealed that a union's institutional muscle memory could be wiped with relative ease, leaving unions' capacity for controlling transnational spaces severely limited. The net result was uncertainty, which contributed to the unravelling of the pro-European consensus, at least in the Irish case.

The financial-cum-sovereign-debt crisis led to a sharp rise in salience around EMU, revealing new lines of conflict, most notably between 'core', surplus countries and 'periphery', deficit countries. 'Political actors had to take a public stance on the EMU under the conditions of strong deadline pressure, dire national economic consequences and often little understanding' (Leupold 2016: 85). Unions, however, can also take their cues from national confederal leaderships or even European leaderships. On 14 November 2012, a co-ordinated general strike was organised by the ETUC. Considered 'a big step forward' (Sheehan, 2016: 55; *see also* Helle 2015) for European trade unions, it is rather surprising that ICTU did not participate in any way whatsoever. This inaction by the Irish labour movement is surprising, given that it had earlier participated in the decentralised European day of action organised by the ETUC on 29 February 2012. The decision not to join November's co-ordinated action must be seen in the context of ICTU's broader 'We are not Greece' strategy. ICTU (2013) was more in favour of engaging the perpetrators of austerity, namely, the Troika, rather than participating in a demonstration of solidarity and mobilising the public. Also, with the Labour party in government there was less of an appetite for mobilisation.

Enjoying 'wide social support', the transnational action is considered to have had 'a very significant impact on contentious politics' and 'transformed the political opportunity structure and encouraged a shift in union strategy and action' (Dias and Fernandes 2016: 34, 31, 35). By and large, it was the national unions in Portugal, Greece and Spain that responded more robustly to the ETUC's call to action. In Italy, CISL and UIL were completely absent from the actions, while the CGIL, on the other hand, were rather uncharacteristically timid, with a four-hour general strike being called.[12] Like ICTU, the Italian confederations did not want to sour relations with the PD, which was supportive of the Monti administration.

Within ICTU, it is possible to identify three factions on EU-related questions. I describe this as *fragmented unity*, which has challenged the pro-European consensus and could serve to undermine ICTU's stance on political questions in the public sphere. Conversely, in Italy, despite the existence of three different confederations, which can be problematic in the national context (Leonardi 2018), paradoxically this is less problematic as all three tend to speak with one voice on big-ticket EU-related issues. I have termed this *centralised pluralism*. In the following sub-sections, I will unpack fragmented unity and the emergence of labour Euroscepticism and centralised pluralism and the enduring pro-European consensus, which cannot be taken for granted.

Fragmented unity and the emergence of labour Euroscepticism

The three different groupings within ICTU emerged during debates on the EU treaties and these divisions were confirmed during interviews with high-ranking union officials. The first grouping consisted of an assemblage of public sector unions, which appeared for all intents and purposes to be pro-Europe; however, as one informant articulated, 'it would be more a case of being pro- whatever the government is pro-' (interview with former General Secretary, SIPTU). Certainly, this left little room for critical engagement. The Charter Group is representative of this grouping, and it organised around the Charter of Fundamental Rights, which the Irish government contemplated side-stepping. Under the rubric of institutionalised social concertation, such a move was never going to wash with the unions. The Charter might have been a welcome development; however, it was a poor replacement for the damage done to Irish industrial relations by the Supreme Court rulings in the Ryanair and the McGowan cases (*see* Chapter Seven), not to mention the plethora of social dumping incidents discussed in the previous chapter. Perhaps this was of less concern for public sector unions? If so, this would be short-sighted, as social dumping also has implications for the exchequer, because it also implies diminished revenue for funding public services (Vaughan-Whitehead 2003).

The pro-government line became particularly evident in the Fiscal Treaty debate, which many on the left referred to as the 'Austerity Treaty'. In real terms, the Treaty meant a financial adjustment for national budgets, which carried far-reaching implications for the public sector (*see* Erne *et al.*, 2024). Notwithstanding this, the Charter Group followed the government line by advocating a Yes vote so as to maximise foreign investment and generate jobs.

The second grouping consisted of unions that adopted a position based largely on the merits of the Treaty in question and the national context, which is embedded in the broader EU context. SIPTU, Ireland's largest general union, and Connect (belatedly) fall into this category, albeit with some differences (*see below*). Between the two Lisbon referendums and the Fiscal Treaty referendum, SIPTU changed its stance three times. Clearly, the Charter alone was insufficient to warrant support from the leadership in the Lisbon debate. All the unions, with the exception perhaps of the Charter Group, felt aggrieved that they were not consulted on the decision to introduce labour mobility in the context of enlargement. Having actively campaigned for the ratification of the Nice Treaty, both SIPTU and ICTU felt aggrieved when the unions were overlooked by the government on opening the Irish labour market to the 'new' member states. This unilateralism by the state marked the beginning of the end for social concertation in Ireland.

'Trade unions are more sceptical and less friendly towards Europe as a result of the evolution of post-Nice Europe' (interview with former General Secretary, SIPTU).

Irish unions, generally, had become alarmed by the proliferation of social dumping episodes already discussed in the previous chapter. Certainly, the Irish Ferries dispute, along with GAMA and Moneypoint, captured the public imagination. More concretely, social dumping 'posed the most serious threat to the survival of the social partnership model in its history' (Roche 2007b: 420) with SIPTU refusing to enter social concertation negotiations without government assurances to address the 'race to the bottom' in labour standards. Adopting a critical stance can be unpopular, resulting in 'orchestrated public opprobrium' (*ibid*.: 419). SIPTU's close ties with the Labour Party made adopting an overt Eurosceptic stance all the more difficult. Its decision not to adopt a formal position on the Lisbon Treaty, led to Labour party members, such as Joe Costello, berating the union for not supporting the position of ICTU and the ETUC. To secure SIPTU's support Labour cajoled the union's leadership by promising to address unions' concerns *if* elected at the next election.

Traditionally, Connect adopted a vocational outlook and rarely entered political debates on the EU, until the Lisbon Treaty. Anecdotally, some have argued that this change in perspective and its critical engagement with the Lisbon Treaty was as a result of a change of leadership. Such a claim, however, is largely spurious as Connect officials had already flagged the problems with social dumping *in the construction sector*, before the change in leadership in 2009. The following excerpt from an ICTU (2008) conference confirms this:

> We need to look at the potential vulnerability of our Registered Employment Agreements, our Employment Regulation Orders arising from the European Court of Justice decision in Laval, Viking and now a worse one in the Rüffert case, where competition is seen, or to put it properly, a race to the bottom is seen and deemed to be more important than anything else to our judiciary; people and the human and fundamental rights of citizens are trampled on in the interests of competition (Owen Wills (TEEU [Connect]), ICTU Special Delegates Conference 2008).

Whilst personal Eurosceptic beliefs may have been held by the new leadership, the line of argument was based entirely upon developments in the construction sector, which, through transnational dynamics, had been disproportionately affected by social dumping (*see* Chapter seven; *see also* Krings *et al*. 2015). Connect (2009) stated that it would reconsider its position, if a social protocol was attached to the Treaty and the Directive on the Posting of Workers was amended to give workers' rights primacy over the interests of the market. Being involved at the EU level would have helped this cause.

Both Connect and SIPTU engaged the government in a bid to strengthen their regulatory coping mechanisms. However, the government would not go beyond what was in the *Towards 2016* agreement for fear of spooking foreign investment, either established or prospective. Whereas a 'solemn declaration' and, more importantly, a promise from the Labour party was enough to convince SIPTU, Connect was not for turning.

The third grouping consisted of British-based unions, 'who are essentially opposed to everything to do with Europe' (interview with former General Secretary, ICTU). This is particularly the case with Unite, whose leadership is ideologically opposed to the EU.

> Where we're coming from is that the people who run the EU, and in whose interests they run it, is, in our opinion, in the interests of capital and we've seen more and more attacks coming on workers' rights, trade union rights, employment rights, etc. ... With the Laval and Viking rulings ... and all those attacks on workers' rights ... we opposed EU treaties on that basis. And unfortunately, we were told lies ... not only is this *not* an attack on workers' rights ... [but] this is going to extend workers' rights ... A Charter of Fundamental Rights ... Of course, we knew that was a pig in a poke ... (interview with Regional Secretary, Unite; *see also* O'Reilly 2019).

The division in ICTU between Irish and British unions is a longstanding one with deep historical roots (O'Connor 2011): 'The split in the 1940s was really over the danger of British-based unions having a majority leadership of the Irish movement' (O'Reilly 2019: 69). Connect is a quintessentially *Irish* union, founded by Countess Markievicz, a leading Irish republican and labour activist, following the quasi-foundation of the state in the 1920s (Yeates 2008; Dineen 2022). Even in the 1990s, Connect's predecessor, the TEEU, was involved in 'all-out-war' with Britain's second largest union (*ibid:* 257–9), the Amalgamated Engineering and Electrical Union, which later became Amicus, before becoming Unite in 2007. Being associated with Unite, a British-based union, was an uneasy position for Connect to find itself in, not least because there were regular turf wars between the two unions for members (Dineen 2022: 272). Whereas Unite's ideologically driven Eurosceptic stance never really came as a surprise, the decision by Connect to maintain an unpopular position would inevitably be interpreted as running counter to the unforgiving 'national interest' and the mainstream political parties, with the important exception of Sinn Féin. Hence, the framing of EU politicisation by underlining the Laval Quartet was of import strategically for Connect. That said, the notion that 'it would be foolish to provide the [EU] institutions with more power' (TEEU 2008a) is shortsighted as only the EU institutions can amend and strengthen (posted-) worker-related legislation (Seliger and Wagner 2018).

Why is the exception of Sinn Féin's standing apart from the political mainstream important? I would argue that how European integration is internalised by the political system will have a bearing on whether unions adopt an overt Eurosceptic stance or not. I will return to this in the following chapter: suffice to say here that Sinn Féin's 'cautious engagement with the EU is predicated on a careful presentation of itself as a resolutely republican and left-wing party' (Maillot 2009: 559). For historical reasons, the soft Euroscepticism of Sinn Féin, which espouses a civic rather than ethnic brand of nationalism, goes some way to legitimise the stance adopted by Connect on EU treaties.

SIPTU's gamble to support the Lisbon Treaty in the second referendum paid off, with the Labour party becoming the minority party in a Fine-Gael-led government in 2011. The front page of its monthly paper, *Liberty* (2015), read 'Collective bargaining at last'. The enactment of the 2015 Industrial Relations Act, which reinstated sectoral REAs, was broadly welcomed by the trade union movement. Whether this legislation strengthened the unions' coping mechanisms remains an open question, but it 'lays down stricter conditions for their [sectoral collective agreements] establishment and operation' (Geary 2016: 138).

Unite had campaigned for statutory union recognition in the run-up to the Lisbon Treaty and this was a right they 'are not prepared to concede' (Kelly 2008). The struggle around trade union recognition rights has been a long and a fraught one. Since the 1980s, unions encountered hostility from US multinationals as well as home-grown multinationals such as Ryanair. ICTU, under different rounds of social concertation, sought to get agreement on mandatory recognition, but without success (Roche 2007b). The prospect of Unite achieving union recognition rights was wishful thinking and its leadership had little confidence in SIPTU's strategy: 'The Labour Party is not going to legislate to underpin those R[egistered] E[mployment] A[greement]s' (interview with Regional General Secretary). On this point, the Unite leadership was proved wrong. I turn now to the Italian unions and their continuing pro-European consensus.

Centralised pluralism and the prevailing pro-European consensus

Italy has undertaken far-reaching 'structural reforms' and consequently undergone significant economic restructuring to ensure its continuing membership of EMU. This was the case in the 1990s and again in the post-2008 period of crisis (Baccaro and Howell 2017; Jordan *et al.* 2021). Prescriptions issued by EU executives even had the temerity to demand the Italian government overturn the result of a positive, abrogative referendum in 2011, which had been organised, *inter alia*, by the unions. The successful referendum reversed legislation to privatise local public services (Bieler 2021). The new economic governance regime's 'continued commodifying bias' consistently called for bargaining institutions to be decentralised to firm level and made it easier for Italian firms to dismiss workers with the abolition of Article 18 (Jordan *et al.* 2021). Notwithstanding, the three Italian confederations remain resolutely pro-EU.

The Italian confederations' stance is underpinned by an ideological commitment to Eurofederalism, which, effectively, is the intellectual heir to Eurocommunism (*see* Chapter Four). However, this credo alone would not sustain a pro-European stance. Importantly, it is, first and foremost, bolstered materially by comparatively robust coping mechanisms (*see* Chapter Seven) and all unions, from federal to confederal level, are actively engaged in trade union structures at the EU level. There is, however, an unwillingness to share the same political oxygen as other Eurosceptic parties (*see below*).

Eurofederalism acts as a unifier amongst the mainstream and even the more radical Italian left. The legacy of Altiero Spinelli and the *Manifesto di Ventotene* is particularly strong amongst the Italian labour movement, including the more radical wing (Mezzadra and Negri 2014). This was one of the first things the General Secretary of CGIL conveyed in an interview, when asked about the union's unwaveringly pro-European stance on European integration: '*noi siamo figli di Spinelli*' ['we are the sons/daughters of Spinelli']. On the question of 'Europe' the three confederations typically speak with one voice, a phenomenon I describe as centralised pluralism.

> We – CISL-CGIL-UIL – are generally in agreement that Europe is a good idea, if anything we would like to see more Europe, more political institutions. We in Italy would never advise the public to vote in a referendum against Europe. We maintain that the European institutions have to be strengthened … Not only strengthened but also imbued with a greater political and social identity (interview with Confederal Secretary, CISL).

These sentiments are regularly expressed, either individually or collectively, in various trade union publications. This remains the case despite the current deep crisis in Italy and Europe. These following extracts are just two examples of many but adequately illustrate the common position shared by the Italian confederations on Europe and their commitment to a United States of Europe.

> UIL believes in the need to have more Europe, more European cohesion and integration policies, going well beyond the Euro area's economic and monetary sphere and aiming at a real political union, with *representative institutions* and wider and

recognized legislative powers. It is an E.U. vision requiring *a transfer or delega-tion of powers to E.U.* institutions on a wide range of matters which currently fall almost exclusively within national competence: suffice to think of economic, fis-cal, social and particularly foreign policies (Rea 2012: 8, emphasis added).

> CGIL, CISL and UIL reaffirm their commitment to deepen European integration by rejecting approaches based on excessive austerity measures not considering social impact and development implications. We call for more economic and political governance of the European Union and *greater involvement of the social partners*. The EU's federal development leading to the construction of the United States of Europe needs to be undertaken immediately and with concrete actions (Rea, Durante and Bonanni 2012: 81, emphasis added).

Italian trade unionists who were interviewed were keen to emphasise that whatever criticism was directed towards 'Europe' it was directed not towards the institutions but towards the politics. On two occasions, to illustrate this point, national examples were given as to why the unions would rather describe themselves as Barroso-sceptic rather than Eurosceptic. On adopting a Eurosceptic stance, the General Secretary of CGIL noted: 'That would be like somebody saying: "seeing that I don't like the current government, I no longer like my country" ' (interview with former General Secretary, CGIL). Building on this analogy, a CISL official noted 'we need a legislature to coun-ter Barroso, Draghi, etc. … we need to change the politics, but the institutions can only be strengthened' (interview with Confederal Secretary, CISL).

Even radical thinkers, such as Mezzadra and Negri (2014), draw on the life and work of Spinelli when advocating the need to politicise the European space. Here, there is a tendency to emphasise the *irreversibility* of European integration and a need for a radical democratic movement as the only solu-tion to breaking the neo-liberal spell. As Mezzadra and Negri (2014) argue, there is a need

> … to rediscover the European space as a space for struggle … Outside of this sphere there is no such thing as *political realism* … Today requalifying a *dis-course of political programme* is crucial, and this is possible only from *within* the European space, and *against* it … It is necessary to immediately reconstruct a general horizon of transformation, to collectively elaborate a new political grammar and a set of elements of a program, that could aggregate strength and power within the struggles (emphasis in original).

Whilst Italian trade union preferences are underpinned by an ideological commitment to Eurofederalism, this credo alone could not be sustained were it not for comparatively robust coping mechanisms, especially at sectoral level, the importance of which are discussed in the previous chapter.

An important difference with the Irish context is that Euroscepticism is synonymous with parties on the right of the political spectrum, in particular the *Lega Nord*, now named simply *Lega* having (almost) abandoned its secessionist position in favour of nationwide representation. Under the leadership of Matteo Salvini, the *Lega* has become increasingly hostile towards the EU and xenophobic towards migrants (Huysseune 2010). For this reason, and others, Italian unions did not want to share a platform with the likes of the *Lega*.

Direct democracy has been an important tool that unions have used to reverse controversial legislation introduced by Italian executives (Erne and Blaser 2018). Following the successful 2011 referendum in Italy, it became a key strategy of a faction within the CGIL to politicise EU questions, albeit with mixed results. As noted above, none of the referendums came to pass but, in the case of joint responsibility, the desired effect was secured. In light of the 2015 Syriza referendum (Sheehan 2016), perhaps this was the best possible outcome.

CONCLUSION

Although attitudes towards the EU vary considerably across member states (De Vries 2018), Italy and Ireland have constantly scored high on being supportive of the EU. Yet, when the Irish public was asked to vote on the Lisbon Treaty, the Eurobarometer data was found wanting. This is because Eurobarometer data is limited methodologically and does not consider broader political developments in the EU, such as the landmark ECJ rulings or, more importantly, the worsening of material conditions for certain sectors of the economy, which can only be articulated by 'organic intellectuals', that is, trade union leaderships, which have to be politically astute.

While EU governance has never been completely free of controversy, the third phase of European integration is certainly synonymous with an increase in the politicisation of the EU from the bottom up (Hooghe and Marks 2007, 2009) and consists of three components: i) increasing saliency of the EU; ii) polarisation of views in relation to the EU and its political and economic direction; and iii) a widening of the number of actors engaging in political interest with the EU (De Wilde and Zürn 2012; *see also* Zürn 2016; De Wilde, Leupold and Schmidtke 2016; Statham and Trenz 2013). This process has occurred incrementally, firstly in the context of 'deepening through widening', the (failed) CT referendums as well as the Lisbon Treaty debates; and secondly in the context of EMU, the financial-cum-sovereign-debt crisis, and the debates on the Fiscal Compact. The analytical distinction between the EU's two flagship projects, the single market programme and monetary union, present unions with different dilemmas, which will have a bearing on their preferences, strategies and the politicisation process. This distinction is rarely acknowledged by politicisation scholars.

Whilst politicisation and labour Euroscepticism is increasingly a feature, to what extent does it constitute a 'constraining dissensus' (Hooghe and Marks 2007, 2009)? Following the double rejection of the CT, the EU simply bided its time by introducing a 'period of reflection' before resurrecting the bones of the CT via the Lisbon Treaty, whose ratification difficulties in Ireland were eventually overcome. Similarly, the country-of-origin principle, dropped following successful transnational counter-mobilisations by unions including the CGIL, was reintroduced by an ECJ wearing a mask for politics (Burley and Mattli 1993). In short, dissensus is only temporarily constraining and needs to be considered in the broader, open-ended process of class struggle (*see* Chapter Two).

Politicisation requires strategic action. This strategic action is in response to 'horizontal' challenges, but is also shaped by political opportunity structures, which in turn are shaped by political or relational factors. Whereas the political opportunity structure is the most obvious difference between Irish and Italian unions when it comes to politicising the EU, that is, Ireland's obligation to hold referendums, this does not explain how or why preferences are adopted. In the context of 'deepening through widening', the policing of a liberal labour market, exposed to transnational socio-economic dynamics, is difficult, as is the politicisation of these dynamics. These pressures, associated with the single market, are 'refracted into divergent struggles over particular national practices' (Locke and Thelen 1994: 4) while at the same time 'reinforc[ing] the opacity of power relations within transnational capitalism' (Szabó *et al.* 2021: 636). Despite social concertation gains 'represent[ing] the single biggest leap forward in social policy initiated in this country' (ICTU 2007), Ireland became an increasingly hostile environment, particularly following the Ryanair judgement[13] (Doherty 2008, 2011; Roche 2007b). In a bid to reverse this, SIPTU, Unite and Connect used the first referendum on the Lisbon Treaty to challenge the political unwillingness of employers and the government to fully address unions' concerns.

The objectives included strengthening workers' rights at the EU level and the granting of trade union recognition rights; but, realistically, neither was going to happen, for two reasons. Firstly, SIPTU's strategy was non-committal and lackadaisical and was pursued so as to avoid a public and political backlash, and to manage its relationship with the Labour party. Connect justified its stance by referring to the contentious Laval Quartet, so as to avoid being the target of public opprobrium, and called for stronger workers' rights at the EU level. Calling for the strengthening workers' rights at the EU level, secondly, is problematic as neither Connect nor Unite are engaged at the EU level. Whilst a trade union remains 'an organization of employees who have combined together to improve their returns from and conditions at work' (Crouch 1982: 13) there are, within a multilevel governance framework, other avenues or 'opportunities' in addition to the national level which need to be explored if one is serious about social Europe. Respectively, SIPTU and ICTU actively engage with the sectoral federations, such as the European Federation of Building and Woodworkers, and the cross-sectoral organisation, namely the ETUC, as do the three Italian confederations, and their respective sectoral federations, which are very active at the EU level.

The pro-European consensus of the Italian unions up to and including the Lisbon Treaty can, in part at least, be explained by their having a Eurofederalist outlook. This alone, however, would not suffice their staunch pro-EU preference and we must also consider their proactive role within trade union structures at the European level and, more importantly, their robust coping mechanisms at the sectoral level, which were the outcome of political exchange during social concertation, and critical in offsetting social dumping practices. However, the Italian unions were hamstrung by the political environment when it came to critiquing the EU, generally, and its new economic governance regime, which was inimical to organised labour's interests, in particular (Jordan *et al.* 2021).

While ICTU and SIPTU did not endorse the Fiscal Compact, Unite, along with Connect, officially rejected it. These unions were also joined by Mandate, which organises the retail sector, and the Civil and Public Services Union (now part of Fórsa). Unite wanted to follow the mass demonstrations in the early part of the crisis with a general strike; however, the leadership of ICTU was not in favour (Kelly 2014). Unite, historically, has stood out from amongst the Irish unions for its constant Eurosceptic stance, which is on ideological grounds. However, the limit of Unite's Euroscepticism became apparent in 2016, when its National Executive voted overwhelmingly to campaign for a 'Remain' vote in the Brexit referendum.

Initially, the Italian unions were restrained and this aspect, particularly the CGIL, puzzled scholars (Castellani and Queirolo Palmas 2018; Gago 2018). For instance, when the ETUC organised an EU-wide campaign to politicise the EU's response to the crisis, the Irish and Italian confederations' involvement, with the exception of the CGIL, was non-existent. Instead, ICTU embarked on a charm offensive travelling to visit, amongst others, the 'reluctant hegemon' (ICTU 2013), Germany, 'which is remaking Europe in its own image[14] (*ibidem*). ICTU did this rather than politicising the EU's new economic governance regime. This substantiates Erne's claim that unions 'lacked the strategic foresight to politicize the transformative, but less visible, changes in Europe's socioeconomic governance regime' (2015: 357).

Factions within the CGIL sought to amend the political opportunity structure by developing direct democracy strategies (Erne and Blasser 2018). A repeat of the successful 2011 referendum was unlikely; however, even the threat of direct democracy was enough to cajole the Gentiloni government into a U-turn on eliminating full joint responsibility in subcontracting: an important coping mechanism in a transnationalised sector (*see* Chapter Seven). Although a referendum on the debt brake never materialised, the pro-European consensus was clearly becoming more difficult to maintain within the CGIL, with FIOM becoming the flagbearer of politicisation.

Its leader, Landini (current General Secretary of CGIL), is clearly inspired by his predecessor Bruno Trentin. Landini (2016: 11) wrote, '[T]he leaders of the European Union seem deaf, blind and, ultimately, indifferent in the face of the Greek drama, the problems of the Spaniards or the Portuguese' [author's translation]. Landini sees politicisation as a part of class struggle and is critical of the 'demonisation of conflict, at every level' which he argues 'is fundamental for the protection of the ruling class because it eliminates the possibility of participating in decisions and identifying solutions' (*ibid.*: 15 [author's translation]). Landini notes that this 'demonisation of conflict, at every level' is also having a bearing on inter-union relations, which have undergone 'a profound mutation' so much so that there has been a 'breakdown of the unity of action between CGIL, CISL UIL' (*ibid.*: 24 [author's translation]). Notwithstanding, Landini (*ibid.*: 43), almost channelling the spirit of Trentin, remains steadfast in his convictions towards the EU and somewhat reluctant to politicise it via direct democracy: 'There is no need for a referendum on the euro to know that the many differences and disparities present in the "old continent" risk destroying the Union even before it really exists. Hence the need for a social battle, including trade unions, to build a Europe based on social solidarity and capable of dealing with difficulties in the world of work' [author's translation]. The burning question, of course, is how might this be achieved?

(Bieler 2006: 130; *see also* 157). That said, social Europe 'is in fact a loosely defined normative concept and, as such, is used with differing meanings in accordance with rather ambiguous definitions' (Jepsen and Serrano Pascual 2005: 232). This implies that its meaning can vary from trade union to trade union (*see* Teague 1989a, 1999b; Bieler 2006; Hyman 2005; Fitzgerald, Beadle and Rowan 2021). As Hyman notes (2001c: 477), the concept or vision 'has generated a polarisation of views' amongst trade unions (*see also* Hyman 2005). Understanding these views might not be as straightforward as one might like.

The power of ideas is seen as being important for informing preference on European integration (van Apeldoorn 2002; Parsons 2003; Morgan 2005; Jabko 2006). Here, I outline two plausible scenarios or polity expectations that envisage either a tighter or a looser form of political integration. These two scenarios are informed by political realism and can be neatly described as 'unity in diversity' and 'ever closer union'. Separately, they act like filters through which European integration is evaluated. There is a greater degree of compatibility between the ideas of 'unity in diversity' and 'ever closer union', than, say, the other way round because the former idea would be considered by proponents of the latter as a stepping stone towards a federal Europe. Such an arrangement, however, would prove a step too far for proponents of 'unity in diversity'. Hence, there is not just one hymn sheet for a socially oriented EU. Instead, there are at least two different ones, albeit with harmonious notes being shared.

In Chapters 7 and 8, I have discussed the importance of industrial relations as an integral component of social Europe. Here, however, I am concerned primarily with the normative value of social Europe

and its justificatory role within discourse on the EU. Hence, social Europe is to 'be regarded as a political construction' and 'as a means of furthering the goal of constructing a European identity' (Jepsen and Serrano Pascual 2005: 232). Within the 'social Europe' discourse, it is possible to discern two competing visions or ideal-types, which correspond to ontologies – basic assumptions about the type of entities that exist and on their relationships – and ideologies as comprehensive conceptualisations of world views. On the one hand, there is European integration as *political unification* and, on the other, there is European integration as *economic and political co-operation.* Whereas the former is espoused by Euro-federalists, who favour 'ever closer union', the latter vision is advocated more by traditional social-democrats, who support what we can term 'unity in diversity' (Morgan 2005). Unlike political parties that might politicise the EU and European integration for electoral gain, unions are more interested in the process of democratisation as a means of embedding the (transnational) market (Erne 2008). The method by which this might be achieved can, however, be shaped by differences in political factors.

In his book *Passage to Europe*, van Middleaar (2013) identifies three 'European' discourses that equate to confederalism, federalism and neo-functionalism. Van Middleaar terms these 'the Europe of States', 'the Europe of Citizens' and 'the Europe of Offices'. As the advocates of the latter 'believe there is no need for any visionary goal' (2013: 3), I will briefly deal with the other two as they map neatly on to the 'unity in diversity' and 'ever closer union' ideals. Advocates of the 'Europe of States' believe that there is most to gain from co-operation between governments. Sovereignty should be pooled in areas of mutual interest, but '[o]nly states have sufficient authority and operational capacity to buttress European unity' (*ibidem*: 2). Advocates of the 'Europe of Citizens' espouse a vision that is 'quite different' (*ibid.*). Here, 'the idea is to detach certain powers from national executive, legislative and judicial authorities and transfer them to a European government, parliament and court, paving the way for federation' (*ibid.*). In short, a United States of Europe becoming 'a democratic society that thinks of itself as a single political – even cultural – entity' (*ibid.*). Whereas Italian unions support 'ever closer union' and political unification; Irish unions are more drawn to the idea of 'unity in diversity' and greater economic and political co-operation.

Both approaches allow unions to view European integration, and the function of the EU, through different lenses. Similarly, their potential remedies for ameliorating tensions or struggles can differ and, despite there being a degree of compatibility between the two approaches, each can find fault with the other's approach. For instance, the 'ever closer union' approach is critical of the 'unity in diversity' approach on the grounds that an evolutionary and piecemeal approach to integration, that is to say, the current approach, produces a glut of problems, including a democratic deficit. The 'unity in diversity' approach is critical of the former on the grounds that federalism is merely code for doing away with nation-state prerogatives and is problematic because political legitimation resides primarily in territorial sovereignty. Here, a greater emphasis is placed on efficiency, or, as Scharpf (1999) terms it, 'output legitimacy'. However, this approach is based on the competence-efficiency formula, which assumes that technical expertise trumps ideology and efficiency trumps democratic legitimacy. Following this logic, political negotiations cannot produce efficiency; but the 'ever closer union' camp might disagree as to what exactly 'efficiency' is and instead argue in favour of effectiveness (Bartolini 2010: 22).

In this book, I argue that organised labour's preferences for a 'social Europe' are shaped by a number of factors. Firstly, there are historical legacies that cast a long shadow. Secondly, there are union–government relations, which are coloured by two aspects. On the one hand, there is the question of social concertation. This was especially important in strengthening Italian unions' so-called 'articulation mechanisms', which enhance the governance capacity of unions at local, sectoral and national levels (Crouch 1993). On the other hand, there is the question of how national governments ratify European treaties. Whereas the presence of social concertation was also significant for Irish unions, having to hold a referendum meant that successive Irish governments could not adopt a minimalist position, particularly on European social issues. The third factor has to do with the changing nature of European integration, which also has two aspects. On the one hand there is the qualitative nature of European integration as a transnational socio-economic process, and its attendant challenges, some of which can be difficult to politicise (*see* Chapter Eight) or even contrary to the interests of organised labour. On the other hand, there are what I term the coping mechanisms of organised labour in a borderless world, and their effectiveness, in particular, in offsetting ethically (and legally) dubious business practices, that is social dumping. Here, I include participation in European trade union structures as well as the development of the EU's social *acquis*, such as the Posted Workers Directive, as coping mechanisms. Fourthly, there is how the question of the EU and European integration has been internalised by the domestic political system. This is important, as preferences are relational.

In the following sections, I will discuss the importance of these factors in shaping the preferences of Irish and Italian organised labour towards European integration. I will conclude the book by returning to the biggest question of all, namely, the future of a post-Brexit EU.

HISTORICAL LEGACIES

Actors' identities were more pronounced in the immediate post-war and emerging Cold War context, which led to divisions within national trade union circles, particularly Italy's. The divisions that emerged within the pluralist Italian trade union system were along classist (CGIL), religious (CISL) and republican (UIL) lines. These divisions were also reflected in the international trade union movement (*see* Carew *et al.* 2000). For the CGIL, its class-based, pro-Soviet ideology underpinned its initial anti-EU stance. That said, the CGIL's opposition is often overstated: once the predicted impoverishment of the Italian working class did not materialise, the leadership of the CGIL found it difficult to maintain its 'orthodox' position and consequently revised its stance towards the EEC from that of outright opposition to one of critical engagement (*see* Chapter Four). Former leader of the influential metalworkers' union (FIOM), and subsequent CGIL leader and MEP, Bruno Trentin, was instrumental in revising the CGIL's position both theoretically and practically. This involved placing the material interests of the workers above the ideological interests of the party–union nexus. Hence, on the question of European integration, the position of the CGIL was closer to that of the *Partito Socialista Italiano*, which in principle held a positive view of European integration, than that of the *Partito Comunista Italiano*. This corroborates the 'fictitious unanimity of democratic centralisation' (Galli 1964: 327). Furthermore, the decision of the CGIL to break rank with the PCI and the communist-led WFTU is not only demonstrative of the value the CGIL places on trade union autonomy but also shows that unions are more responsive to changes in workers' material reality than political parties. In essence, Trentin's influence on the CGIL's Europe policy cannot be overstated.

In Chapter Four, I argued that once the CGIL abandoned its Eurosceptic stance, it advanced the idea of Eurocommunism. Today, Euro-federalism is the intellectual heir of Eurocommunism. This *credo* or *fede* has greatly influenced the Italian left since the 1970s. Its spiritual leader, Altiero Spinelli, started the process of EU constitutionalisation, which culminated with the Lisbon Treaty (Ponzano 2010; Wessels 2014). The legacy of Spinelli and the *Manifesto di Ventotene* is particularly influential amongst the Italian labour movement, including the more radical wing. This sentiment was at its zenith in the late 1980s, when, in an advisory (but unbinding) referendum, Italians voted overwhelmingly in favour (88 per cent) of conferring a mandate on the European Parliament to create a European Constitution. Euro-federalism is best captured by the term 'ever closer union' and whilst the three Italian confederations may well differ on domestic questions, or how to respond to anti-labour government policies, they are very much united in their vision of Europe.

Irish unions, on the other hand, have never really articulated a vision. This is partly because there was such a large number of Irish unions, which prevented a unitary vision from emerging. The Cold War constraints that shaped the preferences of the Italian unions are less relevant in the Irish case. As in Italy, communist thought was utterly abhorred as a Godless doctrine by theo-conservative forces; however, in the Irish context, these forces held a socio-political hegemony. Consequently, the 'red scare' in Ireland was more of a transient affair or, as O'Connor (2011: 174) wittily put it, the Irish communists 'presented no conceivable danger to anything but themselves'. Instead, a brand of conservativism infused with Roman Catholicism was internalised and exalted by the *Irish* trade union movement. Divisions between unions had less to do with ideology and more to do with Irish nationalism. Despite having achieved independence from British rule, little changed on the island of Ireland in terms of industrial relations. Here, it was not as simple as painting the letterboxes green,[1] for there remained British unions which vied for influence within the singular Irish confederation. This resulted in a brief schism in the 1950s, when the native unions attempted to wrong-foot the so-called 'amalgamated' unions; but this strategy ultimately failed and the British unions remained a unique feature of the Irish labour movement.

At the time of the first Irish request for membership of the EU, ninety-five unions were operating on the island of Ireland, twenty-four of which had their headquarters in Britain! When the question of membership became a distinct possibility, ICTU held a special conference, which voted against joining. Clearly, the position of the larger unions, the ITGWU and the British-based ATGWU (now Unite) carried the day. Democratically bound, ICTU campaigned for a 'no' vote in the 1972 accession referendum, albeit in a lacklustre fashion. The latter's disapproval of Irish membership was on the grounds that 'not enough information' (ICTU 1971) from the government was forthcoming. This was clearly a smokescreen for another, more politically sensitive motivation, which was not for public consumption. Here, 'a deterioration of relations' (Murphy 2009: 204) between the hegemonic Fianna Fáil party and ICTU is a possible explanation. Also, this was the first time that Irish trade unions were involved in a political referendum of national significance and their political inexperience in such matters became apparent. Henceforth, in order to understand the position of ICTU on European questions, it is necessary to consider such questions through the prism of ICTU–government relations. In other words, the rhetoric is often not to be taken at face value and there is generally a need to read between the lines. What you see is not necessarily what you get!

By the late 1980s, we see a re-articulation of the positions of both the Italian and Irish confederations on the question of European integration. Here, I identify 1988 as a pivotal year in which strategic steps were taken to forge a pro-European consensus inside the CGIL and ICTU. There were, however, important differences, which speak to the 'ever closer union' and 'unity and diversity' dichotomy. Under the leadership of Bruno Trentin, a devout federalist, the CGIL was being further reformed by strengthening the *European* dimension. The objective of 1988's *Per un Programma Europeo della CGIL* [*For a European Programme of the CGIL*] was to strengthen the case for greater economic, social and political integration of Europe (CGIL 1988). This included developing a European industrial relations system with collective bargaining units at different sectoral levels, so as to address the structural political economy differences between northern and southern Europe. The three Italian confederations expressed a passionate and ambitious vision for the EU. Such passion and ambition were not merely rhetorical: all Italian unions in unison were prepared to make considerable sacrifices, including the abolition of the *scala mobile* (wage index mechanism), in the name of deeper political integration.

If the CGIL's *Programma* expressed an Italian vision *for* Europe, ICTU's *Make Europe Work for Us* conference of 1988 outlined a vision for Ireland *within* Europe. The special ICTU conference involved a Delors-led 'charm offensive', which had the desired effect. The ICTU leadership had a clear eye on '1992' and were keen to address concerns and engender a pro-European consensus in the broader trade union movement. That said, an overly enthusiastic approach was avoided not least because the 'Irish economic performance ha[d] been the least impressive in Western Europe, perhaps in all Europe, in the twentieth century' (Lee 1989: 521). To this end, the arrival of Jacques Delors is a well-documented factor in explaining the shift in trade union preferences (*see*, for example, Jabko 2006; Bieler 2006; Mitchell 2012). Of similar importance is Delors Package I, agreed in February of the same year (*see* Chapter Five).

By the 1990s, the fragmented character of the Irish trade union movement had diminished, following state-led initiatives (Allen 1997). The most significant merger was that of the ITGWU and FWUI in 1990, to create Ireland's largest union, SIPTU. That said, however, historical fault-lines would inevitably resurface, particularly in the European debate, notably between the principal British union, Unite and the *Irish* unions. With the exception of the Maastricht Treaty, Unite opposed every European Treaty. The Maastricht Treaty aberration can be explained by the Delors factor. In the UK, Unite's predecessor, Transport and General Workers' Union, was broadly in favour of EMU, provided public sectoral renewal be completed (Bieler 2006: 155).

Whilst supportive of EMU, Unite, on ideological grounds, remained critical of the relatively good union–government relations which helped to ensure that Ireland (and Italy) met the Maastricht criteria for joining the common currency. This good union–government relationship goes a considerable way towards explaining the emerging pro-European consensus in the Irish trade union movement, which lasted two decades.

UNION–GOVERNMENT RELATIONS

A major factor in explaining the pro-European consensus of trade unions is union–government relations, which were of critical importance in shaping organised labour's preferences towards the EU, generally, and EMU, in particular. Achieving entry to EMU was considerably more difficult for Italy and required greater sacrifices from Italian unions in the name of EMU (Baccaro and Howell 2017), notably, the abolition of the wage-indexation mechanism. That said, in return for this sacrifice, the unions' capacity for labour market governance was strengthened. This would prove important in ensuring that the pro-European consensus continued in the following phase of European integration, and I will return to this in the following sections. Certainly, the commitment of Delors to tripartism at both the European and national levels served to enhance the governance role of organised labour.

On the question of union–government relations within the context of European integration, there are a number of important considerations. Firstly, the formulation and amending of primary legislation, namely, European treaties is the exclusive prerogative of national governments. The work of liberal inter-governmentalists (*see*, for example, Moravcsik 1998; Dimitrakopoulos and Kassim 2004; König and Hug 2006) highlights that EU treaty negotiations are deeply rooted in domestic politics. As Moravcsik (1993: 8) notes, when it comes to the formulation of EU treaties, 'groups articulate preferences; governments aggregate them'. Here, national governments can be targeted by unions, although the latter have been completely overlooked by scholarship as political actors in this process. Certainly, there is evidence that regardless of whether an Italian centre-right or centre-left government was in power, they would adopt a maximalist approach to EU Treaty change (Moravcsik 1998; Moravcsik and Nicolaïdis 1999; Bindi 2011, 2012). For instance, with the Lisbon Treaty, the Italian government 'vehemently supported the extension of QMV' (Quaglia 2010: 98). Hence, the negotiating position of the Italian government is broadly in line with the basic preferences of Italian unions. Typically, the EU treaties do not go far enough.

This differs from Ireland, where the national governments have tended to be centre-right in orientation. On successive EU treaties, Irish governments have typically adopted a mid-way position between the maximalists and mini-malists. This is also evidenced by the submission of the Irish government to the CJEU on the critical Laval case (Lindstrom 2010). Since the mid-1980s, two union-related factors have constrained successive Irish governments from adopting a minimalist position, particularly on European social issues. The first constraint is two decades of institutionalised social concertation, which is seen as being an important factor in the Irish economic miracle (Hastings *et al.* 2007; Regan 2012a; O'Riain 2014; Roche 2009). Were it not for this arrangement, the Irish government would have seriously considered following the UK government by opting-out of progressive EU initiatives, such as the Charter for Fundamental Rights or the Temporary Agency Workers Directive (*see* Chapter Eight). These two decades of institutionalised tripartism came under considerable pressure during the 2006 round of negotiations and as a result of the EU's 'deepening through widening' strategy, which the Irish government and organised capital subscribed to. This aspect, however, is best discussed in the following section on organised labour's coping mechanisms.

The second union-related constraint on the Irish government has to do with how European treaties are ratified. Here, the Irish situation is unique within the EU, much to the vexation of Irish national governments, as well as their European counterparts and EU executives. The first and most significant legal challenge to parliamentary ratification was the case taken in 1987 by Raymond Crotty, challenging the Single European Act, in which the Supreme Court ruled that any EU treaty which surrendered sovereignty must be approved by the Irish people in a referendum. Consequently, Ireland remains an outlier in terms of ratification processes and the Irish government must consider the demands of the Irish public generally, and organised labour in particular, when negotiating an EU Treaty. During the negotiation of the Fiscal Compact, the 'virtuous' countries, Germany *in primis*, were keen to enshrine a debt brake into the 'sinner's' constitutions. The Fine-Gael-led government argued against such a provision, on the grounds that it would be a difficult sell to the Irish public (Gilmore 2016), not to mention an anathema to the majority of Irish organised labour, with perhaps the exception of the public sector unions (*see below*). Whereas two decades of institutionalised tripartism shaped the Irish government's negotiating stance on EU Treaties, the ratification constraint remained important following the demise of tripartism in 2009. This latter development can be explained, at least partly, by the changing nature of European integration as a transnational socio-economic process and the reluctance of the Irish government and organised capital to improve the coping mechanisms of organised labour.

UNION COPING MECHANISMS

The third, and arguably most important, factor in shaping the preferences of organised labour towards European integration has to do with what I term trade union coping mechanisms. Here, it is possible to differentiate between both non-regulatory and regulatory coping mechanisms. Together, these coping mechanisms are key when it comes to ensuring that social dumping practices become less frequent (*see* Bernaciak 2015; Wagner 2018). Measuring their effectiveness is by no means straightforward (*see* Chapter Seven); however, their robustness, particularly that of the regulatory coping mechanisms, can affect government–union relations as well as trade union debates on European integration. Here, Italian organised labour has fared better than its Irish counterpart. This is because the Italian confederations have regularly sought to strengthen their standing in the world of work during episodes of political exchange. Whereas Italian organised labour, partly for historical reasons, had a better understanding of the governance of transnational labour markets and the issue of social dumping, the Irish trade union movement was behind the curve when it came to meeting the challenges associated with transnational labour markets.

The question of coping mechanisms really came to prominence during what I have termed the third phase of European integration, which coincides with the two-term Barroso Commission. The third phase can be sub-divided into two acts: pre- and post-crisis. Whereas the former is characterised by the eastern enlargements of the EU, labour mobility and the contentious 'Laval Quartet' rulings of the CJEU, the latter is concerned primarily with the question of EMU, the financial-cum-sovereign-debt crisis, the Fiscal Compact and the EU's new economic governance regime (Erne 2015). Both 'acts' had implications for the governance of labour markets, albeit with important differences. The EU's eastern enlargement not only carried the threat of downward pressure on wages and working conditions but it also introduced the more insidious practice of social dumping. It is during the third phase that we see the Irish pro-European consensus break down, whilst it remained very strong in the Italian case, despite having been exposed to similar challenges associated with the eastern enlargement and labour mobility. This, I argue, is best explained through the prism of organised labour's coping mechanisms.

The significance of the EU enlargements in the 2000s cannot be overstated. The market-oriented reforms of the Copenhagen criteria and the distinct lack of 'Polanyian fixes' once membership for the former socialist states became a reality (*see* Ó Beacháin, Sheridan and Stan 2012) facilitated the conditions for what I term the EU's 'deepening through widening' strategy. Here, pull factors were strong enough to stimulate East–West labour mobility on a scale never before seen. The 2004 and 2007 enlargements were of particular significance for Ireland and Italy and their respective labour markets, in general, and their construction sectors, in particular (OECD 2012). However, there were important differences between Irish and Italian unions that carried consequences for unions' preferences towards European integration.

The 'deepening through widening' strategy, resulting from the 'big bang' enlargement, inevitably introduced qualitative changes to the nature of the European integration process. This 'horizontal' process had been an incremental one, as each of the 'Four Freedoms' – goods, capital, labour and services – was gradually set free, so to speak. Undoubtedly, the eastern enlargement of the EU had a significant impact in particular on the free movement of labour and services. Understanding how organised labour engages with European integration, as a transnational socio-economic process, is best captured at the sectoral level (Bechter *et al.* 2012). Furthermore, the 'functional equivalence' between Irish and Italian unions means that the sectoral level facilitates comparison (Ragin 1987: 48; Hyman 2001b: 214–17). In using an analytical framework developed in Chapter Seven, I emphasised the importance of construction unions' coping mechanisms, both regulatory and non-regulatory variants, in mediating the socio-economic process of European integration. This was done so as to determine whether or not there was a feedback loop between a union's direct experience with European integration, as a transnational socio-economic process, and their broader preference towards the European project. The simple answer is yes, there was a feedback mechanism; however, it is by no means straightforward and how it was articulated depends on how unions, particularly Connect and Unite, engaged with European trade union structures and how European integration had been internalised by the domestic political system.

The 2004 and 2007 enlargements increased the availability of cheap and mobile labour, creating a division of labour in the construction sector between 'domestic' and 'foreign' labour, where the exploitation of the latter also had an adverse effect on the former (Woolfson and Sommers 2006; Dølvik and Eldring 2006). Hence, the capacity of organised labour to police local labour markets was severely challenged. From the perspective of organised labour in the 'old' member states, labour mobility was a source of concern and strategies to offset the 'negative externalities' varied from country to country. Whilst labour mobility represents the human face of European integration, it was, for some unions, a formal introduction to European integration and the inherent challenges of operating in an increasingly borderless and mobile environment. The EU's deepening through widening strategy was furthered by the CJEU following the 'Laval Quartet' rulings. Two-time Commissioner, Mario Monti (2010), at the behest of Barroso, was commissioned to carry out a report following the Laval Quartet rulings. He found that 'the Court's cases have exposed the fault lines that run between the Single Market and the social dimension at national level'. This fault line varies from country to country and as noted in Chapter Seven, Irish unions found themselves exposed and ill-equipped to deal with the extent of the challenges. Even under the rubric of social concertation, Irish organised labour sought to strengthen their coping mechanisms, ideally by achieving legislation on trade union recognition; however, this was not to be and, consequently, a cohort of unions, rightly or wrongly, choose to politicise the EU and European integration. This differed from the Italian unions, whose construction sector coping mechanisms were more robust; as a consequence, transnational markets were, in the Italian context, more embedded.

Unlike Italy, which, at the behest of organised labour, managed the question of labour mobility, the Irish government, without even consulting ICTU, placed no restriction on the free movement of labour and services in 2004. A disproportionate number of (vulnerable) migrant workers found work in the booming Irish construction industry. Subsequently, a plethora of social dumping cases, ranging from the sublime to the ridiculous, were regularly unearthed, some of which were high profile. A clear indication is the increase in the case load of the Labour Court (2006), which grew by 64 per cent, with a large number of the cases alleging breaches of the collective bargaining agreement in construction. Arqueros-Fernández (2011) also found that the Irish horticulture sector, which also employed large numbers of migrants, similarly experienced extensive social dumping. Irish union officials readily admit that they were unprepared, under-resourced and slow off the mark. It soon

became apparent that what might be termed 'soft' organising, raising awareness about workers' rights and so on was insufficient (*see also* Dundon *et al.*
2007). Once the extent of the exploitation became apparent, clear attempts
were made by the unions to develop their non-regulatory coping mechanisms
and bolster their regulatory ones. Two broad strategies were pursued. The
first involved organising migrant workers. Here, a number of unions grasped
the nettle and followed an organising model, with SIPTU leading the way, as
might be expected since it is the best-resourced and largest general union. For
most Irish unions, this was their formal introduction to migrant labour, which
must be seen as the beginning of a learning process (Erne 2008; Kjeldstadli
2015). Future research will determine whether or not real progress is being
made; however, a recent study finds that SIPTU's organising campaigns have
'registered major achievements' (Geary and Gamwell 2019: 203). This is a
start; but a weak regulatory framework can perpetuate (even invite) social
dumping practices. This brings us to the second broad strategy whereby ICTU
sought to strengthen unions' regulatory coping mechanisms.

This strategy was pursued under the rubric of social concertation. Irish
unions, collectively through ICTU, as well as individually, pressurised the
government to strengthen labour market regulations. This was always going
to be an uphill struggle on account of Ireland's 'light touch' liberal political
economy. Some concessions were made in the 2006 bargaining round, such
as an increase in the number of labour inspectorates, which for ICTU, marked
'the biggest thing we have ever done of our own volition' (ICTU 2007: 16)!
For a number of unions, SIPTU, Unite and Connect, the concessions did not
go far enough, and the divisiveness not only marked the beginning of the end
for two decades of Irish social concertation (*see also* Culpepper and Regan
2014), but it also spilled over into the debate on the Lisbon Treaty.

The Italian unions' regulatory and non-regulatory coping mechanisms
were, by comparison, more robust (see Chapter Seven). A number of strategies were pursued at national, sectoral and workplace level so as to ensure this
outcome. For instance, articulation mechanisms between the various levels
of the industrial relations mechanisms were strengthened during episodes of
social concertation in the 1990s. The agreements signed in 1993, the pension
reform in 1994–5 and the Pact for Employment in 1996 were accompanied
by the creation of a new system of representation in the workplaces. This
meant that unions had a stronger presence at the workplace level and a closer
relationship with the rank and file. In doing so, 'the potential crisis of representation has been channelled and controlled' (Regini and Colombo 2011:
140). On the ground, unions worked in tandem with other 'rival' unions
through the creation of the unitary workplace union representation structure
(*rappresentanza sindacale unitaria*). This differed from the Irish landscape,
in which historical inter-union rivalry persisted into the 2000s and hindered

the effectiveness of trade unions in addressing the challenges associated with a transnational sector (*see* Chapter Seven).

In Italy, the *centro lavoratore stranieri* [foreign workers' centres] established in the 1990s provided an important locus for the provision of legal and social services. Here, the union could engage with the (clandestine) migrant workforce and build trust. This occurred irrespective of the institutional shelter enjoyed by the Italian construction unions. The ethnographic research of Perrotta (2011) also attests to the effectiveness of the Italian construction unions' non-regulatory coping mechanisms, which, I argue, served to maintain a pro-EU preference.

At sectoral level, stronger regulatory mechanisms – in particular the DURC and mutual responsibility in the subcontracting chain – were introduced in the 2000s and subsequently tweaked. Together these provisions, or coping mechanisms, made social dumping more difficult. Also, a 'social clause' is included in public procurement legislation, which requires the full application of relevant collective agreements. This is not to suggest that the Italian situation is ideal, far from it, the threat of social dumping is very real in Italy. Arguably, Italian unions have to be wary of even more sordid features, such as organised criminality, which goes some way in explaining the origins of the DURC. The latter, coupled with mutual responsibility in the subcontracting chain, has been rather successful in thwarting social dumping. Unlike in Ireland, where the legality of the collective agreement (REA) was successfully challenged by a group of rogue employers, no cases have been brought before the Italian Labour Courts, either by foreign undertakings complaining about the binding conditions imposed by the Italian legislation or by Italian undertakings (*see* Pallini 2006). Perhaps it is not so surprising that the European construction union (EFBWW 2008b) lauds the Italian DURC system as 'best practice' in the fight against social dumping.

Returning to the Irish case, SIPTU, Connect and Unite expressed concerns about the lack of consultation on post-enlargement labour mobility, the dearth of labour market regulations and the increasing prevalence of social dumping. With the government unprepared to address these concerns adequately for fear of jeopardising the Celtic Tiger and deterring foreign investment, the unions used their support for the Lisbon Treaty as a bargaining chip. The government, however, was not prepared to negotiate and subsequently the aforementioned unions withheld their support for the Treaty. This stance can be interpreted clearly as an expression of 'soft' labour Euroscepticism, which concluded the pro-European consensus that had existed in Irish organised labour for two decades or so.

Hitherto, the pro-European consensus of Irish organised labour was characterised by three factions within ICTU. The first, so-called permissive, faction can be divided into two groups. On the one hand, there were individual unions, such as Connect, that were resolutely permissive insofar as they took their cues on European questions from the ICTU (pro-European) leadership (interview with ex-General Secretary, Connect). On the other hand, there was a cohort of public sector unions that were unreservedly pro-government. This led to their adopting an automatic, non-critical, pro-European stance, particularly on EU treaties. Hence, it is permissive in the sense of being non-judgmental. The second faction is more inclined to evaluate Europe-related questions on a case by case, or Treaty by Treaty, basis. SIPTU belongs to this faction, although expertise on European affairs remains the preserve of a few within the union's Executive Council (interview with former General Secretary, SIPTU). There is a third faction within ICTU, which is associated primarily with the British-based union, Unite. With the exception of the Maastricht Treaty, Unite has adopted a contrary position on *every* European Treaty, mostly on ideological grounds (interview with former Regional Secretary, Unite).

The two aforementioned permissive factions within ICTU became more vocal over the course of the two debates on the Lisbon Treaty. Connect, which hitherto had never publicly contributed to an EU Treaty debate, felt compelled not only to enter the debate but to do so on a critical platform. In particular, Connect (TEEU 2008a, 2008b) publicly cited the CJEU Laval Quartet rulings as justification for its Euroscepticism. However, these controversial rulings were used primarily as a framing device to avoid the charge from hostile media that unions were putting sectional interests above the so-called national interest. As Begg wrote (2009), this type of 'propaganda is endlessly parroted in certain media outlets' (*see also* Mercille 2014). I argue that if trade unions' demands for better legislation had been met and had more robust regulatory coping mechanisms been implemented by the government, the unions' pro-European consensus would have, by and large, remained intact. As explained in Chapter Eight, this is not what occurred. Instead, the pro-business government was prepared to sacrifice tripartism (Culpepper and Regan 2014) rather than strengthen the regulatory coping mechanisms of Irish organised labour.

In any case, post-referendum analysis of the first Lisbon referendum shows that voting was 'heavily class-correlated' (Storey 2008: 77) and that the single most important issue that concerned voters, regardless of whether they voted for or against, was working conditions (Milward Browne IMS 2008). This fact has been overlooked by a number of post-referendum analyses (for example, Leconte 2010; Quinlan 2009; Barrett 2012). Also, 61 per cent of Labour Party supporters voted against the Treaty. As it happens, the financial-cum-sovereign-debt crisis, paradoxically, came to the rescue, thereby saving the EU from a constitutional crisis.

The second Lisbon Treaty referendum took place in very different circumstances from the first. On the second Lisbon Treaty referendum in 2009, SIPTU was cajoled by its 'sister' Labour Party to support the Treaty in return for the promise of stronger trade union rights. Neither Connect and Unite bought into the Labour Party's promise and instead continued to campaign against the Treaty. The public sector unions, on the other hand, formed the Charter Group, which argued the pro-government line, namely, that the Charter of Fundamental Rights would increase the rights of workers and reverse the anti-labour Laval rulings. This line of argumentation was rejected at the time, not least by Connect; a stance that, to some extent, has been vindicated. As the legal scholar de Búrca (2013) writes, 'the Irish courts have been much less ready to interpret and apply provisions of the EU Charter of Fundamental Rights despite the increasing invocation of the Charter by litigants in Irish cases.'

A sub-component of the third coping mechanisms factor is participation in European trade union structures. The creation of the ETUC in 1972 was an important event from both an Irish and Italian trade union perspective. Unlike the British TUC, ICTU viewed participation in the ETUC as being important not only in terms of access to information but also by way of exposure to other European trade union traditions. ICTU even voted in favour of the admission of the *communist* CGIL to the ETUC (Dølvik 1997: 61). As ICTU did not have the resources to open a Brussels office, the ETUC provided the financial means for disseminating information amongst ICTU's affiliates. This strengthened the role of ICTU *vis-à-vis* the affiliate unions as well as the government of the day and went a considerable way towards ensuring the pro-European consensus among Irish organised labour. However, as noted in Chapter Seven, Irish unions, with the exception of SIPTU, have not participated in the different European trade union federations. This has been to their detriment. As Seeliger and Wagner (2018: 15) note, 'the internal structuring of the European trade union movement plays an important role in advancing European labor's political strategies [and] a shift of loyalties to the EU-level facilitates coordination processes across the different levels'.

A noteworthy distinction between Irish and Italian construction unions is their absence and participation, respectively, in the European trade union federations, generally, and the EFBWW, in particular. While participation in such structures does not automatically imply a pro-European stance, it does allow unions to forge relations with other national unions. This is important in the construction of reciprocal solidarity and the forging of transnational strategies (Erne 2008; Gajewska 2009). The absence of Unite's Irish branch and Connect from trade union sectoral structures at the European level is noteworthy, but also problematic. Surely non-participation is at odds with Unite's *soi-disant* class-oriented trade unionism? London-based Unite participates in all the federal European structures. However, to what extent the interests of Irish workers are represented by London-based Unite representatives is debatable. This very question is what led to the creation of *Irish* unions at the turn of the twentieth century (Yeates 2008).

The Connect union is a progeny of that epoch. Besides 'close ties with the struggle for Irish independence' (TEEU, n.d.), the union is quintessentially nationalist (Dineen 2022), which has prolonged its 'splendid isolation' from the wider European labour movement. Connect has never affiliated to a European trade union federation. However, the union recently noted that they are '*learning* how to harness our collective power creatively, not alone nationally but across the world through the new alliances' (TEEU 2014, emphasis added). In 2012, Connect signed a landmark global federation agreement with the United Association of Journeymen and Apprentices, which represents 370,000 craft workers in the United States, Canada and Australia. Rather bizarrely, this affiliation was chosen over the EFBWW. The question of whether this decision was on account of a hardening labour Euroscepticism remains unanswered.

There remains an important fourth factor when it comes to explaining the re-emergence of labour Euroscepticism in Irish organised labour and its absence in its Italian counterparts and that is how the trajectory of political Euroscepticism in the political system of each country differs.

EUROSCEPTICISM IN THE DOMESTIC POLITICAL SYSTEM

How European integration has been internalised by the national political system can have a bearing on the presence or absence of labour Euroscepticism. In other words, this factor can either constrain a union from or facilitate it in adopting a Eurosceptic position. This aspect, however, is less helpful in explaining the phenomenon that gave rise to labour Euroscepticism in Ireland, that is, ineffective coping mechanisms than it is in explaining *why* it is that labour Euroscepticism was able to emerge in Ireland. As can be seen from Table 9.1, the longstanding faultfinder with the EU in Ireland is Sinn Féin, a leftist-populist-nationalist party by its own definition (Ó Broin 2015), affiliated with the United Left–Nordic Green left bloc in the European Parliament (Maillot 2009; Dunphy 2004). Explaining this stance is beyond the scope of this book: suffice to say that Sinn Féin has opposed every EU Treaty (*see* Table 9.1). That said, on the question of EU membership, 'the litmus test' for 'hard' Euroscepticism (Szczerbiak and Taggart 2008a: 240), Sinn Féin advocated for 'Remain' in the UK's 2016 Brexit referendum. Importantly, however, the programmatic stance of *Sinn Féin* differs from that of

Eurosceptic parties in Italy, primarily the *Lega* and *Fratelli d'Italia*, which, across time, have become increasingly hostile towards the EU on sovereignty grounds (Giordano 2004; Huysseune 2010;). As noted in Chapter Five, joining the Euro was important to Italian unions partly because it put paid to the *Lega's* secessionist plans for Northern Italy (*Padania*) and ensured the integrity of the Italian peninsula, socially, politically and economically.

The question of territorial cohesion is also a political aspiration of *Sinn Féin*, as well as a number of Irish unions, although its realisation has been, until very recently that is, quite unlikely. I will briefly return to this Brexit-related question below but for now the point to make is that Euroscepticism in Ireland's political party system has been constantly expressed by *Sinn Féin*. Importantly, however, *Sinn Féin* is positioned on the left of the political spectrum and espouses a 'civic' nationalism, rather than a *Lega*-inspired ethnic nationalism. Consequently, Irish unions, such as Connect, do not find sharing political space with the likes of *Sinn Féin* awkward or unbecoming. Furthermore, over the past decade, since the onset of the financial-sum-sovereign-debt crisis, Sinn Féin has grown in popularity and is currently the largest party in opposition (Golden 2020b). Conversely, on account of the Italian 'Eurosceptic' political space being filled by xenophobic and neo-Fascist political forces, the Italian unions are very reluctant to publicly critique the EU in any meaningful way for fear of being mentioned in the same breath as the *Lega* or *Fratelli d'Italia*.

Hence, European integration has created tensions between Irish and Italian organised labour and pro-union political parties. In Italy, the rise (and fall) of Renzi affected the relationship between the *Partito Democratico*'s and organised labour (Golden 2013). In Ireland, the Labour Party promised SIPTU that in return for support in the second Lisbon referendum, the union's industrial relations concerns would be addressed. To this end, the Irish Industrial Relations Act was amended in 2015. However, Labour's role as a junior coalition partner in an austerity government put the union–party relationship under duress. In 2015, SIPTU delegates defeated a motion to break ties with the party; however, in 2017, the Labour Party unilaterally amended its constitution, thereby ceasing all organisational affiliations. SIPTU has decided to retain its political fund, which can be used to support any union-related candidates, including from Sinn Féin, whose rise can partly be explained by the decline of Labour's vote from 19.5 per cent in 2011 to 4.5 per cent in 2020. Whilst there are strong historical links between ICTU and the Labour party, there is no official affiliation. Notwithstanding, there is a concern within ICTU regarding the latter's dwindling share of the electoral vote and an equal degree of suspicion of Sinn Féin's rise and of their brand of left-wing populism.

Table 9.1 Irish and Italian political parties on European treaties

Treaty	Parties voting against		Parties abstaining		Parties voting for	
	Ireland	Italy	Ireland	Italy	Ireland	Italy
Accession	Labour, SF	PCI (TEC)	None	PSI	FF, FG	DC
Single European Act	Gr, SF	None	Lab	None	FF, FG, PDs	DC, PSI, PCI
Treaty on European Union	Gr, SF	None	None	None	FF, FG, PDs, Lab	DC, PSI, PD,
Treaty of Amsterdam	Gr, SF	None	None	LN	FF, FG, PDs, Lab	PD, FI, AN, RC
Treaty of Nice	Gr, SF	RC	None	None	FF, FG, PDs, Lab,	PD, FI, AN, LN
Treaty of Lisbon	SF	RC (ECT) LN (ECT)	None	None	FF, FG, PDs, Lab, Gr	PD, FI, AN, LN
Fiscal Treaty	SF	LN	None	None	FF, FG, Lab, Gr	PD, FI, AN,

Source: Adapted from Verney (2013) and own research

Irish Parties: FF, Fianna Fáil; FG, Fine Gael; Lab, Labour; PDs, Progressive Democrats, Gr, Greens; SF, Sinn Féin

Italian Parties: DC, Democrazia Cristiana; PSI, Partito Socialista Italiano; PCI, Partito Comunista Italiano; PD, Partito Democratico; FI, Forza Italia; AN, Alleanza Nazionale; RC, Rifondazione Comunista; LN, Lega Nord

Understanding the importance of social institutions in mediating transnational socio-economic dynamics and weary of workers being drawn to 'populist' politics, ICTU's (former) leader, David Begg (2014b), informed a 2014 Connect conference '[I]f you have free trade and free circulation of capital and people but destroy the social state ... the temptations of defensive nationalism and identity politics will very likely grow stronger than ever in Europe'. Begg expressed concern over the shift towards more radical parties, such as '*Podemos* in Spain, *Syriza* in Greece, the *S*[cotish] *N*[ationalist] *P*[arty] in Scotland and *Sinn Féin* in Ireland' (*ibidem*), at the expense of mainstream social-democratic parties, such as the Labour Party. It is no coincidence that, when speaking to Connect's members, Begg warned of a 'Trotskyite left', whose 'mission is to enter trade unions and social democratic political parties – labour parties if you like – so as to destroy them' (*ibid.*). In other words, entryism. Clearly, this was an attempt by Begg to steer Connect's delegates away from *Sinn Féin* and its brand of republican socialism (*see* Ó Broin 2009). Neither is it coincidental that Begg informed delegates that ICTU 'are part of an international bond of solidarity which joins us to 60 million colleagues in Europe through the ETUC'. As noted above, Connect never participated in European trade union structures. This, I would argue, was an effort by Begg to encourage the leadership towards greater co-operation at the European level. This nudge has thus far amounted to nothing; however, this inaction, for reasons outlined above, could have repercussions.

THE FINANCIAL-CUM-SOVEREIGN-DEBT CRISIS, ORGANISED LABOUR AND POST-BREXIT EU

The year 2012 represents an important year in the relationship between the EU and European organised labour, particularly in the Eurozone countries. Against the onset of the financial-cum-sovereign-debt crisis, the ETUC held five European action days (*see* Table 9.2). At its Congress in Athens in May 2011, the ETUC confirmed its opposition to prevailing neo-liberal economic policies and called for a 'New Social and Green Deal' and a tax on financial transactions. The following year, the ETUC (2012) set a precedent by reject- ing the Fiscal Compact and, to demonstrate its mobilisation power, organised a Day of Action and Solidarity against Austerity for the 14 November 2012. Its co-ordination was without precedent (Dufrense 2015) and is described as 'the most successful mass mobilisation against the crisis and austerity mea- sures' (Müller and Platzer 2018: 323). That said, the transnational mobilisa- tion laid bare a number of puzzling anomalies regarding Irish and Italian organised labour. ICTU, whose leadership had regularly lambasted the EU Commission and compared the Troika's Memorandum of Understanding to the punitive Treaty of Versailles (Begg 2010), did not participate in any way whatsoever in the transnational action! Similarly, in Italy, the response of the unions was subdued and uncharacteristically quiet, with only the CGIL stag- ing a four-hour strike (*see also* Gago 2018). The Italian unions' acquiescence, particularly that of the CGIL, was unusual and perplexing. The only explana- tion is that there was an immobilising sense of dread, given the depth and extent of the crisis. Furthermore, neither the EU authorities nor the national governments were swayed by the protest actions. This raises an important question: *quo vadis, social Europe?*

The fact that labour markets lie at the intersection of the single market and the common currency became all the more obvious against the backdrop of the EU's new economic governance regime (Erne 2015). With EMU hav- ing left national governments bereft of monetary policy, many were coerced into pursuing an 'internal devaluation' strategy, the objectives of which were clearly laid out in in a DG ECFIN (2012: 104) policy paper: 'The new and political instruments of control must be used with the aim of reducing the wage setting power of trade unions.' Reducing the wage-setting capacity of unions inevitably has an impact on their capacity to police and control transnational labour markets, which can, in turn, facilitate social dumping practices. Here, the degree of labour market restructuring went further in the Italian context, with a profound alteration of the sacrosanct Article 18 being the most symbolic example (Rutherford and Frangi 2018; Maccarrone 2019). Furthermore, a debt brake was surreptitiously enshrined into the Italian constitution. Notwithstanding the attack on workers' rights and the debt brake, the Italian confederations remained undeterred in their belief in the European creed. Whilst differences may persist between the Italian unions on domestic and government-related issues, the three confederations remain on the same page when it comes to the political end game of the EU. For the CGIL, CISL and UIL, nothing short of a United States of Europe will do.

On the sixtieth anniversary of the Treaty of Rome, CISL (2017) produced a five-page document, *Manifesto per gli Stati Uniti d'Europa* [*Manifesto for a United States of Europe*], according to which anti-EU and anti-Euro movements are the product of a combination of '*globalizzazione anarchica*' and '*una politica europea miope*' [anarchic globalisation and a European political myopia]. Instead, '[I]t is very necessary and urgent to reopen a passage and to relaunch the "European dream" that designed the United States of Europe project' (*ibidem* [author's translation]). The EU is at a crossroads and will either regress into 'nationalism, xenophobia, racism, ethnic states, protectionism, currency and fiscal wars, with 60 years of social achievements, by the workers and trade union movement, for democracy and peace being put at very serious risk' (*ibid.* [author's translation]). Or alternatively there will be 'an acceleration towards the completion of economic and social Europe, a viaticum [*viatico*] towards the United States of Europe, for a cosmopolitan European and world citizenship, for a government with a global perspective, which the European Union economically and politically represents' (*ibid.* [author's translation]). The term *viatico*, or viaticum, is an antiquated term that has a strong Christian association and refers to the Eucharist administered to or received by one who is dying or in danger of death. The term mirrors CISL's Christian heritage and the *Manifesto per gli Stati Uniti d'Europa* is a formulation of its 'ideas, passion, [and] militancy to keep open a horizon of civilization!' (*ibid.* [author's translation]).

Were such a document produced by an Irish union, they would most likely be ridiculed for fanciful naïveté. That said, by the 2000s, the official Irish discourse on the EU had entered troubled waters. As Hayward notes (2009: 241) there is 'no Irish blueprint for the "ideal Europe"; indeed, Ireland's vision of the EU got more blurred as the EU grew in stature'. Hayward also observes that 'Irish political leaders struggle to articulate to a local audience what kind of Europe they want to see, what limits it should have and what position Ireland should take within it' (*ibidem*). Similarly, at the 2017 ICTU Biennial Conference, a delegate lamented that 'the debate rarely focuses on what kind of Europe we want to live in and how we can participate in the European wide campaigns to achieve those goals' (ICTU 2017). On 18 February 2012, the twentieth anniversary of the Maastricht Treaty, an *Irish Times* headline read: 'We need to talk about federalism.' Whilst there is 'no canonical version of federalism' (*ibidem*), this conversation has yet to be had. This is problematic if we consider Morgan's (2005) argument that the EU requires a 'justificatory fix': 'Unless this question can be answered satisfactorily, there is no good reason for citizens to lend their support to parties, governments and political leaders who favour European political integration' (*ibid*: 3).

Providing this justification is by no means a straightforward exercise, and the leadership of many unions (Hyman 2010), and political parties (Mair 2007), have, effectively, fudged this question. Notwithstanding, adopting an abstentionist position is becoming increasingly untenable, not least because the EU has, since the 2000s, lurched from crisis to crisis. Also, in response to Brexit and the rising tide of Euroscepticism, the French President, Emanuel Macron (2019), argues that it is necessary to rearticulate the underlying purpose of the EU so as to reconnect with its citizens. By calling for a 'European renaissance', Macron, in a widely published opinion piece, argues '[W]e have to establish a Conference for Europe … in order to set out all the changes required by our political project, and do so without taboos, even on treaty revision.' Hence, political actors, including organised labour, have to be able to articulate the 'justificatory fix' on deeper political integration. This is not a question of if, but when.

Table 9.2 ETUC Action Days and demonstrations 2011–2

Date	Place	Slogan
09 April 2011	Budapest	No to Austerity – For Social Europe, for Fair Pay and for Jobs
21 June 2011	Luxembourg	Action and Information Day in Europe
17 September 2011	Wroclaw	Yes to European Solidarity – Yes to Jobs and Workers' Rights – No to Austerity
29 February 2012	Decentralised	Enough is Enough! Alternatives Do Exist. For Employment and Social Justice
14 November 2012	Decentralised	European Day of Action and Solidarity

Source: author's own data

Italy's political maps over the past decade or so have been redrawn. The country underwent a seismic political shift in 2018, when two Eurosceptic parties, *Movimento 5 Stelle* and the *Lega*, formed a government and in doing so made Italy the first EU country to be governed by a coalition of populist parties. Whereas the *Lega* is firmly on the extreme right of the political spectrum, *Movimento 5 Stelle* is a hybrid or cross-cutting party and therefore more difficult to categorise. Notwithstanding, the leaderships of both parties are patently Eurosceptic and *anti-sindacati* [anti-trade union] (*Corriere della sera*, 10 April 2017). The rise of *Prima gli Italiani* ['Italians First'], Lega's electoral sloganeering, is partly laid at the door of the EU by the Italian unions: 'The national anti-European, xenophobic and racist populisms that have grown up across the EU have sprung directly from the interplay between anarchic globalisation and a short-sighted, *cowardly European policy* that, in the past decade, has clashed with the needs, expectations and hopes of wider areas of the population' (CISL 2017, emphasis added).The 'cowardly European policy' is without doubt a reference to the not-so-secret missives sent by the ECB to Berlusconi and the EU's new economic governance regime, which sought to weaken Italian unions' regulatory coping mechanisms (Jordan, Maccarrone and Erne 2020).

Speaking at her final CGIL Congress as General Secretary, Susanna Camusso (2019) stated:

> Europe is not doing well. It is going through a process of weakening of the Parliament and the Commission and has handed over the choices and decisions to the unanimity of the governments. Europe ... has embraced monetary rigor, sacrificing public and social policies, the absence of which feeds the insecurities that are turned into anti-European nationalisms [author's translation].

And on the question of anti-European nationalism, this is what Camusso (*ibidem*) had to say:

> [R]eturning nationalism is the great enemy of humanist development ... [which] is ... touted as an antidote to [workers'] fears. ... In this nationalism, there are no answers for the world of quality work. It does not bring quality jobs, nor does it confront big multinational corporations ... It is a class nationalism that exploits fears and the absence of alternatives [author's translation].

On confronting this 'class nationalism', Camusso (*ibid.*) urged the delegates '[W]e must equip ourselves, choose places, ways, [and] arguments to be actors in a Europe, which is better [for workers]'. In other words, unions have to be able to steer workers away from sovereignist, anti-EU politics. This involves being able to articulate a vision for the EU.

A number of Irish trade union leaders, during interviews, expressed not a desire for federalism but rather a post-Third-Way social-democracy. To what extent a post-Third-Way vision overlaps with the Euro-federalist vision is unclear. However, there appears to be agreement both between Irish trade union leaders and their Italian counterparts on how the EU should respond to the problems facing EMU and its asymmetric construction, which has resulted in a centralised monetary policy, on the one hand, and decentralised economic and fiscal policy, on the other. As Begg (2013a, 2013b) stated in an address to visiting EU Heads of Mission: '[T]he structure of Economic and Monetary Union is defective.' The former leader of SIPTU, Jack O'Connor (2010), called for 'the establishment of a euro bond mechanism combined with a co-ordinated investment strategy for jobs and growth'. During the debate on the Fiscal Compact, ICTU called for 'completing the institutional architecture of economic and monetary union' through the mutualisation of debt, that is, Eurobonds, or the ECB acting as a lender of last resort (Begg 2012d). All three Italian confederations were also in favour of Eurobonds. However, other measures are also proposed by Begg. These include the creation of a robust European budget, in which fiscal autonomy would be secured through a tax on financial transactions, a Carbon tax and national transfers, as well as the establishment of a European Treasury Ministry, integrated into the European Commission and answerable to the European Parliament. In other words, the transformation of the current European Stability Mechanism (ESM), which would then be tasked with the execution of an extraordinary investment plan in infrastructure, amongst other things, to support growth, employment and social cohesion in the Union. Also, there is a need to conclude the current version of the ECB's Quantitative Easing, centred on underwriting national sovereign debts, and replace it with the underwriting of *European* public debt (*see also* CISL 2017).

In Ireland, political maps too have been redrawn, with a realignment of politics along left–right lines instead of the traditional civil war lines. This is the result of, amongst other things, a rise in secularism, two decades of peace in Northern Ireland and strong economic growth, accompanied by an uneven distribution of wealth, which has adversely affected the housing market, resulting in a generation being 'locked-out' (Hearne 2020). Müller and Regan (2020) find that the 'average Irish voter now leans to the centre-left'. Hence, 'Ireland increasingly looks like Western Europe of old' (*ibidem*). That said, Brexit has returned the question of a united Ireland to the Irish political arena. This question must be seen through the prism of the EU. The UK–EU Treaty, much to the anger of Unionists, meant that Northern Ireland remained subject to EU rules for goods so that cross-border trade could continue uninterrupted with the Republic of Ireland, an EU member. For the first time since the signing of the Good Friday agreement, the prospect of a border-poll, that is, a referendum on a united Ireland, has never been closer. A boon for such a vote is the increased trade between Northern Ireland and the Republic: as a recent headline put it 'Britain's loss has been Northern Ireland's gain when it comes to post-Brexit trade with the Republic of Ireland' (*Politico* 15 February 2022). Brexit is still viewed with disbelief, but in this new context Irish labour Euroscepticism could become increasingly problematic on account of Brexit and the Northern Ireland question. Promising one thing and delivering another, the Conservative government in the UK negotiated a hard Brexit, regardless of the implications for Northern Ireland. There was general consensus that the EU was on Ireland's side and, as a result, it increased in the esteem of the general population. Would this also require a reinterpretation also by proponents of labour Euroscepticism? Arguably, this would need a strengthening of trade unions' regulatory coping mechanisms from either the Irish government or the EU.

A group known as Trade Unionists for a New and United Ireland,[2] was established in 2019. The grouping, however, is very broad and consists of 150 trade union officials and activists, including a number of General Secretaries. Spokesman and trade union official Ruairí Creaney stated:

> The debate on the future of Ireland north and south has been escalating significantly against the backdrop of Brexit and the rise of populist right-wing, and borderline fascist, movements in the United States and in a number of EU member states. It is now time to get it out in the open, and to ensure that the voice of trade unionism is to the forefront' (quoted in the *Irish Times*, 25 February 2019).

Surely, the 'voice of trade unionism' will have to have a say on the EU. This could well be problematic for the grouping, which may well be in agreement on the question of a united Ireland, but there are differing political views on the EU (interview with Ruairí Creaney 2020).

For starters, it will be necessary to address the concerns voiced by proponents of labour Euroscepticism around social dumping, which are more than a 'political catchphrase' (Bernaciak 2015). The phenomenon is inextricably linked to the free movement of labour and services, which are two sides of the same labour mobility coin. Unfortunately, 'social dumping has so far received limited scholarly attention' (*ibidem*: 1). We can say the same of political attention. The state is complicit in facilitating the practice of social dumping: 'by allowing particular practices to develop, providing the appropriate legal framework, or failing to combat unfair competition based on much poorer working conditions, they [the state] encourage enterprises to base their operations on social dumping' (Vaughan-Whitehead 2003: 344). Similarly, the ETUC (2015b) points to the role of the state: 'Social dumping can occur because of weak enforcement.' Here, organised labour can play an important role, but this is often a learning experience and an inferior substitute for regulation, preferably at the European level. The latter is also a question of political will, but if the financial-cum-sovereign-debt crisis has taught us anything it is that hard rules, such as state aid, can be quickly overruled. That said, Irish organised labour needs to be proactive on this front and be able to articulate a vision.

Since the bombshell of the Brexit result in 2016, the portmanteau of Ir-exit and It-exit has featured in debates. Following the British vote, former Irish ambassador Ray Bassett (2017) wrote a report for a UK think-tank, Policy Exchange, entitled *After Brexit, Will Ireland be Next to Exit?* Bassett, who appears to favour an Irish exit on account of Ireland's trade ties with the UK and the US, is critical of the 'remarkably little public discussion' on the EU in Ireland. 'The Irish policy in Europe has been very short sighted and gives the impression that it is solely about extracting the maximum short term monetary value from membership' (Bassett 2017: 18). Such instrumentalism is short-sighted and greater engagement with the EU's future is an overdue but all the more necessary of discussion. For instance, the leadership of Irish unions, ICTU *in primis*, admitted to having underestimated the extent to which, in the event of an external economic shock, the full burden of adjustment would be borne by workers (Begg 2013b).

Whereas it was not economically viable for Ireland to join the EU without the UK, Ireland is now entirely capable of remaining in the EU in its own right. However, Ireland's relationship with the EU is 'essentially based on material gain and not on any emotional or symbolic attachment' (Bassett 2017: 6). It is believed that public support for European integration weakened once Ireland became a net contributor to the EU budget in 2013. This does not bode well for the future of Ireland within the EU but, if such a development is true, then an even greater onus is placed on ICTU in articulating a social-democratic vision of the EU. Articulating this 'unity in diversity' agenda is of paramount importance, not least in light of the Brexit debate, in which the dangers of failing to articulate a coherent narrative were laid bare. Certainly, David Cameron and the broader pro-Remain political class failed in this regard as the Brexit debate was framed more successfully on emotive grounds by the Leave camp with the motto 'take back control'. Remain ensconced itself in rationality (and fear) and even in the aftermath of the referendum the tautology of Theresa May's 'Brexit means Brexit' generated more heat than light and will live on in infamy.

Brexit exposed the diversity of views that exist within the British left and beyond and it is important that the Irish labour movement does not repeat the mistakes of the British political class, in general, and the British labour movement in particular. Successive leaders sailed too close to the winds of sovereignist Euroscepticism. For instance, Gordon Brown's 2007 proclamation of 'British jobs for British workers' was a blunder of the highest order and the unsavoury slogan was later used to escalate the EU-related dispute at the Lindsey Oil Refinery (Meardi 2012b). Also, Labour Party senior Peter Mandelson, and Labour's shadow chancellor Ed Balls, both mooted holding an in–out referendum so as to steal a march on the Conservatives (*The Guardian*, 15 May 2012). Lindstrom (2019: 286) argues that '[d]emands from British workers for stronger protection against liberalizing pressure help explain the UK's recent shift towards relaxing its opposition to "market-correcting" EU initiatives like the revised posted worker directive' (Lindstrom 2019: 286). Of course, this is a case of too little too late, as the Brexit result confirms.

Once the referendum was called by David Cameron, further mistakes were made. For starters, and still related to Browne's political gaffe, the impact of labour mobility (that is, migration) on the debate was underestimated by the British unions and there was too much ambivalence in countering the xenophobic narrative. Also, the decision of the TUC to postpone taking a position until Cameron had concluded negotiations with the EU was a mistake, and a costly one. The struggle for social Europe needs to be on the front foot and this requires a constant engagement by organised labour with the mainstream print and broadcast media on EU-related issues. Such is the case in Italy, where the three confederal General Secretaries regularly appear as guests on current affairs programmes. But rarely, if ever, do Irish trade unions' leadership seek the limelight, or put differently, rarely are their opinions solicited.

In what must be a first, the three Italian confederations, along with the Italian employers' association, Confindustria, launched an 'Appeal for Europe' (CISL, CGIL, UIL and Confindustria 2019) in anticipation of the 2019 European elections. Rather than

> ... bringing to life the disturbing ghosts of the twentieth century ... Europe must continue the integration process, it must move forward, complete the economic Union, accelerate the convergence on rights and social protections, strengthen the perspective of the political union. Woe to think that the achievements are sufficient: this would mean not understanding the worries, frustrations, discomfort and social suffering of the many millions of Europeans who are unable to independently manage the complexity of our times (*ibidem*).

To this end, concrete initiatives are proposed, such as completing the Single Market; a European industrial policy; developing an EU foreign policy; and strengthening the European parliament. The cross-class pitch argues that 'the answer is not to retreat but to relaunch the original inspiration of the founding fathers and mothers, the ideal of the United States of Europe' (*ibid.*). Could we expect a similar cross-class vision from organised interests in Ireland? Or would this be too radical?

On the question of radicalism, Italian trade unions recognise the audacity and pluck of their United States of Europe vision, which stands in contradistinction to the Hayekian formulation of market-driven, economic federalism. Camusso (2019), in her parting speech to a CGIL Congress, categorically stated that '*[L]a radicalità non è estremismo*' ['radicalism is not extremism']. Whereas the latter, extremism, is the world of the right-wing *sovranisti* [sovereigntist], radicalism, on the other hand,

> … is knowing that there must be policies that address inequalities at their roots in order to fight and erase them. Radicalism serves in looking at the world and seeing the grave danger of the crisis of multilateralism' (*ibidem*).

A noted difference between Irish and Italian organised labour on the future of the EU has to do with the development of industrial relations institutions. For instance, the aforementioned 'Appeal for Europe' argues in favour of European social dialogue and collective bargaining at the national level. These practices are not seen as mutually exclusive but as complementary and necessary for countering social dumping practices, on the one hand, and building towards the harmonisation of fundamental rights and protections, on the other. Here, a European regulatory framework to support trade unions and collective bargaining is proposed. To this end, enhancing the role of European Works Councils to strengthen industrial relations is envisaged (CISL, CGIL, UIL and Confindustria 2019). Hence, in terms of sketching an idea of what a United States of Europe might look like, the Italian confederations (and Confindustria) present concrete proposals.

The complexity of the EU is an inevitable fact of modern life, and this aspect should not be down-played. Delors is noted as having said that 'Europe does not just need fire-fighters; it needs architects too'. Fire-fighting is a term that is oft-used in trade union circles to describe the nature of their work, that is, going from location to location resolving issues and putting out (transnational) 'fires'. The term is also used to intimate the hecticness of the all-too-often thankless task and the constant struggle to stem the relentless neo-liberal tide. Yet, it is imperative that heads are lifted for eyes to peer through and beyond the eye-watering neo-liberal smoke and towards the horizon, so as to take stock and adjust the direction that the EU is going. As the Schuman Declaration of 1950 states, 'Europe will not be made all at once, or according to a single plan.' The democratisation of the EU starts at the local level with economic democracy. This is because transnational socio-economic processes are too complex to be governed by party politics and electioneering. The idea of economic democracy – defined as 'a system of checks and balances on economic power and support for the right of citizens to actively participate in the economy regardless of social status, race, gender, etc.' (Johanisova and Wolf 2012) – has received less attention than political democracy. Notwithstanding, this aspect needs to be strengthened for two reasons: first, so as to stem the commodification of labour and a growing sense of disempowerment and alienation; and, second, to counter the commodification of public services by constraining fiscal rules. Economic democratisation also serves to strengthen pre-existing cross-border linkages and European trade union structures. As Camusso (2019) stated 'a strong union in one country is an ambition with few prospects.' Hence, there is 'the need to reform Europe as soon as possible, starting with labour rights, wage increases and social security protections. However, we must tell ourselves frankly that if we do not defend Europe, we will not reform it' (*ibidem*). In other words, to paraphrase the Irish republican-socialist, James Connolly,[3] 'the cause of organised labour is the cause of Europe, and the cause of Europe is the cause of organised labour. They cannot be dissevered.'

Bibliography

Abse, T. (2001). 'From PCI to DS: How European integration accelerated the "social democratization" of the Italian left'. *Journal of Southern Europe and the Balkans* 3(1): 61–74.

Adnett, N. (1996). *European labour markets: Analysis and policy.* London: Longman.

Agnoletto, S. (2012). 'Trade unions and the origins of the union-based welfare state in Italy'. *California Italian Studies* 3(2): 13–21.

Ahern, B. (2001). Statement on the Outcome of the Referendum on the Nice Treaty, 12 June 2001.

Ales, E., and Faioli, M. (2008). 'Self-employment and bogus self-employment in the construction industry in Italy'. Report for the European social partners for the construction industry. Brussels: EFBWW and FIEC.

Allen, K. (1997). *Fianna Fáil and Irish Labour: 1926 to present.* London: Pluto Press.

Allen, K. (2000). *The Celtic tiger: The myth of social partnership in Ireland.* Manchester: Manchester University Press.

Allen, K. (2009). 'Social partnership and union revitalization: the Irish case'. In G. Gall (ed.) *the future of union organising: Building for tomorrow.* Basingstoke: Palgrave Macmillan, pp. 45–61.

Allern, E. H., and Bale, T. (eds) (2017). *Left-of-Centre parties and trade unions in the twenty-first century.* Oxford: Oxford University Press.

Almeida, D. (2012). *The impact of European integration on political parties: Beyond the permissive consensus.* London: Routledge.

Almond, P., and Connolly, H. (2019). 'A manifesto for "slow" comparative research on work and employment'. *European Journal of Industrial Relations* 26(1): 59–74.

Amoore, L. (2002). *Globalisation contested: An international political economy of work.* Manchester: Manchester University Press.

Amyot, G. (2004). *Business, the state and economic policy. The case of Italy.* Routledge: London.

Anckar, C. (2007). 'On the applicability of the most similar systems design and the most different systems design in comparative research'. *International Journal of Social Research Methodology* 11(5): 389–401.

Anderson, P. (2009). *The new old world*. London: Verso..

Andretta, M. (2018). 'Protest in Italy in times of crisis: A cross-government comparison'. *South European Society and Politics* 23(1): 97–114.

Andruccioli, P. (2008). *Spine Rosse: Breve Storia della Minoranza Congressuale della CGIL (1978–2006)*. Rome: Ediesse.

Anghel, R. G. (2008). 'Changing statuses: Freedom of movement, locality and transnationality of irregular Romanian migrants in Milan'. *Journal of Ethnic and Migration Studies* 34(5): 787–802.

Armstrong, K. A., and Bulmer, S. (1998). *The governance of the single European market*. Manchester: Manchester University Press.

Arnold, M. (2005). 'Polish plumber symbolic of all French fear about constitution'. *Financial Times*, 28 May 2005.

Arqueros-Fernández, F. M. (2011). Workers against institutions: Power relations and political economy in the Irish mushroom industry. Unpublished PhD thesis, National University of Ireland, Maynooth.

Arrigo, G. (2004). 'Dalla concertazione al dialogo sociale: Europa e Italia'. *Lavoro e Diritto*, 2: 267–76.

Ascoli, U. (1999). 'Il modello storico del welfare state Italiano'. In C. Sorba (ed.) *Cittadinanza. Individui, diritti sociali, collettività nella storia contemporanea*. Rome: Pubblicazioni Degli Archivi Di Stato, pp. 215–24.

Ashford, D. E. (1986). *The emergence of the welfare states*. Oxford: Basil Blackwell.

Aspinwall, M. (2000). 'Structuring Europe: Power-sharing institutions and British preferences on European integration'. *Political Studies* 48(3): 415–42.

Aspinwall, M. (2002). 'Preferring Europe: Ideology and national preferences on European integration'. *European Union Politics* 3(1): 81–111.

Aspinwall M. (2007). 'Government preferences on European integration: An empirical test of five theories'. *British Journal of Political Science* 37(1): 89–114.

Baccaro, L. (2001). 'Union democracy revisited: Decision-making procedures in the Italian labour movement'. *Economic and Industrial Democracy*. 22(2): 183–210.

Baccaro, L. (2002). 'The construction of "democratic" corporatism in Italy'. *Politics and Society* 30(2): 327–57.

Baccaro, L., and Howell, C. (2017). *Trajectories of neoliberal transformation: European industrial relations since the 1970s*. Cambridge: Cambridge University Press.

Baccaro, L., Bremer, B., and Neimanns, E. (2021). 'Till austerity do us part? A survey experiment on support for the Euro in Italy'. *European Union Politics* 22(3): 401–23.

Baccaro, L., Carrieri, M., and Damiano, C. (2003). 'The resurgence of the Italian confederal unions: Will it last?'. *European Journal of Industrial Relations* 9(1): 43–59.

Bachtler, J., Mendez, C., and Wishlade, F. (2013). *EU cohesion policy and European integration: The dynamics of EU budget and regional policy reform.* Surrey: Ashgate.

Bailey, D. (2005). 'Obfuscation through integration: Legitimating "new" social democracy in the European Union'. *Journal of Common Market Studies* 43(1): 13–35.

Bailey, D. (2008). 'Explaining the underdevelopment of "social Europe": A critical realization'. *Journal of European Social Policy* 18(3): 232–45.

Balch, A., Fellini, I., Ferro, A., Fullin, G., and Hunger, U. (2004). 'The political economy of labour migration in the European construction sector'. In M. Bommes, K. Hoesch, U. Hunger and H. Kolb (eds) *organisational recruitment and patterns of migration: Interdependencies in an integrating Europe.* Innsbruck: Imis-Beiträge, pp. 179–200.

Baldwin, R., and Wyplosz, C. (2006). *The economics of European integration* (2nd edn). Maidenhead: McGraw Hill.

Bamber, G. J., Russel, D. L, Wailes, N., and Wright, C. F. (2016). *International and comparative employment relations: national regulation, global changes.* London: Sage.

Ban, C. (2009). 'Economic transnationalism and its ambiguities: The case of Romanian migration to Italy'. *International Migration* 50(6): 129–49.

Barbagli, M. (2007). *Primo rapporto sugli immigrati in Italia.* Rome: Ministry of the Interior.

Barbier, J. C. (2013). *The road to social Europe: A contemporary approach to political cultures and diversity in Europe.* London: Routledge.

Barbieri, G. (2001). 'L'Europa sociale dopo Nizza'. *Euronote* 11 (February 2001).

Barnard, C. (2012). 'The financial crisis and the euro plus pact: A labour lawyer's perspective'. *Industrial Law Journal* 41(1): 98–114.

Barrett, A., Fitzgerald, J., and Nolan, B. (2000). 'Earnings inequality, returns to education and low pay'. In B. Nolan, P. J. O'Connell and C. T. Whelan (eds). *Bust to boom? The Irish experience of growth and inequality.* Dublin: Irish Public Administration, pp. 127–46.

Barrett, G. (2012). 'Lessons from the ratification of the Lisbon Treaty in Ireland'. In F. Laursen (ed.) *The making of the EU's Lisbon Treaty: The role of member states.* Bern: Peter Lang, pp. 273–95.

Barroso, J. M. (2012b). From War to peace: A European tale. Nobel Peace Prize Lecture, Oslo, 10 December 2012.

Barry, F. (2009). 'Agricultural interests and Irish trade policy over the last half century: A tale told without recourse to heroes'. Dublin: Working Papers in British–Irish Studies no. 91.

Bartolini, S. (1993). 'On time and comparative research'. *Journal of Theoretical Politics* 5: 131–167.

Bartolini, S. (2000). *The class cleavage. The electoral mobilisation of the European Left 1880–1980.* Cambridge: Cambridge University Press.

Bartolini, S. (2005). *Restructuring Europe: Centre formation, system building and political structuring between the nation state and the European Union.* Oxford: Oxford University Press.

Bartolini, S. (2006). 'Politics: The right or the wrong sort of medicine for the EU?' Notre Europe Policy Paper, 2006/19.

Bartolini, S. (2010). 'Taking "constitutionalism" and "legitimacy" seriously'. In A. Glencross and A. H. Treschel (eds) *EU federalism and constitutionalism. The legacy of Altiero Spinelli*. Lanham, MD: Rowman & Littlefield, pp. 11–34.

Bassett, R. (2017). 'After Brexit: will Ireland be next to exit?'. *Policy Exchange*, June. Available at: https://policyexchange.org.uk/wp-content/uploads/2017/07/After-Brexit-will-Ireland-be-next-to-exit-1.pdf.

Bechter, B., Brandl, B., and Meardi, G. (2012). 'Sectors or countries? Typologies and levels of analysis in comparative industrial relations'. *European Journal of Industrial Relations* 18(3): 185–202.

Beck, U., and Grande, E. (2007). *Cosmopolitan Europe*. Translated by Ciaran Cronin. Cambridge: Polity.

Beckert, J. (2007). 'The social order of markets'. Discussion Paper No. 07/15, Max Planck Institut für Gesellschaftsforschung (MPIfG). Available at: http://www.mpifg.de/pu/mpifg_dp/dp07-15.pdf.

Begg, D. (2005). 'Barroso intent on shifting EU to right of centre'. *Irish Times*, 7 February 2005.

Begg, D. (2006). Immigration, integration and cultural identity. Speech at MacGill Summer School, Glenties, 17 July 2006.

Begg, D. (2007a). 'Immigration, integration and cultural identity'. *Translocations Online Journal* 2(1): 181–9. Available at: http://www.translocations.ie/docs/v02i01/translocations-v02i01-10.html.

Begg, D. (2007b). Speech made to Biennial Delegate Conference of the Irish Trade Union Confederation (ICTU), Bundoran, 3 July 2007.

Begg, D. (2007c). Managing the labour market: Implications of EU expansion and Ireland's experience. Presentation to Race and Immigration in the New Ireland, University of Notre Dame, 14–17 October 2007.

Begg, D. (2008). The Lisbon Treaty. Presentation to Joint Committee on European Union Affairs Debate on Lisbon Treaty, 18 January 2008.

Begg, D. (2009). 'We won't be cowed by neoliberal lies'. *Union Post*, September 2009.

Begg, D. (2010). Speech to Anti-Austerity Demonstration, O'Connell St, Dublin, 27 November 2010.

Begg, D. (2011a) 'Sharing social responsibility in shaping the future: a trade union perspective'. In B. Reynolds and S. Healy (eds) *Sharing responsibility in shaping the future*. Dublin: Social Justice Ireland, pp. 55–71.

Begg, D. (2011b). Sharing the burden of adjustment to the crisis. Address to EU Economic Forum on Governance, Brussels, 18 May 2011.

Begg, D. (2012a). Speech to Labour Party Conference, Galway, 14 April 2012.

Begg, D. (2012b). The tectonic plates have shifted: Hollande election offers new opportunities to change course in Europe. Speech to CWU Biennial Conference, Galway, 11 May 2012.

Begg, D. (2012c). 'The Fiscal Compact Treaty: A synthesis of views'. Paper presented to the members of the Executive Council of ICTU, 12 April 2012.

Begg, D. (2012d). 'Europe needs a new deal'. Press statement, 17 May 2012.

Begg, D. (2013). 'A social dimension for a changing European Union: The Irish case'. In A. M. Grozelier, B. Hacker, W. Kowalsky, J. Machnig, H. Meyer and B. Unger (eds) *Roadmap to a social Europe*. London: Social Europe Report, pp. 57–61.

Begg, D. (2014a). 'The trade union experience of European integration'. *Administration* 62(2): 131–9.

Begg, D. (2014b). The illusion of fairness: The social and economic consequences of inequality'. Speech at Biennial Delegate Conference of TEEU, Kilkenny, 22 November 2014.

Begg, D. (2016). *Ireland, small open economies and European integration: Lost in transition*. Basingstoke: Palgrave Macmillan.

Béland, D. (2009). 'Ideas, institutions, and policy change'. *Journal of European Public Policy* 16(5):701–18.

Bellamy, R., and Castiglione, D. (2003). 'Legitimizing the Euro-"polity" and its "regime": The normative turn in EU studies'. *European Journal of Political Theory* 2(1): 7–34.

Bellamy, R., and Warleigh, A. (2001). 'Introduction: The paradox and context of European citizenship'. In R. Bellamy and A. Warleigh (eds) *Citizenship and governance in the European Union*. London: Continuum, pp. 1–28.

Bellamy, R., and Weale, A. (2015). 'Political legitimacy and European monetary union: Contracts, constitutionalism and the normative logic of two-level games'. *Journal of European Public Policy* 22(2): 257–74.

Bercusson, B. (1992). 'Maastricht: A fundamental change in European labour law'. *Industrial Relations Journal* 23(3): 177–90.

Bercusson, B., Deakin, S., Koistinen, P., Kravaritou, Y., Mückenberger, U., Supiot, A., and Veneziani, B. (1997). 'A manifesto for social Europe'. *European Law Journal* 3(2): 189–205.

Berman, S. (1998). *The social democratic moment: Ideas and politics in the making of interwar Europe*. Cambridge MA: Harvard University Press.

Bermeo, N. (ed.) (2001). *Unemployment in the New Europe*. Cambridge: Cambridge University Press.

Bernaciak, M. (2015). *Market expansion and social dumping in Europe*. Routledge: London.

Béthoux, É., Erne, R., and Golden, D. (2018). 'A primordial attachment to the nation? French and Irish workers and trade unions in past EU referendum debates'. *British Journal of Industrial Relations* 56(3): 656–78.

Bieler, A. (1999). 'Globalization, Swedish trade unions and European integration: from Europhobia to conditional support'. *Cooperation and Conflict* 34(1): 21–46.

Bieler, A. (2002). 'The struggle over enlargement: A historical materialist analysis of European integration.' *Journal of European Public Policy* 9(4): 575–97.

Bieler, A. (2005). 'Class struggle over the EU model of capitalism: Neo-Gramscian perspectives and the analysis of European integration'. *Critical Review of International Social and Political Philosophy* 8(4): 513–26.

Bieler, A. (2006). *The struggle for a social Europe: Trade unions and EMU in times of global restructuring*. Manchester: Manchester University Press.

Bieler, A. (2009). 'Globalization and regional integration: The possibilities and problems for trade unions to resist neoliberal restructuring in Europe'. In B. van Apeldoorn, J. Drahokoupil and L. Horn (eds) *Contradictions and limits of neoliberal European governance: From Lisbon to Lisbon*. Basingstoke: Palgrave Macmillan, pp. 232–49.

Bieler, A. (2015). ' "Sic vos non vobis" (for you, but not yours): the struggle for public water in Italy'. *Monthly Review* 67(5). Available at: http://monthlyreview. org/2015/10/01/sic-vos-non-vobis-for-you-but-not-yours/.

Bieler, A., and Bieling, H. J. (2019). 'Conceptualising the development of the European political economy from a neo-Gramscian perspective'. In J. Kiess and M. Seeliger (eds) *Trade unions and European integration: A question of optimism and pessimism?* Routledge: London, pp. 51–68.

Bieler, A., and D. Morton (2001). 'Introduction: Neo-Gramscian perspectives in international political economy and the relevance to European integration'. In A. Bieler and A. Morton (eds) *Social forces in the making of the New Europe: The restructuring of European social relations in the global political economy*. London: Palgrave Macmillan, pp. 3–24.

Bieler, A., Erne, R., Golden, D., Helle, I., Kjeldstadli, K., Matos, T., and Stan, S. (eds) *Labour and transnational action in times of crisis*. London: Rowman & Littlefield.

Bieling, H. J. (2003). 'European employment policy between neo-liberal rationalism and communitarianism'. In H. Overbeek (ed.) *The political economy of European employment: European integration and the transnationalization of the (un) employment question*. London: Routledge, pp. 51–74.

Bindi, F. (2011). *Italy and the European Union*. Washington DC: Brookings Institution Press.

Bindi, F. (2012). 'Italy and the Lisbon Treaty'. In F. Laursen (ed.) *The making of the Lisbon Treaty: The role of the member states*. Berlin: Peter Lang AG, pp. 123–42.

Bitumi, A. (2018). '"An uplifting tale of Europe." Jacques Delors and the contradictory quest for a European social model in the age of Reagan'. *Journal of Transatlantic Studies* 16(3): 203–21.

Blackmer, D. L. M. (1975). 'Change and continuity in postwar Italian communism'. In D. L. M. Blackmer and S. Tarrow (eds) *Communism in Italy and France*. Princeton, NJ: Princeton University Press, pp. 21–68.

Blanchard, O., Bean, C., and Münchau, W. (2006). 'European unemployment: the evolution of facts and ideas'. *Economic Policy* 21(45): 5–59.

Blanpain, R. (1998). 'Il trattatodi Amsterdam e oltre: La fine del modello sociale Europeo'. *Diritto delle Relazioni Industriali* 8(1): 11–29.

Block, F. (2003). 'Karl Polanyi and the writing of *The Great Transformation*'. *Theory and Society* 32(3): 275–306.

Block, F. (2007). 'Understanding the diverging trajectories of the United States and Europe: A neo-Polanyian analysis'. *Politics and Society* 35(1): 3–33.

Blyth, M. (2002). *Great transformations. Economic ideas and institutional change in the Twentieth Century*. Cambridge: Cambridge University Press.

Bobek, A., Krings, T., Moriarty, E., Wickham, J., and Salamońska, J. (2008). 'Migrant workers and the construction sector in Ireland'. Dublin: Trinity Immigration Initiative. Available at: https://www.tcd.ie/immig.ration/css/downloads/ConReport03.09.08.pdf.

Bohle, D. (2006). 'Neoliberal hegemony, transnational capital and the terms of the EU's Eastward expansion', *Capital & Class* 30(1): 57–86.

Bohle, D., and Husz, D. (2005). 'Interest group action in accession negotiations: The cases of competition policy and labor migration'. *Politique Européenne* 15(1): 85–112.

Böhning R. W. (1972). *The migration of workers in the United Kingdom and the European Community*. Oxford: Oxford University Press.

Bonefeld, W. (2012). 'Neoliberal Europe and the transformation of democracy: On the state of money and law'. In P. Nousios, H. Overbeek and A. Tsolakis (eds). *Globalisation and European Integration: Critical approaches to regional order and international relations*. London: Routledge, pp. 51–69.

Booth, A., Burda, M., Calmfors, L., Checchi, D., Naylor, R., and Visser, J. (1999). *What do unions do in Europe? Prospects and challenges for union presence and union influence*. A Report for the Fondazione Rodolfo DeBenedetti, Italy.

Börner, S., and Eigmüller, M. (eds) (2015). *European integration, processes of change and the national experience*. Basingstoke: Palgrave Macmillan.

Börzel, T. A., and Risse, T. (2000). 'When Europe hits home: Europeanization and domestic change'. EUI Working Paper RSC No. 2000/56.

Bosch, G., and Weinkopf, C. (2013). 'Transnational labour markets and national wage setting systems in the EU'. *Industrial Relations Journal* 44(1): 2–19.

Boswell, T., and Brown, C. (1999). 'The scope of general theory. Methods for linking deductive and inductive comparative history'. *Sociological Methods and Research* 28(2): 154–85.

Bourdieu, P. (2002). 'Against the policy of depoliticization'. *Studies in Political Economy* 69(1): 31–41.

Bourdieu, P. (2014). *On the state: Lectures at the Collège de France 1989–92*. London: Polity.

Braun, D., and Tausendpfund, M. (2014). 'When European integration becomes costly: The Euro crisis and public support for European economic governance'. *Journal of European Integration* 36(3): 231–45.

Braun, M. (1996). 'The confederated trade unions and the Dini government: The grand return to neo-corporatism?'. In M. Caciagli, and D. I. Kertzer (eds) *Italian Politics: The stalled transition*. Boulder, CO: Westview Press, pp. 205–21.

Breen, M., and Dorgan, J. (2013). 'The death of Irish trade protectionism: A political economy analysis'. *Irish Studies in International Affairs* 24: 1–15.

Breen, R., Hannan, D., Rottman, D., and Whelan, C. T. (1990). *Understanding contemporary Ireland: state, class and development in the Republic of Ireland*. Dublin: Gill & Macmillan.

Brinegar, A. P., and Jolly, S. K. (2005). 'Location, location, location: National contextual factors and public support for European integration'. *European Union Politics* 6(2): 155–80.268

Brouard, S., and Tiberj, V. (2006). 'The French referendum: The not so simple act of saying nay'. *Political Science and Politics* 39(2): 261–8.

Brown, T., and de Rossa, P. (1988). 'Irish foreign policy after the Single European Act [with Response]'. *Studies: An Irish Quarterly Review* 77(305): 21–36.

Bruno, R. (2011). *Breve storia del sindacato in Italia*. Rome: Ediesse.

Bruun, N., Lörcher, K., and Schömann I. (eds) (2009). *Labour law and social Europe. Selected writings of Brian Bercusson*. Brussels: ETUI.

Burawoy, M. (2003). 'For a sociological Marxism: The complementary convergence of Antonio Gramsci and Karl Polanyi'. *Politics and Society* 31(2): 193–261.

Burawoy, M. (2009). *The extended case method: Four countries, four decades, four great transformations, and one theoretical tradition*. Berkeley, CA: University of California Press.

Burgess, M. (1991). *Federalism and European Union: Political ideas, influences and strategies in the European Community, 1972–1987*. Routledge: London.

Burgess, M. (2000) *Federalism and European Union: The building of Europe, 1950–2000*. Routledge: London.

Burley, A. M., and Mattli, W. (1993) 'Europe before the Court: A political theory of legal integration'. *International Organization* 47(1): 41–76.

Cal, L. (2001). 'L'Europa sociale dopo Nizza'. *Euronote* 11 (February).

Camera di Commercio di Roma (2004). Gli immigrati nell'economia Romana: Lavoro, imprenditoria, risparmio e rimesse. Roma: CCIAA.

Camera di Commercio di Verona (2003). 'Quando gli immigrati diventano imprenditori'. Allegato al *Bollettino di Statistica* no. 3–4.

Camusso, S. (2019). Speech at XVIII CGIL Congress, Bari, 22–5 January 2019.

Camusso, S., Bonanni. R., and Angeletti, L. (2012). Letter sent to *Presidente del Consiglio*, Mario Monti.

Caporaso, J. (1998). 'Regional integration theory: Understanding our past and anticipating our future'. *Journal of European Public Policy* 5(1): 1–16.

Caramani, D. (2009). *Introduction to the comparative method with Boolean algebra*. Thousand Oaks, CA: Sage.

Caramani, D. (2010). 'Of differences and similarities: is the explanation of variation a limitation to (or of) comparative analysis?'. *European Political Science* 9: 34–48.

Carchedi, G. (2001). *For another Europe: A class analysis of European economic integration*. London: Verso.

Caren, N., and Panofsky, A. (2005). 'TQCA: A technique for adding temporality to qualitative comparative analysis'. *Sociological Methods and Research* 34(2): 147–72.

Carew, A. (1987). *Labour under the Marshall Plan: The politics of productivity and the marketing of management science*. Manchester: Manchester University Press.

Carew, A. (2000). 'Towards a free trade union centre: The International Confederation of Free Trade Unions (1949–1972)'. In A. Carew, M. Dreyfus, G. van Goethem, R. Gumbrell-McCormick and M. van der Linden (eds) *The International Confederation of Free Trade Unions*. Bern: Peter Lang, pp. 187–239.

Caritas Diocesana di Roma (2009). *XIX dossier statistico immigrazione*. Rome: Idos.

Caritas Diocesana di Roma (2010). *XX dossier statistico immigrazione*. Rome: Idos.

Caritas Diocesana di Roma (2011). *XXI dossier statistico immigrazione*. Rome: Idos.

Caritas Diocesana di Roma (2012). *XXII dossier statistico immigrazione*. Rome: Idos.

Caritas/Migrantes (2008). *XVIII dossier statistico immigrazione*. Rome: Idos.

Caritas/Migrantes (2009). *XIX dossier statistico immigrazione*. Rome: Idos.

Caritas/Migrantes (2012). *XXII dossier statistico immigrazione*. Rome: Idos.

Casadio, G. (2007). *I diritti sociali del lavoro nella costituzione Italiana*. Rome: Ediesse.

Cassells, P. (1988). 'Make Europe work for us'. Paper presented at special ICTU Conference, October 1988.

Cassells, P. (2000). 'Recasting the European social model'. In R. O'Donnell (ed.) *Ireland and Europe – Challenges for a new century*. ESRI: Dublin, pp. 69–75.

Castellani, S., and Queirolo Palmas, L (2018). 'When the spring is not coming: Radical left and social movements in Italy during the austerity era'. In B. Roca, E. Martín-Díaz and I. Díaz-Parra (eds) *Challenging Austerity: Radical left and social movements in the South of Europe*. Routledge: London, pp. 133–51.

Castles, S., and Kosack, G. (1973). *Immigrant workers and class structure in Western Europe*. Oxford: Oxford University Press.

Cavatorto, S., and Verzichelli, L. (2008). 'Italy and the strategy of political appointment'. In S. Fabbrini and S. Piattoni (eds) *Italy in the European Union: Redefining national interest in a compound polity*. Lanham, MD: Rowman & Littlefield, pp. 209–32.

Cedrone, C. (2001). 'L'Europa sociale dopo Nizza'. *Euronote* 11 (February).

Central Statistics Office (2012). *Construction employment index*. Dublin: The Stationery Office.

CGIL (1961). *I congressi della CGIL VI*. Rome: Editore Sindacale Italiana.

CGIL (1969). *Documenti politici dall'XI al XII congresso*. Rome: Editori Riuniti.

CGIL (1977). *La CGIL dall'8° al 9° congresso: Atti e documenti CGIL e documenti unitari*. Rome: Editore Sindacale Italiana.

CGIL (1986). 'Una concertazione su più larga scala'. XI National Congress of the CGIL Rome 28th of February–4th of March.

CGIL (1988). *Per un programma Europeo della CGIL*. Rome: CGIL. Debate available at https://www.radioradicale.it/scheda/28042/per-un-programma-europeo-della-cgil?i=2677682.

CGIL (1989). Il nuovo programma fondamentale della CGIL, Florence 14–16 November 1989.

CGIL (1991). Congresso nazionale, Rimini 23–27 Ottobre. Rome: Editore Sindacale Italiana.

CGIL (2006). XV congress: Riprogettare il paese 1–4 Marzo, Rimini. Rome: Editore Sindacale Italiana.

CGIL (2007). Newsletter del segretariato europa (no date provided).

CGIL (2009). 'Nota Europa sulla situazione rispetto all'entrata in vigore del Trattato di Lisbona'. 8 December 2009.

CGIL (2012). 'La proposta di regolamento Monti II: Brevi note sulla version definitiva'. 23 March 2012.270

Charter Group (2009). Press Release, 22 September 2009.

Charter Group (2012a). Press Release, 28 May 2012.

Charter Group (2012b). Press Release (no date provided).

Chernilo, D. (2006). 'Social theory's methodological nationalism: Myth and reality'. *European Journal of Social Theory* 9(1): 5–22.

Chernilo, D. (2011). 'The critique of methodological nationalism: Theory and history'. *Thesis Eleven* 106(1): 98–117.

Chubb, B. (1969). 'The Republic of Ireland'. In S. Henig and J. Pinder (eds), *European political parties*. London: P.E.P.

Ciampani, A. (2000). *La CISL: Tra integrazione europea e mondializzazione*. Roma: Edizioni Lavoro.

Ciampani, A., and Gabaglio, E. (2010). *L'Europa sociale e la Confederazione Europea dei Sindacati*. Bologna: Il Mulino.

Ciampiani, A. (2013). 'Italian trade unionism and the ETUC: In favour of a European social actor'. In A. Ciampani and P. Tilly (eds) *National trade unions and the ETUC: A history of unity and diversity*. ETUI: Brussels, pp. 67–94.

CISL (1955a). Il congresso nazionale, Roma, 23–27 Aprile 1955: Relazione della segreteria confederale. Roma: Abete.

CISL (1955b). 'Il movimento sindacale e i partiti politici'. *Politica Sindacale.*

CISL (1956a). 'I sindacati Europei e l'integrazione europea e politica'. *Politica Sindacale.*

CISL (1956b). 'Rilancio dell'unitá europea e la posizione della CISL'. *Politica Sindacale.*

CISL (1956c). II congresso nazionale. Rome: CISL.

CISL (2017). Manifesto per gli stati uniti d'europa. Rome: CISL.

CISL, CGIL, UIL and Confindustria (2019). *Appello per l'europa*. Rome: CISL.

Classen, R., Gerbrandy, A., Princen, S., and Segers, M. (2019). 'Rethinking the European social market economy'. *Journal of Common Market Studies* 57(1): 3–12.

CNEL (2008). 'Il contrasto dei fenomeni di illegalità e della penetrazione mafiosa nel ciclo del contratto pubblico'. Rome: CNEL.

Coates, K., and Topham, T. (1986). *Trade unions and politics*. Oxford: Basil Blackwell.

Cofferati, S. (1996). 'Relazione introduttiva, XIII congresso CGIL, Rimini, 2–5 Iuglio 1996'. In *I congressi della CGIL*.

Cohen, J., and Federico, G. (2001). *The growth of The Italian economy, 1820–1960*. Cambridge: Cambridge University Press.

Compston, H. (ed.) (1997). *The new politics of unemployment. Radical policy initiatives in Western Europe*. London: Routledge.

Construction Labour Research (2011). *In search of cheap labour in Europe: Working and living conditions of posted workers*. Brussels: CLR.

Copeland, P., and ter Haar, B. (2013). 'A toothless bite? The effectiveness of the European Employment Strategy as a governance tool'. *Journal of European Social Policy* 23(1): 21–36.

Cordeel, F. (2009). Speech of Dirk Cordeel, FIEC President – Official presentation of the posting database. 25 September, Brussels.

Corso, G. (1979), *L'Ordine pubblico*. Bologna: Il Mulino.

Crafts, N., and Toniolo, G. (eds) (2002). *Economic growth in Europe since 1945*. Cambridge: Cambridge University Press.

Cremers, J. (2009). 'Changing employment patterns and collective bargaining: The case of construction'. *International Journal of Labour Research* 1(2): 201–17.

Cremers, J., Dølvik, J. E., and Bosch, G. (2007). 'Posting of workers in the single market: Attempts to prevent social dumping and regime competition in the EU'. *Industrial Relations Journal* 38(6): 524–41.

Crespy, A. (2010). 'Legitimizing resistance to EU integration'. *Les Cahiers Européens de Sciences Po* no. 03/2010. Available online at: http://www.cee.sciences-po.fr/en/publications/les-cahiers-europeens/2010.html.

Crespy, A. (2012). *Qui a peur de Bolkestein?* Paris: Economica.

Crespy, A. (2016). *Welfare markets in Europe: The democratic challenge of European integration*. Basingstoke: Palgrave Macmillan.

Crespy, A., and Vanheuverzwijn, P. (2019). 'What "Brussels" means by structural reforms: Empty signifier or constructive ambiguity?'. *Comparative European Politics* 17(1): 92–111.

Crespy, A., and Verschueren, N. (2009). 'From Euroscepticism to resistance to European integration: An interdisciplinary perspective'. *Perspectives on European Politics and Society* 10(3): 377–93.

Crotty, R. D. (1988). *A radical's response*. Dublin: Poolbeg Press.

Crouch C. (1982). *Trade unions: The logic of collective action*. London: Fontana.

Crouch, C. (1993). *Industrial relations and European state transitions*. Oxford: Oxford University Press.

Crouch, C. (1999). *Social change in Western Europe*. Oxford: Oxford University Press.

Crouch, C. (2005). *Capitalist diversity and change*. New York: Oxford University Press.

Crouch, C. (2009). 'Privatised Keynesianism: An unacknowledged policy regime'. *British Journal of Politics & International Relations* 11(3): 382–99.

Crouch, C. (2015). *Governing social risks in post-crisis Europe*. Cheltenham: Edward Elgar.

Crouch, C. (ed.) (2000). *After the Euro: Shaping institutions for governance in the wake of the European monetary union*. Oxford: Oxford University Press.

Crouch, C., and Pizzorno, A. (eds) (1978). *The resurgence of class conflict in Western Europe since 1968*. London: Palgrave Macmillan.

CSO (2004). *Statistical yearbook of Ireland*. Dublin: The Stationery Office.

CSO (2005). *Statistical yearbook of Ireland*. Dublin: The Stationery Office.

CSO (2007a). *Statistical yearbook of Ireland*. Dublin: The Stationery Office.

CSO (2007b). *Small business in Ireland*. Dublin: The Stationery Office.

CSO (2008). *Construction and housing in Ireland*. Dublin: The Stationery Office.

CSO (2009). *Construction employment index*. Dublin: The Stationery Office.

Culpepper, P. D. (2008). 'The politics of common knowledge: Ideas and institutional change in wage bargaining'. *International Organization* 62(1): 1–33.272

Culpepper, P. D. (2014). 'The political economy of unmediated democracy: Italian austerity under Mario Monti'. *West European Politics* 37(6): 1264–81.

Culpepper, P., and Regan, A. (2014). 'Why don't governments need trade unions anymore? The death of social pacts in Ireland and Italy', *Socio-Economic Review* 12(4): 723–45.

Cuozzo, F. (1979). 'Trent'anni dopo'. *Rassegna Sindacale* 1 November 1979: 40–1.

d'Art, D., and Turner, T. (2006). 'Union organising, union recognition and employer opposition: case studies of the Irish experience'. *Irish Journal of Management* 26(2): 165–84.

Dahl, R. A. (1965). 'Reflections on opposition in western democracies'. *Government and Opposition* 1(1): 7–24.

Dahlberg, K. A. (1968). 'The EEC Commission and the politics of the free movement of labour'. *Journal of Common Market Studies* 6(4): 310–33.

Daly, M. (2005). 'Recasting the story of Ireland's miracle: policy, politics or profit'. In U. Becker and H. M. Schwartz (eds) *Employment miracles: A critical comparison of the Dutch, Scandinavian, Swiss, Australian and Irish cases versus Germany and the US*. Amsterdam: Amsterdam University Press, pp. 133–56.

Darlington, R. (2008). *Syndicalism and the transition to communism: An international comparative analysis*. Surrey: Ashgate.

de Boissieu, C., and Pisani-Ferry, J. (1998). 'The political economy of French economic policy in the perspective of EMU'. In B. Eichengreen and J. Frieden (eds) *Forging an integrated Europe*. Ann Arbor, MI: University of Michigan Press, pp. 49–90.

De Bréadún, D. (1992a). 'SIPTU, ATGWU back Maastricht despite "many reservations"'. *Irish Times*, 2 May 1992.

De Bréadún, D. (1992b). 'Treaty a good deal: Reynolds tells unions'. *Irish Times*, 13 May.

de Búrca, G. (2001). 'The EU Charter of Fundamental Rights'. *ECSA Review* 14(2): 15–17.

de Búrca, G. (2013). 'The domestic impact of the EU Charter of Fundamental Rights'. *Irish Jurist* 49: 49–64.

de Cecco, M. (2007). 'Italy's dysfunctional political economy'. *West European Politics* 30(4): 763–83.

De Vries, C. E. (2018). *Euroscepticism and the future of European Integration*. Oxford: Oxford University Press.

de Wilde, P. (2011). 'No polity for old politics? A framework for analyzing the politicization of European integration'. *Journal of European Integration* 33(5): 559–75.

de Wilde, P., and Zurn, M. (2012). 'Can the politicization of European integration be reversed?'. *Journal of Common Market Studies* 50(1): 137–53.

de Wilde, P., Leupold, A., and Schmidtke, H. (2015). 'Introduction: The differentiated politicisation of European governance'. *West European Politics* 39(1): 3–22.

de Wilde, P., Michailidou, A., and Trenz, H. J (2012). *Contesting Europe: Exploring Euroscepticism in online media coverage*. Colchester: ECPR Press.

Degryse, C., and Tilly, P. (2013). *1973–2013: 40 years of history of the European Trade Union Confederation*. ETUI: Brussels.

Del Rossi, M. P (2010). 'Dal sindacalismo internazionale alla Confederazione Europea dei Sindacati'. In A. Gramolati and G. Mari (eds) *Bruno Trentin: Lavoro, libertà, conoscenza*. Florence: Florence University Press, pp. 45–66.

della Porta, D. (1995). *Social movements, political violence and the state: A comparative analysis of Italy and Germany*. Cambridge: Cambridge University Press.

della Porta, D. (2015) *Social movements in times of austerity: Bringing capitalism back into protest analysis*. Cambridge: Polity.

della Porta, D., and Caiani, M. (2006). *Quale europa? Europeizzazione, identità e conflitti*. Il Mulino: Bologna.

della Porta, D., and Tarrow, S. (ed.) (2005). *Transnational protest and global activism*. Lanham, MD: Rowman & Littlefield.

della Porta, D., Fillieule, O., and Reiter, H. (1998). 'Policing protest in France and Italy: From intimidation to cooperation'. In D. S. Meyer and S. Tarrow (eds) *The social movement society: Contentious politics for a new century*. Oxford: Rowman & Littlefield, pp. 111–30.

Della Sala, V. (1997). 'Hollowing out and hardening the state: European integration and the Italian economy'. *West European Politics* 20(1): 14–33.

Della Sala, V. (2004). 'Maastricht to modernisation: EMU and the European social state'. In A. Martin and G. Ross (eds) *Euros and Europeans: Monetary integration and the European model of society*. Cambridge: Cambridge University Press, pp. 126–49.

Delors, J. (1985). Speech at first intergovernmental conference (IGC) Luxembourg, 9 September 1985.

Delors, J. (1988). 1992: The human dimension. Speech at ICTU Make Europe Work For Us Conference, October 1988.

Delors, J. (1988). 'Foreword'. In P. Fontaine *Jean Monnet: l'Inspirateur*. Paris: Jacques Grancher.

Delors, J. (1989). Regional implications of economic and monetary integration. Speech at the Collége d'Europe, January 1989.

Delors, J. (1998). 'Preface'. In B. Trentin *La ville du travail. La gauche et la crise du fordisme*. Paris: Fayard.

Dept of Taoiseach (1997). *Partnership 2000*. Available at: https://www.inou. ie/assets/files/pdf/04_partnership_2000.pdf.

Derwin, D. (1976). 'A special survey: the ITGWU'. *International Socialism* 92: 34–6.

DG ECFIN (2012). *Labour market developments in Europe 2012*. Brussels: European Commission.

Di Quirico, R. (2010). 'Italy and the global economic crisis'. *Bulletin of Italian Politics* 2(2):3–19.

Dias, H., and Fernandes, L. (2016). 'The November 2012 general strike and anti-austerity protests – analysis from the Portuguese case'. *International Journal on Strikes and Social Conflicts* 1(6): 16–38.

Diebold, W. (1959). *The Schuman Plan. A study in Economic cooperation 1950–1959*. New York: Frederick A. Praeger.

Dimitrakopoulos, D. G. (2011). 'Introduction: Social democracy, European integration and preference formation'. In D. G. Dimitrakopoulos (ed.) *Social democracy and European integration: The politics of preference formation*. London: Routledge.

Dimitrakopoulos, D. G., and Kassim, H. (2004). 'Deciding the future of the European Union: Preference formation and treaty reform'. *Comparative European Politics* 2(3): 241–60.

Dinan, D. (2004). 'The road to enlargement' In M. Cowles and D. Dinan (eds) *Developments in the European Union*. Basingstoke: Palgrave Macmillan. pp. 7–24.

Dineen, L. (2022). *Connect trade union: A history 1920–2020*. Dublin: Umiskin Press.

Dini, L. (1997). 'The European Union after Amsterdam'. In A. Duff (ed.) *The Treaty of Amsterdam: Text and commentary*. Manchester: Manchester University Press, pp. xxv–xxviii.

DKM Economic Consultants (2005). *Review of the construction industry outlook 2005 to 2007*. Dublin.

DKM Economic Consultants (2006). *Review of the construction industry outlook 2006 to 2008*. Dublin.

DKM Economic Consultants (2007). *Review of the construction industry outlook 2007 to 2009*. Dublin.

DKM Economic Consultants (2008). *Review of the construction industry outlook 2008 to 2010*. Dublin.

DKM Economic Consultants (2009). *Review of the construction industry outlook 2009 to 2011*. Dublin.

Dobson, L. (2006). 'Normative theory and Europe'. *International Affairs* 82(3): 511–23.

Doherty, M. (2008). 'Hard law, soft edge? Information, consultation and partnership'. *Employee Relations* 30(6): 603–22.

Doherty, M. (2011). 'It must have been love … but it's over now: The crisis and collapse of social partnership in Ireland'. *Transfer: European Review of Labour and Research* 17(3): 371–385.

Dølvik, J. E. (1997). *Redrawing boundaries of solidarity? ETUC, social dialogue and the Europeanisation of trade unions in the 1990s*. Oslo: ARENA and FAFO.

Dølvik, J. E., and Eldring, L. (2006). 'Industrial relations responses to migration and posting of workers after EU enlargement: Nordic trends and differences'. *Transfer: European Review of Labour and Research* 12(2): 213–30.

Dølvik, J. E., and Visser, J. (2009). 'Free movement, equal treatment and workers' rights: Can the European Union solve its trilemma of fundamental principles?'. *Industrial Relations Journal* 40(6): 491–509.

Donaghey, J. (2008). 'Deliberation, employment relations and social partnership in the Republic of Ireland'. *Economic and Industrial Democracy* 29(1): 35–63.

Donaghey, J., and Teague, P. (2006). 'The free movement of workers and social Europe: Maintaining the European ideal'. *Industrial Relations Journal* 37(6): 652–66.

Donaghey, J., and Teague, P. (2007). 'The mixed fortunes of Irish unions: Living with the paradoxes of social partnership'. *Journal of Labor Research* 28(1): 19–41.

Doyle, N., Hughes, G., and Wadensjö, E. (2006). 'Freedom of movement of workers from Central and Eastern Europe: Experiences in Ireland and Sweden'. Stockholm: Swedish Institute for European Policy Studies (SIEPS).

Draghi, M. (2012a). Interview with the *Wall Street Journal*, 24 February 2012.

Draghi, M. (2012b). Speech at Global Investment Conference, London, 26 July 2012. Available at: https://www.ecb.europa.eu/press/key/date/2012/html/sp120726.en.html.

Drahokoupil, J., van Apeldoorn, B., and Horn, L. (2009). 'Introduction: Towards a critical political economy of European governance'. In B. van Apeldoorn, J. Drahokoupil and L. Horn (eds) *Contradictions and limits of neoliberal european governance. From Lisbon to Lisbon.* London: Palgrave Macmillan, pp. 1–20.

Drake, H. (2000). *Jacques Delors: Perspectives on a European leader.* London: Routledge.

Drucker, W., and White, G. (2000). *Managing people in construction.* London: Institute of Personnel and Development.

Druker, J., and Dupré, I. (1998). 'The Posting of Workers Directive and employment regulation in the European construction industry'. *European Journal of Industrial Relations* 4(3): 309–30.

Duchêne, F. (1994). 'Jean Monnet's methods'. In D. Brinkley and C. Hackett (eds) *Jean Monnet: The path to European unity.* Basingstoke: MacMillan, pp. 184–209.

Duchêne, F. (1994). *Jean Monnet: The first statesman of interdependence.* New York: Norton.

Dufresne, A. (2015). 'The trade union response to the European economic governance regime. Transnational mobilization and wage coordination'. *Transfer: European Review of Labour and Research* 21(2): 141–56.

Dundon, T., González-Pérez, M. A., and McDonough, T. (2007). 'Bitten by the Celtic Tiger: immigrant workers and industrial relations in the new glocalized Ireland'. *Economic and Industrial Democracy* 28(4): 501–22.

Dunphy, R. (1992). 'The Workers Party and Europe: Trajectory of an idea'. *Irish Political Studies* 7(1): 21–39.

Dunphy, R. (2004), *Contesting Capitalism? Left parties and European integration.* Manchester: Manchester University Press.

Dyson, K. (2002). 'Introduction: EMU as integration, Europeanization and convergence'. In K. Dyson (ed.) *European states and the Euro: Europeanization, variation, and convergence.* Oxford: Oxford University Press, pp. 1–29.

Dyson, K., and Featherstone, K. (1999). *The road to Maastricht: negotiating economic and monetary union.* Oxford: Oxford University Press.

Ebbinghaus, B. (1993). Labour unity in union diversity: Trade unions and social cleavages in Western Europe, 1890–1989. Unpublished PhD Thesis, Department of Political and Social Sciences, Florence: EUI.

Ebbinghaus, B., and Visser, J. (2000). *Trade unions in Western Europe since 1945.* London: Palgrave Macmillan.

EC (European Commission) (1995). 'European Community competition policy'. Brussels: European Commission.

EC (European Commission) (2010). *Employment in Europe.* Brussels: European Commission.

EC (European Commission) (2011). 'Study on the economic and social effects associated with the phenomenon of posting of workers in the EU [Final Report VT/2009/062]. Brussels: European Commission.

EC (European Commission) (2017). White paper on the future of Europe. Brussels: European Commission.

EFBWW (2008a). European implications of the Laval case judgment – Preliminary analysis and proposed strategy for the EFBWW. Brussels: EFBWW.

EFBWW (2008b). Report: Wages in construction. Brussels: EFBWW.

EFBWW (2008c). Strengthening social inclusion of migrant workers in the European construction and wood industries. Brussels: EFBWW.

Eichenberg R. C., and Dalton R. J., (1993). 'Europeans and the European Community: The dynamics of public support for European integration'. *International. Organizations* 47(4): 507–34.

Endo, K. (1999). *The presidency of the European Commission under Jacques Delors: The politics of shared leadership.* Basingstoke: Macmillan Press.

Epifani, G. (2006). Speech to XV National Congress of CGIL Rimini, 1–4 March 2006.

Erdmenger, J. (1983). *The European Community transport policy: Towards a common transport policy.* Aldershot: Gower.

Eriksen, E. O., and Fossum, J. E. (eds) (2000). *Democracy in the European Union: Integration through deliberation?* London: Routledge.

Erne, R. (2008). *European unions: Labor's quest for a transnational democracy.* London: Cornell University Press.

Erne, R. (2015). 'A supranational regime that nationalizes social conflict: Explaining European trade unions' difficulties in politicizing European economic governance'. *Labor History* 56(3): 345–68.

Erne, R. (2018). 'Labour politics and the EU's new economic governance regime: A new European research council project'. *Transfer: European Review of Labour and Research* 24(2): 237–47.

Erne, R., and Blaser. M. (2018). 'Direct democracy and trade union action'. *Transfer: European Review of Labour and Research* 24(2): 217–32.

Erne, R., Stan, S., Golden, D., Szabó, I., and Maccarrone, V. (2024). *European economic governance and labour politics: From the financial crisis to the Covid-19 emergency.* Cambridge: Cambridge University Press.

Esping-Andersen, G. (1990). *The three worlds of welfare capitalism.* Cambridge: Polity Press.

ETUC (2003). Report on activities 1999/2002. Brussels: ETUC.

ETUC (2005). 'ETUC hails victory over Bolkestein and calls for 'Yes' votes on the Constitution'. Press Release.

ETUC (2008a). 'ETUC response to ECJ judgements Viking and Laval'. Brussels: ETUC.

ETUC (2008b). Viking and Laval Cases: Explanatory memorandum (for Executive Committee of the ETUC, 4 March 2008). Brussels: ETUC.

ETUC (2012). Declaration on the Treaty on stability, coordination and governance in the economic and monetary union, 25th of January. Brussels: ETUC.

ETUC (2015a). ETUC action programme 2015–2019: Amendments and Executive Committee recommendations. Brussels: ETUC.

ETUC (2015b). 'Free movement, yes! Social dumping, no!' Press Release.

Etzioni, A. (2007). 'The community deficit'. *Journal of Common Market Studies* 45(1): 23–42.

Eurofound (2005). 'Irish Ferries dispute finally resolved after bitter stand-off'. Available at: https://www.eurofound.europa.eu/publications/article/2005/irish-ferries-dispute-finally-resolved-after-bitter-stand-off.

Eurofound (2007). 'Supreme Court ruling will affect "right to bargain" law'. Available at: https://www.eurofound.europa.eu/publications/article/2007/supreme-court-ruling-will-affect-right-to-bargain-law.

Eurofound, (2002). 'Government and social partners sign Pact for Italy'. Available at: https://www.eurofound.europa.eu/publications/article/2002/government-and-social-partners-sign-pact-for-italy.

European Commission (1993). *Growth, competitiveness and employment*. White Paper. Brussels. CEC.

European Commission (1995). European Community competition policy. Brussels: CEC.

European Commission (2011b). Study on the economic and social effects associated with the phenomenon of posting of workers in the EU Final Report VT/2009/062. Brussels: European Commission.

European Commission. (1985). Completing the internal market. White Paper. Brussels. CEC.

European Council (2000). Lisbon European Council 23–24 March 2000. Presidency conclusions. Brussels: European Council.

European Council (2005) European Council declaration, 18 July 2005. Available at: https://www.consilium.europa.eu/uedocs/cms_data/docs/pressdata/en/ec/85325.pdf.

Ewing, K. (2010). 'The denial by the government and employers of collective bargaining rights for workers is unsustainable under international law'. *Irish Times*, 1 July 2010.

Fabbrini, F. (2013). 'The fiscal compact, the "golden rule" and the paradox of European federalism'. *Boston College International and Comparative Law Review* 36(1): 1–39.

Faenza, R., and Fini, M. (1976). *Gli Americani in Italia*. Milan: Feltrinelli.

Fajertag, G., and Pochet, P. (eds) (1997). *Social pacts in Europe* Brussels: ETUI.

Fajertag, G., and Pochet, P. (eds) (2000). *Social pacts in Europe*. Brussels: ETUI.

Falkner, G. (1998). *EU social policy in the 1990s: Towards a corporatist policy community*. London: Routledge.

Farrell, B. (1970). 'Labour and the Irish political party system – a suggested approach to analysis'. *Economic and Social Review* 1(4): 477–92.

Fassmann, H., and Münz, R. (eds) (1995). *European migration in the late twentieth century: Historical patterns, actual trends, and social implications*. Cheltenham: Edward Elgar.

Fassmann, H., Haller, M., and Lane, D. (eds) (2009). *Migration and mobility in Europe. Trends, patterns and control*. Cheltenham: Edward Elgar.

Favell, A. (2008). 'The new face of East–West migration in Europe'. *Journal of Ethnic and Migration Studies* 34(5): 701–16.

Favell, A. (2010). 'European identity and European citizenship in three "Eurocities": A sociological approach to the European Union'. *Politique Européenne* 30(3): 187–224.

Favell, A., and Guiraudon, V. (eds) (2011). *Sociology of the European Union*. Basingstoke: Palgrave Macmillan.

Featherstone, K. (1988). *Socialist parties and European integration: A comparative history* Manchester: Manchester University Press.

Featherstone, K. (1994). 'Jean Monnet and the "democratic deficit" in the European Union'. *Journal of Common Market Studies* 32(2): 149–70.

Featherstone, K. (2005). '"Soft" co-ordination meets "hard" politics: The European Union and pension reform in Greece'. *Journal of European Public Policy* 12(4): 733–50..

Federal Chancellor, The (2012), 'Continent of peace'. Available at https://www.bundeskanzlerin.de/bkin-en/news/continent-of-peace-604940.

Ferrera, M. (1986). 'Italy'. In P. Flora (ed.) *Growth to limits*. Berlin: Walter de Gruyter, pp. 385–82.

Ferrera, M. (2005). *The boundaries of welfare: European integration and the new spatial politics of social protection*. Oxford: Oxford University Press.

Ferrera, M., and Gualmini, E. (2004). *Rescued by Europe? Italy's social policy reforms from Maastricht to Berlusconi*. Amsterdam: Amsterdam University Press.

Ferrera, M., and Rhodes, M. (eds) (2000). *Recasting European welfare states*. London: Frank Cass.

Fetzer, T. (2012). 'Industrial relations history in transnational perspective: A review essay'. *History Compass* 10(1): 56–69.

Fioretos, O. (2011). *Creative reconstructions: Multilateralism and European varieties of capitalism after 1950*. Ithaca, NY: Cornell University Press.

Fischbach-Pyttel, C. (2017). *Building the European Federation of Public Service Unions: The history of EPSU (1978–2016)*. Brussels: EPSU.

Fitzgerald, I., Beadle, R., and Rowan, K. (2021). 'Trade unions and the 2016 UK European Union referendum'. *Economic and Industrial Democracy* 43(1): 388–409. DOI: https//:doi.org/10.1177/0143831X19899483.

Fitzgerald, M. (2001). *Protectionism to liberalisation: Ireland and the EEC, 1957 to 1966*. Aldershot: Ashgate.

Fitzgibbon, J. (2013). 'Citizens against Europe? Civil society and Eurosceptic protest in Ireland, the United Kingdom and Denmark'. *Journal of Common Market Studies* 51(1): 105–21.

Fitzgibbon, J., Leruth, B., and Startin, N. (2017). *Euroscepticism as a transnational and pan-European phenomenon: The emergence of a new sphere of opposition.* London: Routledge.

Flanders, A. (1970). *Management and unions: The theory and reform of industrial relations.* London: Faber.

Fligstein, N. (2001). *The architecture of markets: An economic sociology of twenty-first-century capitalist societies.* Princeton, NJ: Princeton University Press.

Fligstein, N. (2008). *Euroclash: The EU, European identity, and the future of Europe.* Oxford: Oxford University Press.

Fligstein, N., and Stone Sweet, A. (2002). 'Constructing polities and markets: An institutionalist account of European integration'. *American Journal of Sociology* 107(5): 1206–43.

Fligstein, N., Polyakova, A., and Sandholtz, W. (2012) 'European integration, nationalism and European identity', *Journal of Common Market Studies.* 50(1): 106–22.

Flinders, M., and Wood, M. (2014). 'Depoliticisation, governance and the state'. *Policy & Politics* 42(2): 135–49.

Flood, C. (2009). 'Dimensions of Euroscepticism'. *Journal of Common Market Studies* 47(4): 911–7.

Flora, P. (ed.) (1986). *Growth to limits: The Western European welfare states since World War II*, vol. 2: *Germany, United Kingdom, Ireland, Italy.* Berlin: de Gruyter.

Føllesdal, A. (2006). 'Survey article: The legitimacy deficits of the European Union'. *Journal of Political Philosophy* 14(4): 441–68.

Foreign Affairs Ministers of Belgium, Germany, France, Italy, Luxembourg and the Netherlands (2016). Common statement on British Referendum. Available at: https://www.esteri.it/en/sala_stampa/archivionotizie/comunicati/2016/06/common-statement-by-the-foreign/.

Forfás (2002). Annual report. Dublin: Forfás.

Forfás (2005). Annual report. Dublin: Forfás.

Forlenza, R. (2017). 'The politics of the Abendland: Christian Democracy and the idea of Europe after the Second World War'. *Contemporary European History* 26(2): 261–86.

Fossum, J. E., and Menéndez, A. J. (2011). *The constitution's gift: A constitutional theory for a democratic European Union.* London: Rowman & Littlefield.

Franzosi, R. (1995). *The puzzle of strikes: Class and state strategies in postwar Italy.* Cambridge: Cambridge University Press.

Frege, C., and Kelly, J. (2004). 'Union strategies in comparative context'. In C. Frege and J. Kelly (eds) *Varieties of unionism: Strategies for union revitalization in a globalizing economy.* Oxford: Oxford University Press, pp. 31–44.

Frieden, J. A. (1999). 'Actors and preferences in international relations'. In D. A. Lake and R. Powell (eds), *Strategic choice and international relations*. Princeton, NJ: Princeton University Press, pp. 39–76.

Gabel, M., and Scheve, K. (2007). 'Estimating the effect of elite communications on public opinion using instrumental variables'. *American Journal of Political Science* 51(4): 1013–28.

Gaffney, J. (ed.) (1996). *Political parties and the European Union*. London: Routledge.

Gago, A. (2018). EU ordoliberal intergovernmentalism and the transformation of national political opportunities. Explaining governments' and trade unions' strategies in Portugal, Spain and Italy during the Eurozone Crisis. PhD Thesis. University of Milan.

Gajewska, K., (2009). *Transnational labour solidarity: Mechanisms of commitment to cooperation within the European trade union movement*. London: Routledge.

Galantini, E. (1988). L'Europa del lavoro. Il VI congresso della Confederazione Europea. *Rassengna Sindacale* no. 17.

Galgóczi, B., Leschke, J., and Watt, A. (eds) (2009). *EU labour migration since enlargement: Trends, impacts and policies*. Surrey: Ashgate.

Gall, G. (ed.) (2009). *The future of union organising: Building for tomorrow*. Basingstoke: Palgrave Macmillan.

Gallagher, M. (1982). *The Irish Labour Party in transition 1957–1982* Manchester: Manchester University Press.

Gallagher, M. (1988) 'The Single European Act referendum'. *Irish Political Studies* 3(1): 77–82.

Galossi, E. (2011). I lavoratori stranieri nel settore delle costruzioni'. VI Rapporto IRES-FILLEA Roma.

Garrett, G., and Tsebelis, G. (1996). 'An institutional critique of intergovernmentalism'. *International Organization* 50(2): 269–99.

Garvin, T. (1982). *The Evolution of Irish nationalist politics*. Dublin: Gill & Macmillan.

Garvin, T. (2004). *Preventing the future: Why Ireland was so poor for so long*. Dublin: Gill and Macmillan.

Geary, J. F. (2007). 'Employee voice in the Irish workplace: Status and prospect'. In R. Freeman, P. Boxall and P. Haynes (eds) *What workers say: Employee voice in the Anglo-American world*. Ithaca, NY: Cornell University Press, pp. 97–124.

Geary, J. F. (2016). 'Economic crisis, austerity and trade union responses: The Irish case in comparative perspective'. *European Journal of Industrial Relations* 22(2):131–47.

Geary, J. F., and Gamwell, S. (2014). 'The union organising turn in Ireland?'. Paper presented at IREC annual conference, Dublin 10–12 September 2014.

Geary, J. F., and Gamwell, S. (2019). 'An American solution to an Irish problem: A consideration of the material conditions that shape the architecture of union organizing'. *Work, Employment and* Society 33(2): 191–207.

Gellner, E. (1983). *Nations and nationalism*. Ithaca, NY: Cornell University Press.

George, A. L., and Bennett, A. (2005) *Case studies and theory development in the social sciences.* London: MIT Press.

Geraghty, D. (1992). World class participation. The seventeenth Countess Markievicz memorial lecture. Dublin.

Geyer, R. (1997). *The uncertain union: British and Norwegian social democrats in an integrating Europe.* Aldershot: Avebury.

Gilbert, M. (2008). 'Narrating the process: Questioning the progressive story of European integration'. *Journal of Common Market Studies* 46(3): 641–62.

Gillingham, J. R (2016) *The EU: An obituary.* London: Verso.

Gilmore, E. (2016). *Inside the room: The untold story of Ireland's crisis government.* Dublin: Irish Academic Press.

Ginsborg, P. (2003). *Italy and its discontents: Family, civil society and state 1980–2001.* London: Penguin.

Girvin, B. (2002). *From union to union: Nationalism, democracy and religion in Ireland – Act of Union to EU.* Dublin: Gill & Macmillan.

Girvin, G. (1994). 'Trade unions and economic development'. In D. Nevin (eds) *Trade union century.* Cork: Mercier Press, pp. 117–32.

Glencross, A. (2009a). *What makes the EU viable? European integration in the light of the antebellum US experience.* Basingstoke: Palgrave Macmillan.

Glencross, A. (2009b). 'The difficulty of justifying European integration as a consequence of depoliticization: Evidence from the 2005 French referendum'. *Government and Opposition* 44(3): 243–61.

Gnetti, C. (1991). 'Il grande salto'. *Nuova Rassegna Sindacale* 19, May 1991.

Gobin, C. (1997). *L'Europe syndicale. Entre désir et réalité. Essai sur le syndicalisme et la construction Européenne à l'aube du XXIe siècle.* Brussels: Labor.

Goetschy, J. (1999). 'The European employment strategy: Genesis and development'. *European Journal of Industrial Relations* 5(2): 117–37.

Goetschy, J. (2005). 'The open method of coordination and the Lisbon strategy'. *Transfer* 11(1): 64–80.

Golden, D. (2013). 'Renzi's reforms, Italian trade unions and the EU!'. Available at: https://andreasbieler.blogspot.com/2014/03/renzis-reforms-italian-trade-unions-and.html. and

Golden, D. (2016). Challenging the pro-European consensus: Explaining the uneven trajectory of Euroscepticism in Irish and Italian unions across time. PhD thesis, University College Dublin.

Golden, D. (2020a). 'Has the European semester been socialised? Prescriptions for Germany, Italy, Ireland and Romania in public transport'. Paper presented at European University Institute, Florence, 28 October 2020.

Golden, D. (2020b). 'I gemelli terribili…contro il Sinn Féin'. *Transform Italia*, 24 June 2020. Available at: https://transform-italia.it/i-gemelli-terribili/.

Gorges, M. J. (1996). *Euro-Corporatism? Interest intermediation in the European Community.* London: University Press of America.

Gould, A., Barry, M., and Wilkinson, A. (2016). 'Varieties of capitalism revisited: Current debates and possible directions'. *Relations Industrielles/Industrial Relations* 70(4): 587–602.

Gramsci, A. (1971). 'The intellectuals'. In *Selections from the Prison Notebooks*. Translated and edited by Q. Hoare and G. N. Smith. New York: International Publishers, pp. 3–23.

Gramsci, A. (1971). *Selections from the Prison Notebooks*, ed. and transl. Q. Hoare and G. Nowell-Smith. London: Lawrence & Wishart.

Grande, E., and Hutter, S. (2016). 'Beyond authority transfer: Explaining the politicisation of Europe'. *West European Politics* 39(1): 23–43.

Grande, E., Hutter, S., Kerscher, A., and Becke, R. (2016). 'Framing Europe: are cultural-identitarian frames driving politicisation?'. In S. Hutter, E. Grande and H. Kriesi (eds) *Politicising Europe: Integration and mass politics*. Cambridge: Cambridge University Press, pp. 181–206.

Grande, E., Schwarzbözl, T., and Fatke, M. (2019). 'Politicizing immigration in Western Europe'. *Journal of European Public Policy* 26(10): 1444–63.

Granovetter, M. (1985). 'Economic action and social structure: The problem of embeddedness'. *American Journal of Sociology* 91(3): 481–510.

Grant, A. (2012). *Irish socialist Republicanism*. Dublin: Four Courts Press.

Grant, C. (1994). *Delors: Inside the house that Jacques Built*. London: Nicholas Brealey.

Graziano, P. (2007). 'Adapting to the European Employment Strategy? Recent developments in Italian employment policy'. *International Journal of Comparative Labour Law and Industrial Relations* 23(4): 543–65.

Graziano, P., Jacquot, S., and Palier, B. (2011). 'Introduction: The usages of Europe in national employment-friendly welfare state reforms'. In P. Graziano, S. Jacquot, and B. Palier (eds) *The EU and the domestic politics of welfare state reforms: Europa, Europae*. Basingstoke: Palgrave Macmillan, pp. 1–18.

Greaves, D. (1982). *The Irish Transport and General Workers Union: The formative years 1909–1923*. Dublin: Gill and Macmillan.

Greenwood, J. (1997). *Representing interests in the European Union*. London: Macmillan.

Greer, I., Ciupijus, Z., and Lillie, N. (2013). 'The European Migrant Workers Union and the barriers to transnational industrial citizenship'. *European Journal of Industrial Relations,* 19(1): 5–20.

Grimshaw, D., Willmott, H., Rubery, J., and Marchington, M. (2005). *Fragmenting work: Blurring organizational boundaries and disordering hierarchies*. Oxford: Oxford University Press.

Guasconi, M. E. (2003). 'Paving the way for a European social dialogue'. *Journal of European Integration History* 9(1): 87–111.

Guisan, C. (2013). *A political theory of identity in European integration: Memory and policies*. Abington: Routledge.

Gumbrell-McCormick, R., and Hyman, R. (2013). *Trade unions in Western Europe: Hard times, hard choices*. Oxford: Oxford University Press.

Haas, E. (1958). *The uniting of Europe: Political, social, and economic forces 1950–1957*. Notre Dame, IN: University of Notre Dame Press.

Haas, E. (1968). (2nd edn). *The uniting of Europe: Political, social, and economic forces 1950–1957*. Notre Dame, IN: University of Notre Dame Press.

Haas, E. (1975). *The obsolescence of regional integration theory*. Berkley, CA: Institute of International Studies.

Haas, E. (1976). 'Turbulent fields and the theory of regional integration'. *International Organizations* 30(2): 173–212.

Habermas, J. (1999). 'The European nation-state and the pressures of globalization'. *New Left Review* No: 235, May/June 46–59.

Hall, P. A. (1986). *Governing the economy: The politics of state intervention in Britain and France*. Oxford: Oxford University Press.

Hall, P. A. (1989). *The political power of economic ideas: Keynesianism across nations*. Princeton, NJ: Princeton University Press.

Hall, P. A. (2005). 'Preference formation as a political process: The case of monetary union in Europe'. In I. Katznelson and B. R. Weingast (eds) *Preferences and situations: Points of intersection between historical and rational choice institutionalism*. New York: Russell Sage, pp. 129–60.

Hall, P. A. and Soskice, D. (eds) (2001). *Varieties of capitalism: The institutional foundations of comparative advantage*. Oxford: Oxford University Press.

Hall, P. A., and Franzese, R. J. (1998). 'Mixed signals: Central bank independence, coordinated wage bargaining, and European monetary union'. *International Organizations* 52(3): 505–35.

Hall, P. A., and Taylor, R. C. (1996). 'Political science and the three new institutionalisms'. *Political Studies* 44(5): 936–57.

Hall, P. and A., Jacoby, W., Levy, J., and Meunier, S. (eds) (2014). *The politics of representation in the global age: Identification, mobilization and adjudication*. Cambridge: Cambridge University Press.

Hamann, K., and Kelly, J. (2007). 'Party politics and the re-emergence of social pacts in Western Europe'. *Comparative Political Studies* 40(8): 971–94.

Hancké, B. (2013). *Unions, central banks, and EMU: Labour market institutions and monetary integration in Europe*. Oxford: Oxford University Press.

Hanley, B., and Millar, S. (2010). *The lost revolution: The story of the Official IRA and the Workers' Party*. Dublin: Penguin Ireland.

Hannigan, K. (1981) 'British based unions in Ireland: Building workers and the split in Congress'. *Saothar* 7: 40–9.

Hardiman, N. (1988). *Pay, politics and economic performance in the Republic of Ireland*. Oxford: Clarendon Press.

Hardiman, N. (2002). 'From conflict to co-ordination: Economic governance and political innovation in Ireland'. *West European Politics* 25(4): 1–24.

Hardiman, N. (2006). 'Politics and social partnership: Flexible network governance.' *Economic and Social Review* 37(3): 343–74.

Harmsen R., and Spiering, M. (2004). *Euroscepticism: Party politics, national identity and European integration*. New York: Rodopi.

Harvey, D. (2005). *A brief history of neoliberalism*. Oxford: Oxford University Press.

Harvey, M., and Behling, F. (2008). *The evasion economy: False self-employment in the UK construction industry*. London: Union of Construction, Allied Trades and Technicians (UCATT).

Hassel, A. (2007). 'The curse of institutional security: The erosion of German trade unionism', *Industrielle Beziehungen* 14(2): 176–91.284

Hastings, T. (2008). *The state of the unions: Challenges facing organised labour in Ireland*. Dublin: Liffey Press.

Hastings, T., Sheehan, B., and Yeates, P. (2007). *Saving the future: How social partnership shaped Ireland's economic success*. Dublin: Blackhall Publishing.

Hay, C. (2004). 'Common trajectories, variable paces, divergent outcomes? Models of European capitalism under conditions of complex economic interdependence'. *Review of International Political Economy* 11(2): 231–62.

Hayward, J. (1980). 'Trade union movements and their politico-economic environments: A preliminary framework'. In J. Hayward (ed.) *Trade union and politics in Western Europe*. London: Frank Cass, pp. 1–9.

Hayward, K., (2002). 'Not a nice surprise: An analysis of the debate surrounding the 2001 referendum on the Treaty of Nice in the Republic of Ireland'. *Irish Studies in International Affairs* 13: 167–86.

Hayward. K. (2003). '"If at first you don't succeed …": The second referendum on the Treaty of Nice, 2002'. *Irish Political Studies* 18(1): 120–32.

Hearne, R. (2020). *Housing shock: The Irish housing crisis and how to solve it*. Bristol: Bristol University Press.

Heine, S. (2010). 'Left versus Europe?' *Perspectives on European politics and society* 11(3): 313–32.

Held, D., McGrew, A., Goldblatt, D., and Perraton, J. (1999). *Global transformations. Politics, economics and culture*. Cambridge: Polity Press.

Helgadóttir, O. (2015). 'The Bocconi boys go to Brussels: Italian economic ideas, professional networks and European austerity'. *Journal of European Public Policy* 23(3): 392–409.

Helle, I. (2015). 'A new proletariat in the making? Reflections on the 14 November 2012 strike and the movements of 1968 and 1995'. *Transfer: European Review of Labour and Research* 21(2): 229–42.

Henderman-O'Brien, M. (1983). *The road to Europe: Irish attitudes 1948–61*. Dublin: Institute of Public Administration.

Hendy, J. (2014). The McGowan judgement & collective bargaining. Lecture by J. Hendy, QC, Trinity College, Dublin, January 30, 2014.

Hermann, C., and Hofbauer, I. (2007). 'The European social model: Between competitive modernisation and neoliberal resistance'. *Capital & Class* 31(3):125–39.

Heyes, J., and Hyland, M. (2012). 'Supporting, recruiting and organising migrant workers in Ireland and the United Kingdom: A review of trade union practices'. In Galgóczi, B. (ed.) *EU labour migration in troubled times – Skills mismatch, return and policy responses*. Aldershot: Ashgate, pp. 211–34.

Hine, D. (1993). *Governing Italy*. Oxford: Oxford University Press.

Hix, S. (2007). 'Euroscepticism as anti-centralization: A rational choice institutionalist perspective'. *European Union Politics* 8(1): 131–50.

Hix, S., and Lord, C. (1997). *Political parties in the European Union*. Basingstoke: Macmillan Education.

Hobolt, S. B. (2009). *Europe in question: Referendums on European integration*. Oxford: Oxford University Press.

Hobolt, S. B., and de Vries, C. E. (2009). 'Public support for European integration'. *Annual Review of Political Science* 19: 413–32.

Hodson, D. (2016). 'Jacques Delors: Vision, revisionism, and the design of EMU'. In K. Dyson and I. Maes (eds) *Architects of the Euro. Intellectuals in the making of European monetary union*. Oxford: Oxford University Press, pp. 212–32.

Hodson, D., and Maher, I. (2018). *The transformation of EU Treaty making: The rise of parliaments, referendums and courts since 1950*. Cambridge: Cambridge University Press.

Hoffmann, S. (1966). 'Obstinate or obsolete? The fate of the nation state and the case of Western Europe'. *Daedalus* 95(3): 862–915.

Holmes, M. (2006). *The development of the Irish Labour Party's European policy: From opposition to support*. Lampeter, NY: Edwin Mellen Press.

Holmes, M., and Order, K. (2012). 'The Left from Laeken to Lisbon'. In M. Holmes and K. Roder (eds) *The Left and the European Constitution*. Manchester: Manchester University Press, pp. 1–17.

Holmes, M., and Order, K. (eds) (2012). *The Left and the European Constitution: From Laeken to Lisbon*. Manchester: Manchester University Press.

Hooghe, L. (1998). 'EU cohesion policy and competing models of regulated capitalism'. *Journal of Common Market Studies* 36(4): 457–77.

Hooghe, L. (2007). 'What drives Euroskepticism? Party-public cueing, ideology and strategic opportunity'. *European Union Politics* 8(1): 5–12.

Hooghe, L., and Marks, G. (1999). 'The making of a polity: The struggle over European integration'. In H. Kitschelt, P. Lange, G. Marks and J. D. Stephens (eds) *Continuity and change in contemporary capitalism*. Cambridge and New York: Cambridge University Press, pp. 70–98.

Hooghe, L., and Marks, G. (2001). *Multi-Level governance and European integration*. Lanham, MD: Rowman & Littlefield.

Hooghe, L., and Marks, G. (2005). 'Calculation, community and cues'. *European Union Politics* 6(4): 419–43.

Hooghe, L., and Marks, G. (2009). 'A post-functionalist theory of European integration: From permissive consensus to constraining dissensus'. *British Journal of Political Science* 39(1): 1–23.

Höpner, M., and Jurczyk, D. (2015). 'How the Eurobarometer blurs the line between research and propaganda'. MPIfG Discussion Paper 15/6.

Höpner, M., and Schäfner, A. (2012). 'Embeddedness and regional integration: Waiting for Polanyi in a Hayekian setting'. *International Organization* 66(3): 429–55.

Horowitz, D. L. (1963). *The Italian labor movement*. Cambridge, MA: Harvard University Press.286

Houwerzijl, M., and Peters, S. (2008). *Liability in subcontracting processes in the European construction sector.* Dublin: European Foundation for the Improvement of Living and Working Conditions.

Howlett, M., and Goetz, K. H. (2014). 'Introduction: Time, temporality and timescapes in administration and policy'. *International Review of Administrative Sciences* 80(3): 477–92.

Hughes, G. (2011). *Free movement in the EU: The case of Ireland.* Berlin: Friedrich Ebert Stiftung.

Hutter, S., Grande, E. and Kriesi, H. (eds) (2016). *Politicising Europe: Integration and mass politics.* Cambridge: Cambridge University Press.

Hutter, S., and Grande, E. (2014). 'Politicizing Europe in the national electoral arena: A comparative analysis of five West European countries, 1970–2010'. *Journal of Common Market Studies* 52(5):1002–18.

Huysseune, M. (2010). 'A Eurosceptic vision in a Europhile country: The case of the Lega Nord'. *Modern Italy* 15(1): 63–75.

Hyman, R. (2001a). *Understanding european trade unionism: Between market, class and society.* London: Sage.

Hyman, R. (2001b). 'Trade union research and cross-national comparison'. *European Journal of Industrial Relations* 7(2): 203–32.

Hyman, R. (2001c). 'European integration and industrial relations: A case of variable geometry?'. *Antipode* 33(3): 468–83.

Hyman, R. (2005). 'Trade unions and the politics of the European social model'. *Economics and Industrial Democracy* 26(1): 9–40.

Hyman, R. (2010). 'Trade unions and "Europe": Are the members out of step?'. *Relations Industrielles/Industrial Relations* 65(1): 3–29.

Hyman, R. (2012). 'The labour policies of the European Union: Questions of governance'. In F. Garibaldo, V. Telljohann, C. Casey and M. Baglioni (eds) *Workers, citizens, governance: Socio-cultural innovation at work.* Berlin: Peter Lang, pp. 63–78.

IBEC (2010). 'IBEC sets out opposition to mandatory union recognition'. *IBEC Agenda* Issue 6.

ICTU (1971). The Irish trade unions and the European Economic Community. Dublin: ICTU.

ICTU (1988). Make Europe work for us. Dublin: ICTU.

ICTU (1988a). 'The regional implications of the internal market'. Paper presented at Make Europe Work for Us conference, October 1988.

ICTU (1988b). Information Bulletin: Completion of the internal market, 1992. October 1988. Dublin: ICTU.

ICTU (2005). Towards a strategy for the inclusion of migrant workers in trade unions. Report by S. Phillips. Dublin: ICTU.

ICTU (2006). Observations and recommendations on the application of transitional measures on the accession of Bulgaria and Romania to the EU on 1st January 2007. Dublin: ICTU.

ICTU (2007). 2005–2007 Report of the Executive Council, Dublin: ICTU.

ICTU (2008). Special Delegate Conference, 17 April 2008, Liberty Hall, Dublin.

ICTU (2009). Delivering growth and jobs: Funding a major new investment programme for Ireland. Dublin: ICTU.

ICTU (2012). 'The Fiscal Compact Treaty: A synthesis of views'. Paper presented to ICTU Executive Council.

ICTU (2013). Report of the Executive Council Biennial Delegate Conference, Belfast, 2–4 July 2013.

ICTU (no date). Submission to the taskforce on active citizenship.

Ierarchi, G. (2006). 'Governments, policy space and party positions in the Italian parliament (1996–2001)'. *South European Society & Politics* 12(2): 261–85.

IMF (2012). Euro area policies: 2012 Article IV consultation—selected issues paper. Available at: https://www.imf.org/en/Publications/CR/Issues/2016/12/31/Euro-Area-Policies-2012-Article-IV-Consultation-Selected-Issues-Paper-26075.

IMF (2013). 'The driving force behind the boom and bust in construction in Europe'. IMF Working Paper WP/13/181.

Imig, D. T., and Tarrow, S. (ed.) (2001). *Contentious Europeans: Protest and politics in an emerging polity*. Lanham, MD: Rowman & Littlefield.

Imlay, T. C. (2018). *The practice of socialist internationalism, European socialists and international politics, 1914–1960*. Oxford: Oxford University Press.

Immergut, M. E. (2006). 'Historical-institutionalism in political science and the problem of change'. In A. Wimmer and R. Kössler (eds) *Understanding change: Models, methodologies and metaphors*. New York: Springer, pp. 237–59.

Inglehart, R. F., and Norris, P. (2016). 'Trump, Brexit, and the rise of populism'. Working Paper. Harvard Kennedy School, RWP16-026.

Inglehart, R., and Klingemann, H. D. (1976). 'Party identification, ideological preference and the left-right dimension among western mass publics'. In I. Budge, I. Crewe and D. Farlie (eds) *Party identification and beyond*. London: John Wiley, pp. 243–73.

Inglehart, R., and Welzel, C. (2005). *Modernization, cultural change, and democracy: The human development sequence*. Cambridge: Cambridge University Press.

Ioannou, C. (2012). 'Recasting Greek industrial relations: Internal devaluation in light of the economic crisis and European integration'. *International Journal of Comparative Labour Law and Industrial Relations* 28(2): 199–222.

Irish Government (1963). Second programme for economic expansion. Dublin: Stationery Office.

Irish Government (1987). Programme for national recovery. Dublin: Stationery Office.

Irish Government (1997). Partnership 2000. Dublin: Stationery Office.

ISTAT (2008). *Rapporto annuale sulla situazione del paese*. Rome: ISTAT.

ISTAT (2009). *La popolazione straniera residente in Italia*. Rome: ISTAT.

ISTAT (2010). *Rapporto annuale sulla situazione del paese*. Rome: ISTAT.

ITGWU (1972). 'No to EEC'. Pamphlet on EEC accession referendum.

Ivaldi, G. (2006). 'Beyond France's 2005 referendum on the European Constitutional Treaty: Second-order model, anti-establishment attitudes and the end of the alternative European utopia'. *West European Politics* 29(1): 47–69.

Jabko, N. (2006). *Playing the market: A political strategy for uniting Europe 1985–2005*. Ithaca, NY: Cornell University Press.

Jackson, G., and Muellenborn, T. (2012), 'Understanding the role of institutions in industrial relations: Perspectives from classical sociological theory'. *Industrial Relations* 51(1): 472–500.

Jacobi, O., Jessop, B., Kastendiek, H., and Regini, M. (eds) (1986). *Economic crisis, trade unions and the state*. London: Croom Helm.

Jacobsen, J. K. (1994). *Chasing progress in the Irish Republic*. Cambridge: Cambridge University Press.

Jepsen, M., and Serrano Pascual, A. (eds) (2005). *Unwrapping the European social model*. Bristol: Policy Press.

Jessop, B. (1990). *State theory: Putting the capitalist state in its place*. Cambridge: Polity.

Johansson, K. M. (2002a). 'Another road to Maastricht: The Christian Democrat coalition and the quest for European Union'. *Journal of Common Market Studies* 40(3): 871–93.

Johansson, K. M. (2002b). 'Party elites in multilevel Europe: The Christian Democrats and the Single European Act'. *Party Politics* 8(4): 423–39.

Johnston, M. T. (1994). *The European Council: Gatekeeper of the European Community*. Boulder, CO: Westview.

Jones, E., and Verdun, A. (2003). 'Political economy and European integration'. *Journal of European Public Policy* 10(1): 81–3.

Joppke, C. (1987). 'The crisis of the welfare state, collective consumption, and the rise of new social actors'. *Berkeley Journal of Sociology* 32: 237–60.

Jordan, J., Maccarone, V., and Erne, R. (2020). 'Towards a socialization of the EU's new economic governance regime? EU labour policy interventions in Germany, Ireland, Italy and Romania (2009–2019)'. *British Journal of Industrial Relations* 59(1): 191–213.

Jorens, Y., Peters, S., and Houwerzijl, M. (2012). 'Study on the protection of workers' rights in subcontracting processes in the European Union'. Project DG EMPL/B2 - VC/2011/0015. Brussels: University of Ghent. Available at: https://biblio.ugent. be/publication/8572315.

Josselin, D. (2001). 'Trade Unions for EMU: Sectoral preferences and political opportunities'. *West European Politics* 24(1): 55–74.

Jupille J. (2006). 'Knowing Europe: Metatheory and methodology in European Studies'. In M. Cini and A. Bourne (eds) *Palgrave advances in European Union studies*. Basingstoke: Palgrave Macmillan, pp. 209–32.

Kaiser, W. (2007). *Christian Democracy and the origins of European Union*. Cambridge: Cambridge University Press.

Kaiser, W., and Meyer, J. H. (2010). *Non-state actors in European Integration in the 1970s: Towards a polity of transnational contestation*. Leipzig: Leipziger Univ.-Verl.

Kaiser, W., Leucht, B. and Rasmussen, M. (2008). 'Origins of a European polity: A new research agenda for European Union history'. In W. Kaiser, B. Leucht and

M. Rasmussen (eds) The history of the European Union origins of a trans- and supranational polity 1950-72. London: Routledge pp. 1-11.

Kassim, H., Saurugger, S., and Puetter, U. (2019). 'The study of national preference formation in times of the euro crisis and beyond'. *Political Studies Review* 18(4): 463–74.

Katz, R. S., and Mair, P. (1995). 'Changing models of party organization and party democracy: The emergence of the cartel party'. *Party Politics*, 1(1): 5–28.

Katznelson, I., and Weingast, B. (2005). 'Intersections between historical and rational choice institutionalism'. In I. Katznelson and B. Weingast (eds) *Preferences and situations*. Cambridge: Cambridge University Press, pp. 1–26.

Keatinge, P. (1989). 'Ireland's European policies: The Single European Act and beyond'. *Études Irlandaises* 14(2): 165–76.

Keatinge, P. (1993). 'Ireland's foreign relations in 1992'. *Irish Studies in International Affairs* 4: 69–93.

Kelly, J. (2008). Statement to Joint Committee on European Affairs (Sub-Committee on Ireland's Future in the EU), Debate, Tuesday, 4 November 2008.

Kelly, J. (2014). Speech at Anti-Austerity Alliance meeting, Limerick, 9 July 2014.

Kelly, M. (2009). 'The Irish credit bubble'. Dublin: UCD Centre for Economic Research Working Paper Series; UCD Geary Institute Discussion Paper Series.

Keogh, D. (1997). 'The diplomacy of "dignified calm" – an analysis of Ireland's application for membership of the EEC 1961–1963'. *Journal of European Integration History* 3(1): 81–101.

Kilpatrick, C. (2009). 'The ECJ and labour law: A 2008 retrospective'. *Industrial Law Journal* 38(2): 180–208.

Kindersley R. (ed.) (1981). *In search of Eurocommunism*. Basingstoke: Palgrave Macmillan.

Kirby, P. (2002). 'Contested pedigrees of the Celtic Tiger'. In P. Kirby, L. Gibbons and M. Cronin (eds) *Reinventing Ireland: Culture, society and the global economy*. London: Pluto Press, pp. 21–37.

Kirchner, E. (1977). *Trade unions as pressure groups in the European Community*. Farnborough: Saxon House.

Kitschelt, H. (1994). *The transformation of European social democracy*. Cambridge: Cambridge University Press.

Kjeldstadli, K. (2015). 'A closed nation or an open working class? When do unions opt for including labour migrants?'. In A. Bieler, R. Erne, D. Golden, I. Helle, K. Kjeldstadli, T. Matos and S. Stan (eds) *Labour and transnational action in times of crisis*. London: Rowman & Littlefield, pp. 83–98.

Knight, F. H. (1985[1921]). *Risk, uncertainty and profit*. Boston, MA: Hart.

Koch, H., Sørensen, K. H, Haltern, U., and Weiler, J. (eds) (2010). *Europe: The new legal realism: Essays in honour of Hjalte Rasmussen*. Århus: DJØF Publishing.

König, T., and Hug, S. (2006). *Policy-making processes and The European constitution: A comparative study of member states and accession countries*. London: Routledge.

Korpi, W. (1983). *The democratic class struggle*. London: Routledge.

Kriesi, H., Grande, E., Dolezal, M., Hebling, M., Höhnger, D., Hutter, S., and Wüest, B. (2012). *Political conflict in Western Europe*. Cambridge: Cambridge University Press.

Krings, T. (2007). 'Equal rights for all workers: Irish trade unions and the challenge of labour migration'. *Irish Journal of Sociology* 16(1): 43–61.

Krings, T. (2009). 'A race to the bottom? Trade unions, EU enlargement and the free movement of labour'. *European Journal of Industrial Relations* 15(1): 49–69.

Krings,T., Bobek, A., Moriarty, E., Salamonska, J., and Wickham, J. (2015). 'Large-scale migration in an open labour market: the Irish experience with post-2004 labour mobility and the regulation of employment standards'. In M. Bernaciak (ed.) *Market expansion and social dumping in Europe*. London: Routledge, pp. 25–42.

Krippner, G. R. (2001). 'The elusive market: Embeddedness and the paradigm of economic sociology'. *Theory and Society* 30(6): 775–810.

Kuhn, T., and Stoeckel, F. (2014). 'When European integration becomes costly: The euro crisis and public support for European economic governance'. *Journal of European Public Policy* 21(4): 624–41.

Kunzlik, P. (2013). 'Neoliberalism and the European public procurement regime'. *Cambridge Yearbook of European Legal Studies* 15: 283–335.

Kvist, J. (2004). 'Does EU enlargement start a race to the bottom? Strategic interaction among EU member states in social policy'. *Journal of European Social Policy* 14(3): 301–18.

Labour Court (2006). *Annual report 2006*: Dublin: The Labour Court.

Labour Relations Commission (2005). *Annual report 2005*. Dublin: The Labour Relations Commission.

Lacan, J. (1988). *The seminar of Jacques Lacan, Book 1: Freud's papers on technique 1953–1954*. Edited by J. A. Miller. Cambridge: Cambridge University Press.

Laclau, E., and Mouffe, C. (1985). *Hegemony and socialist strategy*. London: Verso.

Laffan, B., O'Donnell, R., and Smith, M. (2000). *Europe's experimental union. Rethinking integration*. London: Routledge.

Lakatos, I. (1970). 'History of science and its rational reconstructions'. *PSA: Proceedings of the Biennial Meeting of the Philosophy of Science Association*, pp: 91–136.

Lane, F. (2008). 'Envisaging labour history: Some reflections on Irish historiography and the working class'. In F. Lane and N. Purséil (eds) *Essays in Irish labour history*. Dublin: Irish Academic Press, pp. 9–25.

Lange, P. (1993). 'Maastricht and the social policy: Why did they do it?'. *Politics and Society* 21(1): 5–36.

Lapeyre, J. (2018). *The European social dialogue: The History of a social innovation* (1985–2003). ETUI: Brussels.

Larsson, B. (2014). 'Transnational trade union action in Europe. The significance of national and sectoral industrial relations'. *European Societies* 16(3): 378–400.

Laurent, P. H. (1970). 'Paul-Henri Spaak and the diplomatic origins of the Common Market, 1955–1956'. *Political Science Quarterly* 85(3): 373–96.

Laursen, F. (ed.) (2012). *The making of the Lisbon Treaty. The role of the member states*. Berlin: Peter Lang AG.

Leconte, C. (2010). *Understanding Euroscepticism*. London: Palgrave Macmillan.

Leconte, C. (2015). 'From pathology to mainstream phenomenon: Reviewing the Euroscepticism debate in research and theory'. *International Political Science Review* 36(3): 250–63.

Lee, J. (1984). *Reflections on Ireland in the E.E.C.* Dublin: Irish Council of the European Movement.

Lee, J. (1989). *Ireland 1912–1985: Politics and society*. Cambridge: Cambridge University Press.

Legnani, M. (1983). ' "L'Utopia grande borghese": L'Associazionismo padronale tra ricostruzione e repubblica'. In M. Flores (ed.) *Gli anni della costituente: Strategie dei governi e delle classi sociali*. Milan: Feltrinelli, pp. 154–7.

Lehmbruch, G., and Schmitter, P. C (eds) (1982). *Patterns of corporatist policy-making*. London: Sage.

Leibfried, S., and Pierson, P. (2000). 'Social policy. Left to courts and markets?'. In H. Wallace and W. Wallace (eds) *Policy making in the European Union*. Oxford: Oxford University Press, pp. 273–93.

Leonardi, S. (2018). 'Trade unions and collective bargaining in Italy during the crisis'. In S. Lehndorff, H. Dribbusch and T. Schulten (eds) *Rough waters: European trade unions in a time of crises*. Brussels: ETUI, pp. 87–115.

Leruth, B. (2015). 'Operationalizing national preferences on Europe and differentiated integration'. *European Journal of Public Policy* 22(6): 816–35.

Leruth, B., and Startin, N. (2017). 'Between Euro-federalism, Euro-pragmatism and Euro-populism: The Gaullist movement divided over Europe'. *Modern & Contemporary France* 25(2): 153–69.

Leupold, A. (2014). 'The politics of (not) shifting blame onto EMU in the crisis'. Paper presented at ECPR General Conference, 3–6 September 2014.

Leupold, A. (2016). 'A structural approach to politicisation in the euro crisis'. *West European Politics* 39(1): 84–103.

Levinson, C. (1972). *International trade unionism*. London: Macmillan.

Lieberman, E. (2001). 'Causal inference in historical institutional analysis: A specification of periodization strategies'. *Comparative Political Studies* 34(9): 1011–35.

Lijphart, A. (1971). 'Comparative politics and the comparative method'. *American Political Science Review* 65(3): 682–93.

Lillie, N. (2012). 'Subcontracting, posted migrants and labour market segmentation in Finland'. *British Journal of Industrial Relations* 50(1): 148–67.

Lillie, N., and Greer, I. (2007). 'Industrial relations, migration, and neoliberal politics: The case of the European construction sector'. *Politics and Society* 35(4): 551–81.

Lindberg, L., and Scheingold, S. (1970). *Europe's would-be polity: Patterns of change in the European Community*. Washington DC: Prentice Hall.

Lindstrom, N. (2010). 'Service liberalization in the enlarged EU: A race to the bottom or the emergence of transnational political conflict?'. *Journal of Common Market Studies* 48(5): 1307–27.

Lindstrom, N. (2019). 'What's left for "social Europe"? Brexit and transnational labour market regulation in the UK-1 and the EU-27'. *New Political Economy* 24(2): 286–98.292

Locke, R., and Thelen, K. (1995). 'Apples and oranges revisited: Contextualized comparisons and the study of comparative labor politics'. *Politics and Society* 23(3): 337–66.

Ludlow, N. P. (2001). 'The Treaty of Nice: Neither triumph nor disaster'. *ECSA Review* 14(2): 1–4.

Ludlow, N. P. (2009). 'History aplenty. But still too isolated'. In M. Egan, N. Nugent and W. E. Paterson (eds) *Research agendas in EU Studies: Stalking the elephant*. Basingstoke: Palgrave Macmillan, pp. 14–30.

Lukes, S. (2005). *Power: A radical view* (2nd edn). Basingstoke: Palgrave Macmillan.

Maccarrone, V. (2019). A tale of two countries? The impact of the new European economic governance regime on Irish and Italian industrial relations. PhD thesis, University College Dublin.

Macron, E. (2019). 'For European renewal'. 4 March 2019. Available at https://www. elysee.fr/en/emmanuel-macron/2019/03/04/for-european-renewal.

Magnani, S. (1979). 'Elezioni europee. Per un governo democratico dell'europa'. *Rassegna Sindacale*, June 7 1979.

Mahoney, J., and Rueschemeyer, D. (eds) (2003). *Comparative historical analysis in the social sciences*. Cambridge: Cambridge University Press.

Maillot, A. (2009). 'Sinn Féin's approach to the EU: Still more "critical" than "engaged"?'. *Irish Political Studies* 24(4): 559–74.

Mair, P. (1992). 'Explaining the absence of class politics in Ireland'. In J. Goldthorpe and C. Whelan (eds) *The development of industrial society in Ireland*. Oxford: Oxford University Press, pp. 383–410.

Mair, P. (2005). 'Popular democracy and the European Union polity'. European Governance Papers C-05-03.

Mair, P. (2007). 'Political opposition and the European Union'. *Government and Opposition* 42(1): 1–17.

Mair, P. (2013). *Ruling the void: The hollowing-out of western democracy*. London: Verso.

Majone, G. (2005). *The dilemmas of European integration: The ambiguities and pitfalls of integration by stealth*. Oxford: Oxford University Press.

Majone, G. (2009). *Europe as the would-be world power: The EU at fifty*. Cambridge: Cambridge University Press.

Makovec, M. (2009). 'Country study, Italy'. In Brueker, H. *et al.* (eds) *Labour mobility within the EU in the context of enlargement and the functioning of transitional arrangements* Brussels: European Integration Consortium.

Manners, I., and Rosamond, B. (2018). 'A different Europe is possible: The professionalization of EU studies and the dilemmas of integration in the 21st century'. *Journal of Common Market Studies* 56(1): 28–38.

Marginson, P., and Sisson, K. (2004). *European integration and industrial relations: Multilevel governance in the making*. Basingstoke: Palgrave Macmillan.

Marino, S. (2012). 'Trade union inclusion of migrant and ethnic minority workers: Comparing Italy and the Netherlands'. *European Journal of Industrial Relations* 18(1): 5–20.*Bibliography* 293

Marks, G. (1989). *Unions in Politics: Britain, Germany and the United States in the nineteenth and early twentieth centuries.* Princeton, NJ: Princeton University Press.

Marks, G. (1997). 'A third lens: Comparing European integration and state building'. In J. Klausen and L. A. Tilly (eds). *European integration in social and historical perspective: 1850 to present.* Lanham, MD: Rowman & Littlefield, pp. 23–50.

Marks, G. (2004). 'Conclusion: European integration and political conflict'. In G. Marks and M. R. Steenbergen (eds) *European integration and political conflict.* Cambridge: Cambridge University Press, pp. 235–59.

Marks, G., and McAdam, D. (1996). 'Social movements and the changing structure of political opportunity in the European Union'. *West European Politics* 19(2): 249–78.

Marks, G., and Wilson, C. J. (2000). 'The past in the present: A cleavage theory of party response to European integration'. *British Journal of Political Science* 30(3): 433–59.

Marshall, T. H. (1964). *Class, citizenship and social development.* Westport, CT: Greenwood Press.

Martin, A., and Ross, G. (eds) (1999). *The Brave New World of European Labor. European trade unions at the millennium.* New York: Berghahn Books.

Martin, A., and Ross, G. (eds) (2004). *Euros and Europeans: Monetary integration and the European model of society.* Cambridge: Cambridge University Press.

Marx, A., Rihoux, B., and Ragin, C. (2013). 'The origins, development, and application of qualitative comparative analysis: The first 25 years'. *European Political Science Review* 6(1): 115–42.

Marx, K. (1852). *18th Brumaire of Louis Bonaparte.* Available at: https://www.marxists.org/archive/marx/works/1852/18th-brumaire/ch01.htm.

Mathers, A. (2007). *Struggling for a social Europe. Neoliberal globalization and the birth of a European social movement.* Hampshire: Ashgate Publishing.

Mathers, A., Milner, S., and Taylor, G. (2017). 'Euroscepticism and trade unionism: The crisis of "social Europe"'. In B. Leruth, N. Startin and S. Usherwood (eds) *The Routledge handbook of Euroscepticism.* London: Routledge, pp. 331–43.

Matos, T. (2015). 'A pyrrhic victory? A case of national unions and immigrant workers returned'. In A. Bieler, R. Erne, D. Golden, I. Helle, K. Kjeldstadli, T. Matos and S. Stan (eds) *Labour and transnational action in times of crisis.* London: Rowman & Littlefield, pp. 99–114.

Mattina, L. (1993). 'Abete's Confindustria: From alliance with the DC to multiparty appeal'. In Hellman and Pasquino (eds), *Italian Politics VIII.* London: Pinter, pp 151–64.

Mazey, S., and Richardson, J. (1997). 'Policy framing: Interest groups and the lead up to 1996 intergovernmental conference'. *West European Politics* 20(3): 111–33.

McCabe, C. (2013). *Sins of the father: Decisions that shaped the Irish economy.* Dublin: History Press.

McCarthy, C. (1973a). 'From division to dissension: Irish trade unions in the nineteen-thirties (Part One)'. *Economic and Social Review* 5(3): 353–84.

McCarthy, C. (1973b). "From division to dissension the Irish trade unions in the nineteen-thirties (Part Two)'. *Economic and Social Review* 5(4): 469–90.

McCarthy, C. (1973c). *Decade of upheaval: Irish trade unions in the 1960s.* Dublin: Institute of Public Administration.

McDonough, T., and Dundon, T. (2010). 'Thatcherism delayed? The Irish crisis and the paradox of social partnership'. *Industrial Relations Journal* 41(6): 544–62.

McGovern, P. (2007). 'Immigration, labour markets and employment relations: Problems and prospects'. *British Journal of Industrial Relations* 45(2): 217–35.

McLaren, L. (2006). *Identity, interests and attitudes to European integration.* London: Routledge.

McLaughlin, C., and Wright, C. F. (2018). 'The role of ideas in understanding policy change in liberal market economies'. *Industrial Relations* 57(4): 268–610.

McNamara, K. R. (1998). *The currency of ideas: Monetary politics in the European Union.* Ithaca, NY: Cornell University Press.

McNamara, K. R. (2010). 'Constructing Europe: Insights from historical sociology'. *Comparative European Politics* 8(1): 127–42.

Meade, R. C. (1990). *The Red Brigades: The story of Italian terrorism.* New York: St Martin's Press.

Meardi, G. (2011). 'Understanding trade union cultures'. *Industrielle Beziehungen* 18(4): 336–45.

Meardi, G. (2012a). 'Union immobility? Trade unions and the freedoms of movement in the enlarged EU'. *British Journal of Industrial Relations* 50(1): 99–120.

Meardi, G. (2012b). *Social failures of EU enlargement: A case of workers voting with their feet.* London: Routledge.

Menz, G. (2005). *Varieties of capitalism and Europeanization: National response strategies to the single European market.* Oxford: Oxford University Press.

Mercille, J. (2014). *The political economy and media coverage of the European economic crisis: The case of Ireland.* London: Routledge.

Merrigan, M. (1989). *Eagle or cuckoo? The story of the ATGWU in Ireland.* Dublin: Matmer.

Mershon, C. A. (1993). 'The crisis of the CGIL: Open division in the 12th national congress'. In Hellman and Pasquino (eds), *Italian Politics* VII, pp. 87–109.

Mezzadra, S., and Negri, T. (2014). 'Breaking the neoliberal spell: Europe as the battleground'. Available at: http://www.euronomade.info/?p=1417.

Migrant Rights Centre Ireland (2004). *The experiences of twenty migrant women employed in the private home in Ireland.* Dublin: MRCI.

Miliband, R. (1978). 'Constitutionalism and revolution: Notes on Eurocommunism'. *Socialist Register* 15. London: Merlin Press, pp. 158–71.

Milkman, R. (2000). *Organizing immigrants: The challenge for unions in contemporary California.* Ithaca, NY: ILR Press.

Miller, J. A. (ed.) (1988). *The seminar of Jacques Lacan, Book 1: Freud's papers on technique 1953–1954.* Cambridge: Cambridge University Press.

Mills, C. W. (1970). 'The contribution of sociology to studies of industrial relations'. *Berkeley Journal of Sociology* 15: 11–32.

Millward Brown IMS (2008). *Post Lisbon Treaty referendum: Research findings 2008*. Available at: http://www.imsl.ie/news/Millward_Brown_IMS_Lisbon_ Research_Report.pdf,.

Milward, A. S. (2000 [1992]) (2nd edn). *The European rescue of the nation-state*. Routledge: London.

Milward, A. S. (2004). 'Delors agonistes'. *New Left Review* 29 Sept/Oct: 145–52.

Miró, J. (2017). 'European integration, social democratic Europeanism and the competitiveness discourse: A neo-Poulantzian approach to discursive policy analysis'. *Palgrave communications*. DOI: 10. 1057/palcomms.2017.60.

Mitchell, K. (2012). 'From Whitehall to Brussels: Thatcher, Delors and the Europeanization of the TUC'. *Labor History* 53(1): 25–50.

Mittag, J., and Wessels (2003). 'The "one" and the "fifteen": The member states between procedural adaption and structural revolution'. In W. Wessels, A. Maurer and J. Mittag (eds) *Fifteen into one: The European Union and its member states*. Manchester: Manchester University Press, pp 413–54.

Molina, O., and Rhodes, M. (2007). 'Industrial relations and the welfare state in Italy: Assessing the potential of negotiated change'. *West European Politics* 30(4): 803–29.

Monks, J. (2009a). Address to ICTU biennial delegate conference, Tralee, 7th–10th July 2009.

Monks, J. (2009b). 'The British trade unions and Europe'. *Revue Française de Civilisation Britannique* XV(2):160–85.

Monnet, J. (1978). *Memoirs* (trans. Richard Mayne) London: Collins.

Monti, M. (2010). *A new strategy for the single market at the service of Europe's economy and society*. Report to the President of the European Commission. Brussels: European Commission.

Monti, M. (2012a). Speech at European Parliament, 15 February 2012.

Moravcsik, A. (1991). 'Negotiating the Single European Act: National interests and conventional statecraft in the European Community'. *International Organization* 45(1): 19–56.

Moravcsik, A. (1993). 'Preferences and power in the European Community: A liberal intergovernmentalist approach'. *Journal of Common Market Studies* 31(4): 473–524.

Moravcsik, A. (1997). 'Taking preferences seriously: A liberal theory of international politics'. *International Organization* 51(4): 513–53.

Moravcsik, A. (1998). *The choice for Europe: Social purpose and state power from Messina to Maastricht*. London: Routledge/UCL Press.

Moravcsik, A. (2005). 'The European constitutional compromise and the neofunctionalist legacy'. *Journal of European Public Policy* 12(2): 349–86.

Moravcsik, A. (2006). 'What can we learn from the collapse of the European constitutional project?'. *Politische Vierteljahresschrift* 47(2): 219–41.

Moravcsik, A. (2018). 'Preferences, power and institutions in 21st-century Europe'. *Journal of Common Market Studies* 56(7): 1648–74.

Moravcsik, A., and Nicolaïdis, K. (1998). 'Federal ideals and constitutional realities'. *Journal of Common Market Studies* 36 *Annual Review*: 13–38.

Moravcsik, A., and Nicolaïdis, K. (1999). 'Explaining the Treaty of Amsterdam: Interests, influence and institutions'. *Journal of Common Market Studies* 37(1): 59–85.

Moreno, J., and Gabaglio, E. (2007). *La sfida dell'europa social*. Rome: Ediesse.

Morgan, G. (2005). *The idea of a European superstate: Public justification and European integration*. Princeton, NJ: Princeton University Press.

Moschella, M. (2017). 'Italy and the Fiscal Compact: Why does a country commit to permanent austerity?'. *Rivista Italiana di Scienza Politica* 47(2): 205–25.

Mudde, C. (2012). 'The comparative study of party-based Euroscepticism: The Sussex versus the North Carolina school'. *East European Politics* 28(2): 193–202.

Müller, H. (2012). 'The point of no return: Walter Hallstein and the EEC Commission between institutional ambitions and political constraints'. *Les Cahiers Européens de Sciences Po* 3: 1–24.

Müller, S., and Regan, A. (2020). *The compass of Irish politics is moving to the left*. Unpublished manuscript, University College Dublin.

Müller, T., and Platzer, H. W. (2018). 'The European trade union federations: Profiles and power resources. Changes and challenges in times of crisis'. In S. Lehndorff, H. Dribbusch and T. Schulten (eds) *Rough waters: European trade unions in a time of crises*. Brussels: ETUI, pp. 303–29.

Murphy, G. (2009). *In search of the promised land: The politics of post-war Ireland*. Cork: Mercier Press.

Nakano, S. (2014). 'Maastricht social protocol revisited: Origins of the European industrial relations system'. *Journal of Common Market Studies* 52(5): 1053–69.

Napolitano, G. (1978). 'The Italian crisis: A communist perspective'. *Foreign Affairs* 56(4): 790–99.

Napolitano, G. (2008). *Dal pci al socialismo europeo: Un'autobiografia politica*. Rome: Laterza.

Näre, L. (2011). 'The informal economy of paid domestic work: Ukranian and Polish migrants in Naples'. In M. Bommes and G. Sciortino (eds) *Foggy social structures: Irregular migration, European labour markets and the welfare state*. Amsterdam: Amsterdam University Press, pp. 67–90.

National Economic and Social Council (1996). *Strategy into the 21st century*. NESC Report No. 99. Dublin: NESC.

Negrelli, S. (2005). 'The territorial pacts in Italy: The competitive corporatism assumption in question'. In R. Salais and R. Villeneuve (eds) *Europe and the politics of capabilities*. Cambridge: Cambridge University Press, pp. 73–90.

Negrelli, S., and Pulignano, V. (2008). 'Change in contemporary Italy's social concertation'. *Industrial Relations Journal* 39(1): 63–77.

Negrelli, S., and Valeria, P. (2010). 'The evolution of social pacts in Italy: Crisis or metamorphosis?'. In P. Pochet, M. Keune and D. Natali (eds) *After the Euro and enlargement: Social pacts in the EU*. Brussels: ETUI, pp. 137–54.

NESC (2006). *Migration Policy*. Dublin: NESC.

Norris, P., and Inglehart, R. (2019). *Cultural backlash: Trump, Brexit, and authoritarian populism*. Cambridge: Cambridge University Press.

Ó Beacháin, D., Sheridan, V., and Stan, S. (eds) (2012). *Life in post-communist Eastern Europe after EU membership: Happy ever after?* London: Routledge.

Ó Broin, E. (2009). *Sinn Féin and the politics of left republicanism*. London: Pluto.

Ó Broin, E. (2015). 'In defence of populism'. *Magill*, 3 January 2015.

Ó Gráda, C. (1997). *Rocky road: The Irish economy since the 1920s*. Manchester: Manchester University Press.

Ó Riain, S. (2004). *The politics of high-tech growth: Developmental network states in the global economy*. Cambridge: Cambridge University Press.

Ó Riain, S. (2014). *The rise and fall of Ireland's celtic tiger: Liberalism, boom and bust. Cambridge: Cambridge University Press.*

Ó Riain, S., and O'Connell, P. J (2000). 'The role of the state in growth and welfare'. In B. Nolan, P. J. O'Connell and C. T. Whelan (eds) *Bust to boom? The Irish experience of growth and inequality*. Dublin: Irish Public Administration (IPA), pp. 310–39.

O'Brennan, J. (2003). 'Ireland's return to "normal" voting patterns on EU issues: The 2002 Nice Treaty referendum'. *European Political Science* 12(2): 5–13.

O'Connor, E. (2002). *James Larkin*. Cork: Cork University Press.

O'Connor, E. (2011). *A labour history of Ireland: 1894–2000* Dublin: University College Dublin Press.

O'Connor, E. (2015). *Big Jim Larkin: Hero or wrecker?* Dublin: University College Dublin Press.

O'Connor, J. (2010). In place of fear. Statement issued on ETUC Day of Action, 29 September 2010.

O'Donnell, R. (2000). 'The new Ireland in the new Europe'. In R. O'Donnell (ed.) *Europe: The Irish experience*. Dublin: Institute of European Affairs, pp. 161–214.

O'Donnell, R., Adshead, M., and Thomas, D. (2011). 'Ireland: Two trajectories of institutionalization'. In S. Avdagic, M. Rhodes, and J. Visser (eds) *Social pacts in Europe: Emergence, evolution, and institutionalization*. Oxford: Oxford University Press, pp 89–117.

O'Donnell, R., Cahill, N., and Thomas, D. (2010). 'Ireland: The evolution of social pacts in the EMU era'. In P. Pochet, M. Keune and D. Natali (eds) *After the Euro and enlargement: Social pacts in the EU*. Brussels: ETUI, pp 191–222.

O'Donovan P. (1999). 'Irish trade unions and the EU'. In J. Dooge and R. Barrington (eds) *A vital national interest: Ireland in Europe 1973–1998*. Dublin: Institute of Public Administration, pp. 43–54.

O'Donovan, P. (1998). 'Great debate: Three advocates of each vote explain their positions on the Amsterdam Treaty'. *Irish Times*, 6 May 1998.

O'Driscoll, M. (2011). 'The "unwanted suitor": West Germany's reception, response and role in Ireland's EEC entry request, 1961–63'. *Irish Studies in International Affairs* 22: 163–86.

O'Reilly, M. (2001). 'Time has come to reclaim power from corporations'. *Irish Times*, 30 May 2001.

O'Reilly, M. (2016). *From Lucifer to Lazarus: A Life on the left*. Dublin: Lilliput Press.

O'Riordan, M. (1994). 'James Larkin Junior and the forging of a thinking intelligent movement'. *Saothar* 19: 53–68.

O'Sullivan, M., and Gunnigle, P. (2009). 'Bearing all the hallmarks of oppression'. *Labor Studies Journal* 34(2): 252–70.

O'Toole, F. (2018). 'The 1918 election was an amazing moment for Ireland'. *Irish Times*, 8 December 2018..

OECD (1977). *Economic surveys: Italy*. Paris: OECD.

OECD (1982). *Economic surveys: Ireland*. Paris: OECD.

OECD (1991). 'Trends in trade union memberships'. *Employment outlook*. Paris: OECD, pp. 97–129.

OECD (1999). *Economic surveys: Ireland*. Paris: OECD.

OECD (2000). *Economic survey of Italy*. Paris: OECD.

OECD (2001a). *Economic surveys: Ireland*. Paris: OECD.

OECD (2001b). *OECD regulatory reform review of Ireland*. Paris: OECD.

OECD (2002). *Economic survey of Italy*. Paris: OECD.

OECD (2003). *Economic survey of Italy*. Paris: OECD.

OECD (2004). 'Employment protection regulation and labour market performance'. In *OECD employment outlook 2004*. Paris: OECD, pp. 61–125.

OECD (2005). *Economic survey of Italy*. Paris: OECD.

OECD (2006). *Economic surveys: Ireland*. Paris: OECD.

OECD (2007). *Economic survey of Italy*. Paris: OECD.

OECD (2008). *International migration outlook*. Paris: OECD.

OECD (2011). *Ireland: Economic survey*. Paris: OECD.

OECD (2012). *Free movement of workers and labour market adjustment: Recent experiences from the OECD countries and the European Union*. Paris: OECD.

OECD (2013a). *Economic surveys: Ireland*. Paris: OECD.

OECD (2013b). *International migration outlook*. Paris: OECD.

Padoa-Schioppa, T. (1985). 'Policy cooperation and the EMS experience'. In W. H. Buiter and R. C. Marston (eds) *International economic policy coordination*. Cambridge: Cambridge University Press, pp. 331–65.

Padoa-Schioppa, T. (2004). *The Euro and its central bank: Getting united after the union*. London: MIT Press.

Pagden, A. (ed.) (2000). *The idea of Europe: From antiquity to the European Union*. Cambridge: Cambridge University Press.

Pallini, M. (2006). 'Posted workers: Italian regulation and dilemmas'. *Transfer: European Review of Labour and Research* 12(2): 272–76.

Parks, L. (2015). *Social movement campaigns on EU policy: In the corridors and in the streets*. Basingstoke: Palgrave Macmillan.

Parsons, C. (2003). *A certain idea of Europe*. Ithaca, NY: Cornell University Press.

Pasquinucci, D. (2016). 'The historical origins of Italian Euroscepticism'. *Journal of European Integration History* 16(2): 297–392.

Pasquinucci, D., and Verzichelli, L. (2004). *Elezioni europee e classe politica sovranazionale 1979–2004*. Bologna: Il Mulino.

Pasture, P. (2005). 'Trade unions as a transnational movement in the European space 1955–65'. In W. Kaiser and P. Starie (eds) *Transnational European Union: Towards a common political space*. London: Routledge, pp. 109–30.

Patel, K. K. (2020). *Project Europe: A history*. Cambridge: Cambridge University Press.

Patterson, H. (2007). *Ireland since 1939*. Dublin: Penguin.

Pelkmans, J. (2016). 'Why the single market remains the EU's core business'. *West European Politics* 39(5): 1095–1113.

Pellerin, H., and Overbeek, H. (2001). 'Neo-liberal regionalism and the management of people's mobility'. In A. Bieler and A. D. Morton (eds) *Social forces in the making of the new Europe. The restructuring of European social relations in the global political economy.* Basingstoke: Palgrave, pp. 137–60.

Penninx, R., and Roosblad, J. (2000). *Trade unions, immigration, and immigrants in Europe, 1960–1993: A comparative study of the attitudes and actions of trade unions in seven West European Countries.* Oxford: Berghahn Books.

Pernot J.–M. (2001). Dedans, dehors, la dimension internationale dans le syndicalisme français, Doctoral thesis, Université de Nanterre, Paris X.

Perrett, R., Lucio, M., McBride, J., and Craig, S. (2012). 'Trade union learning strategies and migrant workers: Policies and practice in a new liberal environment'. *Urban Studies* 49(3): 649–67.

Perrotta, D. C. (2011). *Vite in cantiere. Migrazione e lavoro dei rumeni in italia.* Bologna: Il Mulino.

Petrini, F. (2005). *Il liberismo ha una dimensione: La Confindustria e l'integrazione europea 1947–1957.* Milan: FrancoAngeli.

Pierson, P. (1994) 'The path to European integration: A historical institutionalist perspective'. Program for the Study of Germany and Europe Working Paper No. 5.2.

Pierson, P. (1996). 'The pathway to European integration: A historical institutionalist analysis'. *Comparative Political Studies* 29(2): 123–63.

Pierson, P. (2004). *Politics in time: History, institutions, and social analysis.* Princeton, NJ: Princeton University Press.

Piketty, T. (2014). *Capital in the twenty-first century.* Cambridge, MA: Harvard University Press.

Pistor, M. (2005). 'Agency, structure and European integration: Critical political economy and the new regionalism in Europe'. In E. Jones and A. Verdun (eds) *The political economy of European integration theory and analysis.* London: Routledge, pp.108–127.

Pochet, P., and Fajertag, G. (1997). 'Social pacts in Europe in the 1990s: Toward a European Social Pact?'. In G. Fajertag and P. Pochet (eds) *Social pacts in Europe.* Brussels: ETUI.

Pochet, P., and Fajertag, G. (2000). 'A new era for social pacts in Europe'. In G. Fajertag and P. Pochet (eds) *Social pacts in Europe–New dynamics.* Brussels: ETUI, pp. 9–40.

Polanyi, K. (2001: [1944]) *The great transformation: The political and economic origins of our time.* Boston, MA: Beacon Press.

Pollack, M. (2000). 'A Blairite treaty: Neoliberalism and regulated capitalism in the Treaty of Amsterdam'. In K. Neunreither and A. Weiner (eds) *European integration after Amsterdam: Institutional dynamics and prospects for democracy.* Oxford: Oxford University Press, pp. 266–89.

Pons, S. (2010). 'The rise and fall of Eurocommunism'. In M. P. Leffler and O. A. Westad (eds) *The Cambridge history of the cold war.* Cambridge: Cambridge University Press, pp 45–65.

Pontusson, J. (1992). *The limits of social democracy: Investment politics in Sweden.* Ithaca, NY: Cornell University Press.

Pontusson, J. (2005). *Inequality and prosperity: Social Europe vs. liberal America.* Ithaca, NY: Cornell University Press.

Ponzano, P. (2010). 'The "Spinelli Treaty" of February 1984: The start of the process of constitutionalizing the European Union'. In A. Glencross and A. H. Treschel (eds) *EU federalism and constitutionalism: The legacy of Altiero Spinelli.* Lanham, MD: Rowman & Littlefield, pp. 3–10.

Popper, K. (1959). *The logic of scientific discovery.* New York: Basic Books.

Pott, A., Rass, C., and Wolff, F. (eds) (2016). *Migration regimes: Approaches to a key concept.* Wiesbaden: Springer.

Pribićević, B. (1981). 'Eurocommunism and the New Party'. In R. Kindersley (ed.) *In search of Eurocommunism.* Basingstoke: Palgrave Macmillan.

Pries, L. (2003). 'Labour migration, social incorporation and transmigration in the old and new Europe: The case of Germany in a comparative perspective'. *Transfer: European Review of Labour and Research* 9(3): 432–51.

Przeworski, A., and Teune, A. (1970). *The logic of comparative social inquiry.* New York: Wiley.

Puchala, D. (1971). 'Of blind men, elephants and international integration'. *Journal of Common Market Studies* 10(3): 267–84.

Putnam, R. (1993). 'Diplomacy and domestic politics: The logic of two-level games'. In P. Evans, H. Jacobson and R. Putnam (eds) *Double edged diplomacy: International bargaining and domestic politics.* Berkeley, CA: University of California Press, pp. 431–98.

Quaglia, L. (2005). 'The right and Europe in Italy: An ambivalent relationship'. *South European Society & Politics* 10(2): 281–95.

Quaglia, L. (2007). 'The politics of financial services regulation and supervision reform in the European Union'. *European Journal of Political Research* 46(2): 269–90.

Quaglia, L. (2010). 'Italy: The importance of party politics in treaty negotiations'. In M. Carbone (ed.) *National politics and European integration.* Cheltenham: Edward Elgar, pp. 90–108.

Quaglia, L. (2012). 'The left in Italy and the Lisbon Treaty: A "political" Europe, a "social" Europe and an "economic" Europe'. In M. Holmes and K. Roder (eds) *The Left and the European Constitution.* Manchester: Manchester University Press, pp.118–35.

Quinlan, S. (2009). 'The Lisbon Treaty referendum 2008'. *Irish Political Studies* 24(1): 107–21.

Radaelli, C. M. (2002). 'The Italian state and the euro: institutions, discourse and policy regime'. In K. F. Dyson (ed.) *European states and the Euro: Europeanization, variation, and convergence.* Oxford: Oxford University Press, pp. 212–37.

Radaelli, C. M. (2002). *Technocracy in the European Union.* London: Routledge.

Ragin, C. C. (1987). *The comparative method: Moving beyond qualitative and quantitative strategies.* Los Angeles, CA: University of California Press.

Ragin, C. C. (2000). *Fuzzy-set social science.* Chicago, IL: University of Chicago Press.

Ragin, C. C. (2008). *Redesigning social inquiry: Fuzzy sets and beyond.* Chicago, IL: University of Chicago Press.

Rassegna Sindacale (1957). La posizione della CGIL sul mercato comune europeo, no. 14, July 1957.

Ravaglia, M. (2009). *Il sindacato e l'autonomia dai partiti.* Rome: Ediesse.

Rea, A, (UIL), Durante, F. (CGIL), and Bonanni, R. (CISL) (2013). 'The Italian unions' proposal for inclusive growth in Italy and Europe'. In A. M. Grozelier, B. Hacker, W. Kowalsky, J. Machnig, H. Meyer and B. Unger (eds) *Roadmap to a social Europe.* London: Social Europe Report, pp. 83–5.

Rea, A. (2012). 'Union reflections from Italy'. *Union reflections on the economic crisis trade unions and EU.* Stockholm: LO Sweden, pp. 7–9.

Recchi, E. (2008). 'Cross-state mobility in the EU: Trends, puzzles and consequences'. *European Societies* 10(2): 197–224.

Recchi, E., and Favell, A. (eds) (2009). *Pioneers of European integration: Citizenship and mobility in the EU.* Cheltenham: Edward Elgar.

Regalia, I., Regini, M., and Reyneri, E. (1978). 'Labour conflicts and industrial relations in Italy'. In C. Crouch and A. Pizzorno (eds) *The resurgence of class conflict in Western Europe since 1968.* London: Palgrave Macmillan, pp. 101–58.

Regan, A. (2012a). The rise and fall of irish social partnership: The political economy of institutional change in European varieties of capitalism. PhD thesis, University College Dublin.

Regan, A. (2012b). 'The political economy of social pacts in the EMU, Irish liberal corporatism in crisis'. *New Political Economy* 17(4): 465–91.

Regini, M. (1996). *Uncertain boundaries: The social and political construction of European economies.* Cambridge: Cambridge University Press.

Regini, M., and Colombo, S. (2011). 'Italy: The rise and decline of social pacts'. In S. Avdagic, M. Rhodes and J. Visser (eds) *Social pacts in Europe: Emergence, evolution and institutionalization.* Oxford: Oxford University Press, pp. 118–46.

Regini, M., and Regalia, I. (1997). 'Employers, unions and the state: The resurgence of concertation in Italy?'. *West European Politics* 20(1): 210–30.

Rhodes, M. (1998). 'Globalization, labour markets and welfare states: A future of "competitive corporatism"?'. In M. Rhodes and Y. Mény (eds) *The future of European welfare: A new social contract?* London: Macmillan, pp. 178–203.

Rhodes, M. (1998). 'Globalization, labour markets and welfare states: a future of "competitive corporatism"?'. EUI Working Paper RSC No. 97/36.

Ricard-Nihoul, G. (2006). 'Is politicisation good or bad for the Union? Initial synthesis of the debates and lines of research'. Notre Europe Working Paper.

Roche, W. K. (1989). 'State strategies and the politics of industrial relations in Ireland since 1945'. In T. Murphy (ed.) *Industrial relations in Ireland: Contemporary issues and developments.* Dublin: Department of Industrial Relations, University College Dublin.

Roche, W. K. (2007). 'Developments in industrial relations and human resource management in Ireland'. *Quarterly Economic Commentary,* Spring 2007, pp. 62–77.

Roche, W. K. (2007b). 'Social partnership in Ireland and new social pacts'. *Industrial Relations* 46(3): 395–425.

Roche, W. K. (2008). 'The trend of unionisation in Ireland since the mid-1990s'. In T. Hastings (ed.). *The state of the unions: Challenges facing organised labour in Ireland*. Dublin: Liffey Press, pp. 17–46.

Roche, W. K. (2009). 'Social partnership: From Lemass to Cowen'. *Economic and Social Review* 40(2): 183–205.

Roche, W. K., and Ashmore, J. (2002). 'Irish trade unions: Testing the limits of social partnership'. In P. Fairbrother and G. Griffin (eds) *Changing prospects for trade unionism*. London: Continuum, pp. 137–76.

Rodrik, D. (2014). 'When ideas trump interests: Preferences, worldviews, and policy innovations'. *Journal of Economic Perspectives* 28(1): 189–208.

Rokkan, S. (1968). 'Nation-building, cleavage formation and the structuring of mass politics'. *Comparative Studies in Society and History* 10(2): 173–210.

Romagnoli, U., and Treu, T. (1977). *I sindacati in Italia: Storia di una strategia*. Bologna: Il Mulino.

Romero, F. (1992). *United States and the European trade union movement 1944– 1951* Chapel Hill, NC: University of North Carolina Press.

Rosamond, B. (1993). 'National labour organizations and European integration: British trade unions and "1992" '. *Political Studies* 41(3): 420–34.

Rosamond, B. (2007). 'European integration and the social science of EU studies: The disciplinary politics of a subfield'. *International Affairs* 83(2): 231–52.

Ross, G. (1995). 'Assessing the Delors era and social policy'. In S. Leibfried and P. Pierson (eds) *European social policy: Between fragmentation and integration*. Washington DC: Brookings, pp. 357–82.

Ross, G. (2011). 'Postscript'. In A. Favell and V. Guiraudon (eds) *Sociology of the European Union*. Basingstoke: Palgrave Macmillan, pp. 215–24.

Ross, G., and Martin, A. (1999). 'Through a glass darkly'. In A. Martin and G. Ross (eds) *The brave new world of European labor: European trade unions at the millennium* Oxford: Berghahn Books, pp. 368–99.

Rossi, N., and Toniolo, G. (1996). 'Italy' in N. Crafts and G. Toniolo (eds) *Economic growth in Europe since 1945*. Cambridge: Cambridge University Press, pp. 427–50.

Ruggie, J. G. (1982). 'International regimes, transactions, and change: Embedded liberalism in the postwar economic order'. *International Organization* 36(2): 379–415.

Rutherford, T. D., and Frangi, L. (2018). 'Overturning Italy's Article 18: Exogenous and endogenous pressures, and role of the state'. *Economic and Industrial Democracy* 39(3): 439–57.

Saba, V. (1992). 'I caratteri originari della CISL in materia di welfare state'. *Oggi Domani Anziani* 4.

Sartori, G. (1970). 'Concept misformation in comparative politics'. *American Political Science Review* 64(4): 1033–53.

Sassoon, D. (1996). *One hundred years of socialism*. London: I. B. Tauris.

Savage, J. D. (2005). *Making The EMU: The politics of budgetary surveillance and the enforcement of Maastricht*. Oxford: Oxford University Press.

Savoini C. (2000). *Con la Cisl verso l'europa sociale*. Roma: Edizioni Lavoro.

Scharpf, F. (1997). *Games real actors play: Actor-centered institutionalism in policy research*. London: Routledge.

Scharpf, F. (1999). *Governing in Europe: Effective and democratic?* Oxford: Oxford University Press.

Scharpf, F. (2000). 'The viability of advanced welfare states in the international economy: Vulnerabilities and options'. *Journal of European Public Policy* 7(2):190–228.

Scharpf, F. (2002). 'The European social model'. *Journal of Common Market Studies* 40(4): 645–70.

Scharpf, F. (2010). 'The asymmetry of European integration, or why the EU cannot be a "social market economy" '. *Socio-Economic Review* 8(2): 211–50.

Schirm S. A. (2018). 'Societal foundations of governmental preference formation in the euro zone crisis'. *European Politics and Society* 19(1): 63–78.

Schmidt, V. A. (2010). 'Taking ideas and discourse seriously: Explaining change through discursive institutionalism as the fourth "new institutionalism"' *European Political Science Review* 2(1): 1–25.

Schmidt, V. A. (2016). 'Missing topic in #euref: neo-liberalism gone too far'. *Social Europe*. Available at: https://socialeurope.eu/missing-topic-euref-neo-liberalism-gone-too-far.

Schmitter, P. C. (1974). 'Still the century of corporatism?' *Review of Politics* 36(1): 85–131.

Schmitter, P. C. (1996). 'Examining the present Euro-polity with the help of past theories'. In G. Marks, F. Sharpf, P. Schmitter and W. Streek (eds) *Governance in the European Union*. London: Sage, pp. 1–14.

Schmitter, P. C. (2000). *How to democratize the EU and why bother*. Lanham, MD: Rowman & Littlefield.

Schmitter, P. C. (2009). 'The nature and future of comparative politics'. *European Political Science Review* 1(1): 33–61.

Schützeichel, R. (2015). 'Europe as process? On the genealogy of a historical-sociological research programme'. In S. Börner and M. Eigmüller (eds) *European integration, processes of change and the national experience*. Basingstoke: Palgrave Macmillan, pp. 26–49.

Sciolino, E. (2005). 'Unlikely hero in Europe's spat'. *New York Times*, 26 June 2005.

Seeliger, M., and Wagner, I. (2018). 'A socialization paradox: Trade union policy cooperation in the case of the enforcement directive of the Posting of Workers Directive'. *Socio-Economic Review* 18(4): 1113–31.

Segni, M. (1994). *La rivoluzione interrotta*. Milan: Rizzoli.

Sheehan, H. (2016). *The Syriza wave: Surging and crashing with the Greek left*. New York: Monthly Review Press.

Silvia, S. J. (1991). 'The social charter of the European Community: A defeat for European labor'. *ILR Review* 44(4): 626–43.

Simms, M. (2010). 'Trade union strategies to recruit new groups of workers'. Eurofound: European Industrial Relations Observatory and Warwick University, UK.

Sinn Féin (2002). 'Alliance against Nice campaigners tackle IBEC on privatisation agenda'. Press release, 16 October 2002.

Sinn Féin (Official) (1977). *Irish industrial revolution*. Dublin: Repsol.

Sinnott, R., and Elkink, J. A. (2010). 'Attitudes and behaviour in the second referendum on the Treaty of Lisbon'. Report prepared for the Department of Foreign Affairs.

Sinnott, R., and Thomsen, R. (2001). 'Why did many not vote?'. *Irish Times*, 23 June 2001.

Sinnott, R., Elkink, J. A., and McBride, J. (2012). Flash Eurobarometer 353: Post- Referendum Survey in Ireland. Report on Stability Treaty'. Report for the European Parliament.

SIPTU (2006). *Guide for shopstewards*. Dublin: SIPTU.

SIPTU (2008). *The Lisbon Treaty: Issues for workers*. Dublin: Trade Union Labour.

SIPTU (2009a). *The Lisbon Treaty: What next? Issues for workers*. Dublin: Trade Union Labour.

SIPTU (2009b). National Executive Council: Statement on the Lisbon Treaty referendum analysis, 3 September 2009. Dublin: SIPTU.

SIPTU (2010). *Changing to win for working people*. Policy Document. Dublin: SIPTU.

SIPTU (2012a). Analysis of the issues around the referendum on the TSCG in the economic and monetary union. 19 April 2012. Dublin: SIPTU.

SIPTU (2012b). Presentation to the Óireachtas sub-committee on the intergovernmental Treaty April 27th. Dublin: SIPTU.

Sitter, N. (2001). 'The politics of opposition and European integration in Scandinavia: Is Euro-scepticism a government–opposition dynamic? *West European Politics* 24(4): 22–39.

Smismans, S. (2006). *Civil society and legitimate European governance*. Cheltenham: Edward Elgar.

Smismans, S. (2008). 'The European social dialogue in the shadow of hierarchy'. *International Journal of Public Policy* 28(1): 161–80.

Smith, M. P. (2005 [1999]). 'EU legitimacy and the defensive reaction to the single market'. In I. Banchoff and M. P. Smith (eds) *Legitimacy and the European Union: The contested polity*. London: Routledge, pp. 26–43.

Spinelli, A. (1957). 'The growth of the European movement since World War II'. In C. Grove Haines (ed.) *European integration*. Baltimore, MD: Johns Hopkins Press.

Spinelli, A. (1972). 'Agenda pour l'Europe'. *Chronique de Politique Étrangère* 25(6): 813–18.

Spinelli, A. (1978). 'How European are the Italian Eurocommunists?'. In G. R. Urban (ed.) *Eurocommunism: Its roots and future in Italy and elsewhere*. London: Temple Smith.

Stan, S., and Erne, R. (2014). 'Explaining Romanian labor migration: From development gaps to development trajectories'. *Labor History* 55(1): 21–46.

Statham, P., and Trenz, H. J. (2013). *The politicization of Europe: Contesting the constitution in the mass media*. London: Routledge.

Steenbergen, M. R., Edwards, E. E., and de Vries, C. E. (2007). 'Who's cueing whom? Mass–elite linkages and the future of European integration'. *European Union Politics* 8(1): 13–35.

Steinnes, K. (2009). 'Socialist party networks in northern Europe: Moving towards the EEC applications of 1967'. In W. Kaiser *et al.* (eds) *The history of The European Union: Origins of a trans- and supranational polity* 1950–72. London: Routledge, pp. 93–110.

Sternberg, C. (2013). *The struggle for EU legitimacy*. Basingstoke: Palgrave Macmillan.

Stolfi, F. (2013). 'Back in Europe? Italy, the Troika, and the Chancelleries'. *Italian Politics* 28(1): 173–87.

Stone Sweet, A., Sandholtz, W. and Fligstein, N. (2001). 'The institutionalization of European space'. In A. Stone Sweet, W. Sandholtz and N. Fligstein (eds) *The institutionalization of Europe*. Oxford: Oxford University Press, pp. 1–28.

Storey, A. (2008). 'The ambiguity of resistance: Opposition to neoliberalism in Europe'. *Capital and Class* 32(3): 55–85.

Streeck, W. (1992). *Social institutions and economic performance: Studies of industrial relations in advanced capitalist economies*. London: Sage.

Streeck, W. (1994). 'European social policy after Maastricht: The "social dialogue" and "subsidiarity"'. *Economic and Industrial Democracy* 15(2): 151–77.

Streeck, W. (1997). 'Beneficial constraints: On the economic limits of rational voluntarism'. J. R. Hollingsworth and R. Boyer (eds) *Contemporary capitalism: The embeddedness of institutions*. Cambridge: Cambridge University Press, pp. 197–218.

Streeck, W. (1998). 'The internationalization of industrial relations in Europe: Prospects and problems'. *Politics & Society* 26(4): 429–59.

Streeck, W. (2010). 'The sociology of labour markets and trade unions'. In N. Smelser, and R. Swedberg (eds) *The handbook of economic sociology* (2nd edn) Princeton, NJ: Princeton University Press, pp. 254–83.

Streeck, W. (2014). *Buying time: The delayed crisis of democratic capitalism*. London: Verso.

Streeck, W., and Schmitter, P. C. (1991). 'From national corporatism to transnational pluralism: Organized interests in the single European market'. *Politics & Society* 19(2): 133–65.

Strøm, K., and Müller, W. C. (1999). 'Political parties and hard choices'. In W. C. Müller and K. Strøm (eds) *Policy, office or votes: How political parties in Europe make hard decisions*. Cambridge: Cambridge University Press, pp. 1–35.

Strozza, S. (2004). 'Immigrati stranieri e inserimento nel mercato di lavoro nella provincia di Roma: La situazione prima e dopo la 'Grande Regolarizzazione'. In E. Zucchetti (eds) *La regolarizzazione degli stranieri. Nuovi attori nel mercato del lavoro italiano*. Milan: Fondazione ISMU, Ministero del Lavoro e delle Politiche Sociali Milano: Franco Angeli, pp. 261–346.

Sunday Business Post (2012a). 'Begg to differ', 22 April 2012.

Sunday Business Post (2012b). 'Politics in focus: getting real in the maelstrom', 13 May 2012.

Sverdrup, C. (2002). 'An institutional perspective on treaty reform: Contextualizing the Amsterdam and Nice Treaties'. *Journal of European Public Policy* 9(1): 120–40.

Sweeney, P. (ICTU) (2012). The Fiscal Compact. Presentation to Joint Committee on European Union Affairs debate on Fiscal Compact Treaty, Thursday, 23 February 2012.

Szabò, I., Golden, D., and Erne, R. (2021). 'Why do some labour alliances succeed in politicizing Europe across borders? A comparison of the Right2Water and Fair Transport European citizens' initiatives'. *Journal of Common Market Studies* 60(3): 634–52.

Szczerbiak, A., and Taggart, P. (eds) (2008a). *Opposing Europe? The comparative party politics of Euroscepticism*, vol. 1: Case Studies and Country Surveys. Oxford: Oxford University Press.

Szczerbiak, A., and Taggart, P. (eds) (2008b). *Opposing Europe? The comparative party politics of Euroscepticism*, vol. 2: Comparative and Theoretical Perspectives. Oxford: Oxford University Press.

Taggart, P. (1998). 'A touchstone of dissent: Euroscepticism in contemporary western European party systems'. *European Journal of Political Research* 33(3): 363–88.

Taggart, P. (2006). 'Keynote article: Questions of Europe – the domestic politics of the 2005 French and Dutch referendums and their challenge for the study of European integration'. *Journal of Common Market Studies* 44(1): 7–25.

Talani, L. S., and Cerviño, E. (2003). 'Mediterranean labour and the impact of economic and monetary union: Mass unemployment or labour-market flexibility?'. In H. Overbeek (ed.) *The political economy of European employment: European integration and the transnationalization of the (un) employment question*. London: Routledge, pp. 51–74.

Tarrow, S. G. (1998). *Power in movement: Social movements and contentious politics*. Cambridge: Cambridge University Press.

Tarrow, S. G. (2005). *The new transnational activism*. Cambridge: Cambridge University Press.

Taylor, G., and Mathers, A. (2004). 'The European Trade Union Confederation at the crossroads of change? Traversing the variable geometry of European trade unionism'. *European Journal of Industrial Relations* 10(3): 267–85.

Teague, P. (1989a). 'The British TUC and the European Community'. *Millennium: Journal of International Studies* 18(1): 29–45.

Teague, P. (1989b). *The European Community: The social dimension*. London: Kogan Page.

Teague, P., and Grahl, J. (1992). *Industrial relations and European integration*. London: Lawrence & Wishart.

TEEU (2008a). 'Country's largest craft union urges 45,000 members to vote No in the referendum on the Lisbon Treaty'. Press release.

TEEU (2008b). *Fusion* January 2008, Issue 8.

TEEU (2009a) 'Statement from TEEU on Lisbon Treaty Referendum', 2 September 2009.

TEEU (2009a). *Ezine*, July 2009, Issue 4. Dublin: TEEU.

TEEU (2009b). 'Race to the bottom can only be defeated with new EU treaty that recognises workers' rights to organise and be represented by unions'. Press release, 1 September 2009. Dublin: TEEU.

TEEU (2011). *Ezine*, Summer 2011, Issue 7. Dublin: TEEU.

TEEU (2012a). 'TEEU to urge "No" vote on Fiscal Compact Treaty'. Press release, 23 April 2012. Dublin: TEEU.

TEEU (2012b). *Ezine*, Winter 2012, Issue 8. Dublin: TEEU.

TEEU (2012c). *Fusion*, Issue 12. Dublin: TEEU.

TEEU (2014). *Ezine*, Autumn 2014, Issue (no number provided). Dublin: TEEU.

TEEU (2015). *Fusion*, Issue 15. Dublin: TEEU.

Tooze, A. J. (2018). *Crashed: How a decade of financial crises changed the world.* London: Allen Lane.

Trentin, B. (1958). 'Il movimento sindacale di fronte alla recessione Americana'. *Rassegna Sindacale* no. 3.

Trentin, B. (1988). L'Europa nel Programma della CGIL. Speech to CGIL Congress, Rome. *Nuova Rassegna Sindacale* no. 25.

Trentin, B. (1991). Introductory speech made at 12th CGIL Congress, Rimini, October 23–27. *CGIL. XXII Congresso.* Roma: Ediess.

Trentin, B. (1992a). 'Ho fatto di tutto. Ho perso. Non posso fingere'. *Corriere della Sera*, 2 August 1992.

Trentin, B. (1992b). *Il coraggio dell'utopia.* Milano: Rizzoli.

Trenz, H. J. (2016). *Narrating European society: Toward a sociology of European integration.* Lanham, MD: Lexington Books.

Treu, T. (1987). 'Italian labor relations: A system in transition'. *Monthly Labor Review* March 1987: 37–9.

Treu, T. (2011). *Labour law in Italy.* Alphen aan den Rijn: Kluwer Law International.

Trichet, J. C, and Draghi, M. (2011). 'Un'azione pressante per ristabilire la fiducia degli investitori'. *Corriere della Sera*, 29 September 2011.

Available at: http:// www.corriere.it/economia/11_settembre_29/trichet_draghi_inglese_304a5f1e-ea59-11e0-ae06-4da866778017.shtml?fr=correlati.

Truger, A., and Will, H. (2013). 'The German "debt brake": A shining example for European fiscal policy?'. *Revue de l'OFCE* 127: 153–88.

Turner, L. (1996). 'The Europeanization of labour: Structure before action'. *European Journal of Industrial Relations* 2(3): 325–44.

Turner, T., d'Art, D., and Cross, C. (2008). 'Polish workers in Ireland: A contented proletariat?'. *Labor Studies Journal* 34(1): 112–26.

Turone, S. (1973). *Storia del sindacato in Italia 1943–1969.* Rome: Laterza.

Tzogopoulos, G. (2013). *The Greek crisis in the media: Stereotyping in the international press.* London: Routledge.

Uleri, P. V. (1996). 'Italy: Referendums and initiatives from the origins to the crisis of a democratic regime'. In M. Gallagher and P. V. Uleri (eds) *The referendum experience in Europe.* Basingstoke: Palgrave Macmillan, pp. 106–25.

Ulivo (2003). Manifesto per l'Italia. Un'altra idea dell'Italia. La libertà, i diritti, la persona. Launched at Convention of Democratici di Sinistra Ulivo programme, Milan, 4–6 April.

Union Post, The (2009a). 'Draft framework for a pact for stabilisation, social solidarity and economic renewal'. February 2009.

Union Post, The (2009b). 'Taking a stand on social Europe'. June 2009.

Union Post, The (2012). 'Fiscal treaty won't create a single job'. 12 May 2012.

Unite the Union (Taft, M.) (2012a). 'The Fiscal Treaty'. Presentation to Joint Committee on European Union Affairs Debate on Fiscal Compact Treaty, 23 February 2012.

Unite the Union (J. Kelly) (2012b). Presentation on the Fiscal Compact to the Joint Oireachtas Committee on European Affairs, 18 April 2012.

Urry, J. (2000). *Sociology Beyond societies: Mobilities for the twenty-first century*. London: Routledge.

Usherwood, S., and Startin, N. (2013). 'Euroscepticism as a persistent phenomenon'. *Journal of Common Market Studies* 51(1): 1–16.

van Apeldoorn, B. (2001) 'The Struggle over European order: Transnational class agency in the making of "embedded neo-liberalism"'. In A. Bieler, and D. Morton (eds) *Social forces in the making of the new Europe: The restructuring of European social relations in the global political economy*. London: Palgrave Macmillan, pp. 70–92.

van Apeldoorn, B. (2002). *Transnational capitalism and the struggle over European Integration*. London: Routledge.

van Apeldoorn, B. (2003). 'The struggle over European order: Transnational class agency in the making of "embedded-neoliberalism"'. In N. Brenner, B. Jessop, M. Jones and G. MacLeod (eds) *State/Space*. Oxford: Blackwell Publishing, pp. 147–64.

van Apeldoorn, B. and Horn, L. (2019). 'Critical political economy'. In A. Wiener, T. A. Börzel and T. Risse (eds) *European integration theory* (3rd edn). Oxford: Oxford University Press, pp. 195–215.

van Apeldoorn, B., Drahokoupil, J., and Horn, L. (2009) (eds). *Contradictions and limits of neoliberal European governance. From Lisbon to Lisbon*. London: Palgrave Macmillan.

van der Pijl, K. (1998). *Transnational classes and international relations*. Routledge: London.

van der Velden, S., Dribbusch, H., Lyddon, D., and Vandaele, K. (2007). *Strikes around the world, 1968–2005: Case-studies of 15 countries*. Amsterdam: Aksant.

van Goethem, G., and Waters, R. A. (eds) (2013). *American labor's global ambassadors: The international history of the AFL-CIO during the cold war*. London: Palgrave Macmillan.

Van Hoek, A., and M. Houwerzijl (eds) *Complementary study on the legal aspects of the posting of workers in the framework of the provision of services in the European Union*. Report for the European Commission Contract VC/2011/0096, University of Amsterdam.

Van Middleaar, L. (2013). *Passage to Europe: How a continent became a union.* New York: Yale University Press.

Varsori, A. (2007). *Alle origini del presente: L'europa occidentale nella crisi degli anni '70.* Milan: Franco Angeli.

Varsori, A. (2010). *La cenerentola d'europa? L'Italia e l'integrazione europea dal 1947 a Oggi.* Soveria Mannelli: Rubbettino.

Vasilopoulou, S. (2013). 'Continuity and change in the study of Euroscepticism: Plus ça change?'. *Journal of Common Market Studies* 51(1): 153–68.

Vauchez, A. (2010). 'The transnational politics of judicialization: *Van Gend en Loos* and the making of a EU polity'. *European Law Journal* 16(1): 1–28.

Vauchez, A. (2015). *Brokering Europe. Euro-lawyers and the making of a transnational polity.* Cambridge: Cambridge University Press.

Vaughan-Whitehead, D. (2003). *EU enlargement Versus social Europe? The uncertain future of the European social model.* Cheltenham: Edward Elgar.

Verdun, A. (1996). 'An "asymmetrical" economic and monetary union in the EU: Perceptions of monetary authorities and social partners'. *Journal of European Integration* 20(1): 59–81.

Verney, S. (ed.) (2011). *Euroscepticism in southern Europe: A diachronic perspective.* London: Routledge.

Visser, J. (1998). 'Learning to play: The Europeanization of trade unions'. In P. Pasture and J. Verberckmoes (eds) *Working-class internationalism and the appeal of national identity.* Oxford: Berg, pp. 231–58.

Vogiatzoglou, M. (2015). 'Workers' transnational networks in times of austerity: Italy and Greece'. *Transfer* 21(2): 215–28.310

Wagner, I. (2014). 'Rule enactment in a pan-European labour market: Transnational posted work in the German construction sector'. *British Journal of Industrial Relations* 12(5): 692–710.

Wagner, I. (2018). *Workers without borders: Posted work and precarity in the EU.* Ithaca, NY: Cornell University Press.

Wallace, H. (2000). 'Studying contemporary Europe'. *British Journal of Politics and International Relations* 2(1): 95–113.

Wallace, W. (1988). Address by William Wallace, President, ICTU, to the Annual Conference, Burlington Hotel, Dublin. 5 July 1988.

Warlouzet, L. (2018) *Governing Europe in a globalizing world: Neoliberalism and its alternatives following the 1973 oil crisis.* London: Routledge.

Watson, A. (1996). 'Thatcher and Kohl – old rivalries revisited'. In M. Bond, J. Smith and W. Wallace (eds) *Eminent Europeans: Personalities who shaped contemporary Europe.* London: Greycoat Press, pp. 264–84.

Webb, B., and Webb, S. (1897). *Industrial democracy.* London: Longman.

Webb, S., and Webb, B. (1894). *The history of trade unionism.* London: Longman.

Weiler, J. H. (2005). 'The European "constitution": requiescat in pace'. In H. Kohl, *et al.* (eds) *The freedom revolution*, pp. 117–131. Available at: https://fundacionfaes. org/file_upload/publication/pdf/00052-11_ _the_european_ constitution. pdf.

Weitz, P. (1975). 'Labor and politics in a divided movement: The Italian case'. *ILR Review* 28(2): 226–42.

Welz, C. (2008). *The European social dialogue under Articles 138 and 139 of the EC Treaty: Actors, processes, outcomes*. Alphen aan den Rijm: Kluwer Law International.

Wessels, W. (2014). 'Revisiting the Monnet method – a contribution to the periodisation of the European Union's history'. In M. Bachem-Rehm, C. Hiepel and H. Türk (eds) *Overcoming divisions: European and international history in the 19th and 20th centuries – A festschrift for Wilfried Loth*. Munich: De Gruyter, pp. 49–61.

Wessels, W., Maurer, A., and Mittag, J. (eds) (2003). *Fifteen into one: The European Union and its member states*. Manchester: Manchester University Press.

White, A. (2011). *Polish families and migration since EU accession*. Portland: Policy Press.

White, J. (2020a). *Politics of last resort: Governing by emergency in the European Union*. Oxford: Oxford University Press.

White, J. (2020b). 'Europeanizing ideologies'. *Journal of European Public Policy* 27(9): 1287–1306.

Wimmer, A., and Glick Schiller, N. (2003). 'Methodological nationalism, the social sciences, and the study of migration: An essay in historical epistemology'. *International Migration Review* 37(3): 576–610.

Woolfson, C. (2007). 'Labour standards and migration in the new Europe: Post-communist legacies and perspectives'. *European Journal of Industrial Relations* 13(2): 199–218.

Woolfson, C., and Sommers, J. (2006). 'Labour mobility in construction: European implications of the Laval un Partneri dispute with Swedish labour'. *European Journal of Industrial Relations* 12(1):49–68.

Yeates, P. (2008). 'Craft workers during the Irish revolution, 1919–1922'. *Saothar, Journal of the Irish Labour History Society* 33: 37–56.

Yondorf, W. (1965). 'Monnet and the Action Committee: The formative period of the European Communities'. *International Organization* 19(4): 885–912.

Zucchetti, E. (ed.) (2004) *La regolarizzazione degli stranieri. Nuovi attori nel mercato del lavoro*. Italiano Fondazione ISMU, Ministero del Lavoro e delle Politiche Sociali. Milan: Franco Angeli.

Zürn, M. (2016). 'Opening up Europe: Next steps in politicisation research'. *West European Politics* 39(1): 164–82.

Zürn, M. (2019). 'Politicization compared: At national, European, and global levels'. *Journal of European Public Policy* 26(7): 977–95.3

Endnotes

Chapter One: Quo Vadis, Europa? The
Politics of European Integration

1 Also, as a former Euro-parliamentarian, Delors was keenly aware of the EU's democratic deficit (Jabko 2006).

Chapter Two: Theories of Political Preferences on
European Integration: A Neo-Polanyian Approach

1 In the 1973 enlargement, Denmark shared a border with another Member State and traditionally was not a labour-sending country. Regarding the southern enlargement, Spain was the only country to share a frontier with another Member States, France. In the fourth enlargement round, only Austria shared a border with an existing Member States and none the three new entrants (Austria, Sweden and Finland) were labour sending countries.

Chapter Three: Studying European Integration
and Preferences across Time

1 SIPTU is the product of a merger between Ireland's two largest unions the Irish Transport and General Workers Union (ITGWU) and the Federated Workers Union of Ireland. The merger happened in 1990, before this the position of the ITGWU will be considered.

2 Unite the Union is also the product of a merger between Amicus and the Transport and General Workers (TGWU) Union in 2007. The Irish wing of the TGWU was the Amalgamated Transport and General Workers Union (not to be confused with the ITGWU).

3 Pierson (1996) levelled this criticism towards liberal intergovernmentalism and Moravcsik (1993) who also used the European treaties in his analysis of national government preferences, and although our unit of analysis is different that criticism is also relevant for our research and therefore heeded. Furthermore, an actor-centred approach casts a different light with regards to an account of European integration such as that by Moravcsik (1993; 1998) or Pierson (1998).

Chapter Four: Italian and Irish Labour on the Supranational Question

1 A word of gratitude to Idar Helle, who allowed me access to his own personal archive.

2 De Gasperi's strategy was undertaken so as to i) improve Italy's damaged international reputation; ii) place Italy on an equal footing with other states, especially Britain and France; and iii) enhance the possibility of clemency regarding the revision of the peace treaty (Varsori 2010).

3 In 1967, The British Labour government and the Danish Social Democrat government both applied for membership of the EEC. Albeit in opposition, the Norwegian Labour party urged that country's centre-right government to submit an application. Steinnes (2009: 105) notes 'that existing accounts of Britain's second application based exclusively on government records [must] be modified'.

4 The defeat of the CGIL in elections to the *commissioni interne* at Fiat in 1955, and the Soviet oppression in Budapest, the following year (1956), caused the CGIL to adopt a more moderate role.

5 Although Larkin has been the subject of vast scholarly attention (e.g., O'Connor 2002, 2015), and his radical spirit summoned more frequently, it is the influence of the more understated O'Brien that has had a more enduring bearing on Irish trade unionism. By and large, historians have been unkind to O'Brien. Greaves (1982), in his seminal study of the formative years of the ITGWU, describes O'Brien as being 'never excessively enthusiastic' and 'unable to inspire people'. Lee (1989: 241) describes O'Brien as 'a classic case of an apparatchik so frequently found in Irish organisations, combining fine administrative abilities with a domineering personality and a narrow mind. He was the type of man, only too common in Ireland, who prefers to wreck a movement rather than lose control of it.' It was his willingness to 'wreck a movement rather than lose control of it' that led to a split in the broader Irish trade union movement.

6 This anti-Britishness mirrored the prevailing mood of the nationalist impulse, which harboured an impatient desire for reform. Courting nationalist governments, the ITGWU sought to undermine the 'amalgamated' unions. Consequently, the legislative programmes of governments were 'of a radical and separatist character' (McCarthy 1973a: 382). The Trade Union Act of 1941, which was introduced to 'ensure that only a small number of Irish-based unions would be allowed to operate in Ireland', is a case in point (Murphy 2009: 42). Wholly unacceptable to the British unions and the WUI, the Act denotes the extent of unvarnished anti-Britishness. In any case the Act failed in its objective and eventually aspects of the Act were found to be unconstitutional. Writing the unofficial history of the ATGWU, Matt Merrigan (1989: 128), former National Secretary, notes that the court's finding 'eased the pressure on amalgamated unions in Éire'.

7 With the creation of the CIU, O'Brien was now 'nearer his ideal of an Irish-based trade union movement ... One could now speak in plain words, demanding the loyalty of Irish workers for Irish trade unions, demanding that British unions should withdraw' (McCarthy 1973b: 472). To that end, a close relationship with Fianna Fáil was established.

8 Agriculture was excluded from EFTA and its inclusion would have only jeopardised Irish exports by increasing competition (Barry 2009).

9 Prior to the four new candidate member states – Denmark, Ireland, Norway and the UK – joining the EEC, France held a referendum on their accession. The French electorate, on 23 April 1972, approved accession by 68.3% in favour.

10 Six of the agreements were bipartite in character, i.e., between the peak labour and employers' organisations. The agreements reached between 1979 and 1980 were the result of tripartite concertation.

11 On the claim that '[O]utside Italy, Eurocommunism rapidly faded from the European scene', (Pons 2010: 65), I belive this to be correct.

12 Interestingly, the PCI had voted against the European exchange rate mechanism (ERM) in 1978. There was a divisive debate in Italy on the question. Whereas the political establishment was typically in favou, technocrats tended to be more divided. Why the PCI adopted this position is possibly a question of politics, i.e., to remain distinct from the rest of the political field; however, this is by no means a definitive answer and requires further research.

Chapter Five: Constructing a Pro-European Consensus

1 Following disagreement between the Commission and the French President, Charles de Gaulle, on the financing of the common agricultural policy, de Gaulle ordered France's representatives not to attend any intergovernmental meetings of the Community bodies in Brussels. Consequently, no decisions could be taken because unanimity was required.

2   Article 118 (and 117) were drafted on the insistence of the French government at Messina. The two Articles were seen as safeguards against a 'race to the bottom' on labour costs between national welfare-state regimes (*see* Moravcsik 1998: 115, 122). Article 22 of the SEA, which amended the EC Treaty in the form of Article 118B, read as follows: 'The Commission shall endeavour to develop the dialogue between management and labour at European level which could, if the two sides consider it desirable, lead to relations based on agreement.'

3   Between 1985 and 1995, the Val Duchesse process generated 21 joint opinions and declarations, two key agreements and seven high-level summits.

4   The articles of the Charter covered, among other things, employment and remuneration, improvement of living and working conditions, freedom of association and collective bargaining, information, consultation and participation rights, gender equality, health and safety at the workplace, and vocational training.

5   The Social Action Programme contained 47 initiatives necessary in implementing the Social Charter, prior to completion of the European common market in 1992. The Action Programme was not binding and each of its proposals would be subject to Council approval.

6   The main Structural Funds are the European Agricultural Guarantee and Guidance Fund (EAGGF), the European Regional Development Fund (ERDF) and the European Social Fund (ESF).

7   Fianna Fáil had fought the 1984 European elections under the slogan of 'We will never join any military alliance'.

8   In January, 1986, the Danish Parliament rejected the SEA by 80 votes to 75.

9   The question asked was as follows: 'Do you think the European Communities should be transformed into an effective Union, with a government responsible to the Parliament, entrusting to the same European Parliament a mandate to draw up a draft constitution for ratification directly, by the competent organs of the member states of the Community?'

10 In Ireland, the European Parliament elections 'concentrated more on national domestic politics than on the European community' (Holmes 2006: 134).

11 Writing on the tenth anniversary of accession, the historian, Joe Lee (1984), was bemused by the 'perspective' of other scholars and elites who sought to sugarcoat the bitter pill that membership of the EU had not delivered on the political promises made a decade earlier.

Chapter Six: Constructing a Social Europe: From Amsterdam to Nice

1   Austria, Belgium, Finland, France, Germany, Ireland, Italy, Luxembourg, Portugal, Spain, and the Netherlands. Greece joined in 2001. Denmark and the UK opted out; Sweden was obliged to join the Euro at an unspecified time in the future. However, Swedes voted against joining the Euro in a 2003 referendum.

2 The National Economic and Social Council (NESC) was established in 1973: however, in the mid-1980s, it 'took on a new role' (Hardiman 2002: 8), which informed the Irish experience of tripartism, in particular, and economic governance more generally.

3 The pact was incorporated into the Amsterdam Treaty in 1997.

4 These sanctions could only be imposed provided the ECOFIN Council approved them.

5 For legal reasons, the refund that Prodi promised, was 'never included in the actual legislative text that created the tax' (Savage 2005: 131). In 1999, the Italian government instituted a tax reduction rather than an actual refund, claiming this substitute effectively served as the reimbursement.

6 This never materialised, as the *Rifondazione Comunista* brought down the *Ulivo* coalition over a much weaker austerity package the following year.

7 Alessio Gramolati and Luciano Silvestri, two CGIL Secretaries, travelled with over 400 workers to join demonstrations.

8 There is an anecdote provided by Hastings, Sheehan and Yeates (2007: 183), relating how, on the announcement of Flynn attending the British TUC conference, British trade union members inquired as to the political orientation of the Irish Commissioner, only to be told 'he's not to the left'. After Flynn delivered an 'incredibly progressive speech', the British trade unionists noted that 'if he [Flynn] is right-wing, what's the [Irish] left like?'.

9 Between the first and second referendum on the Nice Treaty, Mick O'Reilly was controversially suspended from the role of Regional Secretary the week before the biennial conference of the ICTU. On 26 June, O'Reilly received a letter explaining his suspension while an 'administrative audit' was being carried out. No charge of wrongdoing was levelled against him, but the term 'audit' implies improper appropriation of financial funds. Some believe he was suspended for being a constant critic of ICTU's attitude towards tripartism and his negative stance on the EU. Also, an ongoing turf war with SIPTU did not help matters. It is alleged that the SIPTU leadership and Bertie Ahern contacted Tony Blair so as to have Bill Morris, the leader of the British TGWU, suspend O'Reilly.

10 Speakers at the Alliance for Europe launch included Chris Horn, chairman of Iona Technologies; Jack Golden, human resources director of CRH; Sean Melly, chief executive of eTel Group; and Lorraine Sweeney, businesswoman and founding chairwoman of the Small Firms Association (*Irish Times*, 10 October 2002).

11 Having been outvoted in the Council on the Working Time Directive, the Major government brought a failed case before the CJEU on the grounds that the Directive had been issued on a wrong legal basis.

Chapter Seven: Labour Mobility: A Defining Characteristic

1   One example is Polish MEP Danuta Jazlowiecka, who, in the debate for the proposed Enforcement Directive, argued for diminished power for labour inspections, more possibilities for employers to post workers to other member states and more information websites.

2   Article 117 of the Rome Treaty reads as follows: 'Member States agree upon the need to promote improved working conditions and an improved standard of living for workers, so as to make possible their harmonization while the improvement is being maintained. They believe that such a development will ensue not only from the functioning of the common market, which will favour the harmonisation of social systems, but also from the procedures provided for in this Treaty and from the approximation of provisions laid down by law, regulation or administrative action.'

3   According to Vaughan-Whitehead's (2003: 325) definition, illegal social dumping 'would include all situations in which the employer, in order to gain competitiveness, implements working and social conditions that clearly circumvent existing national or international provisions in force in the country where he is operating'.

4   The Taff Vale decision was the principal reason for the creation of the British Labour party.

5   The main unions represented within the CIC are the TEEU, SIPTU, BATU, UCATT and Unite. BATU has recently merged with SIPTU.

6   For a more comprehensive treatment of all the factors, *see* Golden (2016).

7   During these seven years, the transition agreement could be amended; this became known as the '2+3+2' formula. From the formula, we can see that the transitional restrictions were split into three phases. For the first two years after accession, member states either opened their labour markets or maintained restrictions that had been in place since April 2003 and April 2005 regarding the 2004 enlargement and the 2007 enlargement respectively. The second phase lasted three years and member states had the option to lift, modify or maintain restrictions. Regarding the 2004 enlargement, it was largely expected that most member states would have lifted restrictions by this stage, and this was the case, in fact. The final two years afforded member states an additional two years to apply restrictions, provided they could show that they experienced or anticipated 'serious disturbances' in their labour markets.

8   Although the REAs were struck out following a Supreme Court case brought by rogue domestic employers in 2012, they regulated the construction sector over the duration of the study.

9   UCATT merged with Connect in 2017.

10   A good example is the question of subcontracting, which became an issue in the early 2000s. The Irish construction union, BATU, was ideologically opposed to subcontracting in construction and took the view that subcontracting would

only erode working standards and make the sector more difficult to monitor. The Labour Court advised on the inclusion of the subcontracting clause in the REA; however, a legal battle ensued, with BATU arguing that the Labour Court was operating *ultra vires*. BATU sought and was granted a stay by the High Court on the making of the order by the Labour Court. This effectively excluded the subcontracting clause from the REA until 2005. The High Court later held that the Labour Court had followed proper procedures and subcontracting could be included in the frame of reference for the REA.

11 UCATT, OPATSI and Unite.
12 Federazione Italiana Lavoratori Legno, Edili e Affini
13 Federazione Italiana Lavoratori Costruzioni e Affini
14 Federazione Nazionale Lavoratori Edili, Affini e del Legno
15 The other member states are Austria, Belgium, Germany and the Netherlands.
16 *Associazione Nazionale Oltre le Frontiere*
17 *Unione Italiana Immigrati*

Chapter Eight: Lisbon and the Re-Emergence of Labour Euroscepticism

1 An Intergovernmental Conference (IGC) is the formal procedure for negotiating amendments to the EU's founding treaties. Typically, an IGC will bring together member state representatives with the Commission and, to a lesser degree, the Parliament also participating.
2 The full title is *Manifesto per l'Italia. Una società della libertà, dei diritti della persona* ['Manifesto for Italy. A society of freedom and human rights'] and was unveiled as an *Ulivo* programme for government on March 18 2003.
3 This new participatory democracy provision means that one million citizens coming from a significant number of member states can petition the European Commission to address an issued deemed to be of importance.
4 The Labour Court is an independent workplace dispute resolution body concerning industrial relations disputes and (individual) employments rights. Regarding industrial relations the disputes, the Court issues a written recommendation, which the parties 'are expected to give serious consideration to' but that are not legally binding.
5 Under the Lisbon Treaty, the European Commission was to be reduced to 18 members, ending the arrangement of all member states having a permanent Commissioner. Instead, a rotating system was envisaged.
6 These included Ireland for Europe, We Belong, Ireland's Future and Business for Europe. Business for Europe consisted of a number of groups that campaigned in the first referendum as individual groups. The groups include IBEC, the American Chamber Ireland, the Small Firms Association, Irish Exporters Association, Irish Hoteliers Federation and the Irish Food and Drinks Association. Also, individual multinationals such as Ryanair and Intel joined the debate, advocating a 'yes' vote.

7   Thanks to Karen Devine for these estimated figures.

8   This translates as 'Agreements must be kept'. It is a precept of international law underpinning the system of states.

9   The co-ordinators of the 'yes' campaign included Brendan Halligan of the Irish Institute of European Affairs, Brigid Laffan of UCD, Pat Cox, Danny McCoy of IBEC Patricia Callan of the Small Firms Association and Blair Horan of the union IMPACT. The latter was central to the Charter Group and their strategy was in keeping with that of the government and the Yes side, i.e., ratification of the treaty was necessary to ensure Ireland's continued access the ESM and to pay for current government expenditure. 'Stability was the key word for Yes campaigners' (Fitzgibbon 2013: 232), hence the deployment of the sobriquet 'Stability Treaty' by its supporters.

10 ICTU made a similar proposal at the onset of the crisis but with little success. *See* ICTU (2009).

11 The other groups joining FIOM were Libera, Anpi, Articolo 21, and Arci.

12 There were large mobilisations in a number of the bigger Italian cities. This is mainly on account of November being the traditional month for student mobilisations (Vogiatzoglou 2015).

13 The Ryanair and, more recent, McGowan cases ruled on by the Supreme Court provided a serious blow to Irish industrial relations. To this end, ICTU and Connect brought a case to the European Court of Human Rights on the grounds that there were 'major flaws' in the aforementioned Supreme Court rulings resulting in 'tens of thousands of workers being denied the effective right to collective bargaining' (Hendy 2014). This challenge came on the back of an ICTU complaint to the ILO (Doherty 2013), however, both bids were unsuccessful.

14 Paradoxically, it was neither Germany nor the EU that was questioning the logic of austerity or entertaining the prospect of debt relief, instead it was the IMF!

Chapter Nine: Conclusion: Quo Vadis, Social Europe?

1   Following independence from the British Empire, the Irish government did not replace the letterboxes adorned with British insignia. Instead, they simply painted the red letterboxes green.

2   This is not the first time that such an organisation has emerged. A group with a similar name and format, Trade Unionists for Irish Unity and Independence, was launched in Dublin in 1984.

3   James Connolly (1868–1916), born to Irish parents in Scotland, was a trade unionist and with a broad grasp of history, Marxist economics and social theory, a prominent intellectual of the working class. A willing martyr who co-led a failed rising against the British in Dublin, Connolly displayed 'a written style marked by a clarity and strength of purpose that can still grip the reader today' (Newsinger 1983: 153).

Index

www.ingramcontent.com/pod-product-compliance
Ingram Content Group UK Ltd.
Pitfield, Milton Keynes, MK11 3LW, UK
UKHW031346040125
3874UKWH00001B/80

9 781910 259894